WITHDRAWN

CONTENDING ISSUES IN AFRICAN DEVELOPMENT

CONTENDING ISSUES IN AFRICAN DEVELOPMENT

ADVANCES, CHALLENGES, AND THE FUTURE

EDITED BY OBIOMA M. IHEDURU

*Contributions in Economics and
Economic History, Number 219*

Greenwood Press
Westport, Connecticut • London

Library of Congress Cataloging-in-Publication Data

Contending issues in African development: advances, challenges, and the future / edited by Obioma M. Iheduru.
    p. cm.—(Contributions in economics and economic history, ISSN 0084-9235; no. 219)
   Includes bibliographical references and index.
   ISBN 0-313-30961-2 (alk. paper)
   1. Africa—Economic policy. 2. Africa—Social policy. I. Iheduru, Obioma M. II. Series.
HC800 .C6663 2001
338.96—dc21   00-032797

British Library Cataloguing in Publication Data is available.

Library of Congress Catalog Card Number: 00-032797
ISBN: 0-313-30961-2
ISSN: 0084-9235

First published in 2001

Greenwood Press, 88 Post Road West, Westport, CT 06881
An imprint of Greenwood Publishing Group, Inc.
www.greenwood.com

Printed in the United States of America

The paper used in this book complies with the Permanent Paper Standard issued by the National Information Standards Organization (Z39.48-1984).

10 9 8 7 6 5 4 3 2 1

To

Ngozi for teaching me the essence of love
Ozioma for teaching me patience
Adaobi for lessons in endurance

Contents

PART I

Introduction

Conflicts and Convergence in African Development Thinking

Obioma M. Iheduru

African development has been analyzed in various ways. Scholars and policy makers have utilized various approaches to study the dynamics of the African development situation as well as speculate on the particular combination of resources or factors that will facilitate, if not ensure, development. In several of these scholarly and policy endeavors, one thing has, however, remained constant. Dominant analytical variables have almost always centered on certain crucial issues around which any discussions of African development problems have invariably hinged and without which a complete analysis and understanding cannot be made. The question being asked then and now is, are there any unique environmental, cultural, political, and economic issues that undergird and determine the direction of African development? A thorough examination and analysis of these central issues that have hitherto shaped development in Africa form the core of this book.

Several important issues readily come to mind. African polities are said to encompass unstructured economies, hence the need for structural adjustment policies. Other issues include a continuing massive rural to urban migration and its aftermaths of rapid population growth and urbanization; perennial political crises arising from ethnic conflicts and a weak political culture; problems of war, conflict management, and state building; debilitating famine and resultant food scarcity, poverty, authoritarianism, and the absence of a democratic tradition and a bill of human rights; and the lingering problems of the rights and place of women in the African society. Also crucially important is the place of African economies within the world capitalist system and the implications of the neoliberal economic changes it engenders, as evident in most of Africa today. Scholars definitely share a considerable consensus about the centrality of these issues in African development, but most vary as to the scope of the role each should be assigned in explaining the development problem in Africa. The early development theorists, such as Samuel P. Huntington, Cyril Black, Lucian Pye, Gabriel Almond, Claude Ake, Okwudiba Nnoli and others, considered and juxtaposed these issues in their analyses and predictions of future development in Africa. Times have changed, however, and the dynamics of these issues have concomitantly changed, necessitating a reconsideration of the approaches in order to accurately capture the momentum of the new processes of African development.

There is also the issue of ideological disagreement as to what factors are responsible for the development dilemma in Africa today. The radical or neo-Marxist school of thought attributes this to such extraneous issues as foreign capital arising out of the world capitalist system to which African economies were ineluctably linked at independence. This has resulted in a massive capital and resource hemorrhaging that accounts for the ongoing slow rate of development. The neoliberal school of thought, on the other hand, employs the explanatory potentials of structural variables to argue that the extant political and economic arrangements in Africa are the pivotal issues that generate the disabling environment that invariably slows the rate of development. Within this school of thought, the relationship between political liberalization and economic development, as well as its spin-off effects on societal development, is examined. It is argued that, in the long run, a well-structured economy will prosper and spawn a democratic political system.

An examination of the ramifications of these approaches and issues form the core of the work from various contributors in this book. The authors employ varying perspectives derived from several social science approaches in analyzing the way in which these issues are important in understanding the problems of development in Africa. Although the chapters are well researched and based on appropriate theoretical referents, their points of departure are that they trend a futuristic approach by asking such predictive questions as, what next after the theoretical explications? Is there a future for African development? Is the apparent confusion in the analysis and understanding of African development an indication that disciplinary pursuits impose parochial limitations that preclude a better appreciation of the issues involved in the analysis of African development? Would the apparent theoretical consensus of the last thirty, or so, years give way to a convergence of approaches, theories, and action in the third millennium?

The studies here have attempted to deal with specific issue areas and to determine the role of that issue area in the overall development process. This serves a number of purposes. It avoids the mistake of issue-overload of the past, when scholars tended to give comprehensive explanations of development through the use of multiple factors. Simple parsimonious analysis within well-defined disciplinary boundaries is considered a more fitting approach to identifying the effects of certain issues or factors on the development process in Africa. In this respect, this book is divided into four parts dealing with different issues. This is not to say that issues are isolated in themselves. The point is that issues have to be identified and analyzed relative to the areas that they impact in a country's political economy. Once this is done, the functional effects of that issue in development are discerned and analyzed in order to provide a fuller understanding of their contributions to the dynamics of African development. Each part is examined in this chapter within the context of how the chapters revolve around a conceptual and epistemological framework that invariably makes a contribution to the understanding of the African development process.

BRING BACK THE STATE

In examining the current state system in Africa, Kelechi Kalu, Kingsley Harbor, and Ali Mazrui argue that development in Africa cannot proceed in the face of the present stemming of the postcolonial state. There is need, therefore, for a moving away from the state system, as presently constituted, in the light of the enormous problems and challenges facing African economies to a less proactive state that is much less a manager of the economy. There is a need for the state to be reconstituted in order to reorientate what Harbor describes as "the internal dimensions of political instability" that are at the root of the incapacity of the African state to perform its assigned functions. It is this realization of the changes in the state structure that will equip it for the role of selective adaptation of the instruments of development that will ultimately result in development. In this regard, Mazrui, using a comparative analysis of "Westernization" as opposed to "modernization," concepts argues that as a result of European colonization of Africa, neither the Japanese model nor the Turkish models of development have been adopted in Africa. Whereas the Japanese adopted "Western technique," the Turkish adopted "industrial and military modernizations" which fifty years later compromised "cultural authenticity." This seeming "paradox of Westernization without modernization" is counterfactual toward development in Africa. It renders the weak state even weaker. Mazrui's "imperatives" for the modernization of the African states include culturally relative indigenization of the state focusing on cultural expansion, domestication of the foreign to make it as relevant as the local, cultural diversification in order to learn from diverse cultures, horizontal interpenetration of less autonomous cultures, and the counterpenetration of the citadels of power. The question then is, would these obviate the downward trend in economic development that the African countries have been experiencing in the last decade and a half? As a way out, Kalu proposes five superstates—Algeria, Kenya, Democratic Republic of the Congo, Nigeria, and South Africa—to alleviate Africa's problem with instability, bad governance, and development. In a similar fashion, Mazrui suggests that the stability and pan-Africanization of Nigeria, complete liberation of South Africa, and the politicization and sophistication of black America would be the necessary "struggles" that need embarking on to reverse the trend of Westernization without modernization that has not substantially contributed to African development. In other words, it could be argued that the brutal, undemocratic, exploitative, and dehumanizing structural deficiencies that have their roots in colonialism have cumulatively resulted in the absence of development. Similarly is what Harbor calls the practice of "utilitarian journalism" that should move away from what used to be "development journalism," which tended to see the role of the press as being coterminus with the interests of the state. This new model would allow the press to pursue the greatest good of the greatest number of citizens such that they form an effective deterrent to political instability.

The arguments of these authors have parallels with the recent scholarship on the changing nature of the state in Africa. The postcolonial state in Africa embodies contradictory characteristics that inexorably affect both economic and political development. The state is the principal public domain for the setting of the rules, the selection of the officials, and the organization of the competition between the various interests in the polity. The state is also a competitor for the same resources because it has assumed the role of manager rather than that of distributor of resources. The inability, and in some cases incompetence, of the state in the duties it has arrogated to itself have come to question the state's efficiency. The obvious challenge in Africa has been state reconstitution because state consolidation as an instrument of nation building had turned into state deterioration. To this point, the state is unable to carry out its responsibilities, and the contractions of institutional incapacity and political instability resulting from a dysfunctional internal structure plague it. The collapse of the African economies in the 1980s exacerbated this rapid decline of the state and spawned the rise of alternative structures that have come to challenge the state's authority. This and similar challenges arising from the society have led to the delegitimation of the state and its institutions. The new turn of events resulted in a reversal of the expectations of early scholars of African development who had argued and hoped that the building of institutions would set the inevitable stage for development. This was not to be the case, a disappointment that led to a shift of emphasis from integrative studies of development to conflict studies that dealt with "incorporation" into the state and "withdrawal" from it as the inevitable paradigms through which to understand development.[1] In order to resolve the contradictions within it, it is contended that the state must be restructured in order to be reconstituted. This reconstitution must be based on juridical basis of the state rather than from the more pervasive arguments about the "failed" or "collapsed" state.

Regardless of the reasons for its reconstitution or reconstruction, the African state is in need of a thorough reordering for development to be realistically achieved. This realization then is an indication that the state is both structurally weak and deficient and consequently harbors structurally distorted economies that themselves cannot be properly operated given the constriction imposed on the environment of their activity.

BUILDING SOCIAL CAPACITY

The collapse, deconstruction, and reconstitution of the African state was facilitated by changes imminent in civil society, which in itself resulted in the application of neoliberal policies. Neoliberalism dictated political and economic openness to make African economies accessible to international markets and patterned their polities along the lines of Western political democratic governance. It is within this framework that Julius Nyang'oro, Julius Ihonvbere, Harold Fisher, and Vincent Ferrara discuss the prerequisites for building social capacity. Let me here define social capacity as that ability of the political community of active interest groups, professionals, and activist organizations to penetrate the political system and exert as much impact as necessary, not only to change or influence current policies but to substantially alter standards for political practice within a polity.

Nyang'oro's chapter takes a slightly different angle and examines the role of civil societies in the development of democracy and democratic institutions, using the national conference model that started in Benin in 1989 as a beacon. This deliberative conference, summoned to discuss the parameters for a new political arrangement or structure, ushered in a democratic transition for the Republic of Benin and had important implications for change and development on the continent. The role of civil societies in this transformation, and later in the defeat of Kenneth Kaunda in Zambia in 1991, adoption of multiparty politics in Kenya, and the various other calls for political liberalization, took its bearings from Benin. Definitionally classified as nongovernmental organizations (NGOs), civil societies have come to symbolize the demand for change and the pursuit of alternative approaches in policy formulation and implementation. In this way, civil society challenges the environment that sustains a lack of development, what Nyang'oro describes as "challenging the factors responsible for poverty and hence the policies that perpetuate poverty." The push to participate based on one's or a society's self-interest and the struggle to keep open the mode for this participation are essential criteria that collectively characterize civil societies from the National Council of Churches in Kenya to the Lesotho Council of NGOs, resulting in "constructive political engagement" and "unity against government's disintegrative moves."

Nyang'oro is, however, skeptical that the activities of civil societies are sustainable over time and doubts that it could result in the building of social capital. Contrary to expectations but not entirely surprising, current evidence from Africa suggests that there are no guarantees of democratic practice even from governments that came into power on the backs of, and with the invaluable support of, civil societies. This invariably refers to the Federick Chiluba government that, in spite of its populist origins, has become a bugbear of civil society and democratic practice in Zambia. As it were, although the state needs to be challenged and reformed, and considering that civil society has succeeded in fostering this change, the eventual impact of civil societies is no doubt bound to be limited because they lack the organizational clout and resource base necessary to challenge the state, even after they have helped in reinventing it. This inevitable skepticism does not detract from the fact that civil societies in the present context of the African state are a rich source of social capital, perhaps the only effective counterbalance against the state. Social capital is therefore inevitable for the progression toward democratization. It is possible, however, that social capital is underlaid by other factors such as human rights as distinguished from political and civil liberties.

In this respect, the contributions by Fisher, Ihonvbere, and Ferrara are put in perspective as they consider the development of democracy, the state structure and human rights, and a comparative analysis of human rights in the African and Western senses, respectively. Although Fisher recognizes the increasing democratization on the African continent, the point is made that much remains to be done to achieve "true representative democracy." This limitation results from the inability of the electorate to effectively challenge the government that manipulates the electoral system and perpetuates fraud to remain in power. Such manipulation negates the work of civil societies and most importantly upsets the principles and criteria of democratic governance. Single-election analysis as the standard of democratic transition is debunked because, as Fisher maintains, the "democratic process is a continuum" where earlier democratic achievements must cumulate into later democratic accomplishments. In other words, the lack of democratic continuity signifies the inability of civil societies to wage an effective struggle for its opportunity to participate in the political process. On the other hand, the remarkable progress in democratic development made in some African countries between 1989 and 1997 was at least present in those countries. Painfully, the incumbent political leadership that manipulates elections to remain in office vitiates the full development of the social capital necessary for the effective drive toward full democratization. This can only be realized through changes in what Ihonvbere calls "the dynamics of power, politics, production, and exchange relations." Using the dependency approach as his framework of analysis, it is noted that the current popularity of elections and the massive electoral upshot against dictatorial regimes have masked the the wanton violation of human rights in Africa. It is further argued that even the civil society itself is sometimes unaware of violations of human rights because of the underdeveloped state structures, incipient but restrictive political traditions, and above all the survivalist practices that force even the knowledgeable to overlook the human rights abuses. This substructural context is anchored on the "patterns of power, production and exchange, the social relations among and within social classes, and the location of social formations in the international division of labor," which in themselves condition the character of the postcolonial state. The state stands in the way of effective human rights observation through "pedestrian and opportunistic politics." To effectively support democracy, human rights must include social, economic, and cultural rights. The reformation of the African state is the sine qua non for the realization of this democratic objective. Thus, human rights forms a crucial tripod of the conditions necessary for the evolution of social capital. If the components of democracy include free, fair, and periodic elections; popular contestation between at least two political parties; and the lack of constraints on the part of the electorate as to their choice of party or candidate, human rights becomes a very important component for the realization of democratic goals. Without the basic political and civil rights (inevitable ingredients of human rights), the other conditions of democracy cannot be achieved. The freedom of assembly implies a freedom of association and interaction with any persons or groups whose views coalesce. So also is the freedom of choice of the electorate that underlies universal adult suffrage, as well as the freedoms of expression and the press. The guarantees of these freedoms on the one hand facilitate the operation of democracy. Given that the people are the progenitors of the democratic movement through civil societies, the point is made moot that they are contributing toward the establishment of social capital.

The environment of democracy and civil rights then makes relevant Ferrara's contribution in which he argues that the "factual and methodological relations of African and Western views of ethics and rights" exist. In his view, human rights have the capacity of protecting the individual against the intrusion of governmental authority (the negative, governmental restraint sense), but on the other hand it legitimizes the claims of the individual in person and property against the intrusion into personal space and life (the positive sense). Comparatively, Ferrara suggests that the dual interpretation of rights has no bearing as to whether they apply to African (in the community sense) or Western societies (the individual sense) and does not detract from a theory of rights because the very existence of rights is independent of appeals to community or individuality. Therefore, the conceptualization of rights within culturally relative boundaries might be misleading because a common body of transcultural values exists that informs rights, which does not necessarily impose absolute and monolithic parameters for human rights. In reality, there is the possibility of an intercultural dialogue that recognizes the commonality of humans as "individuals and social beings" who reside in communities. Perhaps, therefore, the individual is as important as the community because without the former the latter would not exist. The collectivity of individual rights thus constitutes the foundation of community rights. In essence, the conflict between the African conception of rights based on the rights of the community and the Western conception of rights based on the freedom of the individual results in unnecessary and oftentimes trivial "dialectical opposition." Ferrara is of the view that because none of the two conceptions appear to be committed at the expense of the other (community or individual), the possibility of a cultural dialogue and interchange between Africa and the West on the human rights issue exists and should be explored.

The concern with rights is quite appropriate given that human rights is at the root of the struggles for political space in the African polity. The lack of a deliberative governmental system, which in itself is indicative of the existence of variants of dictatorships until recently, is a consequence of the absence of a civil and political rights framework. The cumulative consequence of this is the absence of democratic forms of government. In other words, the lack of civil and political rights, in turn, results in the absence of democratic governance in most of Africa. Therefore, it is the integration of civil and political rights and the criteria for democratic performance with the current structure of the African state that sets in motion the discourse that these authors adopt. The dialectics of moving from the community-based structure of rights in Africa, incidentally supportive of the state-basis of rights, to the Western-inspired individually based rights form the bulwark for the devolution of powers from the state to the people. This also provides the basis for the challenge of the state and hence its definition of rights. This basic conception of human rights must then be adequately and unambiguously resolved in order to establish the fundamental imperatives of democracy that are in turn hinged on the political and civil rights of the citizens.

POLITICAL ECONOMY AND THE MANAGEMENT OF CHANGE

In this section, Timothy Shaw, Sandra MacLean, and Browne Onuoha discuss the impact of structural adjustment on the development of the African economy. Within this conceptualization, Shaw and MacLean posit that civil societies in African countries exist in dynamic tension with the state but distinguishably remain nonstate actors by their peculiar functions outside, and their interactions with, the state. Shaw and MacLean wonder if the interaction of these groups with international NGOs would not diminish their "democratizing, developmentalist" role. They also wonder if, in the face of the international division of labor and the new international division of power that constituted considerable challenge for Africa, civil societies can be sustained. It is maintained though, that even if structural adjustment policies with which civil societies are closely associated have negative consequences for Africa, they still hold special significance for widespread popular participation. Onuoha uses the case study of the dynamics of agricultural policy in Nigeria at a time it was experiencing political instability, and financial and economic crisis that led to the restructuring of its economy to examine economic and political change.

In challenging agricultural policy during Nigeria's heyday of structural adjustment, Onuoha posits that because "public policy is only an index of the nature and character of the state," Nigeria's agricultural policy from the beginning of structural adjustment policy in 1986 until 1997 reflects the values and perceptions of the political leadership. The nature of the state and the political leadership are inextricably intertwined; hence, an understanding of the dynamics of this relationship informs an appreciation of agricultural policy types of the essentially military regimes that ruled Nigeria during that period. In this way, Onuoha attempts to establish a direct correlation between structural adjustment and agricultural productivity. The Nigerian agricultural policy during the period is examined as to how it responded to the economic changes that were ushered in by structural adjustment. This results in three distinct periods with three varying policy types. Prior to 1970, agricultural policy was "isolated and unarticulated"; from 1970 to 1985, it was piecemeal; from 1985 to 1997, agricultural policy was in consonance with structural adjustment policies epitomized by the 1988 Agricultural Policy of Nigeria. Though agricultural policy was at the time stable and articulated, what was consolidated was a collection of previous policies rather than freshly reformulated ones. Against this backdrop of the changing economic environment, the predicted increase in agricultural production was expected to generate demands by the external market as argued by the defenders of structural adjustment policies and the neoliberal international financial institutions. This reason by itself created contradictions for the local economy with respect to food production and national self-sufficiency because most African countries had barely enough to feed their populace let alone to export into the international market. In this way Onuoha arrives at a confluence of ideas that challenge agricultural, food, and self-sufficiency policies of African countries.

In a germane and timely chapter, April Gordon discusses the misconceptions and misinterpretations about women in Africa. Gordon feels that African women are faced by a "disproportionate lack" of opportunities to participate in education, the economy, and politics, which all lead to the neglect of women's "needs and interests" that feed into that frenzy of Western feminist thinking and writing about African women. Gordon questions what development is and the role of women in it while noting that the gross national product (GNP) is a deceptive measure of development that ignores the "social cost to people" of development, hence the necessity for sustainable development, which must include economic growth, economic equity, and ability to provide basic needs of society, as well as political and social development. Alternatively, a framework that conceptualizes the empowerment of women as one of the measures of sustainable development becomes relevant because in Africa women's roles have been pivotal to economic growth and have become even more so with the advent of structural adjustment policies. This impetus could be accentuated through recognizing women's contributions and empowering them so that they have more access to productive resources, as has been emphasized in the UN's conferences of the 1990s, which link women's empowerment with achieving development objectives. Women, it is argued, have been more receptive than men in agriculture, but colonialism is blamed for the "super-exploitation" of women through emphasis on cash-cropping and "gender division of labor" and for the "double day" of both agricultural and domestic work that women do. This bias also extends to education, and Gordon adds that the lack of education exacerbates population explosion. Thus, women are stereotypified as wives and mothers and not as potential engineers, doctors, teachers, and other professionals, which could call for rational allocation of resources that is gender determined. Therefore, Gordon opines that sustainable development would do well to transform such limitations and inequities and to create an enabling environment because when women are involved in the design and implementation of projects from which they will benefit, they participate actively. Generally, Gordon eloquently makes the point that there is a relationship between project identification and project implementation outcomes, especially on issues affecting women.

REGIONAL INTEGRATION AND SUSTAINABLE DEVELOPMENT

In this part, Aguibou Yansané, Nurudeen Akinyemi, and Aja Akpuru-Aja explore the intricacies in the attempts of African countries to integrate their economies and reap the advantages of economies of scale in the process of development. Whereas Yansané recognizes economic integration as an "important and unavoidable means of development strategy," Akinyemi contends that microlevel integration activities appear to yield more results than macrolevel enterprises. On the other hand, Akpuru-Aja takes a more global approach by examining the "recurrent issues, efforts, limitations, and the prospects" for the realization of regional community set goals. In obvious agreement with Akinyemi on the reasonableness of cooperation, Akpuru-Aja contends that, functionally speaking, it is better for countries to work together in certain technical areas. In saying this, Akpuru-Aja sets the tone for the discussion in the three chapters. He compares and contrasts both the functionalist and neofunctionalist approaches and comes to the conclusion that the latter approach is preferred because it provides institutional mechanisms that promote regional integration and that harmonize the perceptions, intentions, interests, values, and strategies for achieving the goals of integration. However, Akpuru-Aja identifies the lack of trust and confidence-building measures, low-level cross-border trade relations, low-level economic growth and underdevelopment, the lack of political will, and the challenges of globalization and a new world order as the main limitations to economic integration.

Against this backdrop, and in the context of the hopes raised by the 1991 Abuja African Economic Community proposals, Yansané analyzes each subregional economic grouping. The major highlights are that the Economic Community of West African States (ECOWAS) lacks "political will" and suffers from "institutional red tape," the Union Economique et Monétaire de L'Afrique de L'Ouest (UEMOA) duplicates ECOWAS, the Common Market of Eastern and Southern Africa is burdened by ineffective financial policies, and the Southern Africa Development Community (SADC) lacks "an enabling environment and an attractive investment climate" while choked by indebtedness and dependence on the West for the support of its development efforts. The worst of all the integrating regions is the Central African Economic Community (CEEAC) where enthusiasm is clearly lacking among the cooperating countries. Many of the countries are confused as to what exactly they want or expect from the union. In view of these problems, Yansané argues that in spite of the various agreements for the free movement of persons and goods in the said regions, there has been no coordination and harmonization of policies between the various regions to foster the conducive environment for the realization of the objectives of the African Economic Community (AEC). Along the same lines, Akpuru-Aja notes that in spite of the Organization of African Unity's (OAU) 1980 Lagos Plan of Action that supported the existing regional economic communities and encouraged the establishment of new ones, regrettably by 1991, there were no appreciable achievements to show for regional integration. Consequently, this necessitated moving the target dates for the realization of the objectives of the AEC from 2000 to 2035. In the final analysis therefore, the impression is demonstrably created and the facts support same, that to set up laudable objectives might be one thing, but realizing them might encounter enormous obstacles because of the many difficulties besieging African economies.

Akinyemi is a little more optimistic about the success of regional integration observing that the micro approach is the route that would lead to successes and uses the cases of the management of the Senegal and Gambia River basins to demonstrate the efficacy of this approach. In the construction and management of the Manantali and Diamam dams on the Senegal River, the cooperating states' interests were more strongly interdependent than most other broad cooperative schemes, and this understanding permeated the thinking that collective gains were greater than gains ensuing from unilateral actions. When compared with the design and implementation of the Balingor and Kekriti dams on the River Gambia, it was clear that the bureaucratization and politicization of the management structure of this enterprise created clogs that made it impossible to operate. Subsequently, the effort was a colossal failure after eleven years of inaction. In spite of the impressive successes of the microlevel approach, Akinyemi still points out, like Akpuru-Aja, that these economic development projects were still dependent on external funds for implementation. This demonstrates the limited utility of interstate cooperation even in the face of identifiable common interests. The deduction that can be made from these analyses is that it is not that interests cannot be clearly identified and articulated, but that the political will and expertise to manage innovation is evidently lacking in most regions. This resonates with the dominant role of the state in economic development that drives the tendency to politicize and bureaucratize projects and programs of development.

CONCLUSION

In the concluding chapter, Iheduru asks if the restructuring of the African economies that took place in the 1980s was successful in altering the structure of the African state, hence the dynamics in the mix of issues that affected development and that will possibly impact Africa's development outcomes in this millennium. It is contended that the postcolonial state was unstructured but has been forcibly structured by the structural adjustment policies imposed by external capital inflows from the late 1980s to the early 1990s. The imposition of neoliberal market policies that emphasized the use of market-led approaches in the allocation of resources dictated the transfer of responsibilities from the state to the market, which in turn meant the whittling down of the state apparatus. Through the "weakening" of the state and then "retooling" it, Iheduru contends that the state will become stronger and more alive to its responsibilities of policy initiation, policy enactment, and policy implementation. This will wipe out the postcolonial structural deficiencies in the state. In essence then, the constraints imposed by structural adjustment force the state to recede from economic management and in the process abandon the bloated functions acquired during colonialism and subsequent independence. The deconstruction of the state is facilitated by the suspicion, delegitimation, and withdrawal from the state by the citizenry, which in turn challenges the rights of the state to make policy. The rebounding of the state emerges in the form of political capacity by the state, which is the technocratic ability to make and implement policy. This ability will fundamentally alter the issues that the state has to deal with in the subsequent execution of its responsibilities.

Overall, there has been divergence rather than convergence, disagreements rather than consensus, parochialism rather than universalism, and parsimony rather than grandiousness of theory in the development thinking about Africa. Although different issues seem amenable to different paradigms, no single approach exists through which the dynamics of change can be conceptualized and eventually interpreted. The processes of change in all of their components call for varying issue-specific or issue-relevant approaches, as has been adopted in these chapters. In essence, the various epistemological outcomes in the end contribute through their varying approaches to a larger understanding of the African development problems.

NOTE

1. Azarya, Victor, "Reordering State-Society Relations: Incorporation and Disengagement," in Donald Rothchild and Naomi Chazan, eds., *The Precarious Balance: State and Society in Africa* (Boulder, CO: Westview Press, 1988).

PART II

Bring Back the State: From Instability to Consolidation

2

The Political Economy of State Reconstitution in Africa

Kelechi A. Kalu

> The trouble with our new nation—as I saw it then lying on that bed—was that none of us had been indoors long enough to be able to say "To hell with it." We had all been in the rain together until yesterday. Then a handful of us—the smart and the lucky and hardly ever the best—had scrambled for the one shelter our former rulers left, and had taken it over and barricaded themselves in.
>
> Chinua Achebe, *A Man of the People*

INTRODUCTION

Despite increased scholarship on the impact of the post–Cold War situation on states' foreign economic policies, theories for explaining state action, and domestic political and economic development strategies, there is minimal focus on the opportunity the end of the Cold War offers for state reconstitution in Africa. State collapse and/or decay in Somalia, Liberia, Burundi-Rwanda, Sierra Leone, the Democratic Republic of the Congo (former Zaire) and other troubled spots in Africa compels consideration of the extent to which the postcolonial states can be reconstituted to carry out their expected functions. Generally, contemporary African political and economic development strategies are rooted in Western conception of knowledge on and about Africa. Modernization theory approaches development issues from the point of view of Africa's backwardness. Dependency theory advocates present an alternative framework that largely ignores the dynamics of state incapacity characterized by indigenous elite corruption, dependence on foreign economic and political actors, economic and social chaos, systematic repression, and oppression of state "enemies." Although some dependency scholars assess the repressive nature of the state and some articulate the problem as systemic dominance and dependence, most critique colonialism but assume the relevance and viability of the post-colonial state.

Specifically, in the early postcolonial period, the same perspective argued that because of the inchoate nature of African states and the need for economic development and consolidation, it was not necessary to encourage postindependence African governments toward political liberalism and free-market principles. A benign paternalism, this view served the interests of the Western states in a Cold War–structured international system resulting in (unintended?) support for authoritarianism and dictatorship of the few in Africa. Such support is evident in the availability of arms and foreign aid to corrupt leaders in Kenya, Nigeria, Central African Republic, Angola, Zambia, and the Congo who used anti-Communism as a weapon, to suffocate civil society and pillage their countries' natural resources. Consequently, at the end of the Cold War, rather than seeking to understand strategies to empower the state to discharge its functions to citizens in various African countries, this situation has led some scholars to see African states as decaying and collapsing, whereas others argue that what needs further exploration are the triumph of Western liberalism over Eastern socialism/communism, the dominance of Western information technology, and the superiority of Western civilization.

Ideologically driven research on African issues, especially by Western scholars, coincides with the rise to power of conservative governments in Japan, England, and the United States in the 1980s. This is a shift from earlier emphasis from states' involvement in economic development to an assertive neoclassical position for states' withdrawal from the marketplace. Following this shift, the World Bank and the International Monetary Fund (IMF) initiated the Structural Adjustment Program (SAP), which focuses on the utility of states' involvement for the implementation of transitions from autocracy to democratization and from rigid state control of economic redistribution to a market-based rewards system. Thus, with the end of the Cold War, the research focus on Africa's issues moved from (1) modernization to neoliberalism, (2) statist to state collapse arguments, and (3) Western policy makers to international financial institutions (IFIs). These categories reduce the focus on the capacity of the African states in the international political system and ignore questions about the nature of states in Africa, the capacity to implement its functions, and the compatibility of the inherited colonial state to African realities such as diverse ethnic, religious, racial, and cultural differences. Indeed, the turnaround is so compelling that the focus of the World Bank 1997 *World Development Report* is subtitled *The State in a Changing World*.[1]

Deductively, then, discussions about African states are subsumed within Western epistemology with an emphasis on African development framed around civil-society, constitutional governance, free markets, and democratization. In this chapter, I show that states (especially in Africa), by being political rather than social constructions, are featured at the center of political analysis, risking the endurance of societal inequities. Therefore, understanding societal ideas, interests, and institutions are sine qua non to reconstituting the African state. Rather than revealing state decay and collapse, I examine the state collapse arguments on the basis of juridical and empirical definition to show a collapse of authority. Beginning with Western liberal perspectives on development, I then present two contrasting views for state reconstitution in Africa.

MODERNIZATION AND NEOLIBERAL ARGUMENTS

Advocates of neoliberalism or liberal internationalism use these newer concepts of modernization to explore the Cold War basis of contemporary economic and political arguments. Using neoclassical economic theory, these perspectives offer a universal (albeit contested) view of how to maximize states interest and the general welfare within a *free-market* structure. Irrespective of historical differences and social formations of many countries, neoliberalism assumes that its prescriptions can be universally applied. Principally, neoliberalism requires "dogged individualism," an exchange relationship structured around free markets and is built on flexible interactions between buyers and sellers.

Writing against mercantilist policies, Adam Smith argued that state's interest will not be maximized by protectionism and intervention in the market. Instead, the "invisible hand" of the market naturally ensures that the pursuit of self-interest will ultimately maximize efficiency and prosperity. Fundamental to Smith's argument is the notion that "the individual consumer, firm or household is the basis of society . . . [that each] . . . behave[s] rationally . . . to maximize or satisfy certain values at the lowest possible cost . . . on the basis of a cost/benefit or means/ends calculus."[2]

Although Adam Smith recognized the existence of political realities, he argued that trade always benefits all participating states. Using the example that country A's welfare may increase to the detriment of the power position of country B, he argues that however dangerous in war and politics such a condition may seem, it is more advantageous for both countries to trade than to intervene in the market.[3] Whereas Smith's argument is based on the assumption that gains from foreign trade are largely based on absolute advantage, David Ricardo argues that even if a country has no absolute advantage, it can still derive gains from trade.[4] The Ricardian comparative advantage thesis, based on the notion of the market as a self-correcting entity, insists that if all countries specialize in a given economic activity and trade, every participant in the liberal economic marketplace would be rewarded with economic prosperity. As long as trade remains at the center of world affairs, peace and prosperity guarantee the absence of war.

Thus, liberal internationalist theory links theories of economic liberalism and democracy, maintaining that states with similar democratic institutions and open economic systems are more pacific than authoritarian states with centralized economies. Further, the liberal internationalist account, with its emphasis on welfare and peace, is based on the assumption that an open political process and citizens' participation in choosing their leaders encourages such leaders to be more sensitive to public opinion regarding domestic and external economic and political issues that directly affect the citizens. In general, liberal internationalism claims that one state's interest can be realized in cooperation with other states within frameworks of international liberal institutions such as the IMF, GATT (General Agreement on Trade and Tariffs), and the World Bank.

However, from liberal internationalist perspectives, open political and economic systems are more suited to the more advanced and industrialized Western democracies. The less-developed countries are largely viewed by liberal Western social scientists as economically and politically deficient on the basis of the less-developed countries' cultural/traditional characteristics. Walt Rostow,[5] A. F. Organski,[6] and Samuel Huntington[7] are representative of Western scholars who define the political and economic problems of the less-developed countries as functions of internal incapacity and decay. Using the modernization perspective, these scholars generally characterize underdevelopment as an "original state" that every nation goes through. The modernization prescription enjoins "traditional" societies to abandon their "uncivilized" culture for a civilized Western experience in order to attain development.

In the economic sphere, modernization entails application/diffusion of Western technology to the Third World on the one hand and adherence to the principles of comparative advantage on the other. This means that specialization in the production and export of goods with cost-of-labor advantages to the Third World involves concentration on the production and export of raw materials, thus ensuring an effective international division of labor. According to Lofchie and Commins, "This kind of specialization . . . would not only lead to more wealth for all nations, but to the greatest possible improvement in living conditions for their people."[8]

Similarly, analyses of underdevelopment by the modernization school of thought leads them to conclude that feudal or traditional culture is an impediment to development in the Third World. From the modernization perspectives, one of the stages that a less-developed economy has to pass through is the abandoning of traditional customs, norms, and values. In essence, the new nation becomes a "Westernized" state in the image of the European or

American state. And, on the level of the individual, " . . . changes in traditional patterns of behaviour and values, with urbanization, literacy and social mobility [become] characteristic indices of levels of change,"[9] consequently serving as a base for the attainment of modernization.

However, given that modernization and economic development do not occur in a vacuum, its political framework ensures that

modernization involves the development of an institutional framework that is sufficiently flexible to meet the demands placed upon it; the centralisation of power in the state, coupled with a weakening of traditional sources of authority, differentiated political structures, sub-system autonomy, and widened political participation; and an instrumental ideology to give purpose and direction to the processes of change.[10]

From the above perspective, attainment of modernization and or development by Third World countries is premised on two distinct but closely related strategies: the adoption of the neoclassical economic approach as presented by Rostow and the institutionalization of a democratic system of government whose powers are flexible enough to ensure stability and order for market mechanisms to work. Although a stable government is an essential component of the modernization process, the economic growth aspect of the theory insists on avoiding government intervention in the market.

Implicit in the above argument are the following: (1) governments should not interfere with free markets; (2) all states will benefit if they allow "comparative advantage" to shape their economic activity; and (3) the process of modernization is systematic, transformative, and immanent. Consequently, sources of change toward modernization involve pain, patience, and internal behavioral change in the Third World states consistent with the experiences of the Western developed states. Thus, it is to the advantage of the least-developed countries to remain within the international capitalist system in order to ensure access to world markets, capital, and technology, all of which are essential to their industrialization and, by extension, their development.

For African states, therefore, liberal internationalism and its modernization/ neoclassical assumptions would argue that the best chance for economic development in individual states lies in its ability to (1) restrict government intervention in the market place and (2) liberalize the political system sufficiently to allow for protection of property rights and citizens' pursuit of their individual self-interests. For Africa, therefore, development strategies should be based on imitating the free-market system of the industrialized Western countries by adopting their already-developed technology. Also, the wealth generated by economic expansion trickles down to the masses in the form of jobs and economic well-being and benefits ordinary citizens. As evidence for their claims, liberal internationalists point to the successful rebuilding of Europe and Japan following World War II and to the astonishing level of economic growth in the newly industrialized countries (NICs) of Asia within the framework of capitalism. In general, then, and in contrast to dependency theory, liberal internationalism argues that rather than policies that unlink African states from the international system, development depends on Africa's growing integration into the capitalist international economic system.

DEPENDENCY THEORY[11]

Scholars within the dependency school of thought are in agreement with both the realists and the liberal internationalists in their general focus on the international system[12] as a useful analytical framework for understanding the effect of states' behavior on different issue areas. However, most of the dependency scholars, including adherents of the world systems approach, argue that the international system is shaped by the relationship between two classes—the capitalists who own the means of production and the workers whose only product is their labor. Within this framework, relations between states are understood in terms of relations between two classes—the developed capitalist states and the underdeveloped states. This perspective contradicts realists' assumption that states are the dominant actors and central focus of analyses in international politics. It is also at odds with liberal internationalists' viewpoint that individuals and their interactions are the central analytical focus of international relations.

Dependency theory is rooted in Lenin's characterization of the capitalist international system, in which capitalism survives by extending its reaches into the underdeveloped world.[13] Colonial and imperial policies of the industrialized countries result in uneven development, characterized by inequities in the distribution of economic and political power that favor industrialized countries over the Third World.

The historical relationship between the industrialized and underdeveloped countries is further differentiated by "undevelopment" and "underdevelopment." The first term refers to essential state of nature, whereas the second pertains to the structural/infrastructural emanations of industrialization. Andre Gunder Frank argues that the industrialized countries may have been "undeveloped," a phase through which every country must pass, but that capitalist expansion into the peripheral countries of the South resulted in the historical process of "underdevelopment," which is unique to the less-developed countries.[14]

Dependency theory holds that the relationships between the developed countries and the LDCs are largely driven by inequality in wealth and technology. That inequality is also demonstrated by the influence the industrialized countries have in international institutions like the IMF and the

World Bank whose structures advance the developed world's vision of liberal internationalism. As a result, the policies in such international institutions as the IMF and the World Bank constrain the policy options available to the Third World.

The relationship is further characterized by economic and political interdependence emanating from colonial domination. Although the international economic system can be described as interdependent, the nature of interactions between interdependent countries is crucial to the dependency argument. Analyses of interdependence must therefore describe the extent of sensitivity and vulnerability[15] of the developed and less developed countries. To the extent that a developed country's economy is diversified with alternative sources of revenue from effective income and excise taxes, diverse manufactured products with price flexibility, and multiple trade partners across the system, such a country is less sensitive and thus less vulnerable to the fluctuations of international markets. Given their monocultural economies, most African countries lack institutionalized tax-collecting systems, lack alternative revenue-generating activities, and are far more sensitive and vulnerable to fluctuations in price and interest rates. Moreover, those fluctuations are largely driven by the policies of the industrialized countries. As a consequence, the benefits of interdependence described by liberal internationalists go to domestic political and economic elites in alliance with transnational corporations. In this way, overall economic growth masks the impoverishment of the masses within the less developed countries.

Through their structural dependency, the Third World in general, and Africa in particular, continues to be marginalized in an international division of labor where countries like Japan and the United States have moved beyond material-based production toward a growing emphasis on services and information technology. Additionally, as the case of sub-Saharan African countries demonstrates, although some Third World countries have progressed toward the use of synthetic-based materials for production, most are still grappling with their raw material resources.

Implicit in the dependency perspectives are the following: (1) Structural dependency is a general condition affecting all less developed countries; therefore, national and specific conditions are irrelevant for understanding economic underdevelopment. (2) Structural dependency is externally imposed on Third World countries; therefore, underdevelopment is inherently rooted in Third World countries' experience with colonialism, imperialism, and the structural existence of international division of labor. Contrary to liberal internationalists, the problems of development are not rooted in the domestic political, social, psychological, and economic structures of the Third World. Rather, external constraints are direct obstacles to economic development in Third World countries. (3) Structural dependency is largely a problem of economic growth and development exacerbated by declining terms of trade in favor of Western developed countries. (4) Structural dependency is a constraint to development in the Third World. As such, underdevelopment in the periphery and development in the core are two sides of a single process of capital accumulation[16] in favor of the core states.

Adherents of the dependency perspectives argue that capitalist development in the periphery is not possible, largely because of the effect of international division of labor or what Samir Amin refers to as "extraversion."[17] Consequently, reversing the impact of structural dependency on the less-developed states requires a strategy of economic development that is based on self-reliance. Debt repudiation is another strategy suggested for the Third World to pursue economic development. This suggestion is largely driven by dependency scholars' perception that colonialism and imperialism are tools that the core states have used to exploit the Third World, and therefore, debt repudiation is both practical and in the interest of Third World countries. This view is reflected in both the early and contemporary literature on dependency theory.

Revisions within development theory came mainly from scholars with Marxist orientation who argued that the liberal agenda for development based on free-market enterprise is but one approach whose outcome (capitalist development) and its class-based implications are predetermined. Radical Marxists argue that the best strategy is one that offers an alternative path to development whose outcome (socialism) would result in the eventual establishment of a communist economic structure and its political implications for a proletarian revolution. Within structuralism then, both liberal internationalists and the more radical Marxists—in Western cultural spaces—accept "the paradigm of modernity." The major point of disagreement between liberals and Marxists is the nature of the end to be achieved: capitalist or socialist economic structure.[18] Consequently, modernization or development theorists and their critics accept Western experience, culture, and history as universal constants to be replicated in the "backward" societies, insisting that their history move from tradition to modernity, from the use of "crude instruments" to technology, and from communal association to dogged individualism.

As Berman observes, discussions about "culture" are primarily, if not exclusively, an issue of "technology." Also, although African countries are seen as sovereign equals to their Western counterparts capable of taking part in the universal march to "historical development," African societies and cultures are implicitly and explicitly treated as inferior within the Western development paradigm.[19] The assumption that African societies are inferior presupposes their inability to survive in competition with the rational and efficient technology, science, and organizational superiority of Western societies. And, leading these "backward societies" to development requires the identification of important elements such as "indigenous elites, including business elites or capitalists, conceived of as bearers of the necessary universal values of global modernity."[20]

Given the perceived absence of bureaucracy and organizational structure in "primitive societies," nation building became the rational starting point for reconstructing African societies from tradition to modernity. Thus, while the liberal modernizers argue for the utility of "market" mechanisms for capitalist development, their Marxist counterparts seek a reliance on the state. Consequently, discussions about development in the 1960s and early 1970s revolved around state and institution building. Subsequent policies ignored social formations, epistemology, and the nature of postindependence African states. These approaches neglected examination of the concept of state in general and the extent the Western idea of state applies to Africa.

CONCEPT OF STATEHOOD AND ITS APPLICATION TO AFRICA

Writing about the concept of "state" often evokes a dilemma: One either accepts a broad and therefore relatively insignificant definition of the state or agrees that the state is "not a universal concept but rather the product of a specific historical crisis"[21] that gives rise to the social formation and political organization of a given geopolitical experience. The modern state is rooted in a specific Western experience. It came out of the 1648 Treaty of Westphalia that ended the thirty-year war between Catholics and Protestants.

The literature on the nature and functions of the state spans all theoretical and analytical positions.[22] From a sociological perspective (Max Weber), a state exists if it can exercise a monopoly on the use of force in a given territory. Consistent with the language and intent of the 1648 Treaty at Westphalia, the international legal perspective (Ian Brownlie) sees the state as a "legal person" characterized by a given geographical territory, population, government, and political independence. Realists call this sovereignty. For Marxists (Karl Marx/Lenin), although it will eventually "wither away," the state reflects the economic interests of the ruling class. Statists and Realists (Stephen Krasner and others) see the state as a composite of (1) politics more as a problem of rule and control, (2) state as an actor in its own right, (3) formal and informal institutional constraints on individual behavior, and (4) a sense of history, and (5) the state more as disjunctures and stress. Also, in contrast to a Marxist view of the state, Krasner conceives of the state as "a set of roles and institutions having peculiar drives, compulsions, and aims of their own that are separate from the interests of any particular societal group."[23] From that perspective, the state is an abstraction with no particular intent or design to reward any one individual or group in society. The state's generally agreed-on central function of ensuring the national security of its territory and maintaining law, order, and welfare[24] is thus executed without regard to class, coalition, and individual interests. From the Realist perspective, even though the existence of the state is dependent on efficient bureaucracy with the capacity to collect revenues (taxes) and use its natural and human resources, the state is apolitical. If we accept the abstract nature of states from the Realist perspectives, we must conclude that the state is nothing but an umpire in the game of politics where the players are real human beings with, sometimes, bitterly contested interests. It also follows that such a state is autonomous and unaffected by the different political machinations within it. However, we will grant that if such a state is ineffective in its security functions, the likelihood exists that other states, perhaps more efficient, will dominate it. But, at the same, we must also grant that such abstract notions of the state have real and significant consequences for democracy. If in popular sovereignty (the idea that government policies reflect the general wishes of the governed) citizens' choices impact government decisions, and given that the interest of the state is maintained by the government, we must equally conclude that states are antidemocratic and reject the Realist perspective as well as Western liberal prescriptions for Africa.

Rejection of the foregoing perspectives leads to the conclusion that the state as an abstract entity does not exist and an acceptance (if partially) of the Marxists' notion of the state as a reflection of the ruling class. Our choice notwithstanding, the empirical question here is, which perspective gives a plausible road map for understanding the nature of the state in Africa? Most scholars and policy makers on postindependence Africa promote order as a precondition for economic development. Centralized state authority in maintaining law and order is seen as essential, especially by policy makers concerned that political liberalization might result in anarchy and incapacity of the newly independent African states to unify the various nationalities within their territories. Postindependence experiences include central economic planning for national development and nation building supported by the Western and African governments. However, as a number of African states, such as Uganda, Kenya, Algeria, Sudan, Somalia, Congo, Ghana, Nigeria, Central African Republic, Benin, Tanzania, Ivory Coast, Zimbabwe, and Angola, among others, went from hope to despair, from relative political stability following independence to civil wars, coups, and countercoups, the general discussion on Africa shifted from economic growth to political liberalization. Bifurcation of political and economic analysis in international relations theory began to be applied to Africa. The problems were seen as either political or economic. Such bifurcation served not only the interest of donor countries; the Cold War ideologically structured international system facilitated maintenance of growing confusion on and about Africa. And, even though the continent is three-and-half times larger than the United States, analysts, policy makers, and popular media houses tended to approach Africa as if it were a single country whose problems can be easily grasped. Postindependence African leaders were equally involved in the perceptual crisis in which external constituencies found themselves. For instance, military coup d'etats and/or one-man-rule became the prevalent governance structure in Africa. Equally significant was the general acceptance by the leaders that the individual countries needed economic aid from the Western governments in order to survive. Hence, the politics of foreign aid, like those of Arap Moi of Kenya and the late Mobutu Sese Seko's of former Zaire, tried to outdo each other in the level of squandered aid from the West.

It is generally acknowledged that the ongoing crisis in Africa is more than an economic or fiscal problem. It is also a *political* crisis that "besides [being] the usual political instability or crisis of legitimacy" is also evidence of "the pervasive lack of democracy, which some perceive as a conflict between the state and people—a crisis arising from lack of popular partici-pation in the development process."[25] I suggest that the crisis in Africa is deeply rooted in the continent's historical experience, which goes beyond the ongoing democratization processes of African states and leadership in Africa. The political and economic crisis in Africa in the 1990s is directly related to the crises of state and class formation before and during Africa's colonization.[26] To be sure, postcolonial alignment and realignment of socioeconomic and political forces have reproduced inherited conflicts, coalitions, contradictions, and crises.

WHERE THE RAIN BEGAN TO BEAT US[27]

At the birth of the contemporary international political system dating back to the Treaty of Westphalia in 1648, African nations were neither con-ceptually relevant as states nor were Africans seriously considered capable human beings to warrant a seat among the Western colonial powers and, as such, were simply excluded.[28] The partition of Africa by the European pow-ers that followed the Berlin Conference of 1884 to 1885 had two main con-sequences for Africa: (1) the arbitrary merging of several ethnic groups that traditionally had nothing in common and (2) the extension of European political and economic structures into Africa, incorporating the continent in a subordinate role to the European heartland. The forced incorporation of Africa into the international capitalist economic system whose rules favor Africa's former colonizers remains the single most important aspect needing rethinking and transformation.

Although state formation in most other parts of the world, especially in Europe, was a result of class conflicts in which early liberals denounced the "divine rights" of kings to rule, the process of state formation in Africa was stalled by the enforcement of the "white man's burden." The natural processes of class formation reflecting confrontations between communities, and the creation of larger political and administrative units were terminated and distorted by European colonization. New values, institutions, structures, and social relations were then imposed. More devastating for current political and class development in Africa, however, is the process of decolonization, which started at the conclusion of the first World War in 1917. According to Robert Jackson, the birth of African states contrasts with the usual pretwentieth-century sequential birth and death of states based on wars of conquest, colonization, or independence. The concurrent birthdays and uniform excolonial frontiers of African states are connected to a changed doctrine of international legitimacy that occurred in the later half of the twentieth century and were based on the categorical and unrestricted right, colonial (as distinguished from national) self-determination, of overseas colonies to become independent states without regard to preparedness. This is essentially a doctrine of birthright: Territories formed by European colonialism are considered to have a right to become sovereign without regard to precolonial social formations of the different nationalities.[29]

Of course, the implication of this will seem that some states would have opted to remain extensions of the colonial empires, as was the case with a number of French colonies in West Africa. But, that misses the point. If European states decide when and how Africa participates in the international political and economic system whose rules are already established, then the tendency will be toward constraint on the ability of African states to design independent political and economic development strategies in an international system structured for exploitation and marginalization of peripheral countries.

Though sovereignty is a concept emerging from the 1648 Westphalian Treaty, its empowering influence at home and abroad can be either positive or negative. Although the concept of sovereignty recognizes every state in the world system of states as legal equals, the government of state possesses the sole legitimate right and power to use force. Consequently, the influence of sovereignty is twofold: (1) constraints to the development of democracy and (2) good governance in a political space characterized by differences in culture, ethnicity, class, and region.

First, although every state is now politically independent in Africa, the fear of loss of power continues to constrain leadership transitions through the ballot boxes. For example, former autocrats in Ghana, Kenya, Zimbabwe, Nigeria, Benin, and elsewhere have made attempts to turn themselves from autocrats to democrats with few successes in Ghana, Uganda, Benin, and Niger Republic. Political turmoil in Central African Republic, Nigeria, Congo, Algeria, Somalia, Angola, and Guinea Bissau continues because similar autocrats—remain unwilling to preside over fair and openly contested elections. In these instances, the few individuals who hold state power have enormous influence and access to the instrument of force necessary to silence the opposition. Also significant is the role of power, conceptualized as the use of force for material accumulation, corruption, the containment of radicals, violations of human rights, and silencing of the media. To be sure, at independence, the colonial state had badly underdeveloped and marginalized the local elites. Foreign capital dominated all sectors of the respective economies. In the settler colonies, conditions were worse as captured state power became the only institution within the control of the local elites to promote class and clan unity and accumulation and to defend themselves. The state became the bourgeoisie, hence the reluctance to give up power by those privileged to be the first to steer the ship of states in Africa at independence. The nature of this sovereignty makes it difficult for African states to intervene in the internal affairs of member states. Of course, the Tanzanian-led ouster of Idi Amin in Uganda, regional states' support of Laurent Kabila's rise to power in Congo, and the Nigerian-led ECOMOG [ECOWAS (Economic Community of West African States) Monitoring Group] (the West African peacekeeping force) intervention in Sierra Leone remain exceptions to the rule. But these are all interventions of convenience to remove autocrats that do not significantly affect the international community's, especially the Western governments', concern with their "national interests," which, in the case of Africa, is mainly economic.[30] The relationship between Western governments and most of the leaders in Africa is reminiscent of the traditional patronage system, which has been identified by some as a constraint to development in Africa.[31]

Secondly, and more importantly, even when the international community supports democratization in Africa without the obvious class arrangements between the national bourgeoisie and international capital, the problem of social mobilization, essential for participatory democracy, remains. As Karl Deutsch observes, social mobilization

brings with it an expansion of the politically relevant strata of the population. . . . increased political participation. . . . rapid social mobilization to promote the consolidation of states.[32]

And, given that absolute power tends to corrupt absolutely, it becomes obvious why those ethnic groups and individuals that assumed the mantle of political power from Africa's former colonizers accept the principles of participatory democracy but continue to find that it is not in their best interest to share power, and they remain unwilling to preside over power transitions through the ballot box.

For example, nationalistic transitions in contemporary Africa that started in the late 1950s through the mid-1960s involved transitions from colonialism to political independence. In most cases, these country-specific transitions based discussions about unity on the need to end colonialism. Nationalism failed to transform itself into nation building through grassroot participation of the masses; its "unity" became convenient among urban-based elites. Consequently, the masses became irrelevant to state building, and all opposition parties, individuals, and organizations were urged to speak with one voice and eschew differences. Arguably, the unintended consequence of silencing the opposition was the absence of political discourse on matters of the state. With no serious engagement of the military regimes on the necessity for democratic systems, most transitions are from military/one-party rule to competitive party politics. Notable examples of this kind of transition include Nigeria between 1975 and 1979 and again between 1985 and 1993 and Ghana in the late 1970s and its return to civil rule in late 1992. Transitions from one-party rule to multiparty democracy with consequent regime changes are evidenced by Cape Verde in 1990, Benin Republic in 1991, and Zambia in 1991.[33] Although the dictators in Central Africa Republic, Zambia, Nigeria, Sierra Leone, Algeria, and elsewhere aborted and/or compromised those countries' political liberalization processes, some superficial progress allowed for competitive elections in Kenya, Angola, and the Cameroon. Given previous failed attempts at democratic transitions, to what extent are the current externally induced political conditionalities that require political pluralism for foreign aid and the pressures from donors, lenders, and other creditors (including the World Bank and International Human Rights community) likely to result in institutionalization of democratic governments on the continent?

INTERNATIONAL DIMENSIONS OF DEMOCRATIC TRANSITION IN AFRICA

The undemocratic processes adopted by European powers in the scramble for Africa and the impact of consequent authoritarian colonial policies are partial explanations for why most African governance systems are undemocratic. The colonial state (rule), without exception, was brutal, undemocratic, nonaccountable, exploitative, and dehumanizing. Its legacies include a culture of violence, distrust, and divisiveness in Africa. The international system of states within which the African states play subordinate roles not only maintains these undemocratic legacies but serves the interests of the dominant elites in the industrialized or peripheral countries. For example, the weighted system of voting in the World Bank and the IMF, which is based on how much share a member state can buy, subordinates the less-developed states to the interests of the developed. In such contexts, and, as currently constituted, African states will remain irrelevant in their capacity to self-rejuvenate and in negotiations on political and economic matters with the developed Western corporations and states. Further, the politics of trade negotiation in the GATT, which promises nondiscrimination and open access to the international market for goods and services from all countries, does not ensure access for agricultural products, the main export for African countries. The point here is that decision-making structures and policies in the international system in the colonial and postcolonial era continue to be politically motivated, ensuring the marginalization and continued subordination of Third World states to the international capitalist system. Postcolonial states, reflecting the international system and policies, continue to fail to organize and empower citizens to be participants rather than recipients of top-down policies.

For example, even though the Nigerian masses objected to borrowing money from the IMF/World Bank in 1986, the government defied the citizens and accepted the IMF loans and its conditionalities. Although Third World countries that desire to borrow money from the IMF/World Bank are required to liberalize their political and economic systems, it is significant to note that

The emphasis on economic liberalisation and on the autonomy and efficiency of market forces is but the other side of the liberal democracy coin; and the emphasis has come about as a result of the failure of state-directed economic planning in Africa and the consequent pressures on African . . . governments to impose IMF and donor countries' conditionalities in the form of structural adjustment programmes in their various countries.[34]

If the abysmal economic conditions in most African states are a result of poor judgment on the part of their governments, then there is no rationale to expect that new loans will result in improved development in infrastructure or institutionalization of democracy, especially when the loans and SAP are to be managed by the same unstable, nonhegemonic, corrupt, inefficient, and dependent elites and governments. Further, if the international economic system is not characterized by "efficient market forces," as evidenced by the regularly scheduled meetings of the Group of Seven (G7), GATT, U.S. government interventions to shore up the Mexican peso and the Japanese yen, and the frequent utilization of economic statecraft by the industrialized West to promote their interests abroad, then the expectation of economic growth on the basis of Adam Smith's "invisible hand" principle is doomed to fail in Africa.[35] If the failure to sustain economic growth continues to result in increased ethnic tensions and conflicts over the sharing of national resources, then the incentive for the citizens and the ability of the state to sustain democracy will atrophy. As the cases of Kenya and Nigeria illustrate, unabated economic depression result in the development of a political game plan by dominant personalities and ethnic groups to ensure their stay in power. Such circumstances encourage a politics of redistribution that constrains simultaneous attainment of democracy and economic development in multiethnic states whose economic and political decisions are influenced by external interests of the IFIs, local elites, and dominant ethnic groups. Without a visual and concrete transformation of the political and economic structures in Africa, the possibilities that the so-called African renaissance or second independence will lead the continent to the promised land of political and economic development become doubtful.

RECONSTITUTING THE AFRICAN STATES

After several decades, the World Bank notes in the *World Development Report 1997,* that states are *not* merely umpires without economic interests; they are in many instances managed by honest individuals, but, in most cases by corrupt and brutal dictators. Specifically for Africa, and in negation of its neoclassical perspective, the Bank finds that "there is a crisis of statehood in Africa—a crisis of state capability and legitimacy."[36] The Bank is not alone in recognizing that African states suffer from incapacity and are undergoing processes of delegitimation at the end of the Cold War.[37] The analysts with these conclusions are mostly members of the same intellectual community whose theories and measurement instruments do not lend themselves easily to change.[38] Kuhn argues that similar to political revolutions, revolutions in the sciences result from an acknowledged crisis in a segment of the intellectual or political community. Knowledge restricted to a segment of the community often leads to a clear understanding that existing institutions have failed in their expected task. When this knowledge leads to a crisis, how the intellectual or political community responds determines whether the status quo is maintained or changed. The following section looks at the economic crisis facing the African continent, specifies the corpus of existing liberal arguments whose conclusions suggest a no-exit option for Africa, and makes suggestions on reconstituting states in Africa.

THE ECONOMIC CRISIS FACING AFRICA

Empirically, colonial African states were born out of the crisis of European states' needs to exploit other territories to feed their citizens and provide resources for their industries. Similarly, political independence for African states came as a result of crisis in Europe—Hitler's onslaught on his cousins—which made it difficult for Europeans to hold on to their colonial territories, including those in Africa. Since independence in the 1960s, the European-imposed states on various African nations have not enjoyed the stature or respect similar to those of states in Europe. Consequently, African states continue to reflect the European crises that spawned their creation. In the areas of conflict, fourteen of the fifty-three African states were involved in an armed conflict in 1996 alone. Since the 1970s, over thirty wars have been fought in Africa, accounting for "more than half of all war-related deaths worldwide . . . and caused over 8 million people to become refugees, returnees and displaced persons."[39] Economically, African states have become more dependent on Western governments for economic aid and support. Although most regions are experiencing growths and innovations in technology, African economies are still characterized by the use of crude instruments and, in many instances, neglect of the agricultural sectors. As Jon Kraus argues, Africa is increasingly becoming irrelevant in world markets with respect to production, incomes, trade, investments, technologies, and bargaining power it wields.[40] Thus, "while per capita GDP[gross domestic product] income in Africa rose an estimated 1.4 percent in the 1960s and 0.8 percent in the 1970s, it fell to minus 2.4 percent in the 1980s." And as a result of falling terms of trade and debt crises, most African countries experienced a deeper level of poverty and falling incomes in the 1980s. The IMF-imposed SAP reforms of trade liberalization and later political liberalization have not helped either. The result was increased competition from imports, and during 1980–90, forty-three of 139 British firms with industrial investments in Africa withdrew—primarily from Nigeria, Zimbabwe, and Kenya.[41] As most analysts have acknowledged, the 1980s was a lost decade for Africa. More devastating for a continent known to possess enough arable land to feed its population and earn foreign exchange in the early 1960s, on aggregate, "per capita food production in Africa between 1961 and 1995 actually dropped by 12 percent."[42]

Africa's external debt in 1996 stands at over $328.9 billion—debts owed to the Western governments and banks that are managed by the IFIs. Although Africa's external debts are smaller than those of Latin America, as a measure of economic output, African external debt is the highest in the world. Also, although Africa's GDP grew at 5 percent in 1996, it was checkmated by a 3 percent population growth over the same period. Of the 174 countries listed in the 1993 United Nations Human Development Index (HDI), all African countries but three (Mauritius, Seychelles, and Botswana) rank well above 100 with most at the bottom of the list. And, despite the poor showing on the HDI ranking, on aggregate, African countries spent more on defense than on health.[43]

Similarly, using scientific education and acquisition as a measure of technical knowledge, Africa in aggregate terms is well below other regions. For example, regarding the number of scientists and engineers per million of population, Africa has fifty-three compared to 3,548 for Japan, 209 for Latin America, and 202 for Arab states.[44] Indeed, the economic and services data for Africa are so abysmal that Benjamin Barber argues that along with other impoverished Third World countries, sub-Saharan Africa can be realistically called "the Terminal World."[45] As the search continues for the right mix of suggestions and policies for helping African states come out of their crises, we must ask; if modernization and dependency suggestions failed in the past, what are the new and plausible perspectives helpful for reconstituting African states to effectively carry out their expected functions of security, law/order, and welfare?

WESTERN RESPONSE TO THE CRISES OF STATEHOOD IN AFRICA

For the collapsed state thesis, Zartman argues that "It is better to reaffirm the validity of the existing [states] and make it work, using it as a framework for adequate attention to the concerns of its citizens and the responsibilities of sovereignty, rather than experimenting with smaller units, possibly more homogeneous but less broadly based and less stable."[46] Benjamin Barber argues that "Even Africa, although it is falling off the world's economic charts, is to be gathered into McWorld's fold. For in the gunsight of Coke's ambitions, it is not the home of endless poverty, rampant AIDS, and ongoing authoritarianism, but rather a 568-million person soft-drink market featuring warm climates, youthful populations and governments moving toward market economies."[47] The universal free-market perspective expounded by the neoclassical perspectives are therefore targeted at increasing the wealth of transnational corporations whose allegiance is not to their own states, much less to those of Africa. As Barber points out, the new struggle at the end of the Cold War is "about democracy—and the dangers democracy faces in a world where the forces of commerce and the forces reacting to commerce are locked in a struggle"[48] that has the potential to destroy civil society and eventually Western contribution to systems of governance—democracy. From Francis Fukuyama's point of view, the new political discourse at the end of the Cold War is the victory of liberal democracy over other ideological perspectives. Fukuyama states that, "While some present-day countries might fail to achieve stable liberal democracy, and others might lapse back into other, more primitive forms of rule like theocracy or military dictatorship, the *ideal* of liberal democracy could not be improved on."[49] As always, Samuel Huntington is as audacious as ever in his analysis of what Western civilization has done for the rest of the non-Western societies. Huntington asserts:

The concept of a universal civilization is a distinctive product of Western civilization. In the nineteenth century the idea of "the white man's burden" helped justify the extension of Western political and economic domination over non-Western societies. At the end of the twentieth century the concept of a universal civilization helps justify Western cultural dominance of other societies and the need for those societies to ape Western practices and institutions.[50]

Furthermore, "Except for small, isolated, rural communities willing to exist at a subsistence level, the total rejection of modernization as well as Westernization is hardly possible in a world becoming overwhelmingly modern and highly interconnected."[51] Indeed, this is the clearest statement of the intent by advocates of Western culture and practices for the rest of the world. The question is; are non-Western states and civilizations autistic to the arguments and policies emanating from Western institutions of higher learning as well as from international institutions like the IMF and the

World Bank? If autism is out of the question, what strategies will help African states understand the structure of the international political system, how the games are played, and the pay-off structure? The rest of the chapter shall attempt a response to these questions.

IN LIEU OF A CONCLUSION: SUPERSTATES ARE BETTER FOR AFRICA

As Francis Fukuyama argues, "The realm of states is the realm of the political, the sphere of self-conscious choice about the proper mode of governance. The realm of peoples is sub-political: it is the domain of culture and of society, whose rules are seldom explicit or self-consciously recognized even by those who participate in them."[52] Given that states are socially constructed ideas of human organization, participants in such building efforts are self-seeking rather than general welfare-seeking agents. The idea of the state assumes its abstraction only when the members of a given state are in general agreement to be self-restrained from destroying the state and specifically to accept the constraints on individual actions imposed by such a state. Whereas the Western states have attained that high level of abstraction and legitimately serve the interests (albeit unequally) of citizens, the states in Africa have been instruments for class, ethnic and regional intimidation, corruption, and suffocation of civil society by those lucky enough to have received the mantle of leadership from departing colonizers. States in Africa are nonhegemonic in the sense intended by the 1648 Treaty of Westphalia. Indeed, the colonizers of Africa left the continent and its governments with few choices other than to continue the pattern of exclusion practiced by the departing Europeans. This is evident in the granting of political independence without economic strength to sustain the new states. With the end of the Cold War and Western reluctance for involvement in Africa (except for trade), reconstituting the political and economic landscapes in Africa is a prerequisite for advancing the position of the continent in the international political system.

On the basis of either juridical or empirical definitions of state explored here, the state collapse arguments are not adequate for obviating the political and economic weaknesses in Africa. On closer examination, the state collapse arguments reveal a different kind of breakdown. As a conceptual tool for analysis and the center of analytical discourse in international relations, the imposed state in Africa is alive and well. What has collapsed and decayed is the government—the realm of politics—where individuals have a choice of allegiance to the state or to wealth accumulation. Unfortunately, most past and present African heads of governments have chosen the wealth accumulation option, succeeding only in inculcating the culture of separatism, civic irresponsibility, fear, and hopelessness in the citizens. These have engendered

inexcusable levels of poverty, politicized ethnicity, class fragmentations, deep
social and economic deformities, and rigidly maintained power structures
that advantaged the elites over the masses. Collectively, these are the political reasons for the *collapse of authority* in Africa. Against the liberal internationalist accounts of Zartman, Huntington, and Barber, an "exhortation-
ist culture" where corruption is a "structural fact" and bribery is "economic
mugging," the African state cannot be expected to reconstitute itself[53]
because it never had the power to sustain itself.

At this point, two options seem viable—to reconstitute the existing states
on the basis of similarity in culture and language, or, to erase the existing
state boundaries and go back to the drawing boards to create five out of the
existing fifty four states. The option of creating smaller states on the basis
of similarity in culture and language might not solve the problem of African
states' irrelevance in the international system. But, it has the potential of
ensuring more focused relationships at a pace acceptable to specific pre-
colonial social formations like the Yorubas, the Hausas, the Igbos, Kikuyus,
Wolofs, Zulus, Kongos, and Bantus, as well as other groups. It is clear that
such a project would tax the imagination of even the best cartographers; its
greatest weakness is the potential to defeat the social reconstruction agenda
of strengthening the bargaining positions of African states in regional and
international diplomacy.

The existing imposed structures were based on European assumptions of
the absence of institutional and governmental structures in precolonial
Africa. That assumption resulted in the imposition of the idea of states
without regard to cultural ties. Thus, the arbitrary state boundaries separated families, misidentified the depth and length of some rivers (for example, in Cameroon), and politically introduced Machiavellian strategies and
guns for resolving conflicts in Africa. In the ensuing confusion and hostili-
ties, each state was exploited for the benefits it offered to Europe. At the
end of colonialism, transnational corporations carried on the tradition and
pitted states against each other for cheap raw materials and labor. States in
Africa became losers. But, African states can and do have the potential to
be major players in the international system of states. As Western governments and businesses know too well,

Twenty percent of U.S. oil imports come from Africa, and America relies on Africa
for supplies of strategic minerals. Africa possesses 54 percent of the world's cobalt,
32 percent of its bauxite, 52 percent of its manganese, and 81 percent of its
chromium stocks. South Africa alone has 84 percent of the world's reserve of platinum, and Zimbabwe has significant platinum potential. . . . Beyond strategic
metals, Africa's mineral wealth—from West Africa's gold, tin, and iron ore to Southern and Central Africa's industrial and precious diamonds, copper, and gold—is at
least equal to that found elsewhere.[54]

The strategic structure of states in Africa could be changed such that five *superstates* are created around Algeria (United States of North Africa), Kenya (United States of East Africa), Democratic Republic of Congo (United States of Central Africa), Nigeria (United States of West Africa), and South Africa (United States of Southern Africa). The existing major states in Africa will provide the initial administrative and infrastructural support for a Constitutional Convention to harmonize economic, political, cultural, and social issues. By taking advantage of economy of scale and through pooled resources, the superstates will increase economic productivity and opportunities for their citizens. Through increases in the size and scope of the new territories, the superstates will eliminate instances of military coups d'etat that have characterized leadership transitions in Africa since the 1960s. With enhanced human and natural resources in each superstate, business interactions with transnational corporations will largely be dictated by the size of the market and the purchasing power offered by each state. And, significantly, the creation of superstates will have the tendency to eliminate the Machiavellian business strategies that continue to deprive African states of both economic profits and human resources that result in brain drain. Superstates are more likely to institutionalize and operate a more efficient bureaucracy with the capacity to restructure the corporate and income tax collection system in their states. As such, they are more likely to adequately confront and deal with poverty, hunger, and lack of educational facilities/resources as well as general infrastructure than current states.

The issue of governance, which is necessary for realizing the foregoing suggestions, is at the core of reconstituting states in Africa. With Constitutional Conventions for each state, finally, Africans will have the opportunity to determine for themselves what system of government works consistently with continental realities. The absence of political discourse that involved Africans at the Berlin Conference will be rectified. More importantly, introducing politics in its proper context—as the redistribution of scarce economic resources on the basis of value—is predicted to result in the formation of viable interest groups whose activities will impact the formation and enhancement of existing civil institutions—traditional and modern. While resolving issues of political discourse at the Constitutional Conventions, it will become possible for opposition groups in different parts of Africa to articulate and understand the structure of power rather than how individuals acquire power. This is significant because understanding the structure of power and how it works in the political arena is likely to result in losers in a given election accepting their losses while preparing to compete in future elections. The new states will become the new frontiers of influence.

NOTES

1. World Bank, 1997. *World Development Report 1997: The State in a Changing World*. New York: Oxford University Press.

2. Robert Gilpin, 1987. *The Political Economy of International Relations*. Princeton, New Jersey: Princeton University Press: 28.

3. Adam Smith, 1937. *Wealth of Nations*. New York: Modern Library Edition: 461. See also, Albert O. Hirschman, 1945. *National Power and the Structure of Foreign Trade*. Berkeley, California: University of California Press: 6.

4. David Ricardo, 1991. "On Foreign Trade," in George T. Crane and Abla Amawi, eds., *Theoretical Evolution of International Political Economy*. New York: Oxford University Press: 72–82.

5. Walt W. Rostow, 1960. *The Stages of Economic Growth*. Cambridge: Cambridge University Press.

6. A. F. Organski, 1965. *The Stages of Political Development*. New York: Alfred A. Knopf.

7. Samuel P. Huntington, 1968. *Political Order in Changing Societies*. New Haven, Connecticut: Yale University Press.

8. Michael F. Lochie and Stephen K. Commins, 1988. "Food Deficits and Agricultural Policies in Tropical Africa," in Charles K. Wilber, ed., *The Political Economy of Development and Underdevelopment*. New York: Random House: 309.

9. William Tordoff, 1984. *Government and Politics in Africa*. Bloomington, Indiana: Indiana University Press: 16.

10. Ibid.

11. See, for example, Paul Baran, 1957. *The Political Economy of Growth*. New York: Monthly Review Press; Andre Gunder Frank, 1967. *Capitalism and Underdevelopment in Latin America*. New York: Monthly Review Press; Theotonio Dos Santos, 1970. "The Structure of Dependence," *The American Economic Review*, Vol. 60, No. 2 (May); Bill Warren, 1973. "Imperialism and Capitalist Industrialization," *New Left Review*, No. 18 (September/October); Fernando H. Cardoso and Enzo Faletto, 1979. *Dependence and Development in Latin America*. Berkeley, California: University of California Press; Ronald H. Chilcote and Dale L. Johnson, eds., 1983. *Theories of Development: Mode of Production or Dependence?* Beverly Hills, California: Sage Publications.

12. The dependency school maintains that underdevelopment is a historical process of exploitation of the less-developed countries by the industrialized countries of the West. Such a conclusion is similar to realists' assumption that powerful states will tend to dominate the weak. Thus, if industrialized Western countries exploit the less-developed countries, then we must conclude that the basic premise of realism is undisputed by dependency theory. Similarly, liberal internationalists and dependency theorists regard the capitalist world economy as the key feature of the international system. But, for liberal internationalists, capitalism will lift the less-developed countries out of underdevelopment; the dependency scholars argue that capitalism exploits and imprisons the less-developed countries to an unending condition of underdevelopment.

13. See V. I. Lenin, 1939. *Imperialism: The Highest State of Capitalism*. New York: Monthly Review Press: 88–98.

14. See Andre Gunder Frank, 1969. *Latin America: Underdevelopment or Revolution*. New York: Monthly Review Press.

15. For a conceptual clarification of the definition and use of "sensitivity" and "vulnerability," see Robert O. Keohane and Joseph Nye, 1977. *Power and Interdependence: World Politics in Transition*. Boston: Little, Brown and Company.

16. See Alvin Y. So, 1990. *Social Change and Development: Modernization, Dependency, and World System Theories*. London: Sage Publications: 104–5.

17. Extraversion is characterized by the tendency of capitalist activities in the less-developed countries to focus on export products. (cited in Alvin Y. So, op cit.: 102). For a counterargument see Fernando H. Cardoso, 1973. "Associated-Dependent Development: Theoretical and Practical Implications," in Afred Stephen, ed., *Authoritarian Brazil*. New Haven, Connecticut: Yale University Press: 142–76.

18. An important source for the argument being developed here is Bruce J. Berman, 1984. "African Capitalism and the Paradigm of Modernity: Culture, Technology, and the State," in Bruce J. Berman and Colin Leys, eds., *African Capitalists in African Development*. Boulder, Colorado: Lynne Rienner Publishers.

19. Ibid.: 236.

20. Ibid.: 237.

21. See Yale H. Ferguson and Richard Mansbach, 1989. *The State, Conceptual Chaos, and the Future of International Relations Theory*. Boulder, Colorado: Lynne Rienner Publishers: 18.

22. For specific debates and definitions of the state, the following works should be helpful: Max Weber, 1964. *The Theory of Social and Economic Organization*, edited by Talcot Parsons. New York: Free Press; Ellen Kay Trimberger, 1978. *Revolution from Above: Military Bureaucratics and Development in Japan, Turkey, Egypt, and Peru*. New Brunswick New Jersey: Transaction Books; Ian Brownlie, 1979. *Principles of Public International Law*, 3rd edition. Oxford: Clarendon Press; Eric Nordlinger, 1981. *On the Autonomy of the Democratic State*. Cambridge: Harvard University Press; Clifford Geertz, 1981. *Negara: The Theatre State in Nineteenth Century Bali*. Princeton, New Jersey: Princeton University Press; Stephen Skowronek, 1982. *Building a New American State: The Expansion of National Administrative Capacities*. New York: Cambridge University Press; Charles Tilly, ed., 1975. *The Formation of National States in Western Europe*. Princeton, New Jersey: Princeton University Press; Raymond Grew, ed., 1978. *Crises of Political Development in Europe and the United States*. Princeton, New Jersey: Princeton University Press; H. J. Laski, 1935. *The State as a Concept in Theory and Practice*. London: The Viking Press; Frederick M. Watkins, 1934. *The State as a Concept in Political Science*. New York: Harper & Brothers Publishers; Heinz Lubasz, 1974. *The Development of the Modern State*. New York: Macmillan. Also, see Stephen Krasner, 1984. "Approaches to the State: Alternative Conceptions and Historical Dynamics," *Comparative Politics* Vol. 16, No. 2 (January): 223–46; Howard H. Lentner, 1984. "The Concept of the State: A Response to Stephen Krasner," *Comparative Politics* Vol. 16, No, 3 (April): 367–77; Atul Kohli, ed., 1986. *The State and Development in the Third World*. Princeton, New Jersey: Princeton University Press; and V. I. Lenin, 1932. *State and Revolution*. New York: International Publishers.

23. Stephen D. Krasner, 1978. *Defending the National Interest: Raw Materials Investments and U.S. Foreign Policy*. Princeton, New Jersey: Princeton University Press: 10.

24. Howard Lentner, op. cit.: 368.

25. Adebayo Adedeji, 1990. *Development and Ethics: Putting Africa on the Road to Self-Sustaining Process of Development.* Keynote address delivered at the first plenary session of the Thirty-Third Annual Meeting of the African Studies Association, Baltimore, Maryland (November 1–4): 9; *African Renewal* (1997). Report of a conference on state, conflict, and democracy in Africa, Massachusetts Institute of Technology (March 6–9); Goran Hyden and Michael Bratton, eds., 1992. *Governance and Politics in Africa.* Boulder, Colorado: Lynne Rienner Publishers.

26. See also Kelechi A. Kalu, 1995. "Democratic Transitions in African and the 1993 Elections in Nigeria," *CONPO Review* Vol. 4, No. 2 (September): 10–22.

27. For the "rain" metaphor, see Chinua Achebe, 1967. *A man of the People.* New York: Anchor Books edition: 34–35.

28. Robert H. Jackson, 1993. "Sub-Saharan Africa," in Robert H Jackson and Alan James, eds., *States in a Changing World: A Contemporary Analysis.* Oxford: Oxford University Press: 137.

29. Ibid.: 142–43.

30. For an alternative argument, see Kari Levitt, 1990. "Debt, Adjustment and Development: Looking to the 1990s," *Economic and Political Weekly* (July): 1587.

31. *African Renewal,* op. cit.

32. Karl W. Deutsch, 1961. "Social Mobilization and Political Development," *American Political Science Review* Vol. 55 (September): 496–503.

33. See for example, Tunji Olagunju, Adele Jinadu, and Sam Oyovbaire, 1993. *Transition to Democracy in Nigeria: 1985–1993.* London and Ibadan: Safari Books Export Limited: 6–7.

34. Ibid.: 11.

35. In 1994 alone, the Federal Reserve Board intervened five times to shore up the dollar and check inflation rather than let "market forces" do it. As well, the rising relocation of capital abroad, rising inflation, unemployment, crime, etc., show that "market forces" do not automatically bring stability, growth, development, and democracy. I am grateful to Julius Ihonvbere for this insight.

36. World Bank, op. cit.: 162.

37. For example, see I. William Zartman, ed., 1995. *Collapsed States: Disintegration and Restoration of Legitimate Authority.* Boulder, Colorado: Lynne Rienner Publishers; John W. Harberson, Donald Rothchild, and Naomi Chazan, eds., 1994. *Civil Society and the State in Africa.* Boulder, Colorado: Lynne Rienner Publishers.

38. See Thomas S. Kuhn, 1970. *The Structure of Scientific Revolutions,* 2nd edition. Chicago: The University of Chicago Press: 92.

39. See Secretary General's Report, United Nations Security Council, New York, April 16, 1998.

40. Jon Krause, 1994. "The Political Economy of African Foreign Policies: Marginality and Dependency, Realism and Choice," in Timothy M. Shaw and Julius Emeka Okolo, eds., *The Political Economy of Foreign Policy in ECOWAS.* New York: St. Martin's Press: 245–83.

41. Ibid.: 247–49.

42. See "Survey Sub-Saharan Africa," (September 7, 1996), *Economist.*

43. Ibid.

44. Cited in Paul Kennedy, 1993. *Preparing for the Twenty-First Century.* New York: Vintage Books: 216.

45. Benjamin R. Barber, 1995. *Jihad vs. McWorld.* New York: Ballantine Books: 34.

46. I. William Zartman, op. cit.: 268.

47. Benjamin Barber, op. cit.: 70.

48. Ibid.: 298–99.

49. Francis Fukuyama, 1992. *The End of History and the Last Man.* New York: Avon Books: xi.

50. Samuel P. Huntington, 1996. *The Clash of Civilizations and the Remaking of World Order.* New York: Simon & Schuster: 66.

51. Ibid.: 73.

52. Fukuyama, op cit.: 213.

53. See Robert H. Jackson and Carl G. Rosberg, 1986. "Why Africa's Weak States Persist: The Empirical and the Juridical in Statehood," in Atul Kohli, ed., *The State and Development in the Third World.* Princeton, New Jersey: Princeton University Press: 268.

54. David F. Gordon and Howard Wolpe, 1998. "The Other Africa: An end to Afro-Pessimism," *World Policy Journal* (Spring): 49–58.

BIBLIOGRAPHY

Barber, Benjamin R. 1995. *Jihad vs. McWorld.* New York: Ballantine Books.

Caporaso, James A., and David P. Levine. 1992. *Theories of Political Economy.* New York: Cambridge University Press.

Doornbos, M. 1990. "The African State in Academic Debate: Retrospect and Prospect." *The Journal of Modern African Studies* Vol. 28, No. 2: 179–98.

Fatton, R. 1989. "The State of African Studies and Studies of the African State: The Theoretical Softness of the 'Soft State.' " *Journal of Asian and African Studies* Vol. 24, Nos. 3 and 4: 170–185.

Ferguson, Yale H., and Richard W. Mansbach. 1989. *The State, Conceptual Chaos, and the Future of International Relations Theory.* Boulder, Colorado: Lynne Rienner Publishers.

Fukuyama, Francis. 1992. *The End of History and the Last Man.* New York: Avon Books.

Harbeson, John W., and Donald Rothchild, eds. 1995. *Africa in World Politics: Post–Cold War Challenges.* Boulder, Colorado: Westview Press.

———, Donald Rothchild, and Naomi Chazan, eds., 1994. *Civil Society and the State in Africa.* Boulder, Colorado: Lynne Rienner Publishers.

Herbst, Jeffrey. 1996. "Responding to State Failure in Africa." *International Security* Vol. 21, No. 3 (Winter): 120–44.

Huntington, Samuel 1968. *Political Order in Changing Societies.* New Haven, Connecticut: Yale University Press.

——— 1996. *The Clash of Civilizations and the Remaking of World Order.* New York: Simon & Schuster.

Ihonvbere, Julius O. 1994. "The 'Irrelevant' State, Ethnicity, and the Quest for Nationhood in Africa." *Ethnic and Racial Studies* Vol. 17, No. 1 (January): 42–60.

Joseph, Richard. 1997. "Correspondence: Responding to State Failure in Africa." *International Security* Vol. 22, No. 2 (Fall): 175–84.

Kalu, Kelechi A. 1995. "Democratic Transitions in Africa and the 1993 Elections in Nigeria." *CONPO Review* Vol. 4, No. 2 (September): 10–22.

Migdal, Joel S. 1988. *Strong Societies and Weak States: State-Society Relations and State Capabilities in the Third World.* Princeton, New Jersey: Princeton University Press.

———, Atul Kohli, and Vivienne Shue, eds. 1994. *State Power and Social Forces: Domination and Transformation in the Third World.* New York: Cambridge University Press.

Organski, A. F. 1965. *The Stages of Political Development.* New York: Alfred A. Knopf.

Rostow, Walt W. 1960. *The Stages of Economic Growth.* Cambridge: Cambridge University Press.

Rothchild, Donald, and Naomi Chazan, eds. 1988. *The Precarious Balance: State & Society in Africa.* Boulder, Colorado: Westview Press.

Sangmpam, S. N. 1992. "The Overpoliticized State and Democratization: A Theoretical Model." *Comparative Politics* Vol. 24, No. 4: 401–17.

——— 1993. "Neither Soft nor Dead: The African State Is Alive and Well." *African Studies Review* Vol. 36, No. 2 (September): 73–94.

Shaw, Timothy M., and Julius Emeka Okolo, eds. 1994. *The Political Economy of Foreign Policy in ECOWAS.* New York: St. Martin's Press.

World Bank, 1997. *World Development Report 1977: The State in a Changing World.* New York: Oxford University Press.

Zartman, I. William, ed. 1995. *Collapsed States: The Disintegration and Restoration of Legitimate Authority.* Boulder, Colorado: Lynne Rienner Publishers.

3

The Mass Media and Political Stability in Africa: A Utilitarian Theory Approach

Kingsley O. Harbor

INTRODUCTION

For several decades following independence, African nations have known instability—political, social, as well as economic. Whether it is Algeria in the north, Angola in the south, Nigeria in the west, Somalia in the east, or Rwanda in the central, the story is the same. One consequence of this is that in an age of globalization and knowledge explosion, Africa, "the cradle of civilization," lags behind and is even abandoned following the end of the Cold War. Africa's present condition should be cause for somber reflection and deep thought not only for Africans, but also for all well-meaning citizens of the world. The more the world advances in technology, the greater the reality of a global village (as predicted by Marshall McLuhan) where modern communication media would make it possible for "millions of people throughout the world to be in touch with, to affect and be affected by events happening on nearly any spot on the globe," (Littlejohn, 1983, p. 263). No longer can a nation remain insulated from the ramifications of the other's problems. A pertinent and important question here is, why is Africa experiencing persistent instability?

It is generally believed by African scholars, think tanks, and citizens in general (including African leaders) that ethnicity and corruption are among the major factors associated with instability in Africa (Nwankwo, 1972; Obasanjo, 1979; Ngwainmbi, 1995; Musa, 1996; Okoli, 1996). Although the focus of this chapter is on internal dimensions of instability, it is pertinent to state, however, that instability has both internal and external dimensions. The thesis of this chapter is that the mass media, properly conceived and situated, can and should serve as correctors of those problems, such as corruption and ethnic and religious intolerances, which are the precursors of sociopolitical disequilibrium in Africa. So far, the media have been ineffective at this because of state suffocation of mass media operations in Africa.

In view of the foregoing, the purpose of this chapter is to analyze the internal factors associated with instability in Africa and to suggest how the mass media can serve to minimize, if not prevent, future recurrences of these factors. Preventing those factors associated with instability is tantamount to sustaining stability. In doing this, the author revisits the concept of development journalism, arguing that, in its present definition or given its ambiguity, it is dysfunctional to national stability. He introduces the concept of utilitarian journalism derived from John Stuart Mill's theory of utilitarianism (Patterson and Wilking, 1998) as a substitute for development journalism and elucidates the makeup of utilitarian journalism and how it will function to militate against political instability in Africa.

INSTABILITY: DEFINITIONS

Before talking about the origin and components of instability, it is relevant to define the concept. Instability as used here is the unreliability and unpredictability of a system in terms of its continuous and efficient functioning—the system in this case being a nation or nations. Political instability is defined as the absence of a legitimate, orderly, and peaceful process of transferring power (authority) from one leader to the next. This condition ushers in a malaise of cynicism and despair among the masses, the consequences of which include social disintegration, civil unrest, intergroup strifes, economic retrogression, and other attendant social ills. All these translate into an unstable government for the society involved. The situations in many African countries mimic this description, hence the term "political instability" applied to African nations.

What is political instability in the continent of Africa attributable to?

Factors of Instability

As stated earlier, the focus of this chapter is on the internal factors associated with instability in Africa. However, it is important to recognize that instability has both external and internal dimensions. Facts about the external factors—Western contribution (both past and present) to the problems of Africa—are well documented. Essentially, two areas exist within the past thirty years where the industrialized nations are blamed for

Africa's problems—the debt crises and the deteriorating terms of trade— both of which weigh heavily against the already weak African economy. In an article titled, "On African Responsibility for Economic Problems," Richard Mshomba (1997), pointed out that the two most fundamental problems impeding development in Africa are that a high percentage of Africa's GNP is paid to service debts to the West, and at the same time the West pays very low prices for African exports. Worse still, only about half of this payment goes to the principal; the other half goes to interest payments, thus tending to perpetuate the burden of debt and the people's suffering. Furthermore, Africa's debt-service ratio ("the value of a country's external debt payments as a percent of the value of its exports of goods and services," [Mshomba, 1997, p. 50]) remains quite high (currently 14 percent). Given this condition, it is difficult to envisage much economic progress in Africa unless this very serious matter is addressed, and one way to address it is through negotiations between Africa and the West, which will involve debt rescheduling and write-offs.

Returning now to the internal dimension of instability, there is a clear consensus among Africans—officially and unofficially—that the causes of Africa's instability include ethnicity, corruption, and, some will add, religion. In his 1979 New Year address to the nation, Lieutenant General Olusegun Obasanjo (p. ix), the then military president of Nigeria who is currently the civilian president of Nigeria said:

Any government as a human institution will have its shortcomings. But one major cause of failure of civilian administration in this country was that our leaders then concentrated on the part and ignored the whole, hence regionalism, tribalism, sectionalism and ethnicity became the order of the day. Let us now correct that which failed us.

Writing on the Nigeria-Biafra War, a thirty-month-long civil war that ravaged the then secessionist eastern region of Nigeria known as Biafra, Nwankwo (1972) unequivocally identified "the main causes of Nigeria's post-independence crises" as nepotism, tribalism, and corruption (p. 8). The assertions by both Obasanjo and Nwankwo could well be made of several other African countries. Ottoo and Jacobson (1995) put it succinctly but bluntly that: "One grave problem that African countries in general face is ethnicism. The conventional belief is that ethnic affinity in Africa is the number one adversary to good government" (p. 162).

Another politically destabilizing factor in Africa is corruption. Corruption takes varied forms, such as the bribery of public officials (which includes custodians of the law such as the police), embezzlement of public funds by those charged with the responsibility of safeguarding public treasury and other monetary establishments in a nation, cronyism, capital flight (even from debtor countries) to foreign industrialized nations, and other forms of massive abuse of office. Indeed, these kinds of behavior are so prevalent in Africa (and several other developing regions) that the offenders no longer seem to consider their actions an offense. Hence, these reprehensible acts are now carried out with little or no secrecy. It is worse when those who are leaders of nations or other institutions indulge in these kinds of practice because it becomes impossible for them, thus lacking moral authority, to honestly enforce the law against such practices. In some instances, some public officials had become wealthier than the nations they serve. Clearly something is wrong when a part of a body becomes larger than the whole. A clear example of this kind of paradox is the case of the late Mobutu Sese Seko of former Zaire. About the size of Europe, with a population of about 40 million people, and endowed with mineral resources such as gold, copper, manganese, cobalt, zinc, and industrial grade diamonds, Zaire (now the Democratic Republic of the Congo DRC) is naturally not a poor country. This notwithstanding, Mobutu's thirty-two-year rule reduced the DRC to one of the poorest nations in the world while, until his death, Mobutu was one of the richest people in the world with an estimated $2.5 billion in cash and at least twenty expensive properties around the world (Jensen, 1997). It is no wonder that his corrupt practices had orchestrated Zaire's political instability, which gave rise to economic as well as social instabilities, all of which bedeviled the Congo. Eventually, Mobutu was forcibly ousted from power by Laurent Kabila. Mobutu's case is by no means an exception to the rule, but was for more than a decade the rule in Africa. Instability is neither a random act nor a chance occurrence. It has a pattern stemming from enduring practices over time.

A MODEL OF INSTABILITY IN AFRICA

A model is a graphic representation of reality as seen by the presenter of such reality. Such a model tends to present graphically the components of the reality in question in an attempt to explain the relationship, between and among the components, which led to the reality that is being explained.

The model here highlights the internal factors that contribute to instability, delineating their relationships to one another. A knowledge of the factors that lead to a problem and how such factors relate to one another facilitates the process of eliminating the individual or collective root causes of such a problem.

It is germane to point out that a nation can be politically unstable, economically unstable, socially unstable, a combination of these, or all of these. Thus, the figure on the next page depicts the several correlates of instability and the predicted relationships among them.

A model of instability in Africa

MODEL VARIABLES AND DEFINITIONS

Political instability is defined here as the absence of a legitimate, orderly, and peaceful process of transferring authority (power) from one leader to the next.

Ethnicity or ethnic intolerance is defined as the friction between peoples of different ethnic origins based on their ethnic differences.

Corruption is defined as the contravention of accepted social, ethical, and sometimes legal norms in a society.

Economic instability is defined as unreliable market forces that lead to high inflation, high unemployment rate, and the lowering of economic measures such as the GNP and the per capita income of a nation.

Social instability is defined as severe social disorder manifested in the rampant incidence of one or a combination of the following: uncontrolled high rate of robbery (armed and/or unarmed), antigovernment demonstrations and revolts, riotings, and extreme factionalism in a nation.

OPERATION OF THE INSTABILITY MODEL: HOW IT FUNCTIONS

The model here holds that ethnicity leads to political instability. There is a common notion that, in Africa, it is ethnic allegiance, not ideology, that determines where a person stands on issues (Eribo, 1989; Musa, 1996; Okoli, 1996). For instance, Africans tend to vote for a candidate for political office not because the candidate is the most qualified, but because she/he comes from the voters' ethnic group, and so that, if successful, the politician would bring about some development—such as infrastructural and social improvements and job opportunities to that community. This practice, natural as it may seem, leads to diverse problems such as job incompetence, leadership incompetence, and domination of state government by a single group. The distrust and feeling of being cheated (by those groups not favored) inherent in this kind of practice gives rise to ethnic intolerance, which leads to political friction within the ruling echelon, and ultimately contributes to political instability in a nation. The events leading to the 1966 pogrom in Nigeria, which ultimately led to the thirty-month-long Nigeria-Biafra War, was a typical case of ethnicity leading to political instability. The Liberian War, the Rwandan War, the Sierra Leonian War,

and many others in Africa, where ethnic conflicts led to political breakdown and outright war, provide further examples of this relationship
between ethnicity and political instability.

In the instability model, corruption leads to economic instability. Corruption comes in different forms, such as employing someone of the opposite sex in a job (in spite of his/her underqualification) in order to obtain
sexual favor, embezzling public funds, accepting bribe to exonerate someone who committed a crime, cronyism (favoritism to close friends by
extending to them offers they are not qualified for), and many others.
When, for instance, people are employed in jobs for which they are not
qualified, productivity undoubtedly suffers; when public funds are embez-
zled, no matter how small the amount (and they are usually not small),
public revenue is reduced. Cumulatively, these kinds of acts clearly contribute to the destabilization of an economic system. Although the focus
here is on Africa, by no means does Africa hold a monopoly of this canker-
worm. There is little doubt that the economic instabilities that the DRC,
Nigeria, Philippine, and Indonesia (to name a few) continue to suffer today
were in large measure an outgrowth of the corrupt practices of their past
governments—respectively Mobutu's administration, past Nigeria's civilian and most of the military administrations, Ferdinand Marco's long
reign, and Surhato's long reign. Several other African countries and their
leaders (most of them ex-leaders) also fit the above description—Idi Amin
of Uganda, Mengistu Haille Marienne of Ethiopia, and the late John Doe
of Liberia, inter alios.

As the model shows, economic instability will lead to political instability,
which itself will reinforce economic instability (see the return path from
political instability to economic instability). Again, in the examples of
Mobutu and Surharto in the previous paragraph, the economic instability
that was a result of many years of corruption in those countries clearly led
the way to the riotings and political turmoils (in the case of DRC, the military rebellion) that led to the ouster of the two leaders. Similar past cases in
many African countries such as Nigeria, Kenya, Ghana, Zambia, Uganda,
and others, support this relationship. For those countries, such as Ghana and
Zambia, that now have democratically elected governments, essentially it
was harsh economic conditions that led to the change of their former leaders. Indeed, this relationship between economic and political instabilities is
evident even in stable democracies such as the United States, France, Germany, Japan, and others. Especially in the post–Cold War era, any Western
leader is as strong as his/her economy. Former president of the United States,
George Bush, was voted out of office in 1992 for bad economy; over the past
several years, President Clinton has proved to be politically indestructible
because of the excellent U.S. economy. In 1998, following the defeat of his
party, Prime Minister Ryutaro Hashimoto of Japan resigned. At the heart of
his party's defeat was the Japanese economy that was at its worst since the

Second World War. It should be pointed out that political instability as defined here does not apply to these stable democracies, but the relationship between economy and political leadership holds true.

It is predicted in the model that political instability will reinforce economic instability. Usually, any change of government immediately impacts upon market forces such as the stock market. The impact is even greater if such a change is violent, as is usually the case in situations of coups d'etat and military takeovers. Above all, of greater consequence to economic stability is the shock wave that political instability sends to investors (foreign and domestic) who have either invested in the country experiencing instability or who are anticipating to do so. As long as a nation remains politically unstable, no investor would seriously consider investing in that nation's market. Lack of investment coupled with the aforementioned external factors—the debt crises and the deteriorating terms of trade—will certainly bring any nation to its knees economically. Thus, political instability leads to economic instability. Today, this is one of Africa's most serious predicaments—the link between political instability and economic instability. Foreign investors are not just jittery about investing in Africa—most will not even consider it.

The Two-Way Relationship between Economic and Social Instabilities

This model posits a two-way relationship between economic instability and social instability. When the economy is bad, that translates into high unemployment, low wages, high inflation rate, inter alia. Victims of these negative economic conditions are always people living in that country of economic instability. As the cliché goes, "a hungry man is an angry man." An unemployed person after a while becomes both hungry and angry, a socially dangerous combination. When one unemployed person finds many others like him/her who are willing to speak out, stand out, and possibly strike out, they sympathetically join forces to resist the prevailing social order that, in their views, is causing their problems. This is the beginning of social instability.

Demonstrations, especially violent ones, scare businesses that are around the region of action. Strikes cripple one or more segments of an economy. The (1999) UPS (United Postal Services) strike in the United States for instance, had a far-reaching effect not only on UPS (with a loss of several millions of dollars) but also on many other subsidiaries and businesses, such as the U.S. postal services, whose businesses rely on UPS services for their successful operation. Theft and armed robbery threaten and slow down businesses, especially small businesses, which are usually the pillars of most economies—in particular, those of developing nations. All of these are symptomatic of social disorder, and as they occur, they reinforce economic instability.

Economic instability, thus, will lead to social instability, which, in turn, reinforces economic instability as depicted in the previous model by the two-way relationship; the cycle will continue until a stable political system is in place, following which the cycle will begin to recede. Therefore, it seems reasonable to say that the whole problem of Africa's instability hinges on her political instability itself.

The thesis of this chapter is that the mass media have a prominent and important role to play in bringing about stability in Africa. Hence, the focus turns to the mass media next.

THE ROLE OF THE MASS MEDIA IN AFRICA'S POLITICS

The mass media—foreign and domestic—have played a significant role in the history and affairs of Africa. Indeed, the history of Africa will not be complete without that of her mass media. That history of Africa's mass media is evidence that the mass media can be used for good as well as evil purposes, depending on the intent of the user. In his chapter dealing with "Propaganda in a Democratic Society," Huxley (1958) wrote about the duality of mass communication stating that "Mass communication, in a word, is neither good nor bad; it is simply a force and, like any other force, it can be used either well or ill" (p. 43). Africa's press history provides a good example of this duality of the mass media. To look at the role that the media have played in the politics of Africa, the next section will discuss the various stages of the African press from colonialism to the present.

Like the West, Africa's press history is divisible into three epochs: colonial, nationalist, and contemporary. But, unlike the three periods of Western press history (known as absolutism, constitutionalism, and parliamentarism or parliamentary democracy), which reflected the evolution of the Western press from authoritarian to free press (Kepplinger, 1989), the three stages of Africa's press history do not conform to any hierarchical order of freedom for the press. Thus, the three-tier categorization here reflects chronology rather than degree of freedom.

The Colonial Press: The Duality of the Mass Media

The colonial press included, among others, newspapers such as *Courier de l'Egypte, La Decade Egyptienne,* the first two African newspapers published in 1797; the *Cape Town Gazette* published in 1800; the *Royal Gazette* first published in Sierra Leone in 1801; and the *Royal Gold Coast Gazette* published in 1822 (Ochs, 1986). The colonial press was marked by ethnocentrism, catering only to the needs of its home (Western) country, neglecting Africa's interests and aspirations (Ugboaja, 1972; Wilcox, 1975). These papers were characterized by an almost exclusive European elite readership and were mostly used to counter nationalistic activities. To the

African nationalist and freedom fighter, the colonial press represented a "thorn in his flesh." To the foreign colonial administration, however, the same press was a hedge of protection against possible African overthrow of the colonial government. Thus, although the colonial press was functional to the colonial administration, it was dysfunctional to the African nationalist, hence its dual role. Therefore, the dysfunction of the colonial press to the African nationalist created the need among African nationalists for an indigenous African press that would serve the needs of Africans, hence the inevitable birth of the African nationalist press.

The Nationalist Press: Mass Media as Emancipators

Despite colonial resistance in the early 1950s, a nationalist press was born that championed the cause of freedom for Africa and consisted of indigenous African newspapers, such as the *Morning Post of the Gold Coast* (published by Wallace Johnson and once edited by Dr. Nnamdi Azikiwe of Nigeria) and the *West African Pilot* (published by Dr. Azikiwe). The nationalist press became the vehicle that conveyed and raised African nationalism to an unprecedented insurmountable height. The newspaper mastheads of the time ("Independence in All Things and Neutral in Nothing Affecting the Destiny of Africa" and "Pride in Africa and Things African") (Murphy, 1980, p. 4) were among the early signs of the spirit of African nationalism that was to seize and ultimately engulf colonialism.

The collapse of colonialism was seen, in great part, as a consequence of Africa's nationalistic fervor, which found expression through, and was spearheaded by, the nationalist press (Wilcox, 1975; Ochs, 1986) and was perhaps the most "potent instrument" for the dissemination of nationalist fervor. As Africa and her nationalist press survived the onslaught of colonialism, what then became of the African press? This is discussed in the next section.

The Contemporary Press

The contemporary press (the third stage in Africa's press history) here refers to the print media outlets in postindependence Africa. Several African countries, in particular those under British rule (such as Nigeria, Tanzania, Kenya, Ghana, inter alia) eventually at independence inherited a relatively free press system (Wilcox, 1975; Ochs, 1986). As seen today, however, the paradox of Africa's press history is that African leaders, who found the press an indispensable ally in their struggle for freedom, after winning independence, condemned the same press as treacherous. Hence, a postindependence press exists today in most of the continent that enjoys no more freedom than its colonial counterpart.

It was by no accident that several African leaders (ex-presidents) started their careers as newspaper men before their ascendancy to political power. For instance, President Jomo Kenyatta of Kenya was the publisher of the *Muigui Thania* in the 1920s; President Julius Nyerere of Tanzania edited the *Sauti ya Tanu* before independence; President Nnamdi Azikiwe of Nigeria was the publisher of a chain of newspapers in West Africa that included *The West African Pilot;* President Kwame Nkrumah of Ghana started the *Accra Evening News;* President Leopold Senghor of Senegal edited and published *La Condition Humaine;* and President Houphet Boigny of Ivory Coast was also editor of *Afrique Noire* (Ochs, 1986). All these men had seen the power of the media to mobilize public opinion, and they successfully utilized that power to mobilize the support that eventually led to the independence of their various countries. They also understood that the same power could be turned around to be used against them in a free press society, causing later apprehension of the media. President Kenneth Kaunda of Zambia once admitted: "The press is capable of making or destroying governments given appropriate conditions. . . . In this harsh and imperfect world a country can be and often is what the world thinks it is" (Kaunda, 1968, p. 17). In another instance, President Milton Obote of Uganda in 1966 made similar affirmations of apprehension over media activities.

These accounts explain why today, unless they are reconceptualized, the mass media in Africa cannot provide the tool to save the continent from her problems of instability.

THE MASS MEDIA AS AGENTS OF STABILITY

Media Impotence: Why They Are Not Stability Agents

Again, the power of the media is undoubtable. The purpose they can serve is a function of the intent of the user. It is argued in this chapter that the mass media can and should serve as agents of stability (tools for mitigating against instability) in Africa. A pertinent question is; given their ability to mold public opinion, mobilize the masses, and even aid in demolishing colonialism in Africa, why have the mass media not been agents of stability in Africa? The author submits that mass media's impotence or inability to help solve the instability problem in Africa is a result of state suffocation—press control—of mass media operations in most of Africa. Literature on press freedom, albeit defined in Western terms, is replete with data suggesting that Africa has had and still has some of the most serious cases of press control in the world (Nixon, 1960; Lowenstein, 1967; Wilcox, 1975; Ochs, 1986; Merrill, 1988). With such a level of press control in most of Africa, it is no wonder that the mass media in most of Africa remain a toothless mastiff that cannot be the watchdog they are meant to be, much more help to achieve stability in the continent.

Why was free press proper for the continent of Africa during her fight for independence but improper now in her postindependence era? The answer lies in the concept of national development and the role of the media in it.

Development Journalism and National Development

Generally, the common rationale for mass media control in Africa and other developing regions is national development, which demands the practice of what is today known as development journalism. Development journalism is a normative theory that has received a fair share of attention in the literature on communication and national development. Its definitions abound. Some say it is ambiguous and has no definition (Ogan, 1987); others see it as a synonym for press censorship. Whatever the merits and demerits of these criticisms, development journalism is a concept that is dear to the hearts of development theorists and practitioners, especially those from the developing world. Although in practice that theory seems to have run out of steam, its discussions will probably remain alive for some time. In their discussion of development media theory, Otoo and Jacobson (1995) described the principles of development journalism by listing its expectations:

(1) the media is [sic] expected to carry out positive development tasks in line with nationally established policy; (2) freedom of the media is subject to restriction according to economic priorities and development needs of a society; (3) the media should give priority in their content to the national culture and language; (4) the media should give priority in news and information to links with other developing countries which are geographically or culturally close; (5) media workers and professionals have responsibilities as well as freedoms in their information-gathering and dissemination tasks; and (6) the state has the right to intervene in or restrict media operations in the interest of development, through censorship, subsidies or direct control (pp. 153–54).

Chowdhury (1976), another scholar of development theory, defines development journalism as covering news beats that are new in concept and designed to be relevant to socioeconomic changes without stepping on the toes of the government. In yet another definition, Kumbula (1995) in his article on "Media History and Development in Zimbabwe," described the set of criteria that tends to define development journalism in President Robert Mugabe's government. Those criteria include: (1) using the media to promote economic and national development policies; (2) mobilizing the masses in support of government and party policies; (3) explaining government policies and programs; (4) helping in the fight against poverty, ignorance, disease, and illiteracy; (5) not practicing investigative or enterprising journalism; and (6) not criticizing the government.

A common theme runs through these definitions, and that theme seems to be "the lack of the watchdog function of the media." Although some of the criteria stated in the definitions may be subtle in their implication for censorship (for instance, the requirement in Otoo and Jacobson's [1995] definition that "media workers and professionals have responsibilities as well as freedoms in their information-gathering and dissemination tasks"), others were blunt in demanding media's complete allegiance to the state. A clear example of this was Zimbabwe's criteria for development journalism that demanded, according to Kumbula (1995), that the mass media should not practice investigative or enterprising journalism and should not criticize the government. The open and direct demand not to criticize the government is reminiscent of the press printing laws of the sixteenth-century England under King Henry VIII and the Tudor family, during which time it was punishable by law to criticize the crown or to print certain books. This comparison points to how close development journalism is to authoritarian press laws.

Again, the rationale or impetus for development journalism seems to be national development. When a government states that "the state has the right to intervene in or restrict media operations in the interest of development" (Otoo and Jacobson, 1995) and that the media should not practice investigative journalism in the interest of national development (Kumbula, 1995), the question that arises is, what is national development? It seems clear from the foregoing discussion that national development is a name that has no definite meaning and thus can protect any set of rules or policies designed to ensure press censorship. In reality, development journalism could be seen as another name for press control, albeit dressed differently. This, it seems, is the greatest danger and anomaly with the concept of development journalism. It is also the reason why the mass media in Africa, in their present capacity, cannot serve as agents of stability in the continent.

Earlier in this chapter, a model of instability was presented for the purpose of explaining how instability begins in Africa and for demonstrating the relationship between its various components. That model suggests ethnicity and corruption as the precursors of political instability in Africa. It is believed that of the two components, corruption is the greater contributor to instability. It is a known fact that eradication of a problem must begin from the root cause(s) of the problem. If the media cannot practice investigative journalism, clearly they cannot expose corruption; if corruption is unexposed and unpunished, there will be no motivation to deter future perpetrators of corruption. Thus, it is difficult to see how development journalism, as defined here, can aid in saving the African continent from instability.

Consequences of Media Impotence and State Control

The Freedom Forum, an American organization that champions the cause of free press in the United States and around the world, adopts the slogan, "Free press, free speech, and free spirit." When the masses have a right to free speech and the channels of mass communication are free to publish and to broadcast, then the masses can vent their views and opinions through these channels. This creates a free spirit within the masses. Granted, these views may not be what the rulers want to hear, and some opinions truly may not amount to much, but their venting releases the harborer of the burden created by such unexpressed opinions; it creates a free spirit within the harborer. A wise ruler will give due attention to the opinion of the masses. When, on the other hand, the people are not able to freely express their opinions due to state restriction, the suppressed opinion will nevertheless be vented in some other ways, such as the forceful overthrow of that government or through other covert means of subversion. There may be other contributing factors responsible for coups d'etat and military takeovers, but it seems quite plausible that they are evidence of the state of suppressed and hidden public opinion (Ngatara, 1984), and there is almost always loss of lives, although the severity may vary. This is loss of human resources, a nation's most vital and most useful resource. Coups may also lead to loss of major capital resources and investments, such as when banks and other financial institutions are looted, burnt down, or closed. As defined earlier, political instability is the absence of a legitimate, orderly, and peaceful process of transferring political authority (power) from one ruler to the next. A successful coup d'etat signals the beginning of political instability. The higher the frequency of successful coups d'etat in a given country, the greater its political instability. As is well known, coups d'etat and military and/or one-party rulership are common in Africa, hence the alarming state of instability in the continent. Having suggested what factors are believed to lead to instability, it is perhaps, in order to consider possible remedies next.

Propositions for Remedying Instability

In his situational communication theory, Grunig (1983) argues that recognizing a situation as problematic is the beginning of the solution to that problem. One cannot seek a solution to a situation that one does not recognize as problematic. Africa must first recognize instability as a problem, then seek its solution(s). Some people do not seem to recognize instability as a problem, and they may argue that African nations are about forty years old as compared to a country such as United States, which is over 200 years old. Whatever the merit of that argument, Africa has a lot of catching up to do with the rest of the world (economically and technologically), and she does not have the luxury of waiting until her nations are 100 or 200 years old before seriously addressing the problems of instability and embarking on projects that will grant her a steady growth and forward mobility. Development, no matter how defined, is an evolving process. Some might argue that what is happening now in the continent is part of that evolution. True as that may be, three decades of independence is a long time for any efforts not to show some significant progress. A child does not wait until she/he becomes an adult before learning to walk and to walk steadily; otherwise, that child will always remain a child even at an adult age.

For the purpose of this chapter, however, the concern is on how the mass media can use their power of information and persuasion to alleviate instability in Africa. The position of this author is that in their present status, the mass media in Africa are incapable of delivering such a service. To do so, a measure of press freedom is inevitable, and the concept of development journalism in its present form must either be revamped or discarded. There is no reason why a press cannot be both free and useful to its country's development. An inevitable question raised by the last statement becomes, what is a free press?

Freedom of the Press: What Does It Mean?

There is no universally accepted definition of press freedom. Almost every nation on earth has a constitutional guarantee of press freedom. Yet, one does not need to be an international human rights observer to recognize that press control is rampant in the developing world, and occasionally in the developed world too. In reality, press freedom means different things to different people. For example, the former Soviet Union, an archetype of communism, once prided itself as the freest press in the world; of course, article 125 of the then Soviet constitution bore her out as a free press. As Vyshinsky (1948) wrote, for Soviet Union (before perestroika), as for several other Soviet-backed communist regimes, press freedom "consists essentially in the possibility of freely publishing the genuine, not the falsified opinions of the toiling masses, rather than in the absence of preliminary censorship." Hence, it is difficult to fault Soviet Union's claim to freedom of the press so defined.

Contrary to the Soviet concept of free press, the Western definition of free press rejects (at least in theory) any form of censorship of the press. Here, free press is defined to include: (1) the prohibition of government interference with the press in the form of censorship and similar previous restraints and (2) the principles that courts alone have the right to impose penalties if and when it is deemed necessary (Pember, 1987).

The definition of press freedom in the Developing World is even more ambiguous given that the region itself is what Nam (1983, p. 9) described as "a mosaic combination of varied political ideologies." As such, it is erroneous to define press freedom in the Developing World in a monolithic term. Nam identified two distinguishable types of constitutional clauses discernible in the Third World as: (1) that which guarantees the right of free speech and free press to all and (2) that which guarantees it with certain exceptions. He contends that in spite of ideological orientations, efforts at national development preempt other considerations in determining what free press means in a particular Third World country.

The condition is not different in Africa. The diversity of peoples, countries, and cultures of this great continent is extreme, as are their political manifestations. Their mass media, an integral part of their polity, reflect this pluralism, and so does the definition of press freedom. Julius Nyerere, the first president of Tanzania," recognized the necessity of the press to be free, compared the press of a developing nation to that of a nation at war that should accept certain limitations on its freedom (reminiscent of the experience of journalists during the Gulf War). Nyerere described a press not conforming to such developmental dictates as able to "deflect the government from its responsibilities to the people by creating problems of law and order" (Somerlad, 1968, p. 77). From the southern part of Africa, former President Kaunda of Zambia, who once recognized the importance of "an independent press completely objective and free from the influence of government" (Merrill, Bryna, and Alisky 1970, p. 288), later modified that recognition to include that "the government reserves the right to act as arbiter of this freedom." Two contrasting views of the role of the press emerged at one time from leaders of two West African countries. Yakubu Gowon, a one-time military leader of Nigeria, said the press "should tell us off when they feel we are wrong and commend when they feel it's worthwhile: we can take it." An earlier military regime in Ghana, however, had this to say about the press, "We will allow freedom of the press to operate in this country as long as it is consistent with a military government" (Wilcox, 1975, p. 21).

Although there is nearly a universal constitutional guarantee of press freedom by nations, there is no known universal definition of that concept. It is also pertinent to say that there is nothing like an absolute freedom for the press. Even the United States, a champion of freedom, does not have absolute press freedom. The experience of journalists during the Gulf War, when all information coming to them had to be scrutinized by the military, bore witness to this claim of no absolute press freedom. Hence, Africa will not be unique if she defines her press freedom to suit her *genuine* needs.

On this note, the concept of utilitarian journalism will be introduced and recommended as a substitute for development journalism.

THE PROBLEM AND ITS SOLUTION

Before introducing the concept of utilitarian journalism in the next section, it is important to make the point that the problem with African countries is not that they cannot achieve political stability, but that they have not been able to sustain political stability. Every African nation has at one or more times since its independence (for those that once were colonized) achieved a measure of political stability when its government had a peaceful transition from one ruler to the next (whether it was military or civilian). Most African nations, however, have not been able to sustain that stability because such peaceful transitions had at one point or another been replaced by military takeovers with or without bloodshed. Although a host of African countries share this common experience, the frequencies of the takeovers in different countries vary. Countries such as Nigeria and Ghana have had a higher frequency than did the Congo (DRC), Zambia, or Cameroon, for instance. Of course, a higher frequency of takeovers reflects greater instability. Thus, Africa's problem is specifically the lack of sustainable stability rather than the inability to achieve stability. The reason for this lack of sustainable stability seems to have to do with the vacuum created by the absence of a deterrence mechanism in the system. Such a mechanism will incapacitate those factors of instability, especially corruption, which ultimately lead to instability.

Of all the institutions in modern society such as schools, churches, mass media, courts, the military, law enforcement agencies, and others, only the mass media have the capability to provide effective deterrence to political instability. This ability of the media rests essentially on three major qualities: (1) media's ability to engage in investigative journalism, (2) media's information dissemination ability as well as the media's capacity for message ubiquity, and (3) media's ability to mold public opinion, which is a function of the second. Above all, the journalistic philosophy adopted by the media will be critical in determining their success as a deterrent, and this is where utilitarian journalism, discussed in the next section, comes in.

UTILITARIAN JOURNALISM

Utilitarian journalism can be described as useful journalism or journalism that can and will serve the *genuine* needs of Africa and Africans.

Utilitarian theory, based on the principles of ethics, was first articulated by Jeremy Bentham and later taken over by John Stuart Mill. Both of these men were English and lived in the nineteenth century. The main premise of this theory is that "the consequences of actions are important in deciding whether they are ethical" (Patterson and Wilking, 1998, p. 9). Under this theory, the good of the majority takes precedence over that of the minority. This theory, for instance, is the basis for investigative reporting, which may harm an individual but will provide an overall good for the entire society. In their introduction to ethical decision making, Patterson and Wilking wrote about John Stuart Mill's view as expressed in his utilitarian theory that "an act was right in the proportion in which it contributed to the general happiness, wrong in the proportion in which it contributed to general unhappiness or pain" (p. 10).

The detailed definition of utilitarian journalism and the distinction between it and development journalism is better understood by examining the elements of both (see Table 3.1). The model of development journalism

Table 3.1
A Comparison of Development and Utilitarian Journalism

Components of Development Journalism	Components of Utilitarian Journalism
1. The media is [sic] expected to carry out positive development tasks in line with nationally established policy.	The media should carry out positive development tasks in line with nationally estblished policy tasks that satisfy *genuine* African needs.
2. Freedom of the media is subject to restriction according to economic priorities and development needs of a society.	Media should be supported and encouraged to act as economic multipliers through their business enterprising ability.
3. The media should give priority in their content to the national culture and language.	The media should give priority in their content to the national culture and language.
4. The media should give priority in news and information to links with other developing countries which are geographically or culturally close.	The media should adopt a general set of criteria that does not discriminate in its news coverage merely on the basis of geographical proximity or categorization as First, Second, or Third World.
5. Media workers and professionals have responsibilities as well as freedoms in their information-gathering and dissemination tasks.	Media workers and professionals have responsibilities as well as freedoms in their information-gathering and dissemination tasks. These responsibilities should be in consonance with *genuine* African needs.
6. The state has the right to intervene in or restrict media operations in the interest of development, through censorship, subsidies, or direct control.	The state has the right to utilize media services to its advantage in the event of war and in protection of national security in accordance with *genuine* African needs.
7.	The media must be allowed and encouraged to engage in investigative journalism. This should be one of the strengths of utilitarian journalism.
8.	The media should have and exercise the ability to criticize the government, but not necessarily to trivialize the position of those democratically placed in public office.
9.	As with utilitarian theory, utilitarian journalism should be heavily outcome/result-oriented. The consequence of a news item and its utility to the general public should be an overriding consideration in its coverage.

employed here comes from the work of Ottoo and Jacobson (1995, pp. 153–54), which also agrees with Dennis McQuail's (1987) definition of development journalism.

As seen in Table 3.1, utilitarian journalism provides a framework for formulating a definition for press freedom that may suit the genuine needs of Africa without being a replica of either development journalism or the Western definition of free press because the latter in its totality may not necessarily be relevant to the African situation.

Genuine African Needs

As seen in Table 3.1, "genuine African needs" is a phrase that is featured prominently in the definition of utilitarian journalism; hence, it needs some elucidation. The list of what constitutes a genuine African need is hardly exhaustive, so, rather than trying to define what constitutes a genuine African need, the focus will be on what is not a genuine African need.

Corruption in any form is not a genuine African need, and the media should be able to investigate, expose, and challenge corruption. Ethnic intolerance is not a genuine African need; the media should be able to mobilize public opinion against any acts of ethnic intolerance and emphasize national commonalities to the detriment of ethnic divides. The media must also desist from what Musa (1996) described as the "bloc press phenomenon," or the idea of various media outlets forming camps in support of opposing politicians or political parties from their own respective ethnic regions. Religious intolerance, among others, is not a genuine African need.

The Feasibility of Utilitarian Journalism

The definition of utilitarian journalism raises two important and inevitable questions: (1) who should determine what constitutes a genuine African need, and (2) how can utilitarian journalism survive in the face of difficulties posed by harsh economic realities as well as authoritarian regimes in Africa? There are no easy answers to these questions. Just as the problems themselves are complex, their solutions do not lend themselves to any magic-bullet response.

The question regarding who should determine what constitutes a genuine African need? resembles an old debate about the legitimacy of the government or the press as the arbiter of what constitutes public interest: "if it is generally agreed that the press should pursue the public good, and articulate the public interest, who is better qualified to do this"—the government with the people's mandate, or the unelected press? (Ansah, 1991, p. 5). Although this question was posed in a different context dealing with press-government relations in Africa, it may well apply to the case of genuine African need. Considered in this context, this question begins with a false premise that the government has the people's mandate. Self-imposed governments, such as there are in many developing nations today (be they military or civilian), cannot be said to have the people's mandate. Nor can the press. But conventional wisdom suggests that the press is a more manageable institution than any dictatorial regime. The press in a free society worries about public opinion because its existence rests on the mass patronage, which itself is a function of their perception of the press. A dictatorial government cares little about anyone's opinion, which of course is hardly voiced for fear of retribution. The press as a human institution will err, but experience has shown that its excesses can be checked by society's actions.

There are numerous instances of the power of public opinion over the media. A case in point: O. J. Simpson's 1996 acquittal of the murder charge of his ex-wife (Nicole Simpson) and her friend, Ron Goldman—a case that was curiously watched all over the world. Following Simpson's acquittal, public opinion and pressure stopped the media outlets in the United States from airing Simpson's first live television interview. The prevailing perception among many at the time was that he was responsible for the victims' death. The Black Entertainment Network (BET), after a long time, mustered the courage to air this interview first. Although not devastated by this action, BET paid a price for its defiance of public opinion. The reason for its less punitive effect on BET can only be understood against a backdrop of the context of this episode. The Simpson case created racial division between blacks and whites in the United States (with most blacks supporting Simpson, whereas most whites supported the victims). BET is a black-owned network with a predominantly black audience and patronage. Were it otherwise, Simpson's case would perhaps have been sufficient to put BET out of business temporarily (if not permanently), thus teaching it a lesson on the importance of public goodwill. Perhaps nothing other than public opinion could have relented the media from covering an important segment of the "news of the century" (which Simpson's case was called).

Another case—concerning Bill Cosby and NBC—demonstrates that, in stable democracies, when the people speak, the media listen. Bill Cosby is a black comedian and was the producer of *The Cosby Show*, one of NBC's top-rated shows from 1984 to 1992. When, during the apartheid era in South Africa, Cosby demanded that NBC divested in South Africa until apartheid was dismantled, NBC may not have responded immediately, but Cosby's demand weighed heavily on NBC's later decision to distance itself from apartheid. There is yet another case in point—a landmark case, *Food Lion Inc. vs. ABC News, Inc. (PrimeTime Live)* in the United States. ABC, a powerful television network with international reputation, lost a case to Food Lion in their first round (although it was later reversed in 1999). Food Lion, a food chain organization that operates grocery stores, brought a law suit against ABC for employing illegal and unethical tactics in gathering information about Food Lion's business practices, and ABC was fined some millions of dollars as a result. This case clearly had a chilling effect on investigative journalism in the United States in terms of the media's tactics of gathering news. These cases are indications that the excesses of the media can be checked by society; although, for this to happen, media privatization and commercialization are essential. With commercial media comes advertising, and with advertising comes the people power necessary to keep the media in check.

Thus, if dictatorial regimes and the media are considered to be two evils, it seems that the media are the better of the two. If, therefore, society is to err, it should err on the side of the media; until there is a better approach, it seems that it would serve the best interest of the general public for the African media to assume the responsibility of deciding what constitutes a *genuine* African need.

With this level of responsibility placed on the media under this journalistic tradition (utilitarian journalism), the programmatic plan for utilitarian journalism must, of necessity, include an intensive training program for journalists who will practice utilitarian journalism. That training program should be designed to include both academic and philosophical contents. Although the academic content will be almost similar to the traditional journalism curriculum, the philosophical content should be designed to include, inter alia, issues such as: (1) the history of Africa's governance, including her social as well as economic conditions that provided the rationale for the adoption of utilitarian journalism, (2) the qualifications and criteria for practicing as a journalist under this tradition, (3) conditions under which recognition to practice as a journalist can be granted, refused, or withdrawn, and (4) a binding professional code of conduct that takes into consideration the awesome responsibility that this public trust (as the arbiter of what constitutes genuine African need) demands of journalists.

Policy Reform

The second question confronting utilitarian journalism deals with its survival in the face of the realities of poor economy and the reign of authoritarian regimes in Africa. The answer to the economic problems lies in policy reforms in Africa. Prominent economists and developmentalists, Africans as well as non-Africans (Hope, 1997; Mshomba, 1997; Hentz, 1997), have called for economic liberalization as a panacea for Africa's economic problems. Economic liberalization here means engaging in those policies that effectively promote market-oriented principles. This makes sense because the centralized economic planning system adopted in Africa for decades has led only to further economic woes. Above all, African countries must practice regional cooperation and economic integration. Because markets in Africa are relatively weak individually (especially because they are small), they can attract neither domestic nor foreign investments. This means that economic cooperation and integration with other African countries have the potential to provide the economies of scale necessary to achieve a healthy and productive economy.

With foreign debt rescheduling (discussed earlier), economic liberalization, and the consequent economic upliftment of the African society, media commercialization will become a reality. The advent of advertiser-supported media portends to achieve the economic climate capable of fostering the practice of utilitarian journalism. Commercialization will move the media to a new level of self-sustenance and independence capable of enhancing journalistic vibrancy. This new environment thus created for Africa's media can provide the media with the mettle necessary to overcome other political hurdles emanating from the traditional tendencies of the state to suppress the media.

As stated earlier, the first step toward solving a problem is recognizing the existence of that problem. There is evidence that a significant proportion of Africans now recognize that Africa has a serious problem that demands urgent attention. The number of articles and publications on Africa's problems written by Africans themselves both within and outside the continent tends to point to this consciousness. Print as well as the electronic media (the Internet in particular) are replete with heartfelt articles whose content go beyond mere intellectual exercise to suggest deeply felt concerns about Africa. A recent World Bank report shows that there were 2,162 cases of privatization in developing countries between 1980 and 1991, and of that number, 373 (17 percent) were in sub-Saharan Africa (Hope, 1997). This suggests that several African countries are already embracing economic liberalization. This is a good sign because it shows not only the recognition of a serious problem, but also serious efforts to seek its solution. It is only hoped that these deep feelings of African citizens can infect those citizens and leaders at the helm of power in the continent and encourage them to rethink the course of Africa's journey so far.

BIBLIOGRAPHY

Ansah, Paul V. (1991). Africa, Blueprint for Freedom. *Index on Censorship,* 20, 9 (October), p. 3.

Chowdhury, A. (1976). Fiesta of Asian Press Freedom Seen at an End. *IPI Report,* 25(July), 1–2.

Eribo, F. (1989). *Ethnically Simulated Press Freedom in Nigeria in a Positive Context.* Paper presented to the Mass Communication Division of the International Communication Association, San Francisco. May.

Grunig, James E. (1983). Communication Behaviors and Attitudes of Environmental Publics: Two Studies. *Journalism Monograph,* No. 81, March.

Hentz, J. J. (1997). Economic Stagnation in Sub-Saharan Africa and Breaking the Implicit Bargain. *Issue: A Journal of Opinion,* XXV(1).

Hope, K. R. (1997). Development Solutions for Africa: The Need for Policy Reform and Good Governance. *Issue: A Journal of Opinion,* XXV(1).

Huxley, A. (1958). *Brave New World Revisited.* New York: Harper and Brothers.

Jensen, H. (1997). First in Greed. *The Commercial Appeal* (Memphis, Tennessee). May 21, p. A4.

Kaunda, K. (1968). Presidential Address to the International Press Institute 17th Annual Assembly, Nairobi, Kenya.

Kepplinger, H. M. (1989). The Changing Functions of the Mass Media: A Historical Perspective, *Gazette,* 44, 177–189.

Kumbula, T. (1995). Media History and Development Role in Zimbabwe. In Peter Nwosu, Chuka Onwumechili, and Richard M'bayo (eds.); *Communication and the Transformation of Society: A Developing Region's Perspectives.* New York: University Press of America.

Littlejohn, S. W. (1983). *Theories of Human Communication* (2nd ed.). Belmont, California: Wadsworth Publishing Co.

Lowenstein, R. L. (1970). Press Freedom as a Political Indicator. In Heinz-Dietrich Fischer and John C. Merrill (eds.), *International Communication: Media, Channels and Functions,* pp. 129–40. New York: Hastings.

McQuail, D. (1987). *Mass Communication Theory.* London: Sage Publications Ltd.

Merrill, J. C. (1988). Inclination of Nations to Control Press and Attitudes on Professionalization. *Journalism Quarterly,* 65, 839–44.

Merrill, J. C., Bryna, C. R., and Alisky, M. (1970). *The Foreign Press.* Baton Rouge, Louisiana: Louisiana State University Press.

Mshomba, R. E. (1997). On African Responsibility for Economic Problems. *Issue: A Journal of Opinion,* XXV(1).

Murphy, Sharon M. (1980). Nigerian Press and National Development. Paper presented to the International Communication Division of the Association for Education in Journalism and Mass Communication. Boston, MA, August.

Musa, B. A. (1996). *The Bloc Press Phenomenon and Conflict Management in Nigeria.* Paper presented to the Speech Communication Association Convention for its Annual Convention in San Diego, California, November.

Nam, S. (1983). Press Freedom in the Third World. In L. John Martin and Anju Grover Chaudhary (eds.), *Comparative Mass Media Systems.* New York: Longman, Inc.

Ngatara, L. A. (1984). *Why the U.S. Is Right to Quit UNESCO.* Paper presented to the World Media Conference, Tokyo, Japan, November 19–22.

Ngwainmbi, E. (1995). *Communication Efficiency and Rural Development in Africa: The Case of Cameroon.* New York: University Press of America.

Nixon, R. B. (1960). Factors Related to Press Freedom in National Press Systems. *Journalism Quarterly,* 37, 13–28

Nwankwo, Arthur A. (1972). *Nigeria: The Challenge of Biafra.* London: Rex Collins Ltd.

Obasanjo, O. (1979). Make It a Year of Hope, Love. *The Constitution of the Federal Republic of Nigeria.* Apapa, Nigeria: Times Press Limited.

Ochs, M. (1986). *The African Press.* Cairo, Egypt: The American University Press.

Ogan, C. (1987). Coverage of Development News in Developed and Developing Countries. *Journalism Quarterly,* 64(1), 80–87.

Okoli, E. (1996). *The Mass Media and Ethnic Conflict in West Africa.* Paper presented to the Speech Communication Association Convention for its Annual Convention in San Diego, California, November.

Ottoo, M. O., and Jacobson, R. (1995). The Pan-African News Agency: A Manifestation of Development Media Theory. In Peter Nwosu, Chuka Onwumechili, and Richard M'bayo (eds.), *Communication and The Transformation of Society: A Developing Region's Perspectives.* New York: University Press of America.

Patterson, P., and Wilking, L. (1998). *Media Ethics: Issues and Cases* (3rd. ed.). Boston: McGraw-Hill.

Pember, D. R. (1987). *Mass Media Law* (4th ed). Dubuque, Iowa: Wm. C. Brown Publishers.

Somerlad, E. F. (1968). Problems in Developing a Free Enterprise Press in East Africa. *Gazette,* 15(2), 57–77.

Ugboaja, F. O. (1972). Traditional-Urban Media Model: Stocktaking for African Development, *Gazette,* 18(2), 82.

Vyshinsky, A. (1948). *The Law of the Soviet State.* New York: Macmillan Co.

Wilcox, D. L. (1975). *Mass Media in Black Africa: Philosophy and Control.* New York: Praegar Publishers.

4

Africa between the Meiji Restoration and the Legacy of Atatürk: Comparative Dilemmas of Modernization

Ali A. Mazrui

Approximately half a century separated the Meiji Restoration of 1868 in Japan and the rise of Mustafa Kemal Atatürk in Turkey. Involved in those two events were two distinct paradigms of modernization that are of relevance to other nonoccidental societies elsewhere. Of special relevance in this chapter will be the dilemmas of African societies.

What is at stake is the process of modernization, with its baggage of science and technology from the Renaissance to the postindustrial age. Can a non-Western society embrace this heritage of knowledge and modernity without committing cultural suicide? Are we still bedevilled by the question of whether a society can ever modernize without Westernizing? Is modern technology a weapon of cultural genocide in Africa and Asia?

Two separate answers were given to this question by Japan after the Meiji Restoration and Turkey in the wake of the Kemalist reforms. The Japanese after 1868 operated on the conviction that it was possible to embark on an economic and military modernization without simultaneously undergoing cultural Westernization. The economy and the military were figuratively part of the body of the state, but the soul of the state lay in the values, mores, and spiritual culture of the society. Although Shintoist doctrine is less dichotomous than Christian theology, the Japanese did seem to distinguish between the outer functions of the state and the inner spirit of the society.

But in order to perform those functions, the state could indeed borrow specific military or industrial techniques from other societies. That is precisely what Japan after the Meiji Restoration embarked upon. The slogan of "Western technique, Japanese spirit" captured the deliberate selectivity of the Japanese approach to modernization at that moment in time. Economic and military modernization was being undertaken on the assumption that Japanese culture could be held constant.

Fifty years later, Turkey was faced with comparable dilemmas, although the origins of those dilemmas went even further back than the period of the Meiji Restoration. After all, the Ottoman Empire had periodically agonized over Islamic authenticity on one side and Western technical efficiency on the other. These dilemmas among the Turks went back not only to the Young Turk Revolution but also to the Tanzimat and beyond.

However, the moment of ultimate testing came when the Ottoman Empire had disintegrated and Turkey faced the realities of being a distinct and separate nation-state. The Atatürk Revolution took place at a moment of historic decision making; Turkey was at the crossroads between empire and republic.

Would Turkey choose the road of industrial and military modernization combined with cultural authenticity, as the Japanese had done? Or would Turkey decide that the economic and military body could not be modern if the cultural soul was still traditionalist? On the whole, the Kemalist doctrinal assumptions were leaning on these latter directions. Kemal Atatürk was more inclined to equate modernization with Westernization than the Meiji reformers in Japan had been.

Another fifty years later, societies in yet a third part of the world were confronting similar agonizing choices. In this chapter, we are focusing especially on societies in Black Africa south of the Sahara. Can these societies modernize without Westernizing? Should they adopt Atatürk's doctrine that technical modernization was impossible without cultural Westernization? Or should they listen to the nostalgic music of a Japanese slogan in the last quarter of the nineteenth century—"Western technique, Japanese spirit"?

Let us now turn to the African arena of these historic psychological conflicts.

IS WESTERNIZED AFRICA PREMODERN?

In some respects, former colonial territories are fundamentally different from either Turkey or Japan. Far from being a former colony, Turkey after World War I became a former imperial power, an empire that had shrunk into a republic. In 1868, on the other hand, Japan was a potential empire and soon became an empire-in-the-making. Turkey modernized in the wake of territorial shrinkage; Japan modernized in anticipation of territorial expansion. Both Turkey and Japan were of course inspired in part by nationalism. Both sought modernization partly for defensive purposes—to strengthen themselves against the danger of being dominated by others. The history of Turkey after the modernization was a history of trying to abstain from dominating others. The history of Japan after the Meiji Restoration was for a while a history of enhanced appetite for dominion over others.

Black Africa is of course different from both those historic situations. Much of the continent was indeed colonized by outsiders, including the Turks. In North Africa, the impact of the Ottoman heritage was considerable, but it also extended to the Horn of Africa. Indeed, the influence of Islam in Africa during the Ottoman Empire inevitably included an Ottoman component because the Ottoman Empire was at the time the political heartland of the Muslim world.

But from the second half of the nineteenth century, it was Western Europe that gained the ascendancy in controlling the fortunes of the African continent. Britain, France, Portugal, Belgium, and others established varying sizes of empires in the African continent. Part of the legitimation for empire building was Rudyard Kipling's concept of the white man's burden. This included the commitment to "civilize" other societies, which in those days was approximately the equivalent of "modernize." Kipling was calling his racial compatriots to accept the burden of building modern infrastructures for other societies.

The ports ye shall not enter,
The roads ye shall not tread
Go make them with your living
And mark them with your dead.[1]

To this extent, Black Africa had less of a choice as to which direction to take than either Turkey or Meiji Japan. The Western European powers in Africa chose the directions of social, economic, and political change. They also chose the main instrumentalities of change, from missionary schools to multinational corporations. Black Africa was deprived of both the industrial innovativeness of the Meiji reformers and the revolutionary interpreters of Kemalist Turkey. The Africans were not captains of their own destiny. They were not invited to look at historic charts to determine whether they could sail toward modernity without traversing Westernism.

Yet, there is a residual fundamental question that we need to ask. In the literature, the pertinent question has normally been whether one can modernize without Westernizing. The converse has seldom been tackled. Can one Westernize without modernizing?

Part of the answer lies in the African experience. The pace of Westernization in Africa has been faster than the pace of modernization. In some areas of social change, there has therefore been Westernization without modernization—the transmission of culture without a transmission of skill.

The question that now arises is under what circumstances can Westernization take place without modernization. In the African context, a number of discordant processes form part of this basic anomaly.

One anomalous process is urbanization without industrialization. In Western Europe, urbanization gained momentum because industrialization was well under way or because the large-scale agrarian plantation was forcing peasants into wage labor. In Africa, on the other hand, there was no agrarian revolution forcing subsistence farmers into wage labor. The sons of farmers moved to the cities for drastically different reasons.

Within the cities themselves, there was no expanding industrial revolution devouring the workers from the countryside. Industrial change in African cities was relatively modest, and was in any case overwhelmingly in the control of alien hands and under the management of the alien skills.

Whatever it is that generated urbanization in some important centers, it was neither large-scale rural productivity of the kind attained by England during her agrarian revolution nor was it expanding factory productivity that devoured labor from the countryside. African urbanization was fatally disjointed from industrialization. The urbanization helped foster Western tastes, dress, and ghetto lifestyles alongside the Westernized elegance of the elite. But cultural urbanization was not accompanied by real, autonomous, and sustained industrialization.

The other discordant note in the African experience was scientification without secularization. The Western impact fostered the ideology of scientism, a religious belief in the supremacy of science. In the African context, the anomaly arose out of the paradoxical role of Christian missionaries. On the one hand, they were in Africa to propagate a new gospel, asking Africans to exchange old beliefs and traditional religions for the Bible. On the other hand, the same Christian missionaries helped to build schools where Isaac Newton was taught, where mathematics competed with Shakespeare for attention. Out of this paradox of missionary schools propagating a scientific culture emerged the deeper paradox of converting Africans to the ideology of scientism while at the same time capturing their souls for an alternative religious order. The outcome of it all was precisely the process of shallow scientification of African attitudes and values without their translation into technology.

Closely related to this anomaly is the anomaly of education without training. Much of the education that was transmitted in African colonial schools was a process of transmitting values without transmitting skills, acculturation without training.

There were indeed differences among the imperial powers. For example, Belgium in the Congo (Zaire) was widely credited with putting more emphasis on training than acculturation. Vocational training in the Belgian Congo had a higher premium than in either British or French colonies.

But on the whole, schools in Africa were more instruments for transmitting values and lifestyle than for transmitting skills and techniques. Quite often, this meant transmitting to African societies some elements of European traditions, rather than some elements of European modernity.

This element compounded the other anomaly of urbanization without industrialization. African schools seemed preeminently designed to produce rural misfits. An African who completes the equivalent of the Cambridge School Certificate examination, or in some areas the Higher School Certificate examination, is regarded as no longer suitable for residences in the rural areas. The young person's own parents may feel betrayed if the child with such a level of education insisted on remaining in the villages. It was assumed that sacrifices made for higher and higher levels of education were ultimately designed to facilitate urban accomplishments rather than rural performance. Parents who had sacrificed a lot toward their children's secondary education, paying fees in societies without free education, would regard themselves as deeply betrayed if their educated offspring opted for the rural life instead of seeking fortunes in the urban areas.

Had the schools been designed more for training (for example, farming instead of acculturation, through Shakespeare, and the Bible), education in Africa would not be quite as incompatible with rural development as it has tended to be. Once again, Westernization has triumphed over modernization.

Yet another anomaly in the African situation is the promotion of capitalism without entrepreneurship. The profit motive and the quest for maximization of returns are indeed vigorous and widespread in African societies. But genuine entrepreneurship—commitment to risk taking for the sake of psychic performance—is still relatively rare.

Sometimes new wealth mitigates precisely against the spirit of entrepreneurship. For example, oil wealth in Nigeria hovers on the borderline between near capitalism and innovative entrepreneurship. The Nigerian Civil War had generated innovativeness in Biafra especially as the beleaguered community engaged in major areas of self-reliance and inventiveness in order to cope with their own deprivation. One did hope that the Civil War would at least have one beneficial effect—precisely, innovation in desperation, because necessity fosters inventiveness.

Unfortunately, Nigeria missed the opportunity of learning the techniques of creativity from the agonies of destruction, of learning innovation from the deprivations of war. Unfortunately, the Nigerian situation was one in which oil wealth succeeded a Civil War. Although the Civil War created a predisposition toward innovation, the oil wealth in the 1970s created a predisposition toward lethargy. A considerable diffusion and dilution of human energy took place in Nigeria in the aftermath of petroenergy. Incentives for exertion were reduced. Indigenization policies of Nigeria simply resulted in the creation of African directors on governing boards of multinational cooperations, rather than African entrepreneurs in the central areas of economic activity.

These then are the major anomalous processes of Westernization in Africa, devoid of modernization.

In reality, the picture is drawn a little too sharply. Some modernization has, of course, taken place in Africa. A modest level of industrialization has taken place alongside disproportionate urbanization and exaggerated secularization.

As for education in Black Africa, it has disproportionately been acculturation without training, the transmission of Western culture without necessarily transmitting Western skills and technique.

How does this African predicament relate to the comparative scenarios of Atatürk's Turkey and the Meiji Japan? Meiji Japan was a case of attempted modernization without Westernization. The African colonial experience has been so far a case of Westernization basically without modernization. The case of Turkey under the legacy of Mustafa Kemal Atatürk has been a case of modernization through Westernization. Three scenarios are confronting the judgment of historiography.

Are there ways of going beyond these traditional dilemmas of modernity and Westernism? Is there an escape from this paradigm of dilemmas ranging from the Meiji Restoration to the reform of Kemal Atatürk, from the fortunes of former empires to the destinies of former colonies, from the power of political systems like those of Turkey and Japan to the fragility of ex-colonial states?

The quest for a new paradigm may require regional specifity. A preliminary solution may have to be region by region, rather than global in scale; modernization as against Westernization; the struggle for authenticity as against the imperative of change.

MODERNIZATION IN A FOREIGN IDIOM

There is a more pervasive reason as to why the Western impact on Africa resulted in more Westernization than modernization. This was the role of European languages in the whole process of acculturation in the African colonies. In order to understand the implications of this linguistic factor more fully, it is important first to confront the issue of what is modernization.

We have already referred to processes like urbanization, industrialization, and secularization. In fact, these are accompanying characteristics of modernization, rather than defining attributes. Sometimes these are the outer signs of modernization rather than the inner dynamic. In our terms, modernization is to be defined as *change in the direction that is compatible with the present stage of human knowledge, and that does justice to the potentialities of the human person both as a social and as an innovative being.* This definition gives three attributes to modernization. One is compatibility with science and know-how. Secondly, modernity involves expanding social horizons and expanding frontiers of sympathy. Allegiance to clan and tribe is less modern than allegiance to nation; allegiance to nation is less modern than allegiance to continent; allegiance to continent is less modern than sensitivity to the needs of the human race. The second attribute of modernization in terms of doing justice to the human person as a social being carries with it the logic of a constant effort to touch the global village.

The third defining attribute of modernization is acceptance of innovativeness, an encouragement of the spirit that seeks to explore whether things can be done better. Modernization becomes to some extent a readiness to applaud inventiveness, a readiness to encourage discovery.

The outer manifestations of this trinity of modernization can indeed be processes like industrialization. Inventiveness and innovation can accelerate the application of science and technology to the tasks of economic productivity. When industrialization results in urbanization, the ties of clan, tribe, and village could be loosened—and social horizons expanded. But ultimately, modernization is partly measured by its proximity to current levels of awareness and knowledge, ranging from medical science to military capabilities. Secularization can be an outer manifestation of this deepening scientific sophistication.

To an outside observer, Turkey since the Kemalist Revolution has sometimes mistaken the outward trappings of modernization for the inner essence, and sometimes mistaken effect for cause. For example, should Turkey invite science in, or should it simply take religion out? The pursuit of science is a defining characteristic of modernization, but the discouragement of religion is an outer trapping, an accompanying characteristic of modernization at the most.

The legacy of Atatürk has not always been clear whether it is indeed pursuing science or simply diluting the role of religion in society. Major reforms in the Kemalist tradition seem to be obsessed with such trappings as dress and vocabulary as ways of reducing the visibility of religion in Turkish society. The flamboyant trappings of religion were either discouraged or torn asunder, but the essence of science was not necessarily pursued.

In contrast, Japan after the Meiji Restoration focused on the pursuit of technique and know-how rather than the dilution of religion. On the contrary, religious symbolism was mobilized to lend greater legitimacy to the aggressive pursuit of technical efficiency. The religious outlook of the Japanese had varied aspects. The most national was of course the Shintoist tradition, but this was moderated by two other traditions. One had its ancestry in India—Buddhism. The other had its ancestry in China, encompassing both Buddhist and Confucian elements. A synthesis of some kind, or at least a modus vivendi among the different traditions, had evolved over the centuries. The Japanese decision to add a Western component to that diverse heritage did not begin with a decision to secularize Japan; it began with a decision to industrialize Japan. Industrial civilization was pursued not by destroying the Gods of religion but by lighting the fires of science.

Another contrast between Turkey and Japan concerns the issue of expanding social horizons as a defining characteristic of modernization. The Atatürk revolution in Turkey occurred, as we indicated, in the wake of territorial shrinkage. The Ottoman Empire had been disintegrating, and Turkey was shrinking to the size of a solitary republic.

In contrast, the Meiji Restoration was to some extent a prelude to an imperial role. Initially, the primary ambition of Japan, as of Turkey after World War I, was simply protection against an external threat. In the words of Josefa M. Sanial:

Modernization was Japan's response to the nineteenth century challenge caused by the threatened military and economic aggression from abroad at a time when Tokugawa Japan was beset with continued unrest. And after the fall of the *Tokugawa bakufu*, it was a response to the challenge of continued infringement of Japan's sovereign rights by "extra-territoriality" and "uniform tariffs" provisions of her "unequal treaties" with Western powers—for as long as Japanese feudal institutions persisted.[2]

But then Japan became expansionist, looking for a global imperial role. For quite a while, however, she was frustrated by the prior rivalry of Western powers. As Michael Edwards put it:

When Japan felt the impetus of imperial expansion herself—the natural consequences, Marxists would maintain, of her Western capitalist structure—she was continually frustrated by the old colonial powers unless it suited the immediate advantage of imperial rivalries. Japan's position was that of an uninvited guest arriving late at the banquet, only to find that the choicest food was reserved for others.[3]

What is clear from these trends is that Japan's industrialization gradually led to expanding social horizons, with all their frustrations at that stage. On the other hand, Turkey's Westernization seemed to be accompanied by shrinking social horizons, as the legacy of an imperial order gave way to the parochialism of a solitary republic. Japan's expanding social horizons might have aided her capacity to modernize in substance instead of only Westernizing in trappings. Turkey's social shrinkage might have made it more difficult for her to embark on an adequate "takeoff."

In the period immediately following the Meiji Restoration, the Japanese became economically strong, mainly because they wanted to be militarily strong. The impetus for industrialization was, at least in the initial stages, the imperative of national defense.

But then came World War II, Pearl Harbor, and the disasters of Hiroshima and Nagasaki. The American occupation followed, and one product was the constitution of Japan, eventually forbidding Japan from arming itself beyond minimal local defense. A second Japanese miracle occurred. Whereas the Meiji industrialization was the achievement of a militantly militarized Japan, the new industrialization seemed to be the achievement of a militantly pacifist or at least a demilitarized Japan. In the first half of the century, the industrial might of Japan was partly attributed to its warlike determination; in the second half of the twentieth century, Japanese achievements were sometimes attributed to the fact that she spent less money on her own defense and let the United States assume ultimate responsibility for the military protection of Japan.

By the 1980s, pressures were mounting on Japan to spend more on her defense. These pressures were particularly conspicuous in policy statements from Washington. But also in the 1980s, pressures were mounting to get Japan to reduce her export to the United States and Europe. In other words, there was a feeling among Japan's Western friends that Tokyo should become more militarily aggressive and less economically aggressive. Tokyo should spend more money on her military preparedness against the Soviet Union and devote less energy toward capturing economic markets in Europe and North America.

In either case, Japan could not but have her global horizons broadened, with commensurate performance in her productive capabilities. Even without repealing the relevant clause in her constitution, which limits her expenditure on defense, Japan's military capability was already among the top seven in the world when calculated in terms of expenditure and industrial prowess. The three defining characteristics of modernization—responsiveness to know-how, expanding social horizons, and deepening innovativeness—all seem to be supremely realized in the Japanese miracle. What was often lacking was the moral underpinning of expanding social horizons, a moral empathy with other people beyond mere understanding of the behavior of their markets and the dynamics of supply and demand in their societies.

What Turkey and Japan did have in common was the effort to modernize through their own national languages. This was in sharp contrast to colonial situations where educational and scientific change was disproportionately in the imported idiom of the imperial power.

There were indeed differences between Turkish attitudes and Japanese attitudes to language. Both the Turks and the Japanese wanted to make their languages more flexible in order to accommodate both the richness and the specificity of modern scientific discourse. But whereas the Japanese decided to do it mainly through borrowing new words, the Turks decided to do it both through borrowing new words and destroying old usages. The Japanese welcomed such specific Western concepts as *baransu*, meaning "balance," a concept that has had considerable influence in both Japanese economic policy and technological thrust. But the Japanese have also permitted their own linguistic heritage to fare for itself in the new industrial age.

The Turks, on the other hand, have not limited themselves to adopting new Western phrases and concepts; they have at times systematically attempted to purge Turkish of certain older and Arabic-derived concepts. Again, in vocabulary as in lifestyle, the Japanese insisted on introducing new things and letting new things affect the destiny of older ways. The Turks, on the other hand, have sometimes insisted on destroying older ways in the hope that the ashes would be fertile for the growth of new things.

Where does Africa lie between these two paradigms? The most basic factor to be grasped in the African situation is the massive impact of alien languages in precisely those areas that are regarded as central to modernization. For the time being, it is a sociolinguistic impossibility for an African to be a sophisticated physicist without at the same time being supremely fluent in a European language. It is indeed a sociolinguistic impossibility for African physicists to sit together and discuss professional issues in an African language. The business of physics, chemistry, and biology for the time being has to be conducted almost exclusively in European languages. The path to scientific modernization in an African context is for the time being inevitably through linguistic Westernization.

African universities are special arenas for Western acculturation. Outside Arab Africa, the medium of instruction in all departments is a European language, although most first-year undergraduates have still a rather limited command of the imperial medium.

In the specific area of *political* modernization, we once again have to bear witness to the striking role of Western languages. In many African countries that have competitive parties and parliamentary systems, the medium of electoral and parliamentary discourse is a European language, understood only by a limited number of the citizens. In almost all African countries that are governed through the parliamentary system, one cannot be a member of parliament unless one speaks the imperial language (be it English, French, Portuguese, or other). An African potential candidate could speak seven indigenous African languages, but if the imperial language was not among those that the candidate speaks, the candidate would be disqualified. On the other hand, an African parliamentarian can, like the late President Hastings Banda in Malawi, have lost command over his indigenous language, and yet still retain credentials of political prominence. African parliaments are therefore basically political clubs of those who speak English, French, or Portuguese. African conferences of physicists, chemists, zoologists, and botanists are usually dialogues of those in complete command of the relevant imperial language that had previously been used to control the destiny of their own societies.

Is the prominence of the imperial language an aid or a hinderance to keeping up with the present state of human knowledge? In the short run, it is indeed an aid. Mastery over French or English enhances the modernization of the elite in African societies. On the other hand, equating modernization with competence in English or French slows the modernization of the masses in the African context. Modernizing through the imperial language gains speed at the relevant level of elitist change, but it slows the involvement of the masses in the modernizing process.

The masses in Japan have been more speedily involved in the technological age than they would have been had they needed first to learn a European language. The technical modernization of the Japanese language was in part a process of technological democratization, making it possible for more and more Japanese to enter the process of modernization without having to learn an entirely alien linguistic universe.

Kemal Atatürk inaugurated a similar process in Turkey, helping the Turkish language to acquire technological competence, and thereby enabling the Turkish masses to be initiated into the technological age sooner than they might have done had they been forced to learn another language before becoming modern.

The imperial language in ex-colonial states might appear to enhance the capabilities of the elite to expand their social horizons and to understand the wider world. They do indeed understand the wider world, but do they cease to understand their immediate environment? Do the elites of Africa understand London, Paris, and New York more readily than they understand their own villages? If that is the case, there is no real expansion of social horizons; there is only a substitution of alien horizons for indigenous ones. Once again, the African predicament is one of faster Westernization than modernization.

Innovativeness is also sometimes hampered by the illusion of linguistic acculturation. Because Africans are learning new things through their new language, they sometimes think they are learning *original* things. Very often, what is being transmitted is secondhand and sometimes banal, but it is being transmitted in impeccable French. The romance of the French language is mistaken for scientific originality. Once again, modernization lags behind Westernization in Africa.

TOWARD MODERNIZING WESTERNIZED AFRICA

Given that Africa is for the time being sentenced to the apparent paradox of Westernization without modernization, what is the way out of this fate? What lessons can be drawn from the experience of the Meiji Restoration and the reforms of Mustafa Kemal Atatürk?

In an ex-colonial state, the first imperative for modernization in the face of prior Westernization is, paradoxically, the imperative of *indigenization*. On the one side, the Westernization has linked the local psyche, especially among the elite, with the distant world of Europe and North America. But in order to transform cultural substitution into cultural expansion, a connection has to be reestablished with the local scene. The imperative of indigenization seeks to localize resources, personnel, and effective control. The

Atatürk Revolution did include a substantial indigenization. The Meiji Restoration began with the indigenous and proceeded toward mating the indigenous with the stimulus of the alien.

The strategy of indigenization in Africa requires that in situations where African rivers could be converted into hydroelectric power, this should be regarded as more important than establishing instrumentalities of energy that require imported oil or imported uranium. Indigenization is partly an exercise in selecting what is indigenously available and giving that priority over what is exogenously imported.

A second struggle in the pursuit of modernization as against Westernization is the strategy of *domestication*. In this latter sense, what we are looking for is not resurrection or utilization of the indigenous; it is closer to the effort of making the foreign more relevant to the local scene. In Africa, one of the more obvious examples is the African university itself, ostensibly a carrier of modern labels of knowledge and sophistication, a measurement of one of the defining characteristics of modernity. Many African universities were in the first instance subsidiaries of cultural multinational corporations, branches of metropolitan university systems. When I began teaching at Makerere University in Uganda, my students were really students of the University of London. My examination questions at the end of term were subject to the approval or disapproval of the Examining Board of the University of London. My products from Makerere were in the ultimate analysis cultural products—holders of specific London degrees predicated on a satisfactory command of the imperial language and with qualifications based on imperial literary and technical skills.

The strategy of domestication means making these institutions much more responsive to the imperative of local needs. Whereas when I arrived at Makerere the only languages taught were European languages, the Makerere of domesticated sensitivity would permit a greater responsiveness to the linguistic heritage of the immediate local Ugandan scene. Local African languages would thus be studied according to the highest levels of technical proficiency attained by the profession of students of language. Modernization at Makerere University would not mean the triumph simply of the English language—that would be Westernization. Modernization at Makerere would include skills in studying Ugandan and African languages on the basis of the highest levels of the science of languages attained so far.

A third strategy for going beyond Westernization is the strategy of *cultural diversification*. The effort to learn from more than one culture, to respond to the stimulus of creative diversity, is itself a process of minimizing the Western impact while at the same time responding to the impact of modernity. Diversification also aids expansion of social horizons, educating Africans to take seriously not simply what the West has to teach the world, but also what China, Japan, Islam, India, and other civilizations have to contribute to the broad arena of both human understanding and human skills. This degree of diversification has to some extent been deficient in both the examples of Turkey and Japan. On balance, both the Kemalist and the Meiji reforms focused on an immediate marriage between the indigenous and the Occidental heritages.

In the African condition, the diversification needs to go further, linking the African not only with the West, but hopefully also with the Turkish, the Japanese, and other heritages beyond. The beginnings of cultural freedom lie in cultural diversification, responding to the full impact of external plurality combined with national singularity.

Deeply related to this particular thrust is what I have called elsewhere the strategy of *horizontal interpenetration*. This is the mutual penetration of otherwise less privileged societies or otherwise less autonomous cultures. The Japanese had at least a prior synthesis of this kind of interpenetration, ranging from the legacy of India to the legacy of China at a time when Japan was about to experiment with the legacy of Europe.

It is arguable that Turkey did not permit itself to be as culturally promiscuous. Turkey under Atatürk mistrusted the demands of the Islamic heritage, but it was at the same time fascinated by the promise of Western civilization. Modernization under Kemal Atatürk was in part a quest for civilization. In the conclusion of his monumental *Six-Day Speech* of 1927, Kemal Atatürk reasserted his creed that, "We make use of every means solely and exclusively for one purpose: to bestow upon the Turkish nation that position which is its due within the civilized world."[4]

Atatürk's formulation has already been traced to the 1914 decree in Turkey abolishing the capitulations in reviewing the nineteenth century reform efforts:

The Ottoman Empire . . . continues to march in the path of renaissance and reform which it entered upon [with the Tanzimat Decree of 1939] . . . in order to assure for itself the place which was due to it in the family of the civilized peoples of Europe.[5]

Ultimately however, modernization requires responsiveness to more than Western civilization. Neither Turkey with the Atatürk legacy nor Japan in the aftermath of the Meiji Restoration has ever been able to go beyond responsiveness to Western culture as an additive to what had already been accumulated indigenously.

A fifth strategy of conversion from Westernization to modernization involves what I have had reason to call elsewhere *counterpenetration*. This involves penetrating the citadels of power and exerting some leverage over those powers in defense of Third World interests.

The use of OPEC petropower in the 1980s to buy shares in major industries of the Western world, such as Krupp and the Benz mystique, were part of this effort to increase Southern leverage over Northern power.

When Southern money buys up Northern banks, or when Southern professors start teaching in Northern universities, a subtle historic reversal of roles is indeed underway.

Japan has been the most decisive instrument of economic counterpenetration in history. Its ability to enter into the citadels of Western economic power and create consternation in those citadels has been almost unequalled in the history of the Western world's relations with the rest of the universe. Japanese counterpenetration has led to screams for the control of Japanese imports from Detroit to Birmingham, from Minnesota to Munich. Yet, when Japan's economy is in recession, the world holds its breath nervously.

Turkey's economic performance since the Atatürk Revolution has been far less impressive than Japan's performance since the Meiji Restoration. But then, the comparison is less than fair to Turkey because no other country has equalled Japan's industrial miracle.

Turkey's record of counterpenetrating the rest of Europe occurred when the Ottoman Empire was at its height, and Turkish culture and institutions influenced Eastern and Southern Europe. But by the time of the Atatürk Revolution, the impact of Western Europe was gaining ascendancy in Turkey, and the Atatürk Revolution speeded up the Westernization.

Africa's capacity for counterpenetrating the Western world in the future would depend on three possible trends—the stabilization and Pan-Africanization of Nigeria, the more complete liberation of the Republic of South Africa, and the politicization and sophistication of Black America.

Nigeria is by far the largest African country with a population of over 100 million. It is indeed the largest in Eurafrica after Russia. Size, combined with power and with potentially innovative energetic cultures, could in time increase Nigeria's leverage in the global system as a whole. Currently, Nigeria is one of the largest foreign suppliers of oil to the United States. The balance of trade between Nigeria and the United States is heavily in Nigeria's favor. Nigeria's oil power is of course finite, but it could help lay the foundations of sufficient global influence for a counterpenetrative capacity.

The fuller liberation[6] of South Africa would give Africa another potential implement for counterpenetrating the Western world. The mineral resources of South Africa when they are effectively under Black control could form the basis of new African influence in the citadels of global economic power. South Africa's gold resources, if they are indeed maintained and if gold is still monetized, could create credentials for greater participation within the chanceries of the world's monetary system.

As for the potential of Black America, this can best be understood by comparing African Americans with American Jews. Within the United States, Blacks outnumber Jews by a factor of more than four to one. Indeed, there are twice as many Blacks in the United States as there are Jews in the whole world added together, including the Jews of Israel. Yet, the influence of American Blacks on American foreign policy is only a fraction of the influence of Jewish Americans on American foreign policy.

If in time this difference in power between the two groups is narrowed, African Americans could become the most important constituency of the Third World lodged in the heartland of the Western world. With increasing sophistication and politicization, African Americans could become the watchdog of the interests of Africa within the United States the way Jewish Americans have been the watchdog of the interests of Israel.

Culturally, Black Americans have already served as a counterpenetrative device for aspects of African culture, especially African music. The musical impact of African societies has not been directly from Africa to the Western world; it has been indirectly through people of African descent singing and dancing within Western cultural circles and amongst themselves. Jazz, rumba, samba, rhythm and blues, and aspects of rock music are all manifestations of Africa's musical counterpenetration into the lives of young Westerners, and many older ones as well.

It is partly because of these considerations that Africa's future capacity for counterpenetration has to rely not merely on the stabilization and Pan-Africanization of Nigeria and the fuller liberation of South Africa, but also upon the contributions of people of African descent living in the heartland of the Western world.

Counterpenetration helps to make dependence mutual. To that extent, it is the logical conclusion of genuine modernization. We did indicate earlier that modernization is in part a process of expanding social horizons and expanding empathy. Those who are loyal only to their clans and tribes are less modern than those who are loyal to some wider human entity, and the most modern of all are the few who are beginning to perceive the world as a global village. These may regard humankind as a whole as their own clan to help defend and protect without being "clannish."

Reciprocal penetration between societies on terms that are fair and equitable can become the foundations of genuine human interdependence. The expanding horizons and empathy that would in time result from such equitable interdependence could be the ultimate consummation of the process of modernization.

Today, one cannot travel around Africa without witnessing a little bit of the Western world from one African country to another. Perhaps one day it might be true that one cannot travel within the Western world without witnessing a little bit of Africa from one Western society to another.

But before that fully happens, Africa would have to catch up in two areas of modernization—enhanced sensitivity to new levels of knowledge and enhanced capacity for innovation. These two would help facilitate that third process of modernization mentioned earlier—expanding social horizons and empathy. By that time, Africa will have learned not to mistake

Westernization for modernization, not to pursue the trappings of Western cultures at the expense of the substance of modernity.

CONCLUSION

This chapter has attempted to disentangle some of the central dilemmas of modernization and social change that have faced many societies in the last 150 years. We have focused especially on two paradigms of purposeful change—Japan's industrialization after the Meiji Restoration and the reforms of Kemal Atatürk in Turkey after the First World War. We have sought to demonstrate that in at least earlier phases of modernization in Japan, the ambition was to hold a substantial part of Japanese culture constant while the Japanese economy and military modernized. It was believed that technique could be distinguished from essence. Japanese culture was the soul of the society, and the economy, the state, and the military were the equivalent of physical limbs. The limbs could be made stronger with exercise and a change of diet, but ultimately the soul had to remain loyal to itself. Hence, the old Japanese slogan: "Western technique, Japanese spirit"!

The Atatürk reforms in Turkey, on the other hand, started from the premise that neither the state nor the economy could effectively be modernized unless Turkish culture itself was modernized. The soul of the nation was to be converted to a new allegiance before the limbs of the nation could perform their tasks effectively.

In theory, the Atatürk approach seemed the more coherent. Society was an integrated phenomenon, and no easy distinction could be made between culture and economy and between the state and the collective soul.

In practice, the Japanese effort was ultimately a greater transformation and a higher level of performance than anything attained by Turkey since Atatürk. However, the reasons for the difference in performance are complex and cannot be attributed solely to the distinction between modernizing without Westernizing (the Meiji way) and modernizing through Westernizing (the Atatürk way).

In the case of Africa, the trend has been more like Westernizing without modernizing. The trappings of Western culture have gained ascendancy rather than the real substance of modernization. It is time for Africa to go back to the drawing board.

NOTES

This chapter is indebted to earlier work by the author on comparative strategies of development and modernization in a cultural context.

1. Rudyard Kipling, "The White Man's Burden," *The Times* (London), February 4, 1899.

2. Josefa M. Sanial, "The Mobilization of Traditional Values in the Modernization of Japan." In Roberts N. Bellah (Editor), *Religion and Progress in Modern Asia* (New York: The Free Press; London: Collier-MacMillan, 1965), pp. 124–25.

3. Michael Edwardes, *Asia in the European Age, 1498–1955* (New York: Frederick E. Praeger, 1962), p. 278. Consult also Robert A. Scalapino, "Ideology and Modernization: The Japanese Case." In David E. Apter (Editor), *Ideology and Discontent* (New York: The Free Press of Glencoe, 1964), p. 94.

4. Nutuk, 1934, Edn. II, p. 336.

5. Cited in J.C. Hurewitz, *Diplomacy in the Near and Middle East* (Princeton, N.J.: Van Nostrand, 1956), Vol ii, p. 2.

6. Political apartheid has substantially ended, but economic apartheid is still intact. The best lands, the best mines, the best jobs, and the best economic and commercial opportunities are still under white control.

PART III

Building Social Capacity:
Civil Society, Democratization,
and Human Rights

Civil Society and Democratic Development in Eastern and Southern Africa

Julius E. Nyang'oro

INTRODUCTION

The decade of the 1990s will be remembered in the history of the African continent as the decade that witnessed the renewal and rebirth of civil society. It is possible to make such a statement now given what has happened since 1990. For Africa in general, the long national conference in Benin—indeed the first of its kind on the continent—met in 1989 resulting in the first significant political transition in Africa in the post–Cold War era (Bratton and van de Walle, 1997). Through a national conference involving a significant majority of civil society groups and key political figures, the people of Benin were able to replace a military regime with a civilian one without bloodshed. Given the political history of Africa in the 1970s and 1980s, this was indeed a remarkable political feat. In those two decades, the most common mechanism for political change in Africa had been the military coup d'etat. Benin itself had long been known for the frequency in changes of regime through the military. Around Christmastime, one always expected some action by the military in Benin.

The 1989/1990 example of Benin in terms of political transition was quickly repeated in a number of countries, although the results of such effort varied greatly across the continent's political spectrum. In Mali, the national conference led to a new regime. In Congo/Zaire, the political machinations of the former leader Mobutu Sese Seko resulted in a failure of the national conference to usher in a new political dispensation. It took a brewing refugee crisis and a yearlong Civil War to bring an end to Mobutu's regime in 1997. However, the variation of the results of the national conferences notwithstanding, the significance of the Benin experience was a lesson that had far-reaching implications for the practice of politics in Africa. Interestingly, the leader of Benin who had been unceremoniously dumped by the electorate in 1989/1990 was triumphant in the subsequent presidential elections in 1995. The fact that Mr. Kerekou was defeated and then elected to the presidency in Benin in a span of five years may be an important telling point for the reality and complexity of politics in Africa, a reality that requires a closer examination than what has been the case to date. I contend that a closer examination of the political reality in Africa cannot be satisfactorily done unless it is accompanied by a critical analysis of civil society in general and particularly of nongovernmental organizations (NGOs).

In eastern and southern Africa (ESA), examination of such a reality would require a special emphasis on the role of civil society in the political transition of countries that stand out as having undergone significant changes, such as South Africa and Zambia, and those that seem to be marking time and yet are poised for major changes, such as Kenya and Zimbabwe (see for example Nyang'oro, 1999). In all these cases, it is clear from the evidence that civil society in its broadest sense—NGOs, community-based organizations (CBOs), "civics"—has played a critical role in political change. In South Africa, perhaps the best known example of political transition in Africa in the 1990s, civil society groups in terms of CBOs and "civics" played a key role in mobilizing against the apartheid regime, particularly in the 1970s and 1980s (Marx, 1992). The leadership of many of these groups are now occupying important positions in the new political dispensation, a clear indication and acknowledgment of their role in the struggle against apartheid (Naidoo, 1998).

In Zambia, the regime of Kenneth Kaunda was defeated in the October 1991 elections by forces that were principally organized around labor unions (Sichone and Chikulo, 1996). Quite appropriately at the time, Mr. Frederick Chiluba, the leader of the opposition who succeeded President Kaunda, came from the ranks of labor. Here again, civil society had flexed its muscle resulting in a change of regime (Ihonvbere, 1996). Finally, in the case of Kenya, soon after the official banning of political opposition in 1982, the mantle of opposition was assumed by civil society groups. In spite of tremendous repression by the regime of Daniel arap Moi, groups such as the Law Society of Kenya (LSK) and Nairobi University Students stood up in opposition to the politics of repression and exclusion practiced by the regime. In conjunction with other civil society groups—particularly the Church—and through international pressure, these groups managed to force the government to adopt multiparty politics leading to pluralist elections in December 1992 (Mutunga, 1998).

Thus clearly, civil society has been a force to be reckoned with in ESA, a region that is the focus of this study. In broad terms, this study is intended as a critical reflection of the status of civil society in the region with a particular emphasis on NGOs and the critical role that NGOs may play in the region in terms of further political liberalization.

NGOs AS DEMOCRATIZING AGENTS

It is now taken for granted that NGOs are probably the leading agents in the democratization process in ESA. As noted in the introduction, there is a substantial empirical basis for such claims. As Naidoo (1998) has clearly shown, South Africa's "civics" were key players in the dislodging of *apartheid* as they advocated and pushed for democratic rights in South Africa. Indeed, it can be argued that "civics" played a dual role of both pushing for democratic change and also ensuring that the more established/formal anti-apartheid institutions such as the African National Congress (ANC), South African Council of Churches (SACC), and the Congress of South Africa Trade Unions (COSATU) did not sell out to the apartheid regime on key demands for political change. Of course, "civics" had wide-ranging agendas that cannot be captured under one label, except that whatever the agenda was, it was an agenda that had the ultimate objective of creating a democratic society in South Africa.

Given the fact that the antiapartheid struggle ultimately became successful in the advent of multiracial elections in 1994, we can therefore point to civil society as being central to that struggle. Yet, there is a need to take stock of reality of civil society and to disaggregate its composition to determine if indeed we are warranted to maintain the position that civil society is the principal agent of democratization in ESA. A good starting point would be definitional. As is now commonly recognized, "civil society" has been overdefined (Wood, 1990). Yet, many of these definitions shed very little light to the understanding of civil society, and indeed, whether ultimately these definitions can help us to better determine if civil society is an important player in the democratization process in Africa is still an open question. Thomas Callaghy summarizes our dilemma:

Two basic definitions seem to exist in the discussion of civil society in Africa. The first relates to *autonomous societal groups* that interact with the state but delimit and constrain its action; here *associational life* is seen as the core of civil society. The second and less common definition deals with the emergence of *norms* about the nature and limits of state power, including its role in the economy, and about the creation of a public sphere and the political rules that govern its functioning. These two meanings, separately or together, often merge with a third, more general usage—what . . . others have called the "popular upsurge" against despotism (1994, 235).

Callaghy does not think that the broad usage of "civil society" to refer to general associational life can do much to elucidate important processes (that is, democratization) in contemporary Africa. He prefers a restrictive usage that deals with norm creation because that is what is at the heart of the democratization process: the creation of a public sphere and the political rules that govern its functioning.

For NGO practitioners, such a restrictive use of "civil society" may be troublesome given the need to continue large-scale mobilization against despotism. In the long run, however, Callaghy is correct in pushing for using "civil society" in a restrictive sense relating to the emergence of a consensus on norms defining a "civil space." The case of South Africa is illustrative on the need for such restrictions. If we may recall, civil society as an arena (space) that lies between the individual and the state is essentially any kind of associational life that people in a society can envisage, but associational life as such does not have to be a "positive" association to fit into such a category. In South Africa, there was associational life that was (and sometimes still is) hell-bent on maintaining white privilege and using the state to achieve that objective. The underlying principle of such associational life would be parochialism and achieving their objective by essentially undemocratic means. For such a group, the space sought would be highly restrictive and "prebendal" in character (Joseph, 1987). Naidoo (1998) makes the same case for a restrictive use of "civil society" in South Africa, although he does it in a less strident form. Here we have perhaps a classic case of the clash between theory and practice.

This discussion suggests to me that as NGOs become more sophisticated in their understanding of the complexity of civil society, they will become discriminating in their use of the term. The justification for such an approach will be the obvious point that is made quite often by NGOs themselves: that civil society is a diverse space that includes "the good, the bad, and the ugly." So, the struggle for democratic development is not only one of vertical conflict between a controlling state and civil society, but one also of horizontal struggles within civil society itself for its own further democratization. A good reminder to everybody regarding the dangers contained in contradictory sectoral interests within civil society is that even at the height of political repression in Africa in the 1970s and 1980s, there were some civil society groups that actually benefited from such repression, depending on their connection to the state.

Thus, the key to identifying NGOs as agents for democratization in the region would be to first identify those groups that have open and clearly identified agendas pushing for political inclusiveness and a broader social space for views that enhance political participation. In the final analysis, what may at first glance seem an irreconcilable difference between an analytical position, such as the one presented by Callaghy, and that of NGOs practitioners may actually be two points in a continuum for political liberalization and democratization. Ultimately, democratic norms of governance will be created by creating conditions that allow for the expansion of social space for civil organizations.

NGOs AND POLITICS: A CONTRADICTION OF NATURAL EVOLUTION?

Even though NGOs as part of a broader civil society are widely acknowledged to have played a significant role in bringing an end to apartheid in South Africa (and indeed such a role is officially recognized by the government), that is not the case in the rest of the ESA region. The difference in the way governments in the region view NGOs is largely a result of recent political history: For South Africa, NGOs meant an end to *apartheid;* for most of ESA, NGOs have come to symbolize opposition to current regimes and the galvanization of civil society. In almost every ESA country, NGOs insist that governments in their respective countries want to hold them to the abstract notion of *nongovernmental* (meaning for the governments: *nonpolitical*) as a way of controlling their activities (Nyang'oro 1999). The question is, why are governments so keen to control the activities of NGOs?

The answer is to be found in the complex and not so complex nature of political control that states in Africa exercised in years past. This was essentially the reality of authoritarianism in Africa. In the absence of political opposition, NGOs assumed the role of spokesperson for the downtrodden and the oppressed. Although it is generally true that most NGOs in ESA began as voluntary associations to provide welfare services to meet the demands of the poor, many NGOs quickly evolved into organizations that questioned the basis of poverty in society (Mbogori, 1998). It is appropriate at this junction to recall the basis for economic development in most of Africa. Even under conditions of structural adjustment (economic reform), the state in all of Africa still plays a key role in economic organization of society. It is therefore easy to see that once the basis of poverty is brought under scrutiny, it opens a series of questions that are directly related to power relations and resource distribution in society. In retrospect, it is clear that any NGO that engaged itself in attempting to improve the material well-being of its clientele would have to move in the direction of asking questions of power relations in society. This reality should remind us of a Latin American priest's lament: "When I serve the poor, they call me a saint. When I ask why they are poor, they call me a communist."

Because NGOs increasingly have been asking why people are poor, they have been subjected to criticism and harassment by governments. The frequent charge against NGOs has been that they are engaging themselves in politics and thus violating the conditions of their official registration—usually as welfare associations or as organizations that promote "development." In essence, how governments interpret the rationale of NGO activities (that is, *nonpolitical*) and how NGOs view their own role (that is, no distinction between political and nonpolitical) has been at the heart of the struggle for the various pieces of NGO legislation that have either already been enacted or are under review by parliaments in the region. This is particularly the case in Kenya, Uganda, Zimbabwe, and Tanzania. Whereas governments across the board have made the claims that proposed NGO legislation is for purposes of coordinating NGO activities that are mushrooming on a daily basis, NGOs view these attempts as simply desires by governments to *control* them. In an ironic way, in some of these countries, old colonial laws that had been enacted to control voluntary activities of African groups are being invoked to suppress contemporary NGO work (Mutunga, 1998; Mamdani, 1996).

During a research visit to Uganda in July/August 1998, this author was impressed by the sophistication of the discourse on NGOs and their role in society. Almost across the board, a story was recounted to me of a recent consultation between NGOs and government officials whose portfolio includes NGO coordination. At the consultation, it was reported that government officials kept on insisting that the government was at a loss as to what exactly NGOs wanted, thus making it difficult to have a meaningful dialogue with them. Furthermore, these officials complained, NGOs seemed to be eager to get involved in political matters that were "clearly" beyond their mandate. After keeping silent for a while, Professor Jesse Kwesiga, Chairman of DENIVA (an umbrella organization of indigenous NGOs in Uganda) responded to the officials and reminded them that any "development" work to improve the lives of citizens was at its core *political*. Any further pretense that development work was not political, argued Kwesiga, actually undermined the integrity of the work that is being done by NGOs (interview notes, Kampala, July/August 1998).

Clearly in the last decade, there has been a marked shift in the way NGOs—including the Church—consider their role to be in society. In 1993, the All Africa Conference of Churches (AACC) and MWENGO (a study and Reflection Center for NGOs in ESA) published a study that indicated that most NGOs were not willing to consider their work to be *political*. Some National Councils of Churches went as far as suggesting that Churches are a special kind or organizations that do not fit into the generic category of NGOs (MWENGO and AACC, 1993). The resistance by some Church organizations to be called NGOs or dubbed political, however, seems strange in light of activities conducted by organizations such as the National Council of Churches in Kenya (NCCK). From the very beginning of political protest against one-party rule in Kenya, NCCK was on the forefront in organizing seminars and distributing educational materials in favor of multipartyism. The work of NCCK has been praised across the board as being one of the catalysts for political change in Kenya to date (Mutunga, 1998).

If NGOs in some countries have sought to maintain their nonpolitical status, the Lesotho Council of NGOs (LCN) actually decided to adopt a prominent and proactive political stance in the mid-1990s. The proactive role by LCN was prompted by political developments in the tiny mountain kingdom, which is totally surrounded by South Africa. Following a seemingly never-ending political crisis, which was occasioned by disagreements between Prime Minister Ntsu Mokhele's government and the military, King Letsie II suspended the constitution and dismissed the prime minister in what was dubbed a "royal coup" (Nkiwane, 1997). There is still a raging debate in Lesotho as to whether the king had the constitutional authority to suspend the constitution. For purposes of this chapter, what is important is that as the leading political institutions in the country were under crisis, the only credible organization in the country became the LCN under the leadership of its executive director, Mr. Caleb Sello. Mr. Sello, along with other LCN board members, undertook the task of a minishuttle diplomacy between the contending forces in the constitutional crisis, which led to the restoration of the constitutional government (interview notes, Maseru, Lesotho, July 1998).

Although LCN can claim nonpartisanship in its shuttle diplomacy task, its role in the negotiating process was clearly political. The fact that constitutionalism was restored in Lesotho is an indication of LCN's success in its endeavor. But, alas, two years after LCN had done an excellent job in helping to restore political peace it is itself on the verge of disintegration. How did LCN end up where it is today, essentially being under receivership?

The NGO community in Lesotho almost in unison argues that LCN became a victim of its own success. Because it had succeeded in negotiating the political conflict, it was pushed into a prominent role in the country, thus making the government uneasy. LCN was perceived by the public to have the moral authority that the government lacked. The government's response to its lack of moral authority was to systematically destroy LCN. It achieved this by continuously calling LCN "part of the opposition." Further, the government sent "spies" to join LCN and disrupt their normal workings. Allegedly, these "spies" would report back to the government any activity that LCN planned, particularly if it involved exposing wrongdoing by the government. Many in the NGO community in Lesotho claim that as LCN became successful in the political arena, members of the political opposition indeed began to penetrate its ranks, thus making the government's claim of LCN's partisanship partly credible. The last straw for LCN was the recalling back to government service of Mr. Caleb Sello, who had been the most visible representative of LCN in the crisis period. Technically, Mr. Sello had been on loan to LCN since the early 1990s when LCN was perceived to be less threatening by the government.

What lessons can be learned from the Lesotho experience? The *first* lesson to be learned is that there has to be a concerted effort on the part of all

NGOs to band together in light of constant pressure from government. It would seem that even though LCN as an "umbrella" organization was successful in its political activities during the crisis period, when the government struck, none of the constituent member NGOs came to LCN's rescue. In the final analysis, it seemed as if LCN was a rogue organization that did not have the support of its members. Thus, it was badly exposed, resulting in its eventual collapse. Here the old adage of "divide and rule" worked perfectly for the government. The *second* lesson is that there is a need for institution building within the NGO sector. More often than not, NGOs, including umbrella organizations, rely heavily on only one or two key individuals for their success. When these individuals leave for one reason or another, these NGOs end up being seriously weakened. Certainly this was the case with LCN. The *third* lesson is that it is time that NGOs stop hiding behind the label of nonpolitical actors and confront head-on the need to engage the state in a constructive manner. This posture by NGOs would in the long run protect them from periodic accusations by the state that they are being political.

The reality of NGOs being political in a constructive manner was demonstrated by the Zambian experience in the 1996 general elections. After most foreign election observers withdrew their missions from Zambia because of the alleged corruption of the electoral process by the Chiluba government, several NGOs banded together and took the lead in trying to salvage whatever remained of the election that could be termed fair. These NGOs, however, began their work by forming an ad hoc umbrella organization whose specific task was to address issues arising from the election process in a nonpartisan manner. The forming of the umbrella organization was taken as a strategic move by the NGOs, who feared individual persecution by the state. The principle adopted by the NGOs was to "hang together" versus "hanging separately." The umbrella organization conducted seminars, political education, and other activities related to the elections. In the final analysis, the government threatened the coalition with specified and unspecified sanctions, but it could not defeat the purpose for which the coalition was established (CCC-Zambia, 1996).

As in the case of Lesotho, NGOs in Zambia strongly feel that their ranks were penetrated by agents from the state. There is a fairly high level of frustration among NGOs, particularly those that deal with "political" issues such as human rights. The government views them as the effective opposition whenever these NGOs raise issues of corruption, violation of human rights, and the general incompetence of the government. One NGO (Afronet) was actually threatened with deregistration and the freezing of accounts by the government because it was seen as the ringleader in the coalition to monitor the elections. The critical lesson to be learned from Zambia is that even though the government of the day may have origins in the ranks of civil society—as the Movement for Multi-Party Democracy government was from labor—there is no guarantee of democratic practice once the government is in power. There has to be a constant vigilance on the part of civil society to ensure that governments operate at the highest level of accountability.

NGOs AS AGENTS OF DEVELOPMENT: BACK TO THE FUTURE?

With the exception of South Africa's civics and CBOs, which were expressly started as political actors in opposition to *apartheid,* most NGOs in ESA began as welfare organizations to meet the increasing demand for service provision in the late 1970s and 1980s. Most NGOs were thrown into the "lion's den" of service provision when the state began to systematically withdraw from the responsibilities of welfarism promised at the time of independence. The withdrawal of the state was primarily prompted by the overall worsening economic conditions in the aftermath of the 1973/74 oil crisis, the inability of the state to appropriately respond to the crisis, the persistent decline in the prices of primary commodities on the global market, and the subsequent failure of the earlier import substitution development strategy to take off (Nyang'oro, 1989). Thus, the economic failure was generalized, leading to a substantial diminishing in the state's capacity to perform any meaningful management of the economy. As the economic decline continued, the authoritarian tendency of the state increased. Thus, whether consciously or not, any attempt to address the consequences of economic decline would have political implications (that is, power relations) as its core.

Economic decline in Africa elicited a response from the international community, which in many ways remains the hallmark of economic policy on the continent. The response, primarily from the principal international financial institutions (IFIs) led by the World Bank and the International Monetary Fund (IMF), placed much of the blame for economic decline on African states themselves (World Bank, 1981). Although subsequent studies by the World Bank attempted to portion out blame between internal and external factors, the thrust of these studies still was that African states were primarily responsible for the economic crisis by adopting too much centralization of economic activities (World Bank, 1989). The response by IFIs was largely driven by neoliberal ideology, which emphasized a market-driven economic strategy, a strategy that obviously was in sharp contrast to Statist ideology, which had dominated development thinking in Africa since independence. Thus, international actors began looking for alternative avenues for the dispensing of aid to Africa. The rationale for this new strategy by both official/governmental and international nongovernmental agencies was that the state in Africa had become so incompetent and inefficient that it was necessary to find new avenues for providing economic aid. NGOs in Africa became the answer.

Ironically, the displeasure of the state in Africa by IFIs and Western governments coincided with similar displeasure by those who emphasized grassroots development, particularly voluntary organizations who viewed the state with suspicion and disdain for the way it treated its own citizens (Clark, 1990). But more fundamentally, NGOs at the local and national levels were seen as better situated to deliver "development" because of their proximity to the intended beneficiaries at the local level. This comparative advantage of NGOs has perhaps been the biggest selling point for the choice of NGOs as the most appropriate vehicles for delivering economic aid and also as being "genuine" representatives for the oppressed and downtrodden. Thus, in IFIs and grassroots-based development initiatives, we have a case of strange bedfellows who under normal circumstances would have quite opposite agendas.

The emphasis on NGOs as the vehicle for development aid by donor agencies—both official and nongovernmental—has created two essential problems. First, it has made the relationship between the state and NGOs a difficult and contentious one. As the state has come to receive less donor money (partly as a result of shrinking aid budgets in Western countries), it has assumed that all the diverted aid has actually gone to NGOs. The evidence, however, suggests that even though some aid has found its way to local NGOs or branches of international NGOs, the aid received is far less than what previously went to the state (interview notes, Kampala, Uganda and Dar es Salaam, Tanzania, July/August 1998). The reality of less economic aid overall is due more to general declines in foreign assistance than to the diversion to NGOs. Second, although ideologically NGOs may present an alternative to the massive corruption and incompetence of the state, the overwhelming majority of NGOs do not have the capacity to manage large and complex programs in various parts of the country. Although most NGOs do a good job of "connecting" with the intended recipients of aid (Fowler, 1990), they certainly cannot manage large-scale projects, which are essential for overall economic development in African countries. In any case, most NGOs are single-issue or single-development project oriented and thus incapable of processing a large influx of resources (Stewart, 1997).

It would seem then that the most appropriate approach to the development crisis in Africa would be to push for a balance between the work of NGOs, recognizing their comparative advantage, and the activities of the state, which are necessary for purposes of macroplanning and development. One of the consequences of pushing single projects by international donors is that macroplanning by African governments has been thoroughly undermined. In many sectors, such as health and agriculture, one is pressed to find a coherent national strategy in as varied countries as Kenya and Tanzania, where a new word has been coined to describe what is taking place: the NGOnization of development (Stewart, 1997). It seems to me unnecessary, and actually harmful, to draw a sharp dichotomy between NGO and state actions. The challenge is for all sides concerned—donors, NGOs, and states—to evolve a modus vivendi in seeking the best way to uplift the material level of those in whom each sector claims to have an interest. As we have been reminded by Michael Edwards and David Hulme (1996), NGOs are not the magic bullet of development.

CONCLUSION

As we enter the new millennium, NGOs in ESA have already had at least two decades of experience under their belt. In the case of South Africa, it is actually longer then two decades because of its special history. Nonetheless, as in any field of endeavor, good NGOs and similar organizations (that is, NGOs that remain true to their objectives but are also flexible in adjusting to the ever-changing environments in which they operate) will survive. Bad NGOs will of course disappear, because sooner than later they will run out of donor funding. The key for survival for NGOs is not to lose sight of the prize: the uplifting of a lot of the people who are currently being short-changed in all spheres of life—political, social, and economic. Flexibility actually entails capacity building on the part of NGOs. Indeed, the experience that we now have suggests that skills development in the work that NGOs are engaged in—whether it is digging boreholes or pushing for human rights—will go a long way in attaining the stated objectives of NGOs, which on paper always look good.

REFERENCES

Bratton, Michael, and Nicolas van de Walle. (1997). *Democratic Experiments in Africa: Regime Transitions in Comparative Perspective* (New York: Cambridge University Press).

Callaghy, Thomas M. (1994). "Civil Society, Democracy, and Economic Challenge in Africa: A Dissenting Opinion about Resurgent Societies" in John W. Harbesom et al., eds. *Civil Society and the State in Africa* (Boulder, CO: Lynne Reinner Publishers), pp. 231–53.

Clark, John. (1990). *Democratizing Development: The Role of Voluntary Organizations* (West Hartford, CT: Kumarian Press).

Committee for a Clean Campaign, CCC-Zambia. (1996). *Presidential and Parliamentary Elections in Zambia, November 18th 1996* (Lusaka, Zambia: CCC-Zambia).

Edwards, Michael, and David Hulme, eds. (1996). *Beyond the Magic Bullet: NGO Performance and Accountability in the Post–Cold War World* (West Hartford, CT: Kumarian Press).

Fowler, Alan. (1990). "Doing It Better? Where and How NGOs Have a Comparative Advantage in Facilitating Development," *AERDD Bulletin*, 28.

Ihonvbere, Julius. (1996). *Economic Crisis, Civil Society and Democratization: The Case of Zambia* (Trenton, N.S.: Africa World Press).

Joseph, Richard. (1987). *Democracy and Prebendal Politics in Nigeria: The Rise and Fall of the Second Republic* (New York: Cambridge University Press).

Mamdani, Mahmood. (1996). *Citizen and Subject: Contemporary Africa and the Legacy of Late Colonialism* (Princeton, NJ: Princeton University Press).

Marx, Anthony W. (1992). *Lessons of Struggle: South Africa Internal Opposition, 1960–1990* (New York: Oxford University Press).

Mbogori, Ezra. (1998). *NGO Representation and Advocacy in Tanzania* (Unpublished Manuscript) Harare, Zimbabwe: MWENGO February.

Mutunga, Willy. (1998). *The Politics of Constitution Making in Kenya, 1992–1997* (Harare, Zimbabwe: MWENGO).

MWENGO and AACC. (1993). *Civil Society, the State and African Development in the 1990s* (Harare and Nairobi, Africa: MWENGO and AACC).

Naidoo, Kumi. (1998). *The State of Civil Society in South Africa,* a report for Danchurchaid, Johannesburg, South Africa.

Nkiwane, Tandeka. (1997). *My Brother's Keeper: The Lesotho Crisis in Perspective* (Harare, Africa: African Association of Political Science Occasional Paper Series 1,1).

Nyang'oro, Julius E., ed. (1989). *The State and Capitalist Development in Africa: Declining Political Economies* (New York: Praeger).

Nyang'oro, Julius E. (1999). *Civil Society and Democratic Development: Perspective from Eastern and Southern Africa* (Harare, Africa: MWENGO).

Sichone, Owen, and Bornwell C. Chikulo, eds. (1996). *Democracy in Zambia: Challenges for the Third Republic* (Harare, Africa: SAPES Books).

Stewart, Sheelagh. (1997). "Happy Ever After in the Marketplace: Nongovernmental Organizations and Uncivil Society," *Review of African Political Economy,* 71:11–34.

Wood, Ellen Meiksins. (1990). "The Uses and Abuses of 'Civil Society,' " *Socialist Register* (Landem: Merlin), pp. 60–84.

World Bank. (1981). *Accelerated Development in Sub-Saharan Africa: An Agenda for Action* (Washington, DC: World Bank).

World Bank. (1989). *Sub-Saharan Africa: From Crisis to Sustainable Growth* (Washington, DC: World Bank).

6

The State and Human Rights in Africa

Julius O. Ihonvbere

Africa appears to be spawning a unique historical experience, a self-absorbed political elite with no national project whatever, not even an inadequate one. All it has is self-aggrandizement, especially the quest for absolute and eternal power. They know only their interests; it is the only morality they have and their only religion. They hear only echoes of their own voices and see only images of themselves looming to fill every space and every consciousness.[1]

    Freedom of speech and expression means nothing to a largely illiterate and ignorant society and similarly, the right to life has no relevance to a man who has no means to livelihood.[2]

There is a rather innocent tendency in recent times to get carried away with the process of political liberalization in Africa. Even the most ardent of skeptics and Afro-pessimists would agree that there is a lot going on in the continent: the emergence of new voices, organizations, and leaders committed to democratic values; the unpopularity of military dictatorships; elections and party politics; and the changes in the content and context of political contestations. As well, issues of identity, nationality, gender, language, citizenship, rights, and the rule of law now inform political discourses and the struggle for hegemony or power. There is a renewed concern for economic growth and development and the involvement of the people in decision making. With these and other developments, there is a tendency to declare the new millennium not just as one for the African

Renaissance but also of a true second revolution that would usher in all that
has been denied the over 600 million peoples of the continent.

Without doubt, ongoing political reforms and the dynamics of globalization have generated a relaxed interest in human rights. Yet, human rights
are inextricably tied to democracy and democratization. It is even possible
to contend that the future of globalization is tied to what happens to human
rights. If globalization fails to concern itself with rights, then it would be
resisted and would fail to achieve the goal of not just linking markets but
also increasing production and exchange. Unfortunately, human rights discourse in Africa, at least in the contemporary sense, is a recent phenomenon. In Africa, the traditional neglect of human rights discourse and advocacy until about two decades ago has some way enabled dictators and
despots to organize politics and society to suit their reactionary agendas.
The emergence of such ruthless leaders easily gave rise to increasing concerns, which have in turn encouraged the emergence of hundreds of human
rights and civil liberties organizations as well as pro-democracy and popular groups with interest in human rights issues. The activities of these bodies have complemented the works of Amnesty International, Africa Watch,
Africa Rights, Human Rights Internet, and other international human
rights organizations.

The debate on the need for an appropriate definition or conceptualization of human rights has been quite intense.[3] In addition, the issue of
whether it is necessary—indeed, inevitable—to trade political rights for
socioeconomic and cultural rights has been a major aspect of the debate.
Unfortunately, such debates have tended to distract from the real issues:
Why has the African state, its agents, and agencies come to rely heavily on
the abuse of human rights? Why does the state suffocate civil society and
asphyxiate popular groups in spite of the negative implications for change,
stability, resource management, development, growth, and even its own
legitimacy? An appropriate approach to understanding these issues requires
that we locate such debates within the specificities of African social formations as well as the dynamics of power, politics, production, and exchange
relations.[4] As Claude Ake has argued, in the Western world where the level
of development is high, politics is predictable, political values and institutions are consolidated, and a certain rationality guides the relationship
between the custodians of state power and the citizenry.

There is much concern with the right of peaceful assembly, self-determination, free
speech and thought, fair trial, etc. The appeal of these rights is sociologically specific. They appeal to people with a full stomach who can now afford to pursue the
more esoteric aspects of self-realization. The vast majority of our people are not
in this position. They are facing the struggle for existence in its brutal immediacy.
This is a totally consuming struggle. They have little or no time for reflection and
hardly any use for free speech. There is no freedom for hungry people or those

eternally oppressed by diseases. It is no wonder that the idea of human rights has tended to sound hallow in the African context.[5]

The point here is that in the African context, it makes little sense to separate civil and political rights from socioeconomic, environmental, and cultural rights. Although constitutions claim to guarantee civil and political rights, the outright denial of economic and social rights has precipitated contradictions, conflicts, and other forms of violent engagements between the state and the people. In the context of deepening socioeconomic crisis, oppressed constituencies have been forced to resort to armed struggle as the only viable option. A holistic and historical approach to the problem will demonstrate the inextricable linkage between underdevelopment and human rights violations. This is not to excuse the state and its institutions or to contend that because the social formation is underdeveloped, human rights abuses must necessarily take place. On the contrary, we wish to point out that the pressures, contradictions, and implications of underdeveloped state and social structures, poor political traditions, and the preponderance of survivalist strategies among nonbourgeois forces, which become more important in the context of a weak unstable, repressive, and desperate state, make human rights violation inevitable in the African context.

Researchers have tended to overlook these realities when they undertake the more fanciful project of cataloguing the gruesome record of African leaders in the area of human rights.[6] Hence, they frequently miss the fundamental, substructural context of the politics of human rights in Africa. Although such researchers concentrate on political institutions and processes, the existence of more than one political party, periodic elections, and constitutionally guaranteed rights, these might mean very little because they all depend on the patterns of power, production, and exchange; the relations among and within social classes; and the location of social formations in the international division of labor. If the process of growth and development fails to mobilize the people, empower them and their organizations and communities, strengthen democratic and other civil associations, and meet the basic needs of the vast majority, then it can be argued that such a process of development is actually consolidating the narrow and exploitative interest of the minority at the expense of the majority.[7] It is, of course impossible—in fact undesirable—to generalize on the issue of human rights.

Clearly, it is inappropriate to transpose standards of evaluation and determination of human rights from one society to the other. The historical experiences of particular social formations and the consequences of these experiences must be taken into consideration at all levels. Well-worded declarations, charters, covenants, and laws do not necessarily guarantee human rights, as the African situation has clearly shown. Although African states adopted the African Charter on Human and Peoples' Rights in 1981, in which they committed themselves to paying "particular attention to the right to development and that civil and political rights cannot be dissociated from economic, social and cultural rights in their conception as well as universality and that the satisfaction of economic, social and cultural rights is a guarantee for the enjoyment of civil and political rights,"[8] not one African state has lived up to the provisions of the Charter. In fact, not one African state has shown any respect for the Charter, and as Ake has noted "[n]obody can accuse Africa of taking human rights seriously. This remains true whether one is thinking of human rights philosophically, ideologically or politically."[9] To be sure, in countries like Uganda, Eritrea, South Africa, Namibia, Ghana, and Ethiopia where political reforms have begun to emphasize constitutionalism and the rule of law, there is increasing attention to the protection of rights even at the socioeconomic level. What these societies have demonstrated is that the level of rights enjoyed in society reflects the intensity, content, and context of class contradictions and struggles. As well, rights, once won, do not remain static. They change with the times and with the changing character of politics and society. This means that only a strengthened and vibrant civil society can guarantee the sustenance and reproduction of a political environment conducive to human rights protection.[10]

THE HISTORICAL CONSTRUCTION
OF THE AFRICAN PREDICAMENT

It will be valid to argue that the roots of human rights abuses—in fact, of Africa's present predicaments—can be effectively traced to the contact between the precapitalist social formations of Africa and the forces of Western imperialism.[11] This contact culminated in the distortion and underdevelopment of the continent. It also ensured the structured incorporation of the continent into the capitalist-dominated international division of labor. Specially, the contact with the forces of Western imperialism culminated in the following:

1. The creation of a nonhegemonic and unstable state that was incapable after political independence of managing social contradictions and conflicts and thus ensuring the effective reproduction of the respective systemic forces and interests in the continent;[12]

2. The creation of an unproductive, corrupt, and subservient dominant class that lacked effective control of its respective economies and was dependent on the productive activities of the bourgeoisie in the metropole for capital accumulation. This dominant class was equally relegated to unproductive sectors of their respective economies, mostly as "service persons" to foreign interests;[13]

3. The domination of the local economies by profit and hegemony, seeking transnational corporations and the incorporation of the local elites as agents,

representatives, shareholders, partners, and so on. This ensured the effective extraction and repatriation of surpluses and a relative congruence of interests between the respective economies and those of the metropolitan states;[14]

4. A general dependence on foreign aid, trade, expertise, and markets that was designed to generate foreign exchange and to promote growth and "development." This more often than not subjugates national interests to external internal interests, thus promoting vulnerability to external pressure, manipulation, and crisis. The dependence on the production and exportation of a narrow range of cash crops to specific markets in the Western world has deepened the crisis of the continent. Specifically, African nations lack control over the determination of the prices of exports and imports, and generally the international economic environment is a hostile one. The continent is plagued by fluctuating prices, declining terms of trade, increasing debts, declining foreign assistance, frequent foreign interference, and pressures from international finance institutions (IFIs) to implement difficult monetarist policies;[15]

5. Science and technology, which lag behind that of developed nations, engendering not only capital transfer but also a continued inability to harness the forces of nature and protect the environment;

6. Spatial inequalities and rural migration accentuated by the colonial experience. These inequalities programmed the transition to neocolonial dependence as political independence, particularly with the capture of state power by conservative regimes. Corrupt and unproductive dominant forces eroded the limited legitimacy of the postcolonial state and intensified the contradictions and conflicts that the respective African states inherited. The institutions and structures planted in the colonial period and inherited at political independence were not viable enough to ensure the effective mediation of class contradictions and conflicts, especially in view of the limited hegemony of the state. The distortions of the social formation and the failure of colonialism to completely revolutionize the relations of production left Africa with a dual economy and a severely deformed and distorted capitalist system.[16]

In sum, therefore, at political independence the African continent was underdeveloped in all respects. Education was largely dysfunctional, and the institutions and leadership lacked legitimacy, which together with the problem of alienation, instability, mass poverty, and foreign domination, led to near total irrelevance in international relations. Insignificant contributions to world industrial output, illiteracy, rural decay, urban dislocation, and deep-rooted social contradictions characterized African society and politics. Indeed, political independence coupled with the failure of the new elites to carry out an appreciable level of socioeconomic and political transformation generated apathy, opposition, and revolutionary pressures from below.[17] These pressures in turn compelled African leaders to resort to repression; the manipulation of religion and ethnicity; alliances with powerful foreign interests, particularly for military support; ideological containment; and defensive radicalism.[18] As John Hatch noted,

Events during the 1960s largely destroyed the euphoria aroused by independence, replacing expectancy with cynicism or resignation. A score of regimes, created in the high point of anti-colonial nationalism, were unconstitutionally overthrown. The use of violence, actual or threatened, supplanted political processes over large areas of the continent. The goal of pan-African unity, for many nationalists a central objective of the anti-colonial campaigns, receded beyond the horizon, a forgotten Utopia. Instead of national prosperity, anticipated from the collective national efforts released by independence, stagnation in the countryside, massive unemployment in the towns and ostentatious luxury for a tiny minority became the general experience.[19]

Furthermore, because of these challenges and contradictions and the disarticulations in the system, the new governments could not maintain law and order or meet the basic needs of their peoples. Consequently, the leaders "opted for political repression. In the course of this they militarized not only politics—it became a violent struggle with the norms of welfare—but also social life."[20] In addition, "detention without trial, public executions, inter-communal massacres, commonly succeeded colonial rule. Freedom to organize trade unions, political parties or co-operatives was curtailed. The right to publish newspapers, to hold public meetings, was widely curtailed. Theft and rapine violence spread through town streets and country paths. Corruption became rampant, graft commonplace. Africa seemed to be fast imitating not only the societies of New York, Chicago, Dallas, Hamburg, Marseilles or London, but also those of Johannesburg, Cape Town, Salisbury and Bulawayo."[21]

Compared to the contemporary situation, the African condition that Hatch described in the 1960s can be described as a golden age. The fragility of state structures, the occurrence of coups and countercoups, the vulnerability to external manipulations, and the corrupt and unproductive deposition of the dominant forces have continued to deepen contradictions, insecurity, uncertainty, and conflicts.[22] The industrial, agricultural, and service sectors of the various economies are either stagnating or declining. Import substitution industrialization strategy, religiously embraced in the early period of technology transfer, failed to promote an appreciable level of sectoral integration. Periodic improvements in production levels, trade balances, foreign reserves, GDP, and so on were not reflected in the living conditions of the majority of Africa: Poverty, illiteracy, disease, hunger, and marginalization from political and decision-making processes came to characterize life on the continent.[23] As Michael Holman observed, "Today, more people in Africa are poorer, and more children are dying. Other signs of stress are rampant, beginning with the distressing list of countries that have effectively ceased to function as modern nation states: Zaire, Somalia, Liberia, Sudan, Angola. . . . Former 'success' stories and 'role models' of the 1960s have since become cautionary tales. . . . The technological gap between Africa and the world has widened, and the continent's management is weak."[24] The squandering of available limited resources on prestige projects, importation of modern and sophisticated military gadgets, and misplaced national priorities prevent African governments from responding concretely to the contradictions and pressures generated by the continent's backwardness. In the attempt to divert attention and contain popular pressures and opposition, the rights of citizens are wantonly violated.[25]

The point we wish to emphasize here is that wanton human rights abuses in Africa cannot be extricated from the desperate economic and political conditions of the region. As elites find it difficult to run governments, as parastatals crumble due to heavy debt burdens, as foreign exchange earnings go to debt servicing, and as workers, women, students, and peasants engage in open opposition to the state, the governments devise legal and extralegal ways to hold on to power and contain the opposition. In fact, the state becomes the target of all opposition elements, and the custodians of state power see such engagements as direct challenges to them as persons and to their capacities to serve as leaders. In the absence of a democratic political culture and an environment propitious to effective mediation of conflicts and contradictions, the state that monopolizes the means of coercion easily abuses the rights of nonbourgeois forces. To be sure, the crisis of the continent cannot be understood only from the internal perspective. The harshness of the international environment, rising debt-service ratios, frequent increases in the cost of imports, direct military violation of the territorial integrity of African states, until recently, Western support for apartheid in South Africa, and declining foreign assistance have contributed significantly to the plight of the continent. The end of the Cold War and the diversion of interest, investment, and foreign aid to Eastern Europe only laid bare the devastation that the so-called confrontation between the East and the West caused in Africa.[26] Africa was simply a pawn in the East-West game. Although the superpowers never went to war against each other, a poor and underdeveloped region like Africa received high dosages of military aid.

It was not an accident that the most repressive and most corrupt regimes in Africa were the darlings of the West during the era of the Cold War. In Zaire, Kenya, Liberia, the Sudan, and Somalia, leaders threw all ideas about human rights overboard and dealt devastating blows to students, trade unions, academics, social activists, and civil society. They massacred protesting peasants and women, closed universities, executed alleged coup plotters, and plunged their wretched nations into Civil Wars. Scarce resources went into setting up notorious security agencies and in building presidential fortresses. In all these and more activities, which directly and/or indirectly violated all known rules of rational and civilized behavior, the governments of the West continued to give material and diplomatic support to the leaders. Today, although the Cold War has ended and Russia is receiving support from all Western nations, Africa has been left high and dry, and the impact of years of intimidation and harassment of popular forces remain there for all to see.

The marginal location and role of Africa in the international division of labor militates against the region's ability to generate sufficient resources to promote development and thus contain negative political pressures. As well, the domination of African economies by powerful transnational interests erodes the autonomous ability to be creative, and it facilitates massive profit repatriation, technology distortion, corruption of the political elites, taste transfer, cultural bastardization, and general vulnerability of the weak African economy for foreign pressures. As the current "new" world order demonstrates, Africa is an irrelevant actor in the global movement of resources and capital. Its rich resources are merely to be exploited and its market bypassed for those of other regions of the world. Lacking the stability internally and lacking a viable constituency abroad, Africa remains in the backwaters of the policy-making concerns of the developed world. As the Lagos Plan of Action (LPA), adopted by African leaders in 1980, laments: "The effect of unfulfilled promises of global development strategies has been more sharply felt in Africa than in an improvement in the economic situation of the continent, successive strategies have made it stagnate."[27]

The adoption of monetarist policies, particularly those recommended by the World Bank and the International Monetary Fund (IMF), sharpened these tendencies and contradictions within the state structures on the continent.[28] Policies of desubsidization, deregulation, privatization, commercialization, and devaluation among other monetarist programs imposed on already fragile and poverty-stricken African states contributed immensely to the abuse of people's rights and liberties in Africa. As these policies failed to improve the specific and overall conditions of African economies, regimes became the more desperate. Inflation, unemployment, tensions, prostitution, crime, and military coups and countercoups became commonplace. Violent riots organized by trade unions, students, and other vulnerable groups who were left unprotected by structural adjustment made governments insecure and violent in their response to popular challenges. Of course, the IMF and the World Bank had failed to take into consideration the character of domestic constituencies, the ability of nonbourgeois forces to resist adjustment, and the very fragile legitimacy of corrupt and repressive leaders in the region. Thousands of Africans were killed by the police, army, and special security squads during protests against adjustment in Zambia, Zaire, and Nigeria. Human rights activists and intellectuals were harassed and jailed for opposing structural adjustment. The record of adjustment in Africa is one of accentuating already tense situations, promoting the massive and unprecedented abuse of socioeconomic and political rights and widening the gap between an alienated populace and insecure and desperate leaders.[29] Yet, the current orientation of the African economy is mostly one of attempting to service dependent capitalism, implement harsh monetarist programs, and contain popular responses through the use of violence, draconian decrees, repression, diversionary tactics, and outright violation of personal freedoms and liberties.[30] Claude Ake is right when he laments:

We Africans have never had it so bad. The tragic consequences of our development strategies have finally come home to us. Always oppressed by poverty and deprivation, our lives become harsher still with each passing day as real incomes continue to decline. We watch helplessly while millions of our people are threatened by famine and look pitifully to the rest of the world to feed us. Our social and political institutions are disintegrating under pressure from our flagging morale, our dwindling resources and the intense struggle to control them.[31]

THE NONHEGEMONIC STATE AND HUMAN RIGHTS

The end of the 1980s witnessed a largely unanticipated deluge of democratization efforts in Africa. Dictators were swept out of power. Popular forces resisted military regimes. In Zambia, the one-party government of Kenneth Kaunda, which had ruled the country mostly through a state of emergency for almost twenty-seven years, was crushed in popular elections by the Frederick Chiluba–led Movement for Multi-Party Democracy (MMD). In Ghana, Jerry Rawlings, who had earlier boasted that he had little patience with politicians and that a transition to democracy was not on his-agenda, was compelled by donors and pro-democracy groups to organize popular elections and terminate military rule. In Kenya, the repressive and corrupt one-party government of Daniel arap Moi was starved of foreign aid by donor countries and was compelled to open the political system to multiparty elections, which saw the opposition, although divided, win 100 seats. Finally, in Nigeria, the tricks and unending transition to democracy organized by General Ibrahim Babangida were not sufficient to withstand the massive antimilitary and anti-Babangida campaigns of the pro-democracy groups under the umbrella of the Campaign for Democracy (CD), which forced the ruthlessly repressive and corrupt general to resign as president and retire from the armed forces. This struggle for democracy continued until the election of retired General Olusegun Obasanjo in 1999 and the eventual disengagement of the military from active politics. In virtually all African countries, the upheaval was such that the issues of politics and society, which were articulated by the new political actors, challenged existing conditions of inequality, exploitation, marginalization of the poor, corruption, and human rights violations. Rather, human rights associations, trade and students' unions, political parties, pro-democracy groups, peasants' movements, women's organization, and even the unemployed created

new associations, reinvigorated dormant ones that had been driven underground, forged new alliances, and began to express new ideas, ask new
questions, and introduce new issues into the political landscape. Issues of
accountability, empowerment, democracy, participation, social justice,
human rights, gender equality, and environmental protection came to dominate political demands and discourses. Human rights issues took added
prominence not just because human rights groups were in the forefront of
the struggles for democracy, but also because human rights was defined as
part of the package of democratization.

   A major external development at this point, largely facilitated by the end
of the Cold War, was the new insistence by IFIs, Western governments, creditors, and donors that political pluralism or multiparty politics would
become major conditionalities for foreign aid to African states. In fact,
Western governments and international organizations openly declared that
respect for human rights was to become a measure of the reform process
and a determinant of whether foreign aid would flow or not to African
states. These declarations encouraged a more enthusiastic support for
democracy in Africa. It was under this new position that foreign aid to
Malawi and the repressive Kamuzu Banda regime was cut in half in 1992.
Belgium, under pressure from France, also cut off aid to Zaire because of
Mobutu's refusal to respect popular wishes and reach accommodation with
local constituencies. Kenya was equally forced to accept multiparty elections because twelve donor agencies and governments suspended foreign
aid for six months in November 1991 until the Moi regime instituted multiparty politics and allowed for popular elections.[32]

   Many leaders who had reveled in criminal human rights abuse now
found themselves pressured to reach agreement and accommodation with
domestic constituencies, open up the political system, and respect human
rights. They tried to play to the gallery by arguing that such conditionalities amounted to interference in the internal affairs of independent African
states. However, pro-democracy groups argued that it was only through
such internationally imposed conditionalities that stubborn and repressive
African leaders, who had demonstrated no respect whatsoever for their
peoples, could be forced to become politically reasonable. In any case, it
was anachronistic to speak of the "independence" of neocolonial states,
dependent on the outside world for virtually everything and dominated by
foreign capital. Although many African leaders were very uncomfortable
with these political conditionalities, they had little or no choice but to
accept them. This was because they had already accepted the economic conditionalities of creditors and donors through the structural adjustment and
economic stabilization packages of the IMF and World Bank. In fact, in its
1989 report on Africa, the World Bank for the very first time accepted the
argument made already by African and Africanist scholars that the roots of
Africa's economic predicaments were political. It emphasized issues of gov-

ernance, accountability, decentralization, widespread corruption, waste, mismanagement, bureaucratic inefficiency, the overextended role of the state, repression, gender discrimination, and widespread abuse of human rights as major aspects of the African crisis. Among other prescriptions, the World Bank called for the creation of an enabling environment that would allow for democracy, accountability, popular participation in decision making, the rolling back of the state, support for the private sector, building human capacities, protecting the vulnerable during structural adjustment, good governance, and above all, that "ordinary people should participate more in designing and implementing development programs."[33] The sort of "political renewal" demanded by the Bank directly challenged the suffocation of civil society and the privatization of the state and its resources by a handful of elites or by sit-tight presidents for life and military dictators, and it served notice that the current global order would no longer accommodate such political excesses. With debt of over $300 billion, a precipitous fall in foreign aid and investments, and donors complaining of "aid fatigue," African leaders, including those who had boasted previously that democracy did not exist in their dictionaries, were forced to make concessions to civil society and to pro-democracy activists. This singular act reduced—and in many instances, eliminated—the reliance on repression and human rights abuses as a way of retaining political power and excluding the opposition. It forced elections in the majority of countries and allowed popular and opposition groups to organize openly, canvass for public support, generate new political discourses, and set up strategies to check human rights abuses.

Without doubt, these developments and challenges to the state encouraged some respect for human rights in Africa. Yet, the democratization agenda appears to have provided only cosmetic solutions to the problem of human rights abuses as well as to the hopes for democracy. First, democracy has been defined very narrowly as the conduct of elections. Its content is liberal democracy, which is grafted on a sea of dependence, underdevelopment, foreign domination, mass poverty, high indebtedness, declining productivity, and so on. In countries where elections have taken place, democratic processes and institutions have either been rolled back or are experiencing severe political decay as democratic consolidation becomes very difficult. Frederick Chiluba in Zambia was forced to impose a state of emergency on the country in 1993, and as his reform policies failed, he seems more and more irritated by the thirty-four opposition parties that emerged in the country that year. Chiluba has defended corrupt ministers, arrested opponents, tinkered with the country's constitution, and waged an open war against Kenneth Kaunda and the opposition.

A second point is that African leaders seem to have effectively "adjusted" to the new conditionalities. They have taken some break in direct human rights abuses. Most of the repressive politics is not carried out through the manipulation of ethnic, regional, and religious differences and by setting one interest group against the other, dividing the opposition, and creating diversions. Hence, they have allowed the creation of scores of political parties, a condition that ensured victory for Rawlings in Ghana and Moi in Kenya. Thus, democratization is not changing the political landscape in a drastic and fundamental manner, and the survival of the old buzzards of politics continues to pose a challenge to the democratic enterprise.

The third critical point is that support for democratization and human rights from the West has been tenuous. Unlike the support that some East European nations, especially Russia, are receiving, African efforts have been treated with indifference or have received very feeble responses and support. Hence, sanctions on repressive regimes have been light. The military regime of General Sani Abacha, which brazenly terminated democratic processes, received only sanctions from the United States, which hardly affected the regime in any way. Although members of the government were prohibited from visiting the United States, this was not effectively enforced. In Kenya, the Moi regime continues to receive support, as is the Paul Biya regime in Cameroon.

Perhaps the strongest indicator as to the tenuousness of the current tentative break from unmediated repression and exploitation is that the new democratic agenda in Africa does not include in any location the dismantling and recomposition of the exploitative, ruthless, repressive, and non-hegemonic state in Africa. It must be understood that this is a fundamental prerequisite for democracy, democratization, and the ability to create an environment conducive to human rights. The colonial state that had visited untold violence and pain on Africans was not dismantled or restructured at independence. This state, because of its aloof, repressive, and undemocratic character had alienated the masses of Africa. They saw it as nothing but a weapon of oppression, and its institutions and agencies were to be resisted and sabotaged at every turn. This became more prominent during the anti-colonial struggles. At independence, this state structure, along with all its ideological and social apparatuses, was handed over to the new elite that had been groomed under colonialism. The new elite continued to use the state to exploit, intimidate, and repress the people. The people also came to see the new state, manned by local elites, as no different from the colonial state. This accounts for the withdrawal of peasants from the state, the prevalence of the underground economy, scores of peasant and workers' protests and resistance, and the frequent reliance on covert modes of resistance and struggles.[34]

The postcolonial state simply appropriated the institutions of the colonial state and reproduced the underdevelopment of Africa. Its failure in every respect is attested to by the fact that three decades after political independence, as the World Bank has noted, "Africans are almost as poor today as they were 30 years ago."[35] African leaders also confessed to the complete failure of African state to promote development when they noted in the

1980 LPA that "Africa is unable to point to any significant growth rate, or satisfactory index of general well-being, in the past 20 years."[36] This state, which has so failed to improve the lot of the people and which had to rely more on repression, manipulation, and human rights abuses to retain control of the political terrain, is not being restructured or dismantled as part of the democratization agenda in Africa. As Claude Ake noted:

One of the most remarkable features of democratization in Africa is that it is totally indifferent to the character of the state. Democratic elections are being held to determine who will exercise the powers with no questions asked about the character of the state as if it has no implications for democracy. But its implications are so serious that elections in Africa gave the voter only a choice between oppressors. This is hardly surprising since Africa largely retains the colonial state structure that is inherently anti-democratic, being the repressive apparatus of an occupying power. Uncannily, this structure has survived, reproduced and rejuvenated by the legacy of military and single-party rule. By all indications it is also surviving democratization to multi-party elections.[37]

Ake then concludes that the current democratization agenda in Africa is simply replacing "self-appointed military or civilian dictators with elected dictators." The type of democracy that emanates from such programmed efforts, designed often to satisfy donors and lenders, is "not in the least emancipatory especially in African conditions because it offers the people rights they cannot exercise, voting that never amounts to choosing, freedom which is patently spurious, and political equality which disguises highly unequal power relations."[38] It would appear therefore that although the ongoing democratization agenda certainly opens up political spaces for increased political activity, such spaces are in danger of being closed again because the state structure in charge of this political renewal is exactly the same structure that had closed it for decades. The custodians of the state have learned almost nothing and seem to be very unhappy at being unable to repress and intimidate the people with state power because of the new political pluralism. As politicians and ministers in Zambia, Malawi, and Nigeria have clearly shown, the so-called activists are largely political opportunists, persons who had been excluded from the state and its resources by previous regimes, who have very little idea of the meaning of empowerment and democratization, and who have simply joined the bandwagon as an opportunity to move closer to the center of power. Such politicians have practically grounded the government of Frederick Chiluba and turned Zambia into a haven for graft, adultery, drug trafficking, and corruption. In Nigeria, several politicians and leading members of the pro-democracy movement had no qualms about teaming with the brutal junta of General Sani Abacha to abolish the transition to democracy.[39] With such state structures and patterns of pedestrian and opportunistic politics left intact, and with organizations in civil society weak, disorganized, poorly funded, and frustrated by cynical and spasmodic responses to their frequent calls for action from the masses, the return to the earlier conditions of human rights abuses might just be right around the corner.

CONCLUSION

Thus far, we have tried to present the harsh realities of Africa's underdevelopment. We have contended that human rights must necessarily be violated in the context of dependence and underdevelopment. The condition of underdevelopment in itself constitutes a violation of people's rights. Therefore, under conditions where production and exchange patterns and relationships are under foreign control, and the dominant forces are nonhegemonic and largely incapable of mediating the edges of class contradictions and conflicts, human rights for the poor majority cannot be guaranteed. As Julius Nyerere notes: "What freedom has a subsistence farmer? He scratches a bare living from the soil provided the rains do not fail; his children work at his side without schooling, medical care, or even good feeding. Certainly he has the freedom to vote and to speak but these are meaningless."[40] It is our opinion that the Western conception of human rights, which tend to emphasize political and civil rights, are very important but, unfortunately, they are too narrow to inform the African situation.

In Africa, social, economic, and cultural rights are as important as civil and political rights, if not more important. The right to education, housing, food, jobs, and health are critical for the enjoyment of the freedom of movement, speech, organization, and the like. An illiterate person is easily intimidated, misinformed, and misled. A hungry person can hardly take advantage of the freedom of movement and speech. A sick person can hardly be of any use to a political organization. A poor person persistently feels inferior and disillusioned because he or she lacks the capacity to be relevant to the immediate family. These mean that the conceptualization of human rights in Africa must be holistic with particular attention to social and economic rights. The equitable distribution of available wealth, the creation of opportunities, and the availability of opportunities to participate fully in the initiation of the basic needs of the people cannot be negotiated in the process of development.[41] Indeed, unless the majority of the people are mobilized and the rights of the producers of wealth guaranteed, the tendency will be toward deepening alienation and conflicts. The maintenance of political stability, of course, is important to the process of liquidating underdevelopment. Yet, the guarantee of sociocultural rights and economic subsistence of the majority must be a basic right. At the moment, it is quite true that only lip service is paid to subsistence rights. In fact, leaders and politicians use them to lure an alienated and cynical populace into their political games, and then they turn against the people.[42]

Responding to these deprivations and deformities in African social formations requires an agenda for political renewal and the total democratization of the political landscape. Yet, this does not appear to be quite on the agenda. Unfortunately, lenders, donors, and pro-democracy forces in Africa, caught in the euphoria of the pseudopolitical openings and the programmed elections organized thus far, fail to see or appreciate the dangers ahead. In Namibia, Sam Njoma has manipulated the constitution, parliament, and political process for a third term "as a reward" for leading the independence struggle, although this is not provided for in the Constitution. In Egypt, Hossni Mubarak has just been given a fourth term in office. Even the emergence of Thabo Mbeki as the ANC flag bearer in South Africa's June 1999 presidential election cannot be said to have been done in a free and fair way. Africa's dominant classes continue to use the state to accumulate, their politics is still normless, their relation to production is still tenuous, politics is still a business, and the masses are nothing but objects of exploitation and manipulation. Under the guise of strengthening the state and economy, these governing classes have initiated a rather sophisticated and dangerous system of repression that must be dismantled for popular democracy and human rights to thrive.[43]

International declarations, human rights charters, and other well-documented statements on the rights of citizens mean very little to desperate elites who have learned to rely on corruption, repression, and the denial of human rights to reproduce the status quo and maintain their hold on power. Although an acceptable "international morality" might not exist, Africans know all too well about the double standards of Western governments on issues of human rights. As well, to the extent that IFIs continue with policies that alienate and punish disadvantaged groups, international declarations can at best sensitize Africans to the salience of human rights and provide a global basis for articulating domestic programs for challenging the state.[44] What would determine the violation or guarantee of human rights, especially in a crisis-ridden and poverty-stricken continent like Africa, is the extent to which socioeconomic contradictions are resolved. Claude Ake, for instance, has argued that in view of the existing socioeconomic crisis in Africa, fascism is perhaps inevitable: "[A]ll the more dramatic precisely because of the long drawn-out economic stagnation. . . . One thing that would surely be needed in ever increasing quantities in this situation would be repression. As the economic stagnation persisted, the masses would become more wretched and desperate."[45] Ironically, it is exactly in these "desperate" and "repressive" environments that hopes for the guarantee of human rights can be found as each class/social fraction and faction challenge each other for hegemony. As contradictions deepen, nonbourgeois forces will transcend the debates about civil, political, or socioeconomic rights. The struggle will be one of survival or elimination. Given the domestic and international balance of forces, the struggle can be expected to be in favor of nonbourgeois forces. As Ake noted,

Wretchedness and desperation would lead peasants to subversion, workers to induce industrial action, and the lumpen proletariat to robbery and violence. Punitive expeditions would then be sent out to liquidate whole villages, armed robbers would be dealt with by imposing sanctions of exceptional harshness. Striking workers would be chased by police dogs, locked out, starved out, shot at. Any person or group of persons who looked like being a rallying point against the system would be summarily liquidated. All this is already happening. And things are likely to get wrose.[46]

We only need to take a look at Somalia, Rwanda, Togo, Liberia, Angola, the Sudan, and Nigeria to see the validity of this position.

The future will resemble the present if democracy and human rights are pursued outside the context of a structural dismantling of the African state at one level, and the strengthening of civil society at the other. A popular national state that reflects the interests and aspirations of the vast majority must replace the current exploitative, aloof, overblown, inefficient, corrupt, and repressive state in Africa. As Boutros Boutros-Ghali has rightly noted, "Reform of the African state is a prerequisite of reform of the African economy."[47] To buttress the survival of the reformed state structure, civil society must be strengthened. It is precisely the weakness and fragmentation of civil society in Africa that has permitted decades of wanton abuse of human rights. The process of empowerment of the people, their communities, organizations, and civil society entails the "transforming of the economic, social, psychological, political and legal circumstances of the currently powerless." It includes the "emergence of group identities (or community), the development of autonomous and coherent popular organizations, and the defence of, and education about, the legal rights of the popular sectors."[48] This process of empowerment, which is the only way to guarantee human rights and democracy in previously brutalized societies, also involves "access to educational facilities and to the minimum resources needed to sustain households. Illiterate people who must devote all their energies to the bare survival cannot empower themselves. This process further requires that people and their organizations have access to contending opinions and accurate information on the performance of power-holders."[49] It is only through such and other efforts, clearly articulated in the Economic Commission for Africa's African Charter for Popular Participation in Development and Transformation,[50] that African peoples can "become important pillars of the democratic system."[51] It is only such a democratic system that can guarantee human rights in Africa. Any current agenda that overlooks or underplays these prescriptions would be merely addressing the symptoms of the African predicament.

NOTES

1. Claude Ake, "Is Africa Democratizing?" in Nahzeem O. Mimiko (ed.), *Crises and Contradiction in Nigeria's Democratization Programme, 1986–1993* (Akure, Nigeria: Stebak Ventures Limited, 1995), p. 244.

2. Femi Falana, quoted in Babatunde Ojudu, "Nigeria: Morning Yet on Human Rights Day," *African Concord* (June 9, 1987), pp. 6–7.

3. Adebayo Adedeji, "Africa: Permanent Underdog?" *International Perspectives* (March–April 1981), p. 17.

4. For reviews of the various positions on human rights, see R.H. Green, "Basic Human Rights/Needs: Some Problems of Categorical Translation and Unification," *The Review* 24–27 (1980–1981), and Jack Donnelly, "Recent Trends in UN Human Rights Activity: Description and Polemic," *International Organization* 35(4) (Autumn 1981).

5. Claude Ake, "The African Context of Human Rights," in Julius O. Ihonvbere (ed.), *The Political Economy of Crisis and Underdevelopment in Africa: Selected Works of Claude Ake* (Lagos, Africa: JAD Publishers, 1990), pp. 86–87. Ake also notes that the Western notion of human rights has evolved in such a way as to make it "relevant to the African experience, although its relevance still remains ambiguous."

6. For details, see Julius O. Ihonvbere, "Towards a Political Economy of Human Rights in Africa (With Special Reference to Nigeria)," Mimeo, University of Port Harcourt, Nigeria, January 1984.

7. See International Labor Office, *First Things First: Meeting the Basic Needs of the People of Nigeria* (Addis Ababa, Africa: JASPA, 1981).

8. *Organization of African Unity, African Charter on Human and Peoples' Rights* (Geneva: International Commission of Jurists, 1986).

9. Claude Ake, "The African Context of Human Rights," op. cit. p. 84.

10. See Robert Jackson and Carl G. Roseberg, "Why Africa's Weak States Persist: The Empirical and the Juridical in Statehood," *World Politics* 35(1) (1983).

11. See Walter Rodney, *How Europe Underdeveloped Africa* (Enugu, Nigeria: Ikenga, 1981), and Frantz Fanon, *The Wretched of the Earth* (New York: Grove Press, 1965).

12. See Julius O. Ihonvbere and Toyin Falola (eds.), *Nigeria and the International Capitalist System* (Boulder, CO: Lynne Rienner Publishers, 1988), and the works of Hamza Alavi, Colin Leys, Michela Van Freyhold, John Saul, Issa Shivji, Claude Ake, Okwudibia Nnoli, and Paul Nursey Bray on the postcolonial state.

13. See Richard Sandbrook, *The Politics of Basic Needs: Urban Aspects of Assaulting Poverty in Africa* (Toronto: University of Toronto Press, 1982).

14. See the collection in George W. Shepherd, Jr., and Mark O. C. Anikpo (eds.), *Emerging Human Rights: The African Political Economy Context* (Westport, CT: Greenwood Press, 1990).

15. See Julius O. Ihonvbere, "The International Environment and Africa's Deepening Crisis: A Critique of the OAU's Lagos Plan of Action and the African Poverty Program for Economic Recovery," Mimeo, University of Port Harcourt, Nigeria, 1987, and Amadu Sesay, "The Global Economic Squeeze and the Challenges to the Administration of International Organizations: The African Experience," in A.O. Sanda and Olusola Ojo (eds.), *Issues in the Administration of Nigeria's Public Sector* (Ile-Ife, Nigeria: Faculty of Administration, University of Ife, 1987).

16. See the readings in P.C.W. Gutkind and Peter Waterman (eds.), *African Social Studies: A Radical Reader* (New York: Monthly Review Press, 1977).

17. See Claude Ake, *Revolutionary Pressures in Africa* (London: Zed Press, 1978), and his *A Political Economy of Africa* (London: Longman, 1982), Neville Brown, "Underdevelopment as a Threat to World Peace," *International Affairs* 47(2) (April 1971).

18. See "Briefing Paper on Africa's Economic Crisis, No. 1," (Halifax, Nova Scotia. Centre for African Studies, Dalhousie University, Canada, January 1985), and Edward V. K. Jaycox, *The Challenges of African Development* (Washington, DC: World Bank, 1992).

19. John Hatch, *Africa Emergent: Africa's Problems since Independence* (Chicago: Henry Regnery, 1974), p. 5.

20. Claude Ake, "The African Context of Human Rights," op. cit., p. 88.

21. Ibid.

22. See Richard Sandbrook, *The Politics of Africa's Economic Recovery* (Cambridge: Cambridge University Press, 1993), and Rhoda Howard, "The Dilemma of Human Rights in Sub-Saharan Africa," *International Journal* XXV(4) (Autumn 1980).

23. Hugh M. Arnold, "Africa and the New International Economic Order," *Third World Quarterly* 11(2) (April 1980), p. 295.

24. Michael Holman, "Africa Is Striving for a Fresh Start," *Financial Times* (September 1, 1993).

25. Claude Ake, *Revolutionary Pressures in Africa,* op. cit.

26. See Steven A. Holmes, "Africa, from the Cold War to Cold Shoulders," *The New York Times* (March 7, 1993), Salim Lone, "Africa: Drifting off the Map of the World's Concerns," *International Herald Tribune* (August 24, 1990), and Julius O. Ihonvbere, "The Dynamics of Change in Eastern Europe and Their Implications for Africa," *Coexistence—A Journal of East West Relations* 29(3) (September 1992).

27. Organization of African Unity, *The Lagos Plan of Action for the Economic Development of Africa, 1980–2000* (Geneva: Institute for Labor Studies, 1981), p. 1.

28. See World Bank, *Accelerated Development in Sub-Saharan Africa: An Agenda for Action* (Washington, D.C.: 1981). This document, popularly called "The Berg Report," builds on the Lagos Plan of Action. It recommended the dismantling of controls on foreign investment, the collection of user fees for social services, export promotion (cash crops) to earn foreign exchange, devaluation, and more incentives to private investors.

29. Adedeji, "Africa: Permanent Underdog?" op. cit., p. 17.

30. The limits of dependent capitalism and dependent development as a strategy of development are clearly discussed in Peter Evans, *Dependent Development: The Alliance of Multinational, State and Local Capital in Brazil* (Princeton, NJ: Princeton University Press, 1979).

31. Claude Ake, "The African Context of Human Rights," op. cit., p. 88.

32. See Russel Geekie, "Kenya: Split Decision," *Africa Report* (March–April, 1993).

33. World Bank, *Sub-Saharan Africa: From Crisis to Sustainable Growth—A Long-Term Perspective Study* (Washington, DC: World Bank, 1989), p. 1.

34. Unfortunately, since the Bank released the 1989 report, it has not seriously mobilized resources to support grassroots organizations that are ultimately the only credible forces capable of challenging the current custodians of state power and creating an "enabling environment" for stability, growth, and development.

35. World Bank, *Sub-Saharan Africa,* op. cit., p. 1.

36. Organization of African Unity, *Lagos Plan of Action,* op. cit., p. 1.

37. Claude Ake, "Is Africa Democratizing?" *The Guardian* (Lagos) (December 12, 1993).

38. Ibid.

39. See Julius O. Ihonvbere, "Threats to Democratic Consolidation in Africa: The Zambian Experience," Mimeo, Department of Government, the University of Texas at Austin, April 1994, Peter da Costa, "Nigeria: The Politics of 'Settlement," *Africa Report* (November–December 1993), and "Nigeria: Hope Betrayed," Interview with retired Brigadier General David Mark, *Newswatch* (April 11, 1994). For publishing this interview, the editors of the magazine were detained by the Nigerian State Security Services (SSS).

40. Julius Nyerere, "Stability and Change in Africa," address to the University of Toronto, Canada, 1969.

41. Rhoda Howard, "The Full-Belly Thesis: Should Economic Rights Take Priority over Civil and Political Rights? A Discussion from Sub-Saharan Africa," University of Toronto, Development Studies Program, Working Paper, No. A1, April 1983.

42. Adebayo Adedeji, "Perspectives of Development and Economic Growth in Africa up to the Year 2000," in OAU, *What Kind of Africa by Year 2000?* (Addis Ababa, Ethiopia: OAU, 1979), p. 61.

43. Clive Thomas, *The Rise of the Authoritarian State in Peripheral States* (New York: Monthly Review Press, 1984), p. 89.

44. Renate Pratt, "Human Rights and International Lending: The Advocacy Experience of the Task Force on the Churches and Corporate Responsibility," University of Toronto, Development Studies Program, Working Paper, No. 15, February 1985.

45. Claude Ake, *Revolutionary Pressure,* op. cit., p. 105.

46. Ibid.

47. Boutros Boutros-Ghali, *New Concepts for Development Action in Africa* (New York: United Nations Africa Recovery Unit of the Department of Public Information, March 1993).

48. Richard Sandbrook, "Introduction," in R. Sandbrook and Mohamed Halfani (eds.), *Empowering People: Building Community, Civil Associations and Legality in Africa* (Toronto: Center for Urban and Community Studies, University of Toronto, 1993), p. 2.

49. Ibid, p. 3.

50. See Economic Commission for Africa, *African Charter for Popular Participation in Development and Transformation* (Addis Ababa: ECA, 1990).

51. South Commission, *The Challenge to the South* (Oxford: Oxford University Press, 1990), pp. 81–82.

7

Democratization in Sub-Saharan Africa: Problems, Advances, and Prospects

Harold A. Fisher

INTRODUCTION

During the past decade, an increasing number of countries of sub-Saharan Africa, the huge geographic area south of the northernmost tier of Arab states, has been taking steps toward more democratic government. Some commenced representative government earlier. Although the number of forward strides is encouraging, recent advances toward multiparty democracy have been uneven, often moving by forward-backward-forward "stutter steps."

Authorities agree the recent movement toward greater democratic freedoms has been impressive. Widner observes that "Between 1989 and 1992, roughly half the countries of sub-Saharan Africa either installed multiparty governments or embarked on a move toward multiparty governments or embarked on a move toward multiparty rule" (1994, 1). Wiseman (1996, 2) points out that, whereas in 1989 only five states in the region could seriously claim to be governed by even relatively minimal definitions of democracy, by 1995 the situation had remarkably changed in the direction of more liberal government in which people had greater freedom to participate. Other sources confirm such recent progress.

However, even those nations demonstrating the best progress still have a long way to go to achieve true representative democracy. Some that have taken steps forward now find themselves slipping backward. Others are actually regressing. A few have yet to opt for more democratic rule.

Many variables affect a nation's progress toward democracy. After attempting to define "democracy" in the African setting, this chapter will briefly examine historical, geographical, economic, social, and other factors that have complicated sub-Saharan processes and discuss earmarks of gains in countries that have opted for greater freedoms. It will then assess these moves in terms of actual and promised effects and outcomes for their citizens, and how these results measure up to what social scientists consider full, open democracy.

DEMOCRACY IN THE SUB-SAHARAN SETTING: TOWARD A WORKING DEFINITION

Most sub-Saharan African nations reflect a short history of independence. Approximately three-quarters of the countries realized their freedom from colonial dominance between 1956 and 1968. Most have been dominated by military or single-party regimes since their independence. Consequently, political liberalization and participatory democracy are still fairly new concepts. The democratization process is complex, involving many variables aimed at helping citizens to participate in the political process. The citizen must come to feel that he or she has an important role in the society and can take part in governance in some way. Each nation must take an active role in helping the citizen share in the political process. Each nation must begin with practical steps and build on them toward full democracy.

Agunga (1997) indicates democracy must be promoted through the emergence of civil societies by strategies rooted in empowerment of individuals and their participation in the process. According to Drah (1993), a full-blown pluralist democracy is characterized by existence and protection of civil and political rights, free and fair elections, a multiparty system, limits on the powers of government, an independent judiciary, a free press, citizen accountability, decisions by majority procedure, respect for minority views, the right to form independent associations, and supremacy of civil authority over military institutions. Widner adds further considerations: "Broad rights to associate and run for office, freedom of speech, a clear link between the results of elections . . . and the public policy choices governments pursue" (1994, 8). To this list, Wiseman adds the rights of citizens to oppose government officials and inclusive suffrage. Ndegwa (1996) emphasizes the importance of nongovernmental organizations to advance democratization. Such are the tools available to citizens of the pluralistic democracy.

To date, most African nations have taken only first steps toward democracy. In some cases, advances have been reversed. During the past decade, the vast majority of countries underwent political liberalization or reform; however, transition to a fully representative democracy happened far less frequently. Instead, first (and often hesitant) steps were taken to form a democratic regime, defined minimally. Bratton has defined this standard as a democratic transition that "requires only (a) a single election (b) that is open to all parties or candidates, (c) which is freely and fairly conducted, (d) in which the losers accept the results" (1997, 157). He further explains that elections are not full democracy, but they do constitute a minimum to hold leaders accountable. Then he points out that the majority of African countries have not even met these minimal conditions because transitions were flawed by election fraud or blocked by unyielding dictators, military regimes, or civil conflict.

A careful reading of the country-by-country initial moves toward democracy during the past decade recorded later in this chapter confirms Bratton's thesis. The reader will note that the first stuttering steps toward democratization were taken either volitionally by the party in power or after opposition party or citizen pressures. The first action typically was to allow a multiparty system, often by means of a referendum, followed by local, legislative, and/or presidential elections. Strikingly, the incumbent single-party or military leader was often voted back into power. The reader will also note that many of the "conversions" to democracy either moved forward to greater individual freedoms at a snail's pace or stagnated.

FACTORS THAT IMPACT THE SUB-SAHARAN DEMOCRATIZATION PROCESS

A wide range of components have influenced sub-Saharan progress toward representative government. Each has had its own special bearing on African approval of a representative democracy; taken together, they present a unique mixture of factors that have slowed acceptance of democratic rule.

Physical Resources

Availability of land, water, minerals, and other resources vary widely across the vast subcontinent for the seven percent of the region now in cropland. Land is fertile in some areas; in many others, such as West Africa, farmers must use slash-and-burn tactics to produce enough nutrients to raise crops. Desertification caused by overgrazing, drought, and population growth are serious problems in the Sahel, the Horn, and the Namib and Kalahari Deserts. Rainfall varies widely from less than ten inches in desert areas to over eighty in the equatorial region. Tropical forests are rapidly disappearing in the face of export logging and land clearing for agriculture and population growth. Although rich in minerals (copper, iron, gold, diamond, and bauxite and others in lesser quantities), they are distributed unevenly. The region produces about 41 percent of the world's diamonds, 39 percent of its cobalt, 31 percent of its gold, and 18 percent of its uranium (U.S. Department of Interior, 1993).

Historical Factors

Archeological discoveries by Dr. Louis Leakey and others establish that the earliest humans in Africa go back over 4 million years, and the region has been populated by great civilizations throughout its history (Fisher, 1997, 246). Today, well over 600 million people populate the region, with projections that the region's population will reach 867 million by 2010 A.D. and over 1.25 billion by 2025 (Population Reference Bureau, 1996). At present, there is a population explosion of over 3 percent per annum in several countries. Rapid urbanization is taking place as rural people move to cities in search of work. Disease, health care, and education are all shaping today's changes in the region.

Early Civilizations

The Hamites in the Sahel area and the Negroid peoples in the South were often hunters, herders, and farmers; some of their ways exist to this day. Great kingdoms and empires have flourished during the region's more recent periods. Such kingdoms included Ethiopia's Kingdom of Kush, the Nok culture in Nigeria, and empires in present-day Ghana, Mali, Benin, and western Nigeria. In the East and South, the Bantu peoples founded powerful nation-states in Zimbabwe and in southern Africa. Their cultures were affected by regional geographic differences, trading and occupational opportunities, and the influx of Arab cultures from the North. According to Davidson, despite these diversities, Bantu attitudes and beliefs have remained basically similar during the past 1,500 years (1989, 9). Across the continent, the influences of the structures of organization, authority, and individual roles in society of these early kingdoms have endured and continue to this day to shape attitudes of their descendents toward governance and society.

Present-Day Civilizations

The migrations of Africans across the centuries to the present have led to ethnic diversity. Today, over 800 different languages and dialects are spoken. Ethnic groupings remain strong. Two common characteristics are shared by most Africans—respect for elders and a strong extended family, both potentially good building blocks for representative government. However, the demands of modern society are beginning to disintegrate ethnic ties; traditions are becoming subservient to increased urbanization, travel, and the mores and values of life today. Religion, long a characteristic of African peoples, is also changing. Believers in animistic gods and spirits are converting to Islam or Christianity. Both have brought benefits in the forms of schools and hospitals; unfortunately, sometimes missionaries of these two faiths have imposed non-African values. Pentecostalism, by its invocation of spirits, is rapidly gaining new converts. Such ethnic and religious differences affect attitudes to democracy.

Influences of Colonial Rule

Beginning about 1880, several European nations established colonies in the region, bringing changes, some of which persist today. Fisher indicates they brought modern communication and transport systems, introduced the civil service system in which some Africans participated, expanded markets, and improved education and health facilities for some (1988, 231). Agunga (1997) adds that, although the colonialists provided protection, they also dominated and exploited Africans and took material resources for themselves while introducing mercantilism and laissez-faire profit-motivated trade. Davidson says they also ignored African ethnic boundaries "as they erected artificial boundaries that still cause violent disputes" (1989, 11). In the process, the colonialists built railroads and roads for their own use, resulting in a haphazard development of transport systems that disregarded the needs of a country's internal development, a process Ake (1996) calls "disarticulation." The same happened in the development of communication infrastructures—telephony, telex, microwave, and broadcast technologies. Telephone calls, for example, were often routed through the colonial switchboards in Europe.

In addition, colonial rule left a legacy that at times has promoted conflicts and slowed progress toward democracy. The colonials disregarded or cut across ethnic boundaries as they claimed as much territory as their armies could control; consequently, upon independence, diverse African ethnic groups were forced to live together within the confines carved out by the colonial state. Such problems have contributed to a slowdown of shared government; Rwanda and Nigeria are examples of this phenomenon. The colonials' military power also suggested to Africans who traditionally respected tribal chieftain or "strong man" leadership that the military model should be adopted at independence. In addition, the colonial overlords set up a civil service that often failed to allow Africans to rise in the ranks, thus preventing them from gaining experience in the critical decision making needed for democracy.

Economic Woes and Recovery Efforts

At independence, most sub-Saharan countries were predominantly rural agrarian societies with barely viable economies. Up to 70 percent of the populace tilled small farms. Most were subsistence farmers. Most had (and still have) a single raw-material export commodity and frail industries, conditions that lead to deficit spending and large debts. Dia says much of the crisis can be attributed to a "structural disconnect" between the traditional African informal indigenous business institutions and management practices that characterize modern civil society (1996, 36).

The Deficit Crisis

Until independence, most colonial overlords had exported a single raw material purchased for their own industries at cheap prices, failed to develop indigenous industries, and neglected to train African entrepreneurs. The new African governments often compounded their economic woes by poor planning and management. Drought, wars, refugees, migration, and poverty added to their problems and caused a growing economic crisis with spiraling debts, which rose from $5 billion in 1970 to $174 billion in 1990. By that time, the new African nations were making debt payments of over $20 billion annually to creditor nations (Agunga, 1997, 72). According to the World Bank, by 1994 only nine countries had external debt less than their GNP. Efforts were made to correct the situation, and by 1995 "there was positive per capita growth for the first time in many years, associated with trade gains and better fiscal policies in a growing number of countries" (World Bank, 1997a, 28).

Recovery Efforts

Early on, concerned economists began studying the crisis, which was making Africans poorer at an alarming rate. An African proposal, the 1979 Lagos Plan of Action recommended self-reliance and decreasing dependency on exports. The Berg Plan wanted more exports, maximum profits, and free trade. In 1986, the United Nations (UN) adopted a program of international aid combined with responsibility by African governments.

As the crisis worsened, the World Bank and the International Monetary Fund (IMF) offered "structural adjustment" loans based on free markets, reduction of state intervention in markets, financial discipline, and increased exports. Though some African leaders considered the remedy neocolonialistic, their economic conditions forced them to accept these debt-restructuring programs. Beginning in 1980, at least thirty countries adopted the World Bank and IMF proposals. Both programs were economically rigorous; critics said the donors were "calling the shots" (Lewis, 1994, 48). Even by the early 1990s, some nations achieved notable financial improvement under the programs, but most had made only small gains or had even deteriorated financially.

Marked economic improvements began in 1995. Excellent rains increased agricultural output, which accounted for "about 35% of the total GDP, 40% of exports, and 70% of employment" across the region (World Bank, 1997b, 48). Commodity prices rose, grassroots credit unions developed, military expenditures fell, and donor agencies increased their efforts to aid development in the region. The African Economic Research Consortium said the African nations responded with encouraging economic policy changes, among them moves to a more open market–oriented managerial strategy, increased influence of economic experts, liberalization of political systems, growing donor willingness to give recipients a voice in aid strategies, and more media help in heightening public awareness of economic policy issues (Ndulu, 1997). However, to date, in most nations the improvements remain insufficient to cause major reductions in Africa's grinding poverty; GDP, exports, savings, investments, and social indicators all remain below other regions of the world. Economic conditions continue to have a major bearing on political reform.

Social and Cultural Conditions

Social conditions vary widely among the sub-Saharan countries. Problems common to nearly all include ethnic strife, regional conflicts, refugees, availability of resources for the citizenry, and disparities in educational opportunities. But the greatest social impacts have come from a population explosion, rapid urbanization, and health care in the face of a devastating AIDS epidemic.

Fast Population Growth

In 1996, the region's average natural population growth was reported to be 2.9 percent. The World Bank (1997b) indicated ten countries experienced over a 3 percent growth in the same year. The fastest growth tended to be in the poorest countries. The entire population is young; in 1996, the median age was seventeen years. But life expectancy remains far below most of the rest of the world; 1995 estimates showed that the average person would live less than fifty-five years in over half the countries, a contrast to a life expectancy of over seventy-five years for many Western nations. In addition, Africans have large families; most women have four to six babies, and more children are living to maturity. Predictions are that the region will reflect the world's highest growth rates during the coming twenty-five-year period (USAID, 1996).

The population growth has strong economic and political implications. Darnton (1994) said that because of the explosion, African nations would have to move full steam ahead just to avoid standing still economically. Hanley was concerned because "basic resources are being depleted, and environmental pollution is intensifying as a result of unprecedented population growth" (1994, A3). To slow growth rates, strong measures must be taken: Hanley said growth could be stabilized only if births came down to two per couple and if crash birth control educational programs are mounted.

Rapid Urbanization

Since the 1960s, rural people have been migrating to urban centers in search of job opportunities. A rough positive correlation exists between population and urban growth. Urban growth is predicted to be the most rapid in the world in the foreseeable future. African cities are marked by slums and shantytowns with windowless shacks, open sewers, garbage piles, and often no electricity. After a study of urbanization in seven countries, Stren and White (1989) concluded that major factors in rapid urban growth are the population explosion, rural flight to cities, drought, adverse trade for exporters of agricultural products, and government policies that favor city residents over rural dwellers. The bright lights of the city, construction activities, and better education and health facilities are other drawing cards.

The influx has created headaches for city officials. Lacking enough funds, they respond by cutting off free services, such as water standpipes and subsidized housing. Poor sanitation facilities and failure of public transport systems have compounded problems for citizens and officials alike.

Disease, Health Care, and AIDS

After independence, the new nations in the region built clinics, improved health education, and engaged in vaccination campaigns. But when national debts rose, health services declined. Because of poor health education, infant mortality remained high; in 1996, the rate was ninety-six deaths per 1,000 in the first year of children's lives (Population Reference Bureau, 1996). More resistant strains of tropical diseases—malaria, yellow fever, meningitis, tuberculosis, and cholera—are striking children and adults.

HIV/AIDS

In Africa, rapid spread of the human immunodeficiency (HIV) and acquired immune deficiency syndrome (AIDS) viruses is devastating the populace of most nations in the region. The disease is spread mostly by heterosexual contact. A recent UN study concluded that up to one in every four Africans has AIDS. The report indicated 25.8 percent of the people of Zimbabwe are infected. In Botswana, the infection rate doubled from 10 percent in 1992 to 25.1 percent in 1997. Several other countries in southern and central Africa report nearly as many cases. Infection rates run over one in three adults in some large African cities. In some prenatal clinics, tests showed up to 70 percent of women were infected, and many of the infected pass the virus on to their babies. Most of the ill are in the sexually active fifteen- to forty-nine-year-old range. The report also said that in 1997, "30 million people were infected with HIV, the AIDS virus, and that 21 million of them were in Africa" (Altman, 1998, A7). Many children are orphans, having lost their mothers and fathers to AIDS. UN officials attribute the high infection rates in Africa to the facts that women have more children than those in most other countries, that most children are breast-fed, and that drugs and treatment are not readily available.

The AIDS epidemic is slowing moves toward democracy because many are too ill or too close to dying to participate in political activities or pressures. In addition, the disease is a costly burden for the already fragile economies of the region.

Other Social and Cultural Conditions

Still other factors negatively impact the region's advance to political reforms. Illiteracy remains high, schools lack the resources for effective training, classrooms are overcrowded, and there is a lack of trained teachers. Universities lack the faculties, facilities, and financial resources to train adequately a cadre of graduates to lead Africa into full democracy. At the other end of the spectrum, about three-fourths of sub-Saharans are subsistence farmers who produce little more than enough for their own families. The opening of new agricultural lands is inadequate to meet the food needs of a population explosion. Finally, deep-rooted ethnic divisions continue to plague the cooperation needed for representative democracy.

SUB-SAHARAN MOVES TOWARD POLITICAL DEMOCRACY

Given the preceding background, this section provides a synopsis by categories of national moves toward political democracy from the earliest advances since independence to conditions prevailing at present. Because the democratic process is a continuum, the following categories are not necessarily mutually exclusive. However, the typical initial process is a series of steps from initial agreement to establish a multiparty system (often following public agitation for such) to approval of a new constitution to open multiparty elections. This categorization represents information gleaned from Wiseman (1996), Widner (1994), Fisher (1998), Matloff (1997), and other recent academic and news service sources.

Democracy since Independence

Only four small nations chose democratic government at independence. *Botswana:* Has experienced continuous multiparty democracy since 1966. The Democratic Party has governed with no changes or interruptions to date. *Mauritius:* Has enjoyed multiparty liberal democracy since 1968, with open elections and changes via the ballot box in 1982 and 1983. *Senegal:* Multiparty system since 1960, with a reversion to single-party rule from 1974 to 1981; since then, continuous multiparty elections. *The Gambia:* Multiparty liberal democracy governed by the People's Progressive Party since 1965. However, there was a two-year hiatus when a 1994 coup put it under military rule until free elections were restored in 1996.

Democratization Process Undertaken in the 1989–1997 Period

As indicated earlier, there has been a crescendo of moves toward multiparty free elections and other advances since 1989. The following countries are categorized by the year of their initial steps toward democracy. The reader will note that some states have slipped back into single-party or military rule after initial steps toward democracy; some of the backsliders later returned to greater democracy, and others have yet to do so.

1989

The Marxist-Lennist FRELIMO *Mozambique* government agreed to legalize nonviolent parties in 1989. After peace with the opposition REN-AMO party, there was violence, but two-party elections were held in 1994. *Namibia:* People's party SWAPO won the majority of seats in the 1989 preindependence elections. Adoption of a multiparty constitution followed in 1990, free local elections in 1992, and national elections in 1994, again won by SWAPO.

1990

A busy year as thirteen countries began moves to representative government. *Benin:* After a Marxist military regime, a transitional government was installed in 1990, followed by 1991 elections that seated representatives from twelve different parties. *Cameroon:* After a single-party rule under Paul Biya since independence in 1960, a multiparty system was established in 1990. Following boycott by the opposition, Biya won the presidential election with under 40 percent of the vote. *Cape Verde:* A multiparty structure was adopted in 1990, then 1991 legislative and presidential elections led to a peaceful transfer of power. *Comoros:* A single-party state backed by foreign mercenaries allowed the formation of political parties in 1990. After repeated elections, incumbent Mohamed Djohar narrowly won the presidency.

Ivory Coast: After years of one-party state led by Houphouet-Boigny, the government accepted multiparty organization. However, the government won the 1990 elections as the opposition claimed election fraud. *Gabon:* A single-party state led by Omar Bongo and the Democratic Party gave way to a multiparty structure in 1990. Legislative elections were held in 1991, but the opposition claimed fraud as Bongo won the presidency. *Guinea:* In 1990, after military rule under Lasana Conte, the government announced transition to two-party, then a multiparty, system leading to presidential elections in 1993. Conte won amid cries of fraud by the opposition. *Guinea-Bissau:* A single-party military regime led by Joao Vieira gave way to multiparty organization in 1990. Despite opposition by 30,000 demonstrators and an attempted coup that postponed voting, Vieira narrowly won in the 1994 presidential elections. At present, Civil War is being waged in *Guinea-Bissau*.

Madagascar: In 1990, Marxist rule was replaced by a multiparty system. That was followed in 1991 by creation of a transitional government involving opposition groups. After approval of a new constitution, opposition leader Albert Zafy won two consecutive elections in 1992 and in 1993 to become the new president. *Niger:* The military government announced a transition to multiparty rule in 1990 by lifting its ban on parties. A 1992 referendum approved a new constitution, and in 1993 opposition leader M. Ousmane won in an open election for the presidency. *Sao Tome and Principe:* Moved as a single-party state to a multiparty constitution in 1990, which was followed by elections won by the ruling party. When a coup against the government failed in 1995, elected government returned. *Zambia:* Kenneth Kaunda and his UNIP party gave way to the multiparty method in 1990. In 1991, the opposition Movement for Multiparty Democracy party won legislative and presidential elections in a peaceful exchange of power. *Zimbabwe:* Robert Mugabe and his ZANU party allowed multiparty government in 1990. Mugabe, in power since 1980, won national elections again in 1996. ZANU holds 98 percent of the parliamentary seats.

1991

After the 1990 surge toward political liberalization, twelve additional countries took initial steps in the same direction in 1991. *Angola:* After almost continuous Civil War since its independence in 1975, in 1991 the Marxist MPLA and the opposition UNITA parties accepted multiparty elections. The ensuing 1992 election results were contested by UNITA, and Civil War was renewed. Peace agreements of 1993 and 1994 failed. Contention continues. *Burkina Faso:* A multiparty constitution was installed in 1991. Military leader Campaore and his Popular Front won the presidential election despite an opposition boycott. However, the 1992 legislative elections involved twenty-seven parties, who also gained numerous seats in parliament.

Central African Republic: After one-party military rule since 1981, the party system was restored in 1991. In 1993 elections, opposition leader Patasse won the office of the presidency with the support of French troops. *Mali:* In 1991, the military regime ousted leader Moussa Traore and announced its intent to go to multiparty democracy and a new constitution in 1992. The Alliance for Democracy Party won the resulting elections.

Ghana: After military government led by Jerry Rawlings, the government opened to the multiparty approach in 1991. In 1992, Rawlings won the presidential election. However, the main opposition parties boycotted legislative elections, claiming fraud. Despite opposition criticism of Rawling's presidency, he was reelected in 1996, but some opposition pressures continue. *Kenya:* Daniel arap Moi and his KANU party gave in to pro-democracy pressures to allow multiple parties in 1991. However, splits in the opposition allowed Moi to win the 1992 election for president. Moi, who has become increasingly autocratic, was reelected again in 1997. *Rwanda:* The military government led by J. Habyarimana allowed a new multiparty constitution in 1991. Peace agreements made with the Tutsi-led Patriotic Front and elections set for 1995 were cancelled when Habyarimana was assassinated. Civil War resulted, and millions of Hutus became refugees.

Seychelles: The Marxist single party (SPPF) government granted open elections in 1991. A revised constitution was accepted, and SPPF won the presidential and legislative elections in 1993. *Sierra Leone:* The single-party system approved a new constitution in 1991. A 1992 coup delayed the process. In 1993, the government announced it would return to a representative system by 1996, when open and fair elections were held. *Togo:* The military state led by Gnassingbe Eyadema allowed opposition parties in 1991. However, there has been little progress toward democracy or improved human rights since, and most opposition groups are in exile. *Equatorial Guinea:* The military regime approved a multiparty constitution in 1991. However, there has been little progress since toward democracy or improved human rights, and most opposition groups are in exile. *Mauritania:* The military regime, which had allowed municipal elections, agreed in 1991 to a democratic multiparty process. Military leader Ahmed Taya won the 1992 presidential election, but subsequent legislative elections were boycotted. Protests continue.

1992

Burundi: The military regime led by Pierre Buyoya endorsed a new multi-party constitution in 1992. A year later, Buyoya was defeated in presidential elections by opposition leader Melchior Ndadaye, whose party also won the legislative majority. Ndadaye was assassinated in a coup by Tutsi soldiers. Tension between parties remains high. *Chad:* The military regime permitted formation of new political parties in 1992. Ten were formed. Although committed to representative government, security remains unstable.

Congo: Marxist regime referendum approved a new constitution in 1992. Subsequent parliamentary and presidential elections were won by the opposition. After a 1993 no-confidence vote, armed clashes between the army and the opposition have continued. *Ethiopia:* Though never under colonial rule and recently dominated by Marxist rule, the People's Revolutionary Democratic Front (EPRDF) Party intervened in 1992, overthrew the Mengistu regime, gained 90 percent of the vote, set up an interim government, and held regional elections. However, the 1994 elections were boycotted. At present, armed conflict exists with Eritrea.

South Africa: Under white rule after its independence in 1910, blacks and minorities had limited privileges. With Nelson Mandela's release from prison in 1990, repeal of most apartheid laws was planned. In 1992, a white-approved referendum reform led to an interim constitution. The African National Congress (ANC) party won the first-ever nonracial national elections in 1994, and Mandela became president of a national unity government. Under him, open democracy with shared power has prevailed. A Truth and Reconciliation Commission led by Bishop Tutu is seeking justice and reconciliation for offenders under white rule; however, there have been criticisms of the process. South Africa has become a model for democracy for many Africans. *Tanzania:* After Julius Nyerere retired as president in 1990, a multiparty system was introduced in 1992. Orderly elections were held in 1995.

1993

Lesotho: The military regime was overthrown in a coup in 1991. In 1993, the opposition party BCP won a multiparty general election, and its leader became prime minister. Threats to the new democracy by the military and suspension of the new constitution by King Letsie were defeated in 1994, thanks to intervention by other southern African states. *Malawi:* Although long-time President Hastings Banda tried to prevent it, a 1993 referendum prevailed to return the country to a multiparty system, to legalize pluralism, and to repeal the president-for-life status declared by Banda. In 1994, the opposition won national elections, and Baki Muluzi became president. *Eritrea:* In 1993, the Eritrean People's Liberation Front (EPLF) won independence from Ethiopia and opted for representative government. The EPLF declared a four-year transition to full multiparty democracy, and elections were successfully held in 1997. Yet by 1998, Ethiopia and Eritrea were engaged in a fierce war over disputed land.

States Struggling or Straggling in the Democratization Process

Because democratization is a dynamic process, accurate categorization of states on the periphery of moving toward democracy is difficult at best. However, to this author, it appears eight states are either struggling in the initial stages of minimal democratization or have yet to adopt it as a goal. It is a diverse group, each nation with its individual variables that have affected its attitudes and actions regarding democratization. A brief synopsis of each follows.

States Struggling for Minimal Democracy

Three states have taken initial "stutter steps" toward the election box and representative government. *Djibouti:* In 1992, a multiparty constitution was approved in this single-party and highly fractionalized state. In 1993, the ruling Popular Rally for Progress Party won the presidential elections, seating Hassan Aptidon. However, the opposition has continued to accuse the government of electoral fraud and to block further change. The result has been a deadlock, even some retrogression. *Zaire:* In 1990, Mobutu Sese Seko, the leader of this highly militarized single-party state, agreed to a multiparty system. However, the opposition leader's appointment of a transitional prime minister in 1991 was canceled by Mobutu. Anarchy, civil war, and a refugee problem followed until the takeover of the country by Laurent Kabila's forces in 1997, resulting in Mobutu's demise. Kabila has promised to return to democracy, but to date little progress is reported. *Nigeria:* A military-dominated state riddled with corruption and financial crises and struggling with deep, long-held divisions between strong ethnic factions, Nigeria has made initial moves toward democracy. The ban on political parties was lifted to allow local two-party elections in 1990, and legislative elections were held in 1992. But when Social Democratic Party leader Moshood Abiola won a national election for president in 1993, the military rulers annulled the results and installed an interim government. That was overturned by General Sani Abacha, who also imprisoned Abiola in 1994. Recent events have included sudden deaths of Abacha and Abiola. General Abdulsalami Abubakar, who took over quickly organized elections and in May 1999 installed a constitutional democracy headed by Olusegun Obasanjo.

States in which Minimal Democracy Has Yet to Take Roots

Five states either have made feeble efforts to move to political reform only to abandon them or have rejected it altogether. *Sudan:* Amid lengthy Civil War between the northern military-led Islamic government and the partly Christian South, a fragile multiparty system theoretically exists. However, the North dominates, and continued civil conflict hampers further moves toward democracy. *Somalia:* Since its 1960 independence, Somalia was dominated by a single party until 1991, when its leader Siad Barre's overthrow by the military fragmented the country and threw it into anarchy. A three-year intervention by UN forces failed to rectify the situation. The situation remains chaotic.

Liberia: Never under colonial control, a republic was formed in 1947. Under Sergeant Samuel Doe, a multiparty system was set up, but as a military dictator, Doe never allowed it to come into being. Liberia has never risen above chaos, corruption, and ethnic factionalism and has been in various states of civil war since Doe's death, despite intervention from the outside by the UN, the United States, and troops from western African nations. *Swaziland:* Has remained a constitutional monarchy with all political parties banned since independence in 1968, despite some pressures for a multiparty system.

Uganda: After years of despotic rule by dictator Idi Amin and fractious Civil War, Uganda is enjoying both a free-market economy and many benefits of multiparty democracy under the benevolent one-party leadership of President Yoweri Museveni and the National Resistance Council. Although some troubles persist in the North, there is freedom of the press, speech, movement, and interaction. Museveni continues to reject demands for a multiparty system, and Ugandans appear to be too content to protest. Philosophically, Uganda comprises an interesting challenge to often slower and more complicated democratic processes.

CONCLUSION

During the past decade, a majority of sub-Saharan nations have made an initial commitment to political liberalization. The moves have been complicated by numerous problems, among them ethnic divisions and conflict, a legacy of colonialism, desire of military or single-party leaders to remain in power, economic woes, rapid social changes, and an AIDS epidemic.

Most moves have been minimal "stutter steps" involving citizen pressures or a willingness of one-party rulers to allow political reform. This typically has led to a multiparty referendum and subsequent open local, legislative, and/or presidential elections. Although most have not reneged on their initial moves, many states have not moved decisively forward to next steps. On the surface, the progress to date has been quite remarkable. However, achieving full-blown participatory and pluralist democracy is a long, complicated process, and African nations have only begun their march toward it. In the United States, the maturing process has taken well over two centuries, and even to this day, problems continue to surface.

The African nations, having taken initial steps, must now move forward toward more refined and mature democracy with full freedom of speech and press, enthusiasm for the ballot box, and repeated open and fair multiparty elections. Being content to remain on the present plateau will only spell disaster. Given Africa's many problems, there is even danger of slipping backward or failing altogether. Thus there must be a strong will to push forward. Most Africans are energetic and resourceful people, and this writer is cautiously confident the sub-Saharan states will move forward, perhaps first by more "stutter steps," and later by firm strides as they gain confidence in political freedom for all.

REFERENCES

Agunga, Robert A. *Developing the Third World: A Communication Approach* (Commack, New York: Nova Science Publishers, 1997).

Ake, Claude. *Democracy and Development in Africa* (Washington, D.C.: The Brookings Institution, 1996).

Altman, Lawrence. "AIDS Scourge Rivals Worst Yet," *Oregonian* (Portland, Oregon), June 24, 1998, A1 and A7.

Bratton, Michael. "International Versus Domestic Pressures for Democratization in Africa." In Hale, William, and Eberhard Kienle, *After the Cold War: Security and Democracy in Africa and Asia* (New York: Tauris Academic Studies, 1997).

Darnton, J. "Survival Test: Can Africa Rebound?" *Oregonian* (Portland, Oregon), June 28, 1994, A7ff.

Davidson, Basil. "Africa in Historical Perspective." In *Africa South of the Sahara,* 18th Edition (London: Europe Publications, 1989).

Dia, Mamadou. *Directions in Development: Africa's Management in the 1990s and Beyond* (Washington, D.C.: The World Bank, 1996).

Drah, F.K. "Civil Society and the Transition to Pluralist Democracy." In Ninsin, Kwame, and F.K. Drah, *Political Parties and Democracy in Ghana's Fourth Republic* (Accra, Ghana: Woeli Publishing Services, 1993).

Fisher, Harold A. "Sub-Saharan Africa: Problems, Progress and Potentials." In Gonzalez, Alfonso, and Jim Norwine (eds.), *The New Third World,* 2nd Edition (Boulder, Colorado: Westview Press, 1998).

Fisher, Harold A. "Sub-Saharan Africa: Barriers and Prospects." In Norwine, James, and A. Gonzalez (eds.), *States of Mind and Being* (Boston: Unwin Hyman, 1988).

Hanley, C. "The Human Tide," *Oregonian* (Portland, Oregon), September 2, A3, 1994.

Lewis, Peter. "Politics of Economics," *Africa Report* 39:47–49, 1994.

Matloff, Judith. "Suddenly Africa's Conflicts Aren't So Local," *Christian Science Monitor,* February 7, 1997, pp. 6ff.

Ndegwa, Stephen. *The Two Faces of Civil Society: NGOs and Politics in Africa* (West Hartford, CT: Kumarian Press, Inc., 1996).

Ndulu, Benno. 1997. Editorial, *World Development,* 25, (5):627–630.

Population Reference Bureau. *World Population Data Sheet* (Washington, D.C.: Population Reference Bureau, June 1996).

Stren, Richard E. and Rodney R. White, eds., *African Cities in Crisis: Managing Rapid Urban Growth* (Boulder, Col.: Westview Press) pp. 11–19.

United States Agency for International Development, 1996. *World Population Profile,* Washington, D.C.: USAID.

U.S. Department of Interior. *Minerals Yearbook, Africa* (Washington, D.C.: Author, 1993).

Widner, Jennifer (ed.). *Economic Change and Political Liberalization in Sub-Saharan Africa* (Baltimore: The Johns Hopkins University Press, 1994).

Wiseman, John A. *The New Struggle for Democracy in Africa* (Aldershot, England, and Brookfield, VT: Avebury, 1996).

World Bank. *World Bank Atlas* (Washington, D.C.: Author, 1997a).

World Bank. *World Development Report* (New York: Oxford University Press, 1997b).

8

Prolegomena to an African-Western Ethics and Theory of Rights

Vincent J. Ferrara

INTRODUCTION

Cultural relativism can be examined politically, methodologically, and through its critique of ethical criteria. The first protects ethical differences against the hegemonic dogmatism of the powerful. The second denies the possibility of adjudicating among competing claims. The third points to ethical criteria as culturally generated and hence as culturally limited. In this light, a cross-cultural ethics appears both undesirable and impossible. However, hegemonic dogmatism is weakened in the presence of culturally ethical similarities, and intercultural dialogue methodologically permits transcultural values through identification, recognition, modification, and exchange, while both make feasible the claim of culturally independent criteria. This chapter explores the factual and methodological relation of African and Western views of ethics and rights as a response to the claims of cultural relativism, and it seeks to show that criteria need not be culturally limited. Rights generally denote what protects the bearer against general and specific intrusions by authority or others regarding the domain of what is protected on the one hand, while endorsing, legitimizing, and giving authority to the bearer's varying claims concerning person or property on the other. Viewed in this twofold way, rights are negative against power and are positive as empowering. But when rights are defined exclusively or predominantly in this way, they appear essentially protectionistic. These negative and positive meanings hold whether we understand rights in the Western sense as primarily concerned with individuals or in a Third World sense where rights address the concerns of community. In both cases, rights, functioning for-the-self over against others, or for-the-whole de-emphasizing the priority of individuality, appear essentially to support an objectionable protectionism. That rights might function in either of these two ways does not mean that a theory of rights demands we equate rights with such objectionable positions. A theory of rights need not rest either on appeal to solipsistic individualism or to a homogeneous communalism. A theory of rights need not be divisive. An examination of the African and Western emphases on rights is prologue to a dialogue in which a more balanced view of rights can be created.

RELATIVISM, MULTICULTURALISM, AND A COMMON ETHICS

The experiences of Africa and the West reveal a seemingly incompatible difference in their approaches to rights—the former emphasizing community, the latter, the individual—making it appear not only that the two traditions are irrevocably distinct but that they ethically pull in opposite directions. Do the dynamics of these two views preclude the possibility of dialogue issuing in some noncontingent commonality? Can the two traditions meet in a transcultural position faithful to both, or must any found similarities be nothing more than contextualized accidents?[1] Cultural relativism, linked to one variation of multiculturalism, argues the latter because it denies the existence of transcendent cross-cultural values obligating all humans, holding that values are immanent to culture in origin, justification, and applicability. Dialogue so premised can only achieve compromises internally validated by each side linked to a political practicality of mutual accommodation. But multiculturalism is inherently transcultural even when it opposes intracultural marginality, and its principle of inclusiveness is equally applicable to what is intercultural. If relativistic, it could not condemn, as it does, marginalization or hegemonic practices because such condemnation assumes a transcultural perspective. This chapter seeks a beginning for a common ethical theory faithful to the particularities of specific cultures through an African-Western dialogue leading to a common understanding of rights. It argues for a theory taking advantage of the best insights of both traditions. Accordingly, it revisits the debate about relativism, and this preliminary groundwork coupled with the positive suggestions of the chapter's last section justifies the title.

Theoretically, cultural relativism precludes adjudicating differences cross-culturally and constitutes a form of moral isolationism. Ethical similarities are no more than accidental occurrences and not revelatory of cross-cultural applicability. They do not justify an objective, universal rule, or principle legitimately binding both because all moral rules are only validated for, and within, each separate cultural group. Thus, relativism argues that appeals to supposed similarities do not affect the debate because relativism's position does not demand a denial of similarities (any more than absolutism does regarding differences). Because relativism can claim similarities are coincidental, it continues to maintain that justification of all values, similar or not, must be intracultural. As an aside, one might note that if found similarities do not argue for transcultural values, comparably found differences should not be used to argue their denial. Still, from a relativist viewpoint, existent similarities provide no justification for epistemological or valuational obligations for those external to the justifying culture, nor do they permit argumentation for, or importation of, values across cultures because these cannot be justified within the context of the imported culture. In this regard, relativism denies a transcultural methodology. If valuational similarities exist, it is not because a culturally independent argument can be found that justifies them *for both* cultures, but because *each* culture internally justifies what empirically *happens* to be similar. Now this position is appealing because it supports cultural autonomy and opposes cultural hegemony, making it politically, methodologically, and critically attractive. But such an appeal is not relative regarding the correctness and value of what it proposes or the purpose for which it is used. Relativism holds that values are only applicable and justifiable within, and not independently of, culture. *In principle,* no ethical principle is transcultural, a principle itself transcultural. On this point, and on the values relativism implicitly argues are limited to each culture, the appeal to relativism is not relative.

Politically, the appeal to relativism protects ethical differences against the hegemonic dogmatism of the powerful. Methodologically, it prevents reducing variability to an authoritatively common, yet alien, standard that would adjudicate competing claims. Critically, it argues that value criteria are culturally generated and, therefore, culturally contextualized and limited. In this light, a cross-cultural ethics appears both undesirable and impossible, because absolutism appears with the introduction of cross-cultural values, and absolutism supposedly signals a stability linked to exclusivity, the implied justification of power to support itself, and a monolithic view of what is right and proper for human action. That such absolutisms have appeared in history is not contested. That missionary activity to the Third World assumed such an excluding absolutism is admitted. That European intrusion into an Africa viewed as a "dark continent" in need of enlightenment cannot be questioned. That the West claimed it owned and could trade territories in the lands that it "discovered" is a matter of record. In light of such historical phenomena, it might be argued that absolutism factually and necessarily limits autonomy and independence and unjustifiably denies variability because the assumed rightness of its specific code supposedly justifies the rightness of imperialistic actions carried out in its name. Thus spake the gospel of Absolutism. Thus must it always speak.

However, to argue that every form of absolutism entails hegemonic dogmatism with its accompanying negatives can be countered in a number of ways.

First, it is not true that absolutism denies the cultural differences that relativism and multiculturalism recognize. But it does argue for a standard discriminating among differences. Asserting that some ethical positions are wrong, ignorantly held, or simply evil and wicked is not inconsistent with acknowledging that the criticized differences exist. There is a difference between recognizing that differences exist and evaluating them. Nor can one deny a priori the possibility of such evaluative judgments or assume hegemony because such judgments are made.

Second, an appeal to principle is not in and of itself hegemonic. Absolutism is not an ethical totalitarianism. The latter would entail a mindless and simplistic dogmatism equitable with exemption from criticism, expressible in an unqualifiedly detailed code indifferent to circumstances and modifications, and rigidly applied. Such a "dogmatism" would constitute an intolerant absolutism. But this pejorative use of "dogma" as entailing intolerance must be distinguished from a reasonable adherence to principle. "Dogma" has a legitimate meaning, and misusing a term does not justify the critical application of such misuse. "Dogma" need not mean inflexibility. As indicating religious orthodoxy (and thereby supposedly "invariant"), "dogma" has not always ruled out doctrinal modification through a deepening of insight and understanding. That it need not mean intellectual blindness and intractability is revealed in Christianity's fruitful debate between faith and reason. The point is that not all meanings of "dogma" are pejorative. Its various meanings center around the notion of stability, but stability is not synonymous with intransigence. However, although the critical use of "dogma" connotes negativity, "tolerance" appears positive. But it is equally "dogmatic" in that the appeal to tolerance is not intended as a defense of evil or wrongdoing or as a toleration of intolerance. Tolerance is not equatable with ethical laissez-faire.

Third, absolutism is consistent with accepting differences originating within, and limited in their applicability to, a particular culture. It is not the case that absolutism requires ethical practices to be identical in every culture. The issue is not whether practices are the same or different, but whether they are ethical. To state that the use of transcultural standards necessarily means unwarranted imposition of extracultural values begs the question because the issue is not whether such a principle or rule is applied but whether it is a justifiable moral principle justifiably applied. To deny the applicability of any extracultural principle to a culture means it is impossible for such a culture to be mistaken about any of its moral positions and to exempt it from any criticism it is unable or unwilling to make. Only what the culture's ethical code sanctions or condemns is a legitimate standard, but this asserts cultural infallibility regarding its moral norms, the very "dogmatism" charged against absolutism.

Fourth, absolutism does not rule out the possibility of discourse about the positions it takes. To assert a position is true is not inherently objectionable, and where self-examination and criticism are part of ethical doctrine, adopting a position is not objectionable merely because it is adopted. Strong positions coupled with constant reexamination are a legitimate part of scientific doctrine. Absolutism can permit the same.

Fifth, a distinction needs to be made between the *theoretical* correctness of absolutism and the social and political *use* of unjustified absolutes. Criticism of applying values cross-culturally must not assume that in and of itself such an application must be hegemonic because this assumes that the only principles to which appeal may be made are the ones an agent accepts. If this is true, then any agent could claim the agent's belief justified the action, and the belief would constitute a sufficient reason for exemption from criticism. Thus, no application of any principle external to an agent's ethical perspective could ever be justified. Denying the possible use of transcultural principles regarding cultures parallels denying the applicability of transindividual principles to individuals. If any use of transcultural principles is hegemonic, would it not be legitimate to argue hegemony exists when individuals are criticized by principles to which they do not subscribe? For individuals and groups, any criticism based on an external principle would mean the principle is used hegemonically.

Sixth, there is an internal criticism that absolutism must face. Absolutism has a potential for vacuousness when it attempts to create ethical generalities flexible enough to take account of situations and circumstances. But absolutism can deal with this by qualifying the limits within such generalities function and by constantly examining the specific rules of its ethical code. Absolutism needs to ask what its general principles mean, the scope of their applicability, and the conditions under which they are conceptually defined or challenged by counterexamples. Absolutism also needs to examine the applicable range of specific ethical rules consistent with its general norms. An internal dialectic arises between absolutism's meaningful generalities and their possible ethical specification, and it must be sensitive to how its metaethical norms relate to such specifications. Hence, absolutism would be substantially weakened if it did not examine its metaethical principles in terms of definitional and instantiated specificity. Absolutism's internal weakness can be offset by an internal strength.

Seventh, the charge that absolutism is monolithic does not address the difference between a general core principle with a variety of meanings and its variable specifications. The variability of a general rule does not indicate an inherent defect denying the possibility of absolutes, but it does indicate the existence of a range of meaning within which a moral principle functions. General principles are flexible within a determined range. This is a constant matter for investigation, and no ethical principle is immune to this. The full implications of a principle are not explicit when it is first discovered or at any point in its use. Principles are never totally explicated at any point in time. Understanding of them expands, deepens, and is redefined through examination and use. This does not indicate a mere relativity to time and place, but it does indicate that a range of meanings exists within stable conceptual boundaries. That such boundaries historically and experientially expand and change does not necessitate denying their existence. Similar phenomena are found when defining art, religion, or any profound cultural reality. That such realities grow and develop in meaning does not mean they lack identity. Development does not equate with epistemic chaos.

Relativism's weakness lies in its restrictive assumption that only ethical differences count in cultural analysis, and that difference itself must be normatively interpreted so as logically to deny any form of absolutism. In spite of opposing, and even incompatible, differences, relativism cannot use the mere fact of difference as the basis for its position or make a selective appeal to facts that are only revelatory of difference because such an appeal and selectivity preclude recognition of ethical commonalities. If it does this, it is both empirically and logically flawed because it denies ethical similarities as evidential for absolutism while using differences to justify its own position. In short, if it does not permit common ethical beliefs to support a transcultural ethics, it cannot appeal to found differences to support ethical contextualism. Thus, its use of facts is arbitrarily exclusive, and its judgment of their epistemic value is logically inconsistent. Because it appeals to experience, it cannot preclude the possibility of factual value identities across a wide variety of cultures or merely appeal to selected facts to conclude ethical identities are no more than the result of happenstance. Mere appeal to facts does not decide this question either way because it is in their interpretation that the absolutism-relativism debate is centered. A perusal of the moral values that humans hold shows it is empirically untrue that no substantial body of common values exists. The crucial question is how to understand these facts.

There are three objections to relativism's failure to acknowledge any global form of human valuation. The first is conceptual in that relativism does not appreciate that the recognition of difference is not an evaluation of what is recognized as different. The second is its infidelity to its use of empiricism because it does not acknowledge and coherently explain the manifest ethical agreement existing among members of the human family. The third is found when it permits itself the type of argument it denies absolutism.

Against these failures, three approaches argue the legitimacy of possible transcultural values. The first two may be termed *extensive* in nature because they indicate a range and a commonality of types, respectively. Initially, we witness adherence to specific common values such as justice, love, trust, loyalty, truthfulness, respect, devotion to family and tradition, and secondly, specific common value types such as the aesthetic, political, ethical, religious, and social. A third consideration is *intensive* in that the specific values are held as important, significant, binding, and subject to accountability when violated. These facts indicate broad agreement at a general or metaethical level. Examples of these can be found by examining the rituals, art, literature, oral traditions, and religions of various cultures. In addition to such conceptual similarity, the possibility of intercultural dialogue exists, methodologically opening up the possibility of discovering transcultural values through mutual identification, recognition, modification, exchange, and justification. The presence of found commonality and critical and charitable dialogue, and even confrontational disagreements, attests to the feasibility of culturally independent, yet mutually recognized, values and criteria. That some forms of commonality exist can be seen when nations appeal to values they expect other nations to acknowledge and share. Even aggressor nations argue for their independence, autonomy, sovereignty, and the rightness of their actions; when appealing to these, they assume the appeal is meaningful and ought to be accepted by other nations. Here, their value, however defined or perverted, is advanced as a recognizable universal claim. In international matters, difference does not preclude action in light of common principles not limited to the perspective of agents. Otherwise saying so makes it justifiably so. One does not expect relativism to defend the view that the violated are to be tolerant of their violation because those violating defend a different moral view, or that a commitment not to be violated fails on the grounds of dogmatism. This does not mean that every ethical claim is valid or that every selected principle is defensible, but there are occasions when appeal to principle does not permit compromise, and where such a justifiable lack of compromise is found, we might understand this as some form of absolutism. The appeal to relativism is often made in support of cultural autonomy and against the legitimacy of hegemonic domination. If this is true, then this use of relativism covertly constitutes an appeal to a transcendent principle. If this is not implied, the appeal to relativism becomes so relativized as to lose value because, as a claim, it would be no better or worse than any other.

If the use of relativism is to be more than a simple citation of culturally contextualized differences, then the use of its recognition of legitimate variability is made against the background of some larger valuational framework. In a nonbeggingly way, we ask whether this framework excludes or permits some form of agreement and cooperation. How do we hold to a larger common valuational framework while doing justice to an instantiated variability while not fragmenting the whole into disconnected and separatist differences or submerging the parts in an amorphous and abstracted totality? We need some principled ethical vision compatible with specific variability. This kind of absolutism can respect the worthwhile concerns of relativism, one of which is the necessity of doing justice to people's different ethical concerns and principles. If absolutism does this explicitly, relativism does it implicitly. If absolutism did not argue for such a variegated justice, it would forfeit the validity of relativism's recognition of differences, and if relativism did not argue for justice at all, it could not avoid making difference a mere end in itself. Relativism uses difference to make the significant point that difference matters, and this is used to take a stand against marginality and exclusion, while fostering recognition of otherness. If it does not do this, its moral force is annihilated, and it simply becomes a cataloguing of variability. On the other hand, the major weakness of absolutism's appeal to some "principled ethical vision" raises the problem of vacuousness, and it must come to terms with "contextualism" if it is to avoid holding to nothing more than a vague concept of goodness as such. A move toward solving this problem is found by posing the question in the concrete. One place to test out the social-political-valuational possibility of valuational sameness and difference is through a comparison of African and Western views on ethics and rights. Their compatibility *without reduction* to some amorphous unity without difference would undercut a simplistic and dogmatic relativism on the one hand, and a hegemonic and totalitarian absolutism on the other, thereby pointing to the possibility of developing a theory of values and rights that transcends cultural boundaries while permitting differences. This is valuable because it simultaneously makes possible maintaining the rightness of cultures to be themselves, with the possibility of interacting with each other at a level of common principle. It would save cultures from cultural imprisonment.

RIGHTS

Viewed generally, we may say that rights protect the bearer against general and specific intrusions by authority or by others regarding a protected domain on the one hand, while endorsing, legitimizing, and authorizing the bearer's varying claims concerning person or property on the other. The bearer might be either an individual or a group. Viewed in this twofold way, rights are negative against power and are positive as empowering. But, rights now appear essentially divisive and adversarial. Is this the case, and does this mean rights constitute an isolating protectionism? Must a theory of rights entail a dichotomizing of interests where individual is pitted against individual or group, group against group? Does a theory of rights mandate either the egoism of the individual or group? Are rights incompatible with loyalty to others and to groups, and must groups as groups be antithetical to the individuals who compose them? That this might be the case is not denied. The question is not whether we must forgo recognizing (and criticizing) imperfect, unbalanced, or poorly realized views of rights, but whether rights as rights must entail such an opposing divisiveness. Can individuals still find themselves a part of, and be loyal to, community, and can the community still care for the independence and differences among individuals? This is the most pressing of political concerns because it addresses the tension that always exists between the private concerns of individual self-determination and freedom, and the public human need to relate to, and be part of, a larger human life. The existence of such an individual-social tension leads to three questions. The first asks whether an objective value theory is possible because the question of rights is asked in terms of international considerations. The second is whether the protection that rights affords entails a debilitating protectionism weakening either the status of the individual or group. The answers to these questions lead to the third, which asks whether the different emphases in African and Western views permit an accommodation of the two, while preserving significant differences.

A CASE FOR CROSS-CULTURAL VALUES

Multiculturalism's recognition of diversity appears to support both relativism's denial of absolute or transcultural values and its claim that values apply exclusively to their place of origin, thereby confusing origin with worth or possible applicability. On the other hand, the use of cross-cultural values seems to be hegemonic because of the values selected and seems to constitute an ethical imperialism regarding their application. Relativism's values lie in its covert appeal to such democratic ideals as independence and autonomy and in its recognition of the factual variability of values themselves. But democracy's values are not relativistic because it strongly espouses specific values and condemns others. Negatively, it is antihegemonic; positively, it supports freedom, autonomy, and self-determination, the values that multiculturalism and relativism espouse. Second, a culture's independent status does not preclude its adherence to what is unethical, nor does difference as such indicate the specific worth of what is different. Third, factual variability does not indicate the nature of what is variable. That one might build a house in a number of possible ways does not state the goodness or badness of any of these ways. It is possible none, some, or only one way is good. This illustrates the possibility of asserting legitimate variability within the context of some restraining absolute, in this case what is needed to build a house successfully. We do recognize well-built houses and poorly built ones, and we need not conclude that such determinations rest on whimsy or arbitrary declaration. The builder's claims must be substantiated. Variability as such is only an empirical factor, not a judgment of worth. The latter requires justification of what is different, and not all justifications are equally successful. Thus, it is possible to determine what constitutes a good and healthy regimen for eating that can be set out according to fairly rigorous standards. But this does not determine what anyone will or must eat on a given occasion, nor does it rule out the possibility of a variety of different, but more or less equally enticing, cuisines. What has been said thus far constitutes a propadeutic, opening the way for positive and substantive questions regarding African and Western views.

Variability of ethical beliefs notwithstanding, it is an ethical commonplace that all humans are entitled to respect, that fairness and justice are universally applicable, and that these need not be articulated without deference to distinctions and variations among those who would endorse such values. It is not the case that all the values of every culture are in disagreement with all those of every other. The arguments for ethical differences and multiculturalism's inclusiveness ultimately appeal to cross-cultural values founded in the democratic ethical ideals of freedom, autonomy, and self-determination. Difference is linked to inclusiveness and is opposed to marginality. Substantive concrete ethical differences can be consistent with commonality—even though this is not true of all differences—or where mere self-evaluation claims them to be so, or else legitimate condemnation of Nazi atrocities, apartheid in South Africa, and American racism would be impossible. If all values were of equal worth, Martin Luther King's stand against segregation would be no more right than wrong, and if values were only supportable on the basis of what is culturally accepted, King would have been an ethical and political outlaw. On such an assumption, his position would have been a minority's moral variation, but it would not have been ethically superior to racism.

Yet, difference still attracts and disturbs. Although the lack of a common moral standard inhibits critical attack on the evil actions others permit themselves, arguing for any form of absolutism still appears at odds with the prime values of freedom and autonomy because absolutism appears to mandate ethical hegemony. On the other hand, if relativism claims its position is correct, then it takes a stand and claims superiority to absolutism. But this assumes what it denies, namely an absolutist basis for its position. If not, it is no more or less true than absolutism and forgoes possible criticism of the latter. And what would happen to its criticism of absolutism's appeal to transcultural values? Relativism cannot argue absolutism is incorrect while relativizing any claim to resolving the question of ethical differences and commonality in favor of commonality because that is the question it both poses and purports to resolve. Relativism's claims are not neutral or relativistic. Its strong point is its intuitive appeal to the validity of at least some ethical differences.

An approach to the issue of handling such ethical differences is to find a way to justify their coexistence (that is, to validate the legitimacy of cultural differentiation as compatible with a defensible version of moral absolutism). In this way, some different values could be traced to, and seen to rest within, a common moral view, albeit one permitting different applications. Such a solution will not reconcile all ethical conflicts, but it would function in many instances where we find our ethical positions different, and even in conflict with each other. This is not a formula for universal reconciliation on all issues because some activities are evil and wrong, such as South African apartheid, the Holocaust, and American slavery.

The Yanomamo: Overcoming Substantial Differences

One instance revealing the compatibility of substantial differences under a general moral principle is found in the Western and Yanomamo rituals regarding the dead. Because this involves two vastly different cultures in terms of some basic categories, it provides an excellent illustration of the problem. The Yanomamo ritual involves drinking a potion containing the ashes of the dead. In the West, the common practice is to embalm and bury. From an aesthetic, ethical, religious, cultural, and gastronomical perspective, the two practices seem completely antithetical. The purpose of the Yanomamo practice is to make certain the soul of the dead finds its way to *hedu,* which is a Yanomamo paradise existing above the earth. In both Yanomamo and traditional Western practice, there is concern and respect for the dead and a sense of obligation regarding their well-being after death. Common principles function in both, but not so as to demand an identical practice or as a basis for condemning or changing either ritual. Even if we assume neither culture could adopt what the other does, it is not intuitively obvious either group is ethically bound to change or condemn the other's practice. Acculturation would make cross-cultural adoption difficult, if not impossible, but, neither ritual inherently violates the value of persons or the metaethically shared value of respect and concern for the dead. Neither ritual violates the democratic value of an individual's worth (and thus the West need not object), nor is either practice blasphemous or irreligious, nor do either impose psychological guilt. But although both rituals accord respect to the dead, it is a respect differently realized. Most importantly, the principle of respect as found (or contextualized, if one prefers that expression) in the practice of each culture can be justified *without appeal to either culture,* and this possibility of justification lifts the principle from mere immersion in the cultures utilizing it. In light of this, one may ask what principle would justify mandating that either the Yanomamo or the West forfeit their respective practices and adopt the other's, where both employ a reverential attitude regarding the dead and where neither ritual violates the memory or personhood of the deceased? Thus, whether viewed at the metaethical level of respect for the death or at the specific level of substantial different realizations actually involving common principles, both cultures exhibit a transcultural metaethical similarity supporting, and not negating, their wide differences. Criticism of either by appeal to strong negative emotions does not constitute a basis authorizing condemnation or sanction, unless we are willing to endorse emotional antipathy as a basis justifying other value judgments, such as racism, prejudice, or colonialism. That one might be emotionally hostile or prejudicial to equality of races is no justification for the hostility or the prejudice. If appeal to emotion in and of itself sufficed, it would authorize condemnation of differences in dress, food, and other social practices, or support for racism and sexism. The only criterion would be emotional response. Such an appeal intuitively reveals its inherent weakness. Thus, the example of the Yanomamo illustrates that specific and substantial differences that are apparently incompatible can ethically and socially coexist, and this instance is especially relevant even where neither side might be able to institute the practices of the other into its culture. Although such an example is encouraging, it is true that not all value differences permit this type of resolution.

Cross-Cultural Appreciation of Cultures

Another approach to justifying possible communal values exists when we attempt a cross-cultural appreciation of what different cultures have produced. This approach places cultural achievements in an imaginary locus where all coexist and interact. In his *Voices of Silence*, Andre Malraux noted photography had changed our appreciation and understanding of the visual arts by creating what he termed a "museum without walls."[2] Extending this concept to all aspects of culture, an imaginary discursive framework can be instituted regarding values, which I call *dialogic morality*. Through this technique, we can examine, compare, and appreciate a wide variety of cultural expressions. Malraux's artistic museum without walls finds its counterpart in the areas of world literature and comparative religion. Here, familiarity has not bred contempt, but respect, understanding and love, and we no longer respond through attitudes based on the exotic or the strange. The value of such an enlarged appreciation lies in the fact that our vision is no longer myopically focused on our differences, ignoring what we have in common. It is not true that peoples exist in separate and isolated confines. The history of conquest shows the cross-fertilization of cultures throughout history. The development of language shows internalization of what was originally external. Where language goes, so go ideas and attitudes, beliefs and values. Peoples of all kinds and in all ages can appreciate the Egyptian *Instruction of Ptah-Hotep,* Akan and Yoruba wisdom, the epics of Homer, the *Bhagadva-gita, Qu'ran,* Bali music, Eskimo carvings, the insights of the *Tao Teh Ching,* and the ethical wisdom of Confucius, the latter having been rightly compared to Socrates, as Socrates has been to Jesus. In the case of the arts, differences of age and place are overcome through a common love and understanding regarding a wide variety of artistic realizations, and this is neither limited to, nor dependent on, the time and place in which such art was created, nor in which individuals or groups exist. All humans can perceive the beauty of Hiroshige's prints or Rembrandt's paintings, Persian miniatures, and late medieval manuscripts. Cross-cultural influences enrich the cultures so influenced, and cross-cultural fertilization is apparent when peoples come into contact with each other whether through conquest, trade, or discovery. At the beginning of the twentieth century, Western art discovered the vitality and poetry of African art. Today, African master-pieces such as the Benin *Head of the Queen Mother* and *Pendant Mask* are given a place of honor in world art. Even African art objects far removed from any Western style move and inspire awe, and we are able to respond to their beauty. Western aesthetics itself is now returning to the view that art cannot be divorced from ceremony and cultural values, such values never having been foreign to African art. With this, we find the more communally oriented African tradition recalling us to our own Greek tradition of community ameliorating the excessive individualism that the West has developed. At the same time, Africa is finding value in an emergent individualism it is hoped will avoid the presently defective Western realization.

Multiculturalism's argument for inclusion of a variety of values assumes that what is included, ought to be—and can be—appreciated and valued. One does not argue for the legitimacy of a change if the change is impossible or indefensible. One cannot ethically demand what cannot be. One ought not ethically demand what cannot be ethical. Thus, multiculturalism's argument is possible because what is to be included can be included, and most importantly, because it warrants inclusion. The pointed question is whether what is to be included is argued for because it is good, or whether it is good merely because one wants to include it. Multiculturalism's argument implies the former because it does not seek to import into a schema of values such cultural variables as slavery, torture, or the "right" of colonialism, etc. In the appeal to multiculturalism's values, the appeal is to a limited and selected number of values.

What this reveals is a form of absolutism acknowledging the reality of some cross-cultural values and an appreciation of them, and it criticizes the view cultures are necessarily alienated and isolated ideologically, ethically, or factually. The last is the rarity rather than the norm, and even the isolation of the Yanomamo does not preclude an ethical compatibility and commonality. If all values, though culturally inaugurated and instantiated, are not culturally limited, it is possible for cultures to share values and outlooks, even when they are modified and adapted to the culture.

PROTECTIONISM AND RIGHTS

Rights are valuable because they afford a moral and legal basis for the weak, whether they are individuals or groups. Rights protect against the strong's misuse of power. Rights act as a moral force when rights are not legally recognized. As such, they permit criticism of human rights violations and provide an argument to garner world opinion. Failure in the long or short term is not a sufficient argument against appeal to rights because the appeal possesses moral validity, and in many cases it compels the violator to adjust action so as to avoid criticism. Partial success attests to the practical value of rights, but one ought not measure his or her worth even if only some humans are protected by them. The inherent worth of protecting any human life ought to be the measure of the value of rights, not some impersonal statistic. Saving one person is still supremely important.

The question is whether the protection rights afford constitutes an objectionable protectionism.[3] Are all forms of protection objectionable, and if so, why and in what way? Disvalue exists where protection disproportionately advantages some at the expense of others, where it involves unjustified use of power, where employment of power entails abuse, or, where a majority, or powerful minority, determine on their own, and unjustifiably for others, the ideal and direction of human life. Thus, to protect a racist or sexist system disadvantages those excluded and abused, and to prevent citizens from voting denies equal participation in the exercise of political power. Here, protection maintains privilege for some while disadvantaging others. But there is another and significant disadvantage where a communal spirit is destroyed or weakened because rights, devoid of responsibilities, are understood only in terms of protecting private concerns. In this case, individual life, in general, is seen as antithetical to a charitable regard for others and for the social whole, and societal duties and obligations are ignored or grudgingly carried out. In these cases, rights do constitute an indefensible protectionism. They defend only one side (that of egoistic individuality) or constitute an imbalance that does not do justice to the dual nature of humans as both social and individual. But outside the individual's justifiably circumscribed and limited societal obligations, rights protect the individual's prerogative to live in an independent and self-determining way.

Humans are individual and social beings who require moments of privacy and independence, as well as a communal framework within which to interact with, and benefit from, others. The thesis adopted is that only a rights theory that addresses both is humanly adequate.

What follows argues the correctness of this thesis. Within this framework, protection as such is not objectionable but its kind, and this raises the issue of whether protection must necessarily mean advantaging one side at the expense of another. If rights are valuable, it is because they make possible a genuinely human life, provide for the enrichment and enhancement of that life, and support the requisite autonomy and self-determination without which all humans forfeit their selfhood. Selfhood is not identifiable with individuality, although the concepts do interrelate. The focus on individuality as presently understood is divisive: individuality as individualism. At its extreme, individualism is a practical solipsism. But individuality defined in terms of the value and autonomy of the person is identical with the integrity of each self. To value individuality is to value every individual self. Now, if society possesses worth, it is not because it is valuable for its own sake. To make society an end in itself is to subordinate individual value to the social organization individuals create. The social whole is valuable because it is the framework within which individuals exist and because it serves the needs of individuals. Societies undergo changes, as individuals do, but they are formed because individual humans are social, need each other, and must contend with the imperfections of others. But above all, humans form social wholes not merely for the protection they afford, but because when they live with other humans, the potential for human achievement and growth is expanded. Societies exist for the enhancement of the humanness of human beings. Societies are not ends in themselves. They exist so humans may be fully persons and may be fulfilled as persons. Because of the duality of human nature, the hermit is an anomaly; the social human individual is the norm.

Given this, and the fact that societies and individuals do not act in exemplary and moral ways and legal systems do not create perfect or just laws, it is reasonable to regard human rights as necessary to sustain individuals and communities. Communities can appeal to rights to protect themselves against more powerful communities, as individuals can against groups and other individuals. Protection becomes objectionable when it is used in a way that is inequitable and unfair. But in itself it need not entail an objectionable protectionism. The distinction between the two is maintained when we correctly define the meaning of being an individual as the free self in contradistinction to that of solipsistic individuality.

The assertion that rights are essentially protectionistic, and inherently objectionable, is based on the assumption that the protection rights provide entails social division. Such a view fails to appreciate that in the individual-social relationship there is a need for mutual restraint on individuals and the social whole. If individuals can be wayward, authority can be corrupt. If individuals follow their own vision of the good life, this does not mean its exercise cannot deny the same to others. If individuals need to be autonomous or separate, this should not be unmindful of the fact that others may have to assume some or all of the responsibilities of those exercising such independence. Individual exercise of freedom cannot become license negating the freedom of others. On the other hand, if the whole protects itself, it can do this at the expense of individual lives. If policies advantage the many, this does preclude their endangering or abusing the few. If the generalities found in policies cover the widest range of applicability, this does not prevent their imperfections from excluding those whom the policy does not address. In this regard, rights are adjustments made to offset the imperfections of individual actions and of social generalities.

Protection does not equate with protectionism, and the protection rights afford must itself be weighed in terms of the moral good that ethical positions and legal systems seek to enforce. It is difficult to grant the greatest protection to both the social whole and each individual so that societal oppression and individualistic anarchy are never de facto possible or de jure condoned. But the answer is not to annul rights because of correctable defects.

AN AFRICAN-WESTERN VIEW OF RIGHTS

With this in mind, we now present some reflections leading toward a possible African-Western view of rights. We ask whether the distinct emphases of these two traditions preclude some commonality in outlook that will simultaneously preserve the distinctive character of both cultures.

We have already seen rights may be defined in terms of individuals or groups so that power does not oppress individuals or groups, and so that other groups within a community, or the world at large, do not endanger the social fabric.

Since the end of WW II, the concept of rights has come to the forefront of international legal concern. Given what took place during that war, the United Nations incorporated rights language into its Charter as protection for nations and individuals. Including individuals under the protection of international law extended its range in a bold, new way. At the war's end, African nations developed a consciousness of their own traditions, and in action, if not in explicit language, asserted their right to independence. International law was now expanded to protect the rights of colonies and various peoples to independence and self-determination. The latter right is definitionally troublesome because territorial divisions made in Europe and Africa by a variety of powerful factions render some claims ambiguous and uncertain. But it is the awareness of this right that has changed the postwar political landscape and that occasions some of the most pressing of contemporary problems. The problem for Africa lies in giving to the rights of individuals the value it accords the rights of peoples. What peoples constitute a given nation? What is the fate of individuals when powerful political factions seek to maintain or come to power? The plight of the refugee makes concern for the well-being of ordinary individual humans a pressing matter because it is the individual who is without food, a home, medical and educational needs, and who hopes for an end to pain and suffering. Within the Western view, there is a paradox regarding individual rights because their proliferation jeopardizes both rights themselves and the social fabric by trivializing the former and undermining the latter. Thus, a dialogue between Africa and the West must involve recognition of where each is at this moment in history.

In 1945, the existent divisions and territorial boundaries in Africa, along with their proposed justifications, continued to be maintained legally, though with a growing cultural and moral demand not to do so. The legal and moral status of colonies was called into question. Such an appeal rested

on cultural and moral reasons outside the status of "legality." The justification for this is found in the argument that although a nation may be
deprived of recognized autonomy and independence, this does not constitute forfeiture of its claims to either. Whether these will eventually be recognized is a matter of history. That the claim is made constitutes an ethical
and cultural demand. This does not deny the possibility of a legal defense,
but it shows that where the latter is missing or debatable, a strong moral
rights argument may nevertheless exist. Because of this, appeal to rights
becomes more pressing even though the multiple appeals by individuals and
groups to extension of possible rights might seem to trivialize the appeal.
That not every claim to a right justifies its existence is no argument that
new justifications cannot be found, or that traditions must persist because
they are traditional. At the same time, the proliferation of rights can be contained if appeal is initially limited to basic principles. Internationally, this
involves appeal to existent and newly argued international law, generally
utilized moral principles, and an assessment of recent history. In cases
where outside nations have drawn new boundaries, one can compare what
native divisions existed before such partitions. The former Yugoslavia is a
case in point. Its national "unity" was the result of decisions made at the
end of WW I. The unity was created and imposed, not on the basis of some
national justification, but because it was politically expedient. In Africa,
colonialism's territorial divisions impacted that continent in extreme ways.
With little understanding of the native populations and traditions, the continent was divided arbitrarily, from an African perspective, although justifiably from a European one. The result was Africa's peoples were denied the
basic right of self-identification and autonomy. Criticism founded in human
rights provides an argument against whatever legalities Europe might cite
to justify its actions. The fact that time passed before the argument was
seriously taken does not invalidate it. The African continent is no longer
territorially defined as it was at the end of WW II, and we no longer refer
to such national designations as the Belgian Congo. There is a startling difference between an African map of 1945 and 2000. What is African, one
hopes, is now rightly African, or, at least within African determination.

But does this affect the question of commonality between an African and
a Western theory of rights, and if so, how?

In *The Open Sore of a Continent,* Wole Soyinka graphically describes the
horrors of the present Nigerian military dictatorship.[4] Soyinka is pro-
foundly humane and centers his argument around the plight of individuals.
It is not merely the nation that occupies his attention because such a restriction would soften any response to the pain of an abstract many and would
dull sympathy for the real agonies of pained individuals. Humanity never
suffers. Individuals do. Soyinka avoids insensitivity to individual pain
because his concern for the nation does not neglect concern for the individual; he sees the individual as within, and as a member of, the nation. This

demonstrates that concern for the nation does not have to be at the expense of the individual, any more than the autonomy of individuals necessitates a denial of the nation. The human being is an individual existing within a social context and is, therefore, a social individual. In the light of this, rights provide a basis to criticize violations of individuals, from whatever source. Although the traditional African view of rights looks to the group rather than the individual, the changes that have taken place in Africa point toward a new understanding of rights, which includes concern for the individual. In contrast, the West has persisted in its excessive concern for individuality as individualism, causing deep rifts in the relationship of individual to individual and to society as a whole. This is seen in the increasing litigious nature of American society and in the increasing disintegration of the bonds among government, business, and one's fellow citizens. Thus, the question of how to integrate a legitimate concern for individual rights with an appreciation of communal rights is a pressing American problem. An American appreciation of the African tradition would place the problem in a new setting.

Each tradition can look to the values best exemplified in the other. This does not mean that new emphases must be subversive of either culture. What is needed is to ask how one might inaugurate a dialogue between them to inaugurate new perspective on rights.

Conceptually, rights involve both a subjective and objective moment. The subjective moment is that aspect of rights that addresses the one who enjoys rights—the bearer of rights. From this perspective, the bearer enjoys the benefits of rights by limiting whatever would intrude on what the right protects. The subject may be either an individual or a group. Benefit is contrasted with obligations on the part of those who must recognize the authority of rights to place limits. A problem arises when this is defined in ways that destroy relationships between the bearer of rights and those who are obligated to respect the rights. Where a tradition emphasizes community, the individual appears to stand against the group, and the group against the individual. Where a tradition emphasizes the individual, the group appears as alienating and opposed to the freedom and autonomy of the individual. Understanding rights in this confrontational way gives primacy to either individual or group regarding the other, justifying that a relationship has negative consequences for cooperation between the two. In Western liberal thought, the individual is accorded priority, and the group is valued in terms of its ability to sustain and permit individual development. In the Third World, the community is accorded priority, and individuals live lives in terms of the framework and values of the group. But the notion of emphasis can be understood as a means of situationally prioritizing, a tilting toward the individual or the community. Such a prioritizing is not fixed and not hierarchically oppressive. Context and tradition would point to a rationale indicative of what is needed for a specific people at some moment in their development. It would indicate what the particular moment in time requires because it exists under specific historical conditions. This does not argue mere expediency, but for the necessity of reasonable decisions made in light of defensible principles. If the community denigrates individuality, then an emphasis on individual rights would act as a counterbalance. If individuality threatens to weaken or destroy the social bond, then emphasizing the rights of community would redress this excess. How this is to be realized in specific cases is a community responsibility exercised in light of the nature of the imbalance, the severity of the evil to be redressed, the moral standing of the means chosen, and the morality of its ideal goal. A theory of rights would specify general principles and guidelines. The value of a body of rights at the level of a political-cultural code supplements and corrects a defective constitution or functions in its absence. But its specific realization can, and must, be left to the democratic decisions of each group. This does not mean that what emerges is necessary justifiable. What is created is always subject to moral examination that raises the question of diverse ethical codes within a defensible metaethics. The present point merely indicates specificity is to be determined in terms of legitimate group autonomy. The language of the American Constitution's Bill of Rights shows that it is not possible to create formulations of specific rights to cover every contingency without requisite interpretation, nor to make an exhaustive list. Such a list would be too long and imply completeness precluding future possibilities. Ethics, like politics, is not static; it is capable of growth. History reveals an ethical development about the nature of the person, condemnation of slavery, torture, and "racial" and gender discrimination. What theory can do is offer general principles. The social order is governed by law, but the body of laws is limited in its capacity to determine rights, has sometimes failed to protect rights, and has created "rights" that are unethical privileges or justifications for some. In the United States, Jim Crow laws are an example of the latter. This means the notion of legal rights cannot afford a complete protection to individuals or citizens or nations. But even assuming the morality of existent legal rights such as codification would be too complex, and if made too specific, problematic regarding individual needs and in constant need of emendation. The extension, criticism, and guarantee of legal rights will always need the complementary support of moral and human rights, but more importantly, the vigilance of moral justification. This points to the general limitation of law itself and its need for a coexistent morality. The complex relationship of individual and group must be constantly and consistently addressed. Through such an approach, a more balanced and refined concept of rights can be developed in which neither individual nor group is given the kind of priority that would necessitate a moral, social, or legal domination of one over the other. The prolegomena to such a theory could be found in a dialogue between African and Western views of rights so as to see how the relationship between individual and social whole might be developed. What themes might such a prolegomena consider?

Five Prolegomic Themes

The first theme would be that of priority itself. Replacing the hierarchical power relationship of superiority-inferiority and authority-subordination, prioritization would result from an assessment of how interrelated necessities function optimally in concrete situations. Multiple requirements often require strategies of choice. Such strategies might require either/or decisions, or decisions in which some ranking takes place (for example, in terms of structure, procedure, or goal). Whether correctly or incorrectly, the decision to postpone the question of slavery to guarantee ratification of the U.S. Constitution is an example of the first. An example of the second joined to the third is found in Martin Luther King's decision to bring about civil rights through nonviolence. Here, morality was given priority over political necessity. In this way, prioritization became comparative, and what was not prioritized was not rejected or denied. Thus, King's emphasis on the morality of his strategies did not indicate any weakness regarding his commitment to the goal of civil rights. The status of what is given priority is understood relationally in terms of other elements so that all factors are examined in terms of their operative contextual roles. Prioritizing is justifiable as a needed form of situational reevaluation, acting as support for what is functionally required and as a constraint on legitimate importance, where this is imbalanced or taken to excess.

Applying this view to the relationship between individual and group reveals its value. Emphasizing the group, values encompass cohesiveness supporting wholeness, providing direction to its members in terms of vision and goal, and most importantly, constituting the group's identity. Emphasizing individuality gives value to difference, autonomy, freedom, the worth of individual experimentation in ways of living and thinking. Here, openness is valued in terms of a freedom and independence, seemingly leading to societal anarchy. But the balance of individual and group values is precarious and is not permanent. In the language of art, such a classicism constantly tilts toward an academic formalism or an overly emotive romanticism. Prioritizing counteracts excess where the focus on either individual or group is extreme or denies the value of one in order to preserve the other. Prioritizing can redress such an imbalance and permit an assessment of how to relate the two so as to maintain the worth of both. Prioritizing addresses overall worth as realized in specific social contexts. Because it is functionally defined, it is not a static ideal, but one constantly tested by lived realities. In this model, the issues do not involve an antagonism between individual and group, and the variety of relations between the two need not be mandated in terms of a detailed code of binding international laws or moral imperatives so specified as to rule out differentiation and emendation. What is needed is a relationship of generality and specificity to permit individual cultures the possibility of creating the details of that relationship.

This requires some generally agreed upon principles, as well as some subordinate ones leading to specification. These principles can be found in the common ethical stances that do exist among cultures utilizing the technique of dialogic morality. It is not the case that diversity necessitates antithetical difference, or that legitimate differences militate against any more generalized commonality. The commitment to values is a commitment to what is generally true, and true for the most part, but which must also recognize and permit ethical latitude. This does not mean the collapse of values into an extreme and permissive relativism, but an understanding of what is involved in creating a value system. Ethics is not like mathematics. It examines values, not formulae, and the values examined are those of interacting humans existing in a changing and multiple world, one that humans change and diversify and in that diverse humans are themselves changed. In such a world, historical rigidity is generally out of place. But although this sounds dangerously like an ethical contextualism devoid of transhistorical principles, it is an attempt to address nonreductively the perplexing problem of continuity and change. This demands considering the dialectical complexity that ethical thinking involves, the difficulty of making moral judgments in light of principles instantiated into a changing and complex world, and the existence of legitimately different moral judgments of moral individuals. Finally, it is the attempt to recognize that this complexity generates a tension between the defense of human dignity at the level of principle and to acknowledge the various ways in which that dignity is manifested.

A second theme raises the question of why priority as emphasis must be understood as denigrating what is not prioritized. In the comparison of what is given priority to what is not, the nonprioritized value can still remain valuable. This takes place in those cases where it possesses inherent value, or where it instrumentally complements directly or indirectly what is taken as primary. Thus, the prioritized value is emphasized in light of a deemphasized, but not negated, value. Applied to the individual-community question, the focus on community can still be consistent with a commitment to the value of the individual because individuals constitute the community. The reality of a community is based on the integrated reality of the individuals who constitute it. On this reading, emphasis on group values is a universal assurance of the value of each individual life within the community as worthy of such universal protection. It is not a valuing of community for its own sake. Prioritizing as a way of emphasizing is a way of stressing what is important. Prioritizational justification lies in the attempt to correct an existing imbalance, to indicate the worth of what is prioritized by highlighting, recalling, or introducing a needed value, or to gain a moral insight that nonemphasis would miss. A comparative and relational view indicates that valuing in more complex ways is consistent with the various and changing possibilities of being human. Thus, priority as emphasis is not priority as hierarchically hegemonic. This is a point implicit in Soyinka's position.

A third theme addresses how individual and community are defined relationally, and this appears as the central question. How the African tradition will ultimately define the place of the individual in society is directionally different from how the West will accommodate its strong emphasis on the individual to a more communal outlook. The specifics cannot be mandated for either tradition. This is a matter for the moral, social, and political development by the parties involved. No theory can provide this for at least two reasons: It is not possible, in advance, to take into account the myriad of particulars only the choices made in the face of the future will reveal, and secondly, such an attempt would be tyrannical. What theory can do is provide suggestions, possibilities, conceptual models and explore the consequences of these in variable contexts. Thus, a theory of rights is a complex conditional in which general principles are examined, defined, defended, and tested and in which the consequences following from them are examined in moral experiments. Creating cases in which principles function under stringent conditions shows the latitude or limitation of a principle, its possible integration into—or its opposition to— other principles, and its standing within moral theory as a whole. For the African-Western dialogue appeal to the history of each with its triumphs and failures, its achievements and tensions provide a factual and experimental basis to test the possibilities of ideas. An initial step would be to outline what questions need to be asked in the light of past realities and theoretical possibilities. Thus, the West would have to ask how the concept of individuality, which has developed to the point of a disintegrating isolationism, can be rethought. In this, it may look to the fact that humans are social by nature, use a language they have not invented, and are protective of, and educated within, their culture so as to provide a direction toward a definition of community supporting the actual living of individual lives. Within the African perspective, one could examine how strong individuals have come to power and imposed authoritarian regimes, how individual artists have created works of beauty, how wise persons have provided a special talent benefiting the social whole, or how individual leadership has been exemplary and moral. Here, the value of autonomous individuality emerges in both good and bad forms. Each tradition has within itself instances and examples of what makes individuality and the social whole valuable and worthwhile, or negative and destructive. This is because all humans are both individual and social, and as such, transcend the boundaries of time, place, culture, and race. The dialogue between Africa and the West can begin with the self-reflection of each.

A fourth theme concerns what happens when the emphasis on either individual or group effects a loss rather than a gain. There will be either a loss of community through societal dissolution brought about by individuality interpreted individualistically or the submersion of the individual in an oppressive collectivism. If we look at the West and the Third World, we see two different strains. Yet, if both individuality and community are values, then a view of rights that gives primacy to either at the expense of the other lacks what a relational view of them demands. The emphasis on individuality attests to the value of the person. But the notion of personhood is not identical with an unqualified notion of individuality. Although individuality does not rule out possible individualism, the personhood of the person indicates an intrinsic value in being a person and that all persons are to be valued. Raw individualism is a potential disvalue within the notion of individuality. It does not exist within the notion of person. The disvalue comes about because a person is seen in terms of egoistic individuality understood in terms of an excessive differentiation from others. Being a person is being with others, along with recognition of the personhood of others. In terms of personhood, other individuals are also persons and, as such, are worthy of respect. This means the freedom of the person is a freedom bound to, and limited by, the freedom of other persons. As such, all persons may rightfully demand respect, and in this we find a basis for the rights of all persons. Where there are persons, there are rights; where there are rights, the community must secure such rights and recognize the value of the individual-as-person existing in community, whose existence is to be preserved by community. In this light, the community does not deny the value of individuality in community, but recognizes this value because it is the value of the members who are itself. Through its communal protection of individuals, the community protects itself. The individual in turn sees the self as valued by community and can give its loyalty to such a community. Such a community argues for a defensible place for individuality and for individual dedication to community. Although the community protects, fosters, secures, and provides a basis for individual development and achievement, the individual serves, supports, protects, and is loyal to community. Such a self is a communal self, and such a community is a community of autonomous and loyal selves.

A fifth theme concerns the dangers that threaten both individuality and community. The first danger lies in a protectionistic-divisive view of rights weakening and dissolving community. The second danger lies in a denial of rights leading to repression and collectivity. A proper notion of rights does not lead to either of these. The argument is that being a bearer of rights would be meaningless without community. A community that is not a community of free and autonomous individuals is nothing more than a soulless collective. How do we understand rights if either the individual or the community is defined without relation to each other? It might seem one cannot speak about the communal status of a prisoner in solitary confinement, but this is not true—there are issues about justification, length, the conditions of such incarceration, and the fact that this is done to the prisoner by others. Thus, the rights of one in solitary confinement are not the rights of a being totally unconnected to community. The one in solitary confinement is a communal being because isolation is imposed to deny access to community, and one evaluates such confinement in terms of the loss of community. A more appropriate example might be that of a solitary astronaut stranded on an uninhabited asteroid. In this instance, the astronaut's rights seem incapable of being affirmed or denied. For what would such supposed rights be? In what context would such rights exist? What would be their nature? What would be their content? They would not be rights regarding a relationship to others because no others exist. Although such a person might have duties to self, in what meaningful sense can one say such a one has rights over self or with respect to nonexistent others? Claimed rights might be rights that are capable of being rescued, or the guarantee upon return of rights formerly possessed. But these do not exist without others who must respect such rights. The concept of rights is meaningful and functional only within a framework where there are others and were others exercise and are obligated to recognize similar rights in others, so that the appeal to rights is made within a universalization of rights. Rights are not arguable where the other is not responsible toward others who also are bearers of rights. Rights are meaningless without a corresponding notion of community.

But, this states the case at the highest level of abstraction and without all the necessary qualifications that avoid reduction of a right to a factor in a utilitarian calculus or to an absolutism in which rights become nothing more than solipsistic claims. It is for this reason that the concept of rights must be seen as correlative with the concept of individual responsibility, which entails exercising rights within a realm where others also have rights. If freedom is meaningless when taken as license (because then the freedom of others is negated), rights without responsibility entails the totalitarianism of one bearer of rights over another. In such a case, one would have rights but not the other, and for any one to be denied rights where claimed by another is to make such a bearer of rights a tyrant. Limiting rights to selected agents is a mandate for their abuse. To have rights without recognition of the rights of others reduces rights to a demand that can only be secured by force, because as the privileges of some, others would have no reason to recognize the validity of rights benefiting the few. Those with such "rights" would be lead to use force to have them recognized. The notion of rights without restraint is isomorphic with the notion of freedom without limitation. Rights become a form of tyranny.

Two ideas appear in dialectical opposition. On the one hand, the notion of rights appears as a safeguard against intrusion into individuality, and rights function as the guarantee of the autonomy and independence of the individual as individual. This is the moment of privacy, the moment in which one's self exists in and for oneself alone. Without this, the individual becomes a member of the collective, and rights are necessary to preserve this autonomous independence as founded on the value of the person as both unique and independent. On the other hand, we are not solipsistic beings, and sociability is part of what we are as humans. This is evidenced in our use of language, our functioning within culture, and our need for the education that human experience provides. Our lives are enriched by the aggregation of past successes and our knowledge and sensitivity to the consequences of human failures. In this we find human sociability. Kant expressed this human duality when he referred to our "social unsociability," indicating a dialectic pull in the opposing directions of what is private and what is public.[5] On the one hand is the deep human directedness toward self as the individual selves we are. On the other hand, an equally deep directedness exists toward communion with others who are like ourselves. This dialectical tension does not function in the same way in all individuals. Some persons are more private; some are more social. But relatively few go to either extreme. It is the argument of this chapter that neither extreme is viable for a culture. The dangers involved in this dialectic come about when a move is made to either of the extremes. Individualism leads to pure or mixed forms of isolation, hostility, or alienation. Dostoevsky portrayed this type of individuality in *Notes from the Underground*. It appears meaningless to speak of this type of individuality in terms of rights (although the Underground Man would have rights). How is this so? For the Underground Man to make a claim for rights, he would have to acknowledge his connection with others.

At the other extreme, we have the suppression of individuality in the name of the social. This would entail the demise of the individual for the sake of the collective. The notable examples here are Aldous Huxley's *Brave New World* and George Orwell's *1984*. The notion of the collective presents us with the denial of rights in its most extreme form because there is no dialectical relation between the social and the individual. Instead, there is the submersion of individuality in a nondiscriminating and reductive holism.

A third possibility emerges. It is unclear how it will ultimately be realized. But however described, negatively, it must oppose and deny any form of totalitarianism; positively, it must permit the relation of our two opposing forces. This emerges from Kant's notion of unsocial sociability in which individuality exists but is protected and fostered within the realm of community. Community is essentially different from collectivity, which argues the good of the whole through the sacrifice of the individual. This does not mean that one might not sacrifice oneself for the whole, as those do who protect a country in time of war. Neither the African nor Western traditions appear ideologically committed to collectivity at the expense of individuality. This does not preclude an imbalance between individuality and community at some point in time. What it does mean is that neither tradition has excluded the possibility of the other and that a dialogue between the two can be mutually productive. Both traditions are involved in consensus, and this differentiates the commonality that could be argued for both as different from collectivity. Collectivity's essential unity is not the result of consensus, but an imposition that does not permit rights. Issues of individuality and community raise questions of the range of freedom and control, or freedom and law. If the social good is to be maintained, the individual must be limited in some way. If the individual is to be sustained, the social good must be modified so as not to be oppressive.

It is easy to state the problem as a dialectical tugging of freedom and law or of individuality and sociability. This merely presents a formalism inviting endless specific objections. What needs to be addressed is how to indicate some concretization that is sustainable both conceptually and in the face of serious objections.

There is no glorious and free individualism as there is no unifying and supportive communitarianism. What exists is a mixture of individualism defending or abusing the sustaining of freedom, and community suppressing or supporting human solidarity and individuality. Good and evil coexist, but neither individualism at the expense of other individuals (which means no concern for community) nor commonness to sustain the whole and its parts at the expense of an individuality that follows the different drummer is ethically defensible. Community must be sustained to the straining point of suppression, and individuality must be protected to the bursting point of anarchy. Only posed in terms of these tensions does the question of the relation of the self to the whole emerge as the problem it is. It is a matter of degree. It is not that the individual will not survive with all the force of its uniqueness and autonomy. It is not that the community will not survive with all the force of its identity and unity.

Given the distinct emphases found in Africa and the West, a dialogue between these two traditions appears to be a realistic way of advancing the question.

NOTES

1. The term "similarities" will be used to indicate a broad range of values common to two or more traditions. Its meaning can range from weak to strong "identities." This chapter does not explore the difficult issue of how to define when two values are "different," as relativism would use the term, or "identical" in absolutism's usage. The sense of "similarities" best approximate "cultural transcendent values."

2. Andre Malraux, *Voices of Silence,* trans. Stuart Gilbert (New York: Doubleday & Company, Inc., 1956), p. 16.

3. The difference between protection and protectionism lies in the fact that the latter advantages some at the expense of others, or is functionally or structurally inequitable or unfair.

4. Wole Soyinka, *The Open Sore of a Continent* (New York: Oxford University Press, 1946).

5. Immanuel Kant, "Idea for a Universal History with a Cosmopolitan Purpose," *Kant's Political Writings,* ed. Hans Reiss, trans. H.B. Nisbet (Cambridge: Cambridge University Press, 1970), p. 44. Kant's point is that human nature exhibits a duality, a tendency toward privacy that threatens social cohesiveness, and a tendency toward social unity that tends to suppress individuality.

PART IV

Political Economy and the Management of Change

9

Toward Democracy and Security in Africa: What Prospects Exist for the Sustainable Development of Civil Societies?

Timothy M. Shaw and Sandra J. MacLean

> There are good reasons for thinking that the twenty-first century will be a realist century.
>
> (Dunne 1997:120)

> West Africa is becoming *the* symbol of worldwide demographic, environmental and societal stress, in which criminal anarchy emerges as the real "strategic" danger. . . . West Africa provides an appropriate introduction to the issues, often extremely unpleasant to discuss, that will soon confront our civilization.
>
> (Kaplan 1994:46)

> For all that one must retain scepticism about the intentions of major world actors, it remains true that in 1990 the world does enjoy a privileged democratic moment.
>
> (Foltz 1993:133)

At the end of the millennium, structural adjustment and changes in both Africa and the global political economy that became apparent in the 1980s became undeniable. Yet, during this period, which has been aptly if somewhat ambiguously termed the "New" World (Dis)Order (Shaw 1994c), the uncertainties regarding Africa's future have intensified. Optimism about the possibilities for renaissance through a "third wave" of democratization has been replaced in some quarters by a growing pessimism caused by the examples and possible spread of regression toward corporatism, authoritarianism, and anarchy. Within this unsettled environment (and within related discourses), civil society has gained a central position, consequently stimulating prolonged debates about the role that nonstate actors may play alongside states and companies in Africa's prospects for good governance, economic growth, and human as well as national security in the twenty-first century.

As a contribution to these debates, this chapter focuses on nongovernmental organizations (NGOs) as central actors within new and reestablished civil societies in Africa and elsewhere in the South. Much of the "first wave" of contemporary literature on the contributions of NGOs (and the civil societies that these organizations partly comprise) to the theories and practices of democratization and development posits their uncontradictory association with the institutions of liberal democracy. However, NGOs are an extremely diverse group, and the idea that they possess a simple congruity with democratic process needs to be questioned if not disputed. Therefore, although acknowledging the relevance and necessity of constitutions, multipartyism, and elections for the consolidation of democracy, this chapter is concerned to go beyond the formal processes and institutions of governance to underlying economic and social structures. Hence, it commences with an overview of Africa's political economy at the end of the twentieth century, seeking to situate the continent in the New International Division of Labor (NIDL) and of Power (NIDP) after more than a decade of externally dictated but internally digested adjustment "reforms" as well as several complex emergencies that embroiled myriad actors—both indigenous and external, formal and informal. It then proceeds to an analysis of the possibilities and constraints involved in the revitalization of African civil societies, and concludes by identifying major challenges and opportunities confronting the continent as we enter this new millennium.

AFRICA'S POLITICAL ECONOMY AND CULTURE IN THE 1990s

The political economy and political culture of Africa at the end of the twentieth century were quite different from those inherited at the end of the colonial era. Such changes are as much a function of the evolution of national and international economies and civil societies as of national policies or preferences; hence the relevance of international political economy perspectives rather than that of rational choice. Indeed, without discounting the continuing relevance of state intervention to recent events in Africa, of greater salience are structural changes, the incidence and intensify of which have increased with the new conditionalities of the present "neoliberal" period (that is, since the start of the 1980s). To some extent, the "lost decade" of structural adjustment programs (SAPs) was an extension of pre- and post-independence dependency, the negative effects of which had been initially camouflaged by postwar growth and the postindependence honeymoon. However, as the latest formulation of dependency, SAPs coincided not only with the height and then demise of the Cold War but also, unfortunately, with profound structural change and contraction in the global economy.

Initially, in the first half of the 1980s, SAPs designed by the international financial institutions (IFIs) in Washington—the World Bank (International Bank for Reconstruction and Development) and the International Monetary Fund (IMF)—were confined to "economic" policies and terms, but their range of conditionalities recently grew to include "political," ecological, and military elements, such as democratic constitutions and elections, and increased environmental and decreased strategic expenditures. In short, the early stages of SAPs created the need for subsequent revisions and extensions. To be sure, SAP agreements are often not implemented, with Western allies securing preferential treatment until the end of the Cold War. However, in an era of neoliberal hegemony, some SAP agreements are implemented as aspects of contemporary policies, often following informal as well as formal direct or indirect negotiation.

The negative effects of SAPs on "vulnerable" groups, such as the very poor, are now widely recognized. Much less acknowledged are their equally negative implications for middle and even upper classes. The declining quality and availability as well as escalating costs of basic welfare—education, health, and infrastructure like electricity, housing, and water—have hit the working class, the unemployed, and the underemployed severely and incrementally since the early 1980s. But the middle classes have also been affected negatively albeit belatedly as (1) real incomes have declined precipitously, especially in terms of foreign exchange, and (2) costs of goods and services have escalated as inflation and user fees have risen. This group's decline in prosperity has profound implications for redevelopment as well as for democracy; without a strong middle class, sustainable democracy is unlikely. The assumption that SAPs would ultimately contribute to the emergence of thriving bourgeoisies throughout the continent involves a fallacy of social composition that parallels the economic fallacy that unlimited opportunity for diversification and expansion of exports exists even when most other Third World states are subject to similar SAP conditionalities.

In the initial postindependence period, most African regimes had sought to maximize their control over the hitherto colonial or settler state by interventions for indigenous power and property. These were relatively noncontroversial at that time, given the prevailing social democratic environment in a global system that favored state control, whether capitalist or socialist. Even declaring a "people's" or "communist" system was considered to be quite normal given the nature of some liberation struggles as well as of the bipolar system. In the absence of regular democratic elections, nationalist leaders were changed only by coups or by death. Thus, until the end of the

1970s, most African states were classic one-party or military regimes characterized by a relatively high degree of centralization and regulation, extending into the parastatal nexus.

Such postindependence regimes were neither developmental nor democratic. Wherever or not they could do so, they placed severe limits on the role of civil society as well as on private capital. Such concentration of power was excused as a necessary reaction to previously exclusive colonial or settler orders in a Cold War era in which large parts of the world enjoyed state communist government. Notions of democratic development or human rights were rejected as mere Western attempts to maintain economic influence and strategic balance.

At the level of the polity, the 1970s seemed to be a decade of continuity of African state control, but at the level of the economy this decade constituted the beginning of a discontinuity. Although some African countries, communities, and classes grew along with most of the world economy in the 1960s—reinforcing orthodox notions of international assistance and exchange as the means to growth if not development—the subsequent "shocks" of the 1970s wrought havoc even among the minority of "oil producers," let alone among the majority of importers. Exponential rises in the prices of both oil and money in the 1970s sowed the seeds of the debt "crisis" of the next decade and made the continent vulnerable to hegemonic neoliberal pressures.

The 1980s were marked by the appearance of two contradictory visions for post nationalist Africa: the Organization of African Unity's "orthodox" pro-state or state-centric Lagos Plan of Action (LPA) and the IBRD's International Bank for Reconstruction and Development "radical" pro-market Agenda for Action, otherwise known as the Berg Report. Despite widespread support in Africa for the former and despite initial resistance toward the latter from both inside and outside the continent, the neoliberal doctrines of both the World Bank and the IMF became the new orthodoxy throughout Africa by the second half of the 1980s, in part because the conditionalities were effective in some cases, but also because, in actuality, there was often little policy choice. Given escalating debt obligations as well as foreign exchange shortages, most regimes buckled under and began negotiations with the Paris and/or London Clubs as well as with the IFIs in Washington.

In the process, the nature of the development discourse was transformed from acceptance of state intervention in the economy to a mix of deregulation, devaluation, privatization, user pay etc. (in other words, to a diminishing role for the state) (Nyang'oro 1993). The space for non-state actors and activities expanded as it had done in the final day of colonialism when the nationalist movement successfully demanded a voice. Thus, by the start of the 1990s, African states in general, however reluctantly at first, were moving toward liberalization in both economics and politics, whether or not these were complementary or compatible. In part, this was in response to increasing northern conditionalities or interventions, which insisted on "democratic" governance as well as open economies.

The IFIs' new focus on governance in the early 1990s emphasised democratic practices, legitimacy, accountability, and civil liberties, recognizing that multiparty constitutions and elections may not be enough to sustain "new" democracies into the next century. National conventions, constitutions, and elections are crucial elements in any democratic system in the North as well as in the South, but they are only sustainable if continuously reinforced and supported by myriad non-state actors and activities (that is, the civil society). Toward the end of the 1990s, as the promises of structural adjustments—first of economies and then of governance—faded in many countries, to be replaced by the imperatives of conflict and emergency, the position of African civil societies became more prominent than ever, and the roles of NGOs in processes of peacekeeping and peacebuilding as well as democratization became more necessary and controversial.

CIVIL SOCIETY ON THE CONTEMPORARY AFRICAN CONTINENT

Civil society is usually conceived as the web of voluntary association composed of the various NGOs, human rights groups, cooperatives, unions, media, religious assemblages, professional associations, among others, through which individuals collectively and voluntarily carry out their social enterprises. As its organizations tend to exist in dynamic tension with the state, analytical treatments of civil society have tended to correspond to various definitions and theories of state. For instance, liberals have tended to see state and civil society as distinct and oppositional—the state, possessing final coercive authority, mediates among competing interest in civil society, whereas the latter, protected by the rule of law, collectively limits the power of the state. By contrast, in the Marxist tradition, the state is subordinate to civil society, which is considered to be the realm of economic relation. Meanwhile, Gramscians accept the Marxist idea of the primacy of a materialist base but place civil society in the superstructure along with the state and include ideology with economics as primary forces (Carnoy 1984:65–68).

With the recent revival of interest in civil society, these conceptual differences have not been resolved. If anything, with the latest resurrection of the concept, the intensity of the debate has intensified, and scholars strongly disagree about the nature of civil society's relationship and its point of division with the state as well as on its content (for example, whether criminal groups are or are not included; whether market relations are integral or merely affiliated; or whether churches are voluntary associations that are part of the civic realm or exist alternatively in a separate moral realm). Indeed, the discussions on civil society have become increasingly contentious, even to the point that some scholars argue that, in current usage, the idea is too imprecise, ambiguous, complex, or normative to be of significant value to scholarship (Hall 1995). The issues surrounding the "argument" (Walzer 1992), the "ambiguities and historical possibilities" (Blaney & Pasha 1993), and the various "uses and abuses" (Wood 1990) of civil society are not entirely new, but the heightened level of controversy in the contemporary debate is exacerbated by dilemmas associated with economic globalization. Not only does the latter undermine state-societal relations as they have been conventionally understood, but references to the possible existence of a "global civil society" raise questions about fundamental concepts especially because there is no corresponding sovereign and legal equivalent of the state at the global level.

Analytical interest in civil society has reemerged largely because of the latest wave of democratization, the proliferation over the past two to three decades in the numbers and activities of NGOs, and the rise and responses of various "new" social movements. It is not particularly surprising, therefore, that the current discourse surrounding the concept is contentious and somewhat arcane. Trends in theory reflect corresponding events and processes in political economy and political contestation. Therefore, as relations within civil society as well as between civil society and the state are always at least potentially competitive, it is not surprising that antagonisms would become more prevalent and apparent as a result of the profound transformations in the new post–Cold War divisions of labor and power. Hence, although it would be a mistake to romanticize civil society by raising undue expectations about its potential role in performing developmental or democratizing miracles, the *idea* of civil society needs to be taken seriously at the present time. Scholars who discount the importance of the current debate tend to ignore the significance of events and the novelty of the social processes that have brought the concept back recently into analytical focus.

These events and processes affect Africa as elsewhere, and the complexity and intensity of the civil society debate are prevalent also on that continent, although, as it is frequently observed, the traditional political culture of Africa as well as the colonial and postcolonial political structures have prevented the development of robust civil societies. However, claims that African civil society either does not exist at all or exists in some rudimentary or pre-political form (Gyimah-Boade 1996:128–29) need to be questioned. To deny the presence of civil societies in Africa ignores the highly politically and/or state-conscious actions of many associations. Some aspects of associational life of Africa may remain enmeshed to varying degrees in familial and ethnic linkage group, and interest representation often takes on personalistic and/or patrimonial forms rather than the secular, impersonal, and bureaucratic characteristics that have been associated with traditional (liberal) conceptions of civil society. However, as Osaghae (1995:194) asserts, the question is not whether civil society exists in Africa, but what the form is in which it exists. In Africa, Osaghae argues, the term "civil society" often "applies more to ethnic, cultural, hometown, women's and other kinship based organizations rather than politically active and watch-dog students, professional, civil liberties and other civic organizations," but association here as elsewhere is motivated by communal instincts as well as human needs for material gain and power maximization (that is, stimulants for the development of civil society).

To understand postindependence state-societal relations in Africa, the concept of hegemony, which distinguishes the Gramscian notion of civil society from both liberal and Marxist versions, is useful. Whereas the term refers to the leadership by dominant classes by virtue of the subordinate classes' submission—confirmed through consent rather than coercion—any hegemonic order that may have prevailed in countries in the early postindependence period was based on the unifying ideologies of nationalism and developmentalism, which were unsustainable and short-lived. Although the characteristic African one-party and one-man state attempted in this period to monopolize political, economic, and social life, it rarely achieved total, authoritarian control; weak economies do not allow for strong states. Although hegemony in the Gramscian sense may have been fleeting in at least some of the postindependence societies, the combination of authoritarianism and weakness that ensued resembled a Gramscian crisis of authority. Such a crisis resulted from the inability of the dominant class to maintain social consensus, following which control of civil society can be maintained only through coercion.

Nevertheless, while postindependence African states became increasingly adept at suppressing many of the institutions of their civil societies, some features of the latter persisted, whether cooperatives, service clubs, trade unions, professional associations. religions, or social organizations (sometimes based on ethnic solidarity). In the late 1990s in response to comparative state weakness, the range and diversity of forces in contemporary civil society expanded once again. In particular, there was a proliferation of NGOs ranging from the small-scale indigenous associations, which are the building blocks of effective local democracy, to global NGOs, which serve ideally in facilitating roles (constituting perhaps another international division of labor). Also in the 1990s, various formations from grassroots organizations and national structures to continental alliances represented a revival of civil society. In this reconstruction of societal relations, local and national, regional and global, NGOs together with the media and religious institutions had a major part to play because reconstruction depends upon pluralism as well as capitalism.

The essential feature that NGOs share with each other and with other elements of civil society is that they are nonstate institutions beyond the family or household. Otherwise, they are characterized by heterogeneity. Some of the diversity is a function of the evolution in behavioral practices

within the NGO community, although much is due as well as to changes—
in the form of both demands and opportunities—that have been presented
by new divisions of labor and power. Therefore, just as African political
economies have now to be recategorized in relation to their changing positions within the NIDL and NIDP, there is a need for a new typology of
NGOs in Africa because they vary in terms of their functional attributes
and their political character. One helpful attempt at categorization (for
NGOs generally rather than African ones specifically) was offered by Korten (1990) at the beginning of this decade, when he distinguished four "generations" of NGOs: (1) relief and welfare, (2) small-scale: self-reliant/local
development, (3) sustainable: systems development, and (4) North/South
partnership. Yet, although its comparative aspect was useful, this somewhat
linear typology fails to treat adequately the complexities involved in the
current changes in both external (global and international) contexts and
internal (national and subnational) structures. Both types of change can
lead to complications and/or contestations in relations among NGOs or
between NGOs and institutions of governance, thereby encouraging not
only the advances that Korten describes in scaling up of NGOs' development impact, but regressions as well.

Some distinctions found in other southern regions may be relevant to
Africa given their greater longevity and the impact of NGOs, as in parts of
Asia and Latin America. Drawing on other comparative analyses (such as
by Cleary 1997; Dicklitch 1998; Heyzer et al. 1995; Macdonald 1994;
Weiss, 1998; Wellard & Copestake 1993), we can suggest the following set
of overlapping categories for African NGOs, which complement Korten's
Asia-centric list of NGO generations:

1. local versus national, international, regional, and/or global;
2. specific sector or multisectoral (for example, agriculture, environment, education, gender, health, human rights, media, religion, etc.);
3. advocacy, communications, educational, welfare, and/or production oriented;
4. democratic or not in structure;
5. primarily concerned with development issues and/or projects;
6. part of broader NGO/civil society coalition or not;
7. instant or long-established NGO;
8. political orientation—conservative, mainstream, neutral, and/or progressive;
   antagonistic, cooperative, or dependent relations with governments and/or
   transnational organizations;
9. autonomous or "subcontracting" NGOs, especially in recent initiatives by international agencies in peacekeeping and peace building on the continent.

In short, NGOs are distinguished not only by their normative commitments
and functional operations but also by the nature of their relations with

other actors in both domestic and international environments. NGOs may exist in contradictory or complementary relationship with the state or, in Bratton's words, "engagement between state and society . . . may be congruent as well as conflictual" (1989:418). The state-societal relationship may even degenerate to disengagement or anarchy, although hopefully not inevitably, as Robert Kaplan's (1994) pessimistic and rather stereotypical perspective of Africa suggests.

But even if the maintenance of a democratic social order implies some measure of engagement, by most definitions NGOs are distinct from the state. Indeed, autonomy is essential for the authority and integrity of such groups; popular or civic associations that fail to retain their independence are in reality only quasi- or seminongovernmental. However, creating and maintaining distance from partisan politics, government interventions, and powerful economic interests is not easy. Government attitudes toward NGOs extend from support through toleration to suspicion and outright hostility. Frequently, governments resort to various methods to coopt, control, or repress, in which case many of the actions tend to blur the legal and/or de facto distinction between state and societal organizations (MacLean 1993). Some elements in civil society have particular difficulties in maintaining their separateness from the state. For example, those that had been part of broad nationalist movements in the 1950s and then in democratic movements in the 1980s have had to distinguish themselves from political parties, especially those formally in power or in opposition. Such has been the challenge for the civic movement in South Africa; its close alliance with the transitional Government of National Unity causes difficulties in shifting to playing the role of watchdog/conscience.

In some instances, NGOs' lack of autonomy from the state is influenced by parochial interests. Because external lending agencies now frequently fund NGOs directly, government officials in some countries have set up rival structures, awkwardly termed governmental-nongovernmental organizations (GONGOs)(Fowler 1992). The proliferation of such quasi-NGOs (QUANGOs) is frequently a response to external pressures or incentives to liberalize political economies and political cultures. Indeed, as Bebbington and Farrington (1993:202, 216) suggest, such conditions have even fostered the growth of a type of so-called NGO that they describe as "technocratic," These tend to result from the "economic displacement of middle class professionals from both public and private sectors"; any criticisms of government from them is "on the grounds of its inefficiency rather than its distributional and political biases." Bebbington and Farrington go on to suggest in this context that "Technocratic is a generous term. They might also be called opportunistic NGOs . . . [even] 'yuppie' NGOs."

This observation reflects that the NGO world has become big business, especially since the start of the 1980s and SAPs: At least 5 percent of official development assistance (ODA)—over $US2 billion annually—is now distributed by NGOs (ODI 1995; Fowler 1992). These transfers of funds are mainly through some 200+ northern NGOs, but they are increasingly also via myriad southern NGOs, hence the controversies over an equitable and sustainable division of labor among them (Kajese 1987). Many NGOs in both the North and South now depend on ODA rather than upon private or members' donations. In turn, they are becoming more professional and bureaucratic, undergoing evaluations and upgradings themselves.

There is also a tendency toward greater specialization. Especially with the advent of the growing "market" in peace-building "services" from confidence-building measures (CBMs) and "track two" diplomacy, to refugees, rehabilitation, reconstruction etc., NGOs have increasingly "diversified" their activities toward cooperation with blue-beret/helmet operations. Thus, if NGOs have become crucial in terms of sustainable development on the continent in general, they are even more so in terms of sustainable peace-building partnerships. States and militaries need NGO involvement at each stage—from CBMs through peacekeeping operations (PKOs) to postconflict reconstruction and in various initiatives from early warning to refugees and reconciliation (MacLean, Orr, & Shaw 1998). Divisions of labor among individual states, international agencies, and NGOs vary between cases and stages, but between 1989 and 1999, there are no instances where one of this trio of types of actors has been absent or excluded altogether from PKOs.

Yet, NGOs (and civil societies generally) play ambiguous roles in the peace-building nexus and in development processes, generally. Recognition of the importance of local initiatives to peacekeeping, peace building, democratization, and sustainable development has enhanced the profile of indigenous NGOs although, these organizations are usually heavily dependent upon international NGO (INGO) "partners," who, in turn, gain their visibility and resources through partnerships with official actors (McDermott 1997). NGO and INGO relations with interstate organizations and individual (donor and/or recipient) states are fraught in peace-building as well as other "developmental" sectors. Thus, Paul Nelson (1995) distinguished between "advocacy" and "program" (I)NGOs. Pre-SAP, NGOs tended to be concentrated in the former category. Subsequently, with the pressure toward "subcontracting" (Weiss 1998) under a neoliberal global regime, many NGOs were moving toward the program end of the spectrum (Hulme & Edwards 1997). The majority of these have been concerned with basic needs like education, health, and infrastructure, such as housing (to some extent, a reversion to functions defined by Korten as first and second generation).

The growing involvement of NGOs in the wide array of postconflict activities added fuel to the ongoing debate on whether NGOs serve mainly as delivery agents for more powerful states, IFIs, and/or IGOs, or whether they maintain a democratizing, developmentalist role in policy and/or political protest. Even if NGOs resist cooption or external control, any active involvement in policy debates with state and interstate agencies is complicated. On the one hand, if they focus exclusively on "microlevel" projects, then their efforts may be rendered pointless by macropolicies, such as SAPs or PKOs. On the other hand, if they deal only with macropolicy issues, then local development may be neglected, particularly in the short term. Clearly, some mix of macro- and microlevel roles, however elusive and problematic in practice, may be imperative for the sustainability of both civil society and development.

CHALLENGES FOR AFRICAN DEVELOPMENT IN THE TWENTY-FIRST CENTURY

The NIDL and NIDP have together thrown up considerable challenges for the continent that are likely to persist well into this century (Shaw 1994c):

1. *new states,* from the regions of the Baltic and Turkic states to the former Soviet Union and Yugoslavia to Eritrea and Somaliland;

2. *new factors* ranging from the resurgent interest in democracy, concern for environmental issues such as biodiversity, ozone depletion, and global warming; the emergence of gender as a political issue and force; the increase in informal sector activity, including drug trafficking and other crime; intense intrastate conflict; the growing problem of social emergencies, such as AIDS and migrations of people; to dramatic changes in production and labor practices, especially flexibility and feminization of work;

3. *new institutions* including the diversity of intergovernmental (for example, G-7, G-15, and G-24), regional (for example, African Economic Community, Asian Free Trade Agreement, North American Free Trade Agreement, Southern African Development Community, etc.) and transnational organizations (from multinational corporations, especially now from Asia, and trade unions to global religious arrangements and "ethnic" communities, such as the Inuit Circumpolar Conference);

4. *new relations,* especially globalization, regionalization, hierarchization, and differentiation between and within states, notably the rise, then crisis of the newly industrializing countries (NICs) and near NICs and the role of "middle powers" like China and India along with the continuing relative decline of the Fourth and Fifth Worlds; and

5. *new responses or perspectives* from civil society, such as alternative global conferences on the environment and women or at IFI annual meeting (that is, global mobilization by NGOs rather than by states), along with the (re)emergence of analytical or ideological formulations, which include civil society at the center of analysis and/or focus on issues of popular participation, democratic development as well as conflict, complex crises, and reconstructions.

Such changes present numerous development and foreign policy challenges, but they also offer some favorable conditions as well. Assuming the
continuing global recession and restructuring, international and national
aid agencies may not be able to maintain SAP terms much longer. Indeed,
these agencies have already proliferated conditionalities in part to disguise
their inability to meet their terms of the apparent development "contract"
involving promises for more assistance by external donors in exchange for
less intervention in economies and reduced measures of oppression by
recipient states. Regimes have had to meet a gradually extended range of
political, ecological, and strategic requirements as well as the economic
ones. Meanwhile, economic contraction and aid fatigue in the North, along
with diversion of attention to the East, mean that the South might still be
able to seize opportunities that arise out of the current conjuncture to
advance its self-reliance.

Much of the euphoria that was associated with the collapse of socialist
regimes at the turn of the decade has since dissipated. Although "a degree
of ideational convergence" may signal "the 'triumph' of neoclassical economics" on a global scale, there is evidence that neoliberal confidence has
also evaporated, symbolized by the Clinton White House's preoccupation,
first, with jobs rather than debt and, more recently, with some support for
the so-called Third Way to economic growth. In these circumstances,
encouraged by the first post–Cold War conference of the Non-Aligned
Movement (NAM) in September 1992 that focused on the Challenge to the
South (which should now include NAM's own internal democratization),
the South, including Africa, might still advance its national and collective
self-reliance, thereby ultimately advancing global as well as Third World
sustainable development.

Global change after the Cold War can no longer be the exclusive preserve
of either states or interstate organizations such as UN and IFI systems and
continental or regional institutions; it includes nonstate actors as well.
Although most institutions at all levels have been resistant to popular pressures, it is now widely recognized that sustainable development in Africa
cannot occur without widespread popular participation in official decision-
making processes. Also, pressure at the official level has changed both the
normative framework and the institutional environment in a way that
would allow an increased role for nonstate actors. In particular, partly
through the efforts at various UN conferences as well as by organizations
such as the United Nations Development Program (UNDP) and the United
Nations Research Institute for Social Development (UNRISD), the security
and development agendas are being broadened to include human as
opposed to only state-centric concerns. Indeed, the current climate of democratic goverance constitutes a unique conjuncture at which civil society
can demand attention at inter- and transnational as well as local, national,
and regional arenas.

Yet, to be sure, established agencies have not exactly brought international peace or development, and unless global institutions are changed, they will continue to advocate inappropriate policies like SAPs. Moreover, if NGOs do not insist on a direct role in international as well as national decision making, they will run the risk of being co-opted in such inappropriate projects on terms dictated by the UN, IFIs, etc., in addition to the dangers of co-optation at national and local levels. This dilemma extends also to African continental and regional organizations, from the Economic Commission for Africa and the Organization of African Unity to the Economic Community of West African States and the Southern African Development Community. How can transnational connections among civil societies as essential elements in any sustainable pattern of integration be facilitated and reinforced? The challenge posed by the continental conference organized in 1989 by the OAU in Arusha on popular participation cannot be avoided by African (and other Southern, like NAM and G-77) intergovernmental organizations.

The second chance for the South to introduce democracy may be its last. Just as novel multiracial and multiparty constitutions and elections disappeared in the 1960s, the current trend toward pluralism may also evaporate. Given the largely negative consequences of SAPs, the environment for democracy is hardly propitious, despite neoliberal rhetoric to the contrary. Declining levels of living and basic needs satisfaction along with increasing inequalities and under/unemployment do not advance democratic practice. Exponential inflation along with the disappearance of the middle class undermine prospects for sustainable development, whether brokered by NGOs or not.

If democracy proves to be unsustainable, in part because political and economic liberalization are incompatible, then a return to authoritarianism or a retreat to anarchy are possible, particularly in the more marginal Fourth or Fifth World states. Alternatively, especially in the more developed Third World political economies, forms of *corporatism* are likely to emerge. Corporatism consists of a set of structured social relations that revolves normally around a convergence of interests among capital, labor, and state. Although it may include connections with media, churches, professional organizations, and other institutions of civil society, it also excludes many groups. There are already corporatist systems in some African states such as Zimbabwe (Nyang'oro & Shaw 1989), and others may be anticipated, perhaps in a postapartheid South Africa (Shaw 1994b). As Baskin (1993:i) suggests: "There is a trend towards bargained corporatism in South Africa. . . . An institutionalised role for labour and capital in the formulation and regulation of economic policy is emerging." This conclusion is echoed from a more radical, materialist perspective by Johann Maree (1993:24) who indicates that the combination of corporate concentration and high levels of unemployment and underemployment are likely to lead to both macro- and intermediate-level corporatism, such as from the National Economic Forum (now NEDLAC) to sectoral groups and summits:

There is a remarkably strong corporatist current flowing in South Africa. The major actors—labor, capital, and the state—are so caught up in it that they are hardly aware of the fact that they have become part of the current. Not all such possible scenarios—from democratization at global as well as local levels, through national corporatism and authoritarianism to anarchy—are incompatible; there may be a mixture or sequence of them depending on national and international contexts and pressures. Although the cycle of state nationalization and liberalization may be repeated at the start of this new century, further *divergence* of African political economies is more likely, in part as a consequence of adjustment reforms and external market opportunities, such as authoritarianism or anarchy in the Fourth and Fifth Worlds and corporatism in the Third. Such differences would present problems throughout the continent for civil society in general, and for NGOs in particular, as they would tend to become stronger in some states and weaker in others, retarding prospects for regional and continental roles, at least at the formal, official polity levels.

Whatever the specific character of internal social forces (such as the balance between civil society and the state) as already suggested, a range of relatively "new" issues confronts contemporary African political economies. These have typically been treated previously as "foreign policy" matters, open only to exclusive elite decision making: the myth of "national security." However, in a postbipolar and postadjustment period, characterized by growing irrelevance of national borders and expanding transnational relations including "new" security threats, these increasingly become the concern of civil society as well, even if they lack sufficient technical and financial resources to resolve them all at once. Elements in local or national civil society may, of course, seek to respond to many of these contemporary issues through regional or global levels of civil society, such as international NGOs or international cooperative, media, religious, and professional organizations. Complemented by pressure applied from such external sources, revitalized civil societies may yet force hitherto recalcitrant states into new, more democratic associations.

CONCLUSION: WHAT PROSPECTS EXIST FOR SUSTAINABLE DEMOCRACY IN THE TWENTY-FIRST CENTURY?

SAP conditionalities and consequences have contradictory implications for African political economies/cultures. On the one hand, they have led to lower levels of basic human needs satisfaction as well as to greater degrees of inequality. On the other hand, positively, they have legitimized political as well as economic liberalization, creating both demand and space for nonstate actors and activities (Bratton 1990). However, the extent to which the latter promote peace as well as sustainable democratic and developmental institutions and political cultures in particular countries varies, depending upon unique sets of state, societal, and external relations (Cox 1987).

Establishing appropriate civil society alliances surely constituted the major challenge confronting civil society, and especially the developmentalist NGOs within it, at the end of the twentieth century: how to articulate and sustain local and global attention and resolution to critical issues. To be sure, it is quite unfair for the state system to deny its responsibility and capability, especially given the paucity of NGO resources. Yet although this challenge was rather unanticipated, the international context was never more favorable, given the new ideology and practice of democratic government on the continent. If the 1980s in Africa was the pessimistic decade of SAPs, hopefully the 1990s and beyond can be the more optimistic one of the NGOs and of African "renaissance."

Such a possibility needs to be noticed and encouraged by both academic and policy analysts. Even now, the tenuous rise of pluralism in the continent tends to be overlooked by scholars and practitioners alike, particularly its civil society/NGOs if not so much its multiparty/elections aspects. Although they now symbolize the diminished stature and ambition of the hitherto dominant and dominating African state, the current dynamism of pluralism as well as capitalism herald the possibility of future democratic alliances between revitalized civil societies and reformed states. However, although the present conjuncture may offer opportunities to create such alliances, the possibility for less attractive scenarios is a troubling reality: corporatism, authoritarianism, and anarchy remain as potential and, in some countries, likely alternatives to democratic multipartyism and constitutionalism.

BIBLIOGRAPHY

Adedeji, A. 1990. "The African Challenges in the 1990s: New Perspectives for Development," *Indian Journal of Social Science,* 3:255–69.

"Africa in a New World Order." 1991. *Review of African Political Economy, 50.*

African Leadership Forum. 1991. "Kampala Document." Conference on Security, Stability, Development and Cooperation in Africa. Kaupala, Uganda

All Africa Conference of Churches. 1992. "Emerging Power of Civil Society in Africa." Report of Workshop on Approaches and Skills in Advocacy for Development, Nairobi.

Anyang' Nyong'o, P. (ed.). 1987. *Popular Struggles for Democracy in Africa* (London: Zed Books for UNU).

Archibugi, D., and Held, D. (eds.). 1995. *Cosmopolitan Democracy* (Oxford: Polity Press).

Atkinson, D. (ed.). 1992. "Special Issue on the State and Civil Society," *Theoria,* 79:1104.

Baskin, J. 1993. "Corporatism: Some Obstacles Facing the South African Labour Movement." Research Report No. 30. Johannesburg: Centre for Policy Studies.

Bebbington, A., and Farrington, J. 1993. "Governments, NGOs and Agricultural Development," *Journal of Development Studies,* 29, 2:199–219.

Blaney, D. L., and Pasha, M. K. 1993. "Civil Society and Democracy in the Third World: Ambiguities and Historical Possibilities," *Studies in Comparative International Development,* 28, 1:3–24.

Bratton, M. 1989. "Beyond the State: Civil Society and Associational Life in Africa," *World Politics,* 41, 3:407–30.

————1990. "Non-Governmental Organizations in Africa: Can They Influence Public Policy?" *Development and Change,* 21, 1:87–118.

Burbridge, John (ed.). 1997. *Beyond Prince and Merchant: Citizen Participation and the Rise of Civil Society* (New York: Pact Publications).

Carnoy, Martin. 1984. *The State and Political Theory* (Princeton, New Jersey: Princeton University Press).

Chazan, N. 1992. "Africa's Democratic Challenge: Strengthening Civil Society and the State," *World Policy Journal,* 9, 2:279–307.

Clark, J. 1991 *Democratizing Development: The Role of Voluntary Organizations* (London: Earthscan).

Clayton, A. 1996. *NGOs, Civil Society, and the State: Building Democracy in Transitional Societies* (Oxford: INTRAC).

Cleary, S. 1997. "In Whose Interest? Authoritarian Social Organisation, NGO Advocacy Campaigns and the Poorest: An Exploration of Two Indonesian examples." In *The Role of NGOs under Authoritarian Political Systems* (London: Macmillan): 14–58.

Cohen, J., and Arato, A. 1992. *Civil Society and Political Theory* (Cambridge, MA: MIT Press).

Cornia, G., and Helleiner, G. (eds.). 1994. *Adjustment and Development in Africa: Is the Current Approach Satisfactory?* (London: Macmillan for UNICEF).

Cox, R. 1987. *Production, Power, and World Order: Social Forces and the Making of History* (New York: Columbia University Press).

Dicklitch, S. 1998. *The Elusive Promise of NGOs in Africa: Lessons from Uganda* (London: Macmillan).

Dunne, Timothy. (1997). "Realism." In J. Baylis and S. Smith (eds.), *The Globalization of World Politics: An Introduction to International Relations* (New York: OUP): 109–24.

Economic Commission for Africa. 1989. *African Alternative Framework to Structural Adjustment Programmes for Socio-Economic Recovery and Transformation* (Addis Ababa, Ethiopia: OAU).

———— 1990. *African Charter for Popular Participation in Development and Transformation,* Arusha, February 1990. (Addis Ababa, Ethiopia: OAU).

Edwards, M., and Hulme, D. (eds.). 1992. *Making a Difference: NGOs and Development in a Changing World* (London: Earthscan for SCF).

Fatton, R., Jr. 1990. "Liberal Democracy in Africa," *Political Science Quarterly,* 105, 3:455–73.

————. 1995. "Africa in the Age of Democratization: The Civil Limitations of Civil Society," *African Studies Review,* 38, 2:67–99.

Foltz, W. 1993. "Democracy in Post-Apartheid South Africa: External Influence." In J. Chipasula and A. Chilivumbo (eds.), *South Africa's Dilemmas in the Post-Apartheid Era* (Lanham: UP); 127–38.

Fowler, A. 1992. "Distant Obligations: Speculations on NGO Funding and the Global Market." *Review of African Political Economy,* 55:9–29.

———. 1997. *Striking a Balance: A Guide to Enhancing the Effectiveness of Non-Governmental Organisations in International Development* (London: Earthscan).

Friedman, S. 1991. "An Unlikely Utopia: State and Civil Society in South Africa," *Politikon,* 19, 1:5–19.

Gellner, Ernest. 1994. *Conditions of Liberty: Civil Society and its Rivals* (London: Hamish Hamilton).

Gibbon, P. (ed.). 1993. *Social Change and Economic Reform in Africa* (Uppsala: Scandinavian Institute of African Studies).

———. 1997. "Civil Society, Politics & Democracy in Developmentalist States." In S. Lindberg and A. Sverrisson (eds.), *Social Movements in Development: The Challenge of Globalization and Democratization* (London: Macmillan): 78–98.

Gibbon, Peter, Yusuf Bangura, and Arve Ofstad (eds.). 1992. *Authoritarianism, Democracy and Adjustment: The Politics of Economic Reform in Africa* (Uppsala: Scandinavian Institute of African Studies. Seminar Proceedings 26).

Ginifer, J. 1997. "Emergent African Peace-Keeping: Self-Help and External Assistance." In Anthony McDermott (ed.), *Humanitarian Force* (Oslo: PRIO. Report 4/97): 71–98.

Gyimah-Boade, E. 1996. "Civil Society in Africa." *Journal of Democracy,* 7, 2 (April):118–32.

Hall, J. (ed.). 1995. *Civil Society: Theory, History, Comparison* (Cambridge: Polity Press).

Harbeson, John W., Donald Rothchild, and Naomi Chazan (eds.). 1994. *Civil Society and the State in Africa* (Boulder, CO, and London: Lynne Rienner).

Heyzer, Noeleen, Riker, James V., and Quizon, Antonio B. (eds.). 1995. *Government-NGO Relations in Asia: Prospects and Challenges for People-Centered Development* (London: Macmillan for APDC).

Hyden, G., and Bratton, M. (eds.). 1992. *Governance and Politics in Africa* (Boulder, CO: Westview).

Hulme, D., and Edwards, Michael E. (eds.). 1997. *NGOs, States & Donors: Too Close for Comfort?* (London: Macmillan for SCF).

Hutchful, E. 1995–96. "The Civil Society Debate in Africa," *International Journal,* 51:54–77.

Kajese, K. 1987. "An Agenda of Future Tasks for International and Indigenous NGOs: Views from the South," *World Development,* 15:79–85 (Special issue).

Kaplan, R. D. 1994. "The Coming Anarchy," *Atlantic Monthly,* 273, 2 (February):44–75.

Korten, D. 1987. "Third Generation NGO Strategies; A Key to People-Based Development," *World Development,* 15:145–59 (Special issue).

———. 1990. *Getting to the 21st Century: Voluntary Action and the Global Agenda* (West Hartford, CT: Kumarian).

Kumar, K. 1993. "Civil Society: An Inquiry into the Usefulness of an Historical Term," *Journal of Sociology,* 44, 3:375–95.

Lewis, P. 1992. "Political Transition and the Dilemma of Civil Society in Africa," *Journal of International Affairs,* 46, 1:31–54.

Macdonald, L. 1995. *Supporting Civil Society: The Political Role of NGOs in Central America* (London: Macmillan)

MacLean, S. 1993. "North-South NGO Relations and Sustainable Development in Africa: Towards a Study of Canadian and African Partnerships," ASA Conference, Boston.

———. 1997. " 'Managing' Development in Sub-Saharan Africa in the 1990s: States, Markets and Civil Societies in Alternate Paradigms." In R. Siddiqui (ed.), *Challenges to Democracy and Development: Sub-Saharan Africa in the 1990s* (Westport, CT: Greenwood).

MacLean, S., Orr K., and Shaw, T. M. 1998. "Teaching African Peacekeeping/Making/Building." In J. Parpart and M. Bastian (eds.), *Teaching Africa: African studies in the New Millennium* (Boulder, CO: Lynne Rienner).

Maree, J. 1993. "Trade Unions and Corporatism in South Africa," *Transformation,* 21:24–54.

Mawlawi, F. 1993. "New Conflict, New Challenges: The Evolving Role for Non-Governmental Actors," *Journal of International Affairs,* 46, 2:391–413.

McDermott, A. 1997. "The UN & NGOs: Humanitarian Interventions in Future Conflicts." In *Humanitarian Force* (Oslo: PRIO. Report 4/97).

Najam, A. 1996. "NGO Accountability: A Conceptual Framework," *Development Policy Review* 14, 4,(December)339–53.

Nelson, P. 1995. *The World Bank & NGOs: Limits of Apolitical Development* (London: Macmillan).

"NGOs and Official Donors." 1995. *ODI Briefing Paper,* 4(August).

Nyang'oro, J. 1989. *The State and Capitalist Development in Africa: Declining Political Economies* (New York: Praeger).

———. 1993. *The Receding Role of the State and the Emerging Role of NGOs in African Development* (Nairobi: AACC).

Nyang'oro, J., and Shaw, T. (eds.). 1989. *Corporatism in Africa: Comparative Analysis and Practice* (Boulder, CO: Westview).

———. 1992. *Beyond Structural Adjustment in Africa: The Political Economy of Sustainable and Democratic Development* (New York: Praeger).

Onimode, B. 1992. *A Future for Africa: Beyond the Politics of Adjustment* (London: Earthscan).

Osaghae, E. 1995. "The Study of Political Transitions in Africa." *Review of African Political Economy,* 22, 64:183–97.

Rothchild, D., and Chazan, N. (eds.). 1988. *The Precarious Balance: State and Society in Africa* (Boulder, CO: Westview).

Rupesinghe, K. 1994. "Advancing Preventive Diplomacy in a Post–Cold War Era: Suggested Roles for Governments & NGOs," *RRN Network Paper,* 5 (September).

Shaw, T. M. 1989. "The Non-Aligned Movement and the New International Division of Labour." In R. Onwuka and T. Shaw (eds.), *Africa in World Politic* (London: Macmillan).

————. 1990. "Popular Participation in Non-Governmental Structures in Africa: Implications for Democratic Development," *Africa Today*, 37, 3:5–22.

————. 1993. *Reformism and Revisionism in Africa's Political Economy in the 1990s: Beyond Structural Adjustment* (London: Macmillan).

————. 1994a. "Beyond Any New World Order: The South in the 21st Century," *Third World Quarterly*, 15, 1:139–46.

————. 1994b. "South Africa: The Corporatist/Regionalist Conjuncture," *Third World Quarterly*, 15, 2:243–55.

————. 1994c. "The South in the 'New World (Dis)Order': Towards a Political Economy of Third World Foreign Policy in the 1990s," *Third World Quarterly*, 15, 1:17–30.

————. 1997. "Beyond Post-Conflict Peacebuilding: What Links to Sustainable Development & Human Security?" In Jeremy Ginifer (ed.), *Beyond the Emergency: Development within UN Peace Missions* (London: Frank Cass): 36–48.

Shaw, T. M., MacLean, S. J., and Orr, K. 1998. "Peace-building and African Organisations: Towards subcontracting or a 'new' and sustainable division of labour?" In K. van Walraven (ed.), *Early Warning and Conflict Prevention: Limitations and Possibilities* (Dordrecht: Kluwer).

Stewart, F. 1991. "Are Adjustment Policies in Africa Consistent with Long-Run Development Needs?" *Development Policy Review*, 9:413–36.

Stewart, F., Lall, S., and Wangwe, S. (eds.). 1992. *Alternative Development Strategies in Sub-Saharan Africa* (London: Macmillan).

Vakil, A. C. 1997. "Confronting the Classification Problem: Towards a Taxonomy of NGOs," *World Development* 25, 12, (December):2057–70.

Walzer, M. 1991. "The Idea of Civil Society," *Dissent*, 38, 2:293–304

————. 1992. "The Civil Society Argument." In Chantal Mouffe (ed.), *Dimensions of Radical Democracy: Pluralism, Citizenship, Community* (London: Verso).

Weiss, T. G. (ed.). 1998. *Beyond UN Subcontracting: Task-Sharing with Regional Security Arrangements & Service-Providing NGOs* (London: Macmillan).

Wellard, K., and Copestake, J. (eds.). 1993. *NGOs and the State in Africa: Rethinking Roles in Sustainable Development* (London: Routledge for ODI).

Wood, E. M. 1990. "The Uses and Abuses of Civil Society," *The Social Register 1990*, 60–84.

10

Nigeria: The Dynamics of Agricultural Policy in a Restructuring Economy

Browne Onuoha

INTRODUCTION

In one of his early propositions on development in the poor nations of the world, Baran remarked:

[W]hether there will be meat in the kitchen is never decided in the kitchen; nor is the fate of agriculture under capitalism ever decided in agriculture. Economic, social and political processes unfolding outside of agriculture, and in particular the accumulation of capital and the evolution of capitalist class . . . become, with the outset of capitalism the prime movers of the historical development. (Baran, 1978: 308)

In this citation, Baran captures the crucial role of public policy on agricultural productivity. Besides policies on agriculture, there are certain state policies in other sectors of the economy that become incentive or disincentive to agricultural development. If they are disincentive, they obviously become disruptive to agricultural development. For instance, a state policy on commercial activities or importation of goods and services may become a disincentive to agricultural productivity. The situation thus sketched appears to constitute one of the principal contradictions to agricultural policy (and productivity) in most parts of Africa including Nigeria. Also emerging from the citation of Baran is that public policy is only an index of the nature and character of the state as well as a demonstration of the values of the policy makers.

The primary concern of this chapter, therefore, is to examine critically the contribution of the public policy of structural adjustment to agricultural development in Nigeria. This is with the understanding that whatever policies on agriculture reflected the values and perceptions of the policy makers during the years of structural adjustment, and also the nature of the state they presided over. Both the nature of the state and the values of the policy makers are intermeshed, and they coalesce to illumine arguments to be raised in the development of the discourse.

The work is done in three parts. The first part discusses background to agricultural development in Nigeria. The second part analyzes the nature of Nigeria's postcolonial state and how this may have impinged on the character of agricultural policies formulated. The third part discusses the nature and state of agricultural development in Nigeria, particularly the contribution of the structural adjustment program (SAP) to the overall development of the agricultural sector. The fourth and final part evaluates agricultural policy and implementation from 1985 to present and suggests measures toward improving and sustaining agricultural development.

AGRICULTURE AND NATIONAL DEVELOPMENT

The importance of agriculture in national development, particularly those of the poor nations, is widely recognized. What does not appear to be as widely resolved is the attempt to build a framework for the modernization of agriculture, which includes agricultural technology, productivity, storage, and processing. The attempt at building a framework is said not to have proceeded appreciably beyond the cataloguing of relevant inputs, a recognition of important complementaries, and general diagnostic studies indicating which inputs are most likely to be limited under various circumstances (Elegalam, 1980: 181).

In relation to the developing economies, the major issue appears to be how best or most efficiently to produce sufficient food for the population and fibre for the industries, and at the same time develop other sectors of the economy—thus an integrated development of agriculture, industry, and people.

In order to resolve this problem, Myint (1958, 1964), Helleiner (1966), and Hill (1963, 1970) suggest that the primary motive force to the positive contribution of agriculture in the economy is the surplus-incentive mechanism. The mechanism ascribes increased agricultural productivity to the reason of profit, which the farmer makes or is likely to make at the end of the season. Consequently, the higher the price or economic benefit resulting from productivity, the higher the acreage the farmer is likely to employ. Also, if price falls or there are indications of low income from farm produce, the incentive to cultivate the land drops (Eicher and Liedholm, 1970). In effect, if the development must be sustained, agricultural development must of necessity imply sustained growth in output, increased productivity per worker and per hectare, and constantly changing technology (Elegalam, 1980: 181).

The concern of the radical views about agricultural development may be reduced into two: firstly, how to modernize agriculture, and secondly, and equally important, the question of who expropriates the profit from agricultural mechanization. The latter was not adequately addressed by the developmentalists. However, the current emphasis on the development of agriculture involves the integration of all sectors (the backward integration paradigm) into farming for the provision of food for the population and raw materials for the industry, which in turn lead to industrial expansion, which will further provide employment for the rural poor.

But what the experience in the formulation of framework for successful agricultural development appraises is the role of the state and the policy makers in the formulation of policies that are apt for the development of agriculture. In the first instance, the nature, and a major character of developing states like Nigeria, is the lack of autonomy (Gramsci, 1971; Miliband, 1969; Poulantzas, 1974, 1975, 1978). As variously analyzed, the states are dominated by the interests of the policy makers made up of technocrats, merchants, and bureaucratic—military collaborators. By their internal relations and subordination to international economic system, the policy makers in the developing states are weak, and they depend largely on the multinational corporations for their subsistence and for their ability to even maintain power (Ake, 1981).

Their policies, which included agricultural policies, might have to be formulated in a way that such policies would be acceptable in some degree to the multinational corporations on which the policy makers rely for their success. Also, the maintenance of the dependent policy makers rests largely on the fast-growing investment capital, which is characterized by economic activities directed toward services, trade, commerce, and other economic activities requiring a short gestation period before profit is made (Turner, 1978). Incidentally, agricultural productivity requires a long gestation period in order to begin to make profit. The implication is that policies of agriculture in some developing states like Nigeria most often give way to activities that yield fast turnover and that most of the time are not central to fundamental changes needed in agriculture.

Also, the so-called principle of comparative advantage in international economic relations (center-periphery relations) has created a situation where the center or their agents, including the World Bank (and their Agricultural Development Projects [ADPs], formulate agricultural policies, which benefit the developed world by means of determining cropping and providing inputs. Accordingly, a review of the literature on agriculture and agricultural policies in Nigeria since the 1970s contains a reoccurring observation (that is, the continuous fluctuation of agricultural prices because of externally oriented policies) and the dominance of commercial capitalism in international commodity prices. (Onimode, 1983; Turner 1978, Beckman, 1982).

The primary concern of this chapter, therefore, is to examine critically what has been the agricultural situation since the implementation of SAP (1986–1998) in Nigeria, why it has been so, and what could be done to improve and sustain high agricultural productivity and stable agricultural prices. This naturally leads to a review of the state of agriculture prior to 1986. Thus, the period of 1960–19985 may constitute a point of departure for a proper appraisal of the development of agriculture between 1986 and the present.

AGRICULTURE IN NIGERIAN ECONOMY

It is now almost a cliché to observe that agriculture has remained for a long time the economic mainstay of Nigeria. By 1960, it made up 63 percent of the gross domestic product (GDP) and 83 percent of the export (Nigeria: First National Development Plan 1962–68—First Plan). Between 1960 and 1966, it was still responsible for 58 percent of the GDP and 70 percent of the export products. During the same period, it provided over 80 percent of the employed labor as well as 95 percent of the total Nigerian food consumption (Nigeria: Second National Development Plan 1970–74—Second Plan). The overall economic development (manufacture, transportation, education, health, housing, etc.) of the regional governments (1960–66) depended almost entirely on agriculture (First Plan). By 1975–83, agriculture still constituted 60 percent of the employed labor (Nigeria: Third National Development Plan 1975–81—Third Plan). This was in spite of the drop in agricultural productivity of 1966–70 as a result of the Civil War and the 1970–74 drought in the northern belt of the country (Central Bank of Nigeria [CBN] Annual Report, 1975–83).

This crucial position of agriculture in national development rested immensely, among other considerations, on four interrelated roles. Firstly, the rural sector, populated by more than 70 percent of the entire national population, depended almost entirely on income from agriculture and livestock production. Secondly, a large portion of the low-income population of the urban sector depended primarily on employment generated by the secondary and tertiary activities that arise from the processing and marketing of agricultural products. Thirdly, the entire population in the urban and rural sectors depended for their sustenance on the food and fibre supply, which come mainly from the rural sector where agricultural activities take place. Fourthly, the importance of agriculture also rests on its general contribution to the country's foreign exchange earnings.

Regardless of these considerations, neglect of agriculture increased in the 1970s, perhaps because of the mineral oil boom of that period, during which time oil became the principal source of national revenue. The situation did not improve with the indigenization exercise of the 1970s. Thus, in spite of public policy instrument on agriculture, like the river basin and rural development authorities, agriculture declined. Therefore, by the 1980s, agriculture had dropped to less than 3 percent of total export earning; agricultural production not only remained insignificant to GDP and export earning, but food import bills rose astronomically, which was followed closely by high demand for food and corresponding increase of the cost of food materials. Almost every single food item and industrial fibre was imported, in spite of the government's several—though isolated and unarticulated—policies on food production. However, most of those policies were either duplications or outrightly contradictory to each other (CBN Annual Report, 1975–97).

AGRICULTURAL POLICY, 1970–85

Agricultural policies from the beginning of the 1970s to the end of the 1980s were piecemeal and haphazard. There was no coordination of one policy and another. Also, because they were isolated and duplicated, a lot of waste seemed to have occurred in their implementation. Prominent ones among these policies and programs are listed in Table 10.1.[1]

In 1973, the Nigerian Agricultural and Cooperative Bank (NACB) was established to assist agricultural development with necessary funds. Also along the need of funds, the Nigerian Bank for Commerce and Industry was established in 1973 to assist, among other industries, the agro-allied industry with fund.[2] These policies and programs were designed to achieve food sufficiency and general agricultural development, but the policies and programs added too little to reduce the decline in agricultural productivity in spite of huge financial investments, as Central Bank Annual Reports clearly show (CBN Annual Report, 1972–97; Onuoha, 1988:274–94).

Studies carried out so far indicate that the performance of agriculture from the 1970s to the 1990s were decidedly in shortfall. One of the reasons for the severe decline at the period, besides the oil boom, was the high technology that the state employed in its mechanization process (Wallace, 1980; Okello, 1982; Adams, 1983; Beckman, 1985a, 1985b). The high technology, particularly at the River Basin Authorities, ignored the labor and activities of the peasantry who constituted the largest single class of the farming population. The farming technology was so highly capitalized in a manner that it could not be replicated; the farmers themselves could not manipulate the farm machines. Also, the repair and maintenance of the technology could not be guaranteed. Agricultural activities also got bogged down by bureaucratic procedures. It became clear, therefore, that the agricultural plans and development were designed for emergent private large-scale farmers composed of retired high-ranking military officers and civil servants (Onimode, 1983; Turner and Baker, 1984; Emekekwe and Turner 1984).

Table 10.1
Agricultural Policies/Programs

1. The Nigerian Agricultural and Cooperative Bank (NACB) established in 1973; enlarged in 1978
2. Fertilizer and tractor hiring scheme; most of the two were state governments' schemes
3. The National Accelerated Food Production Program (NAFPP), 1973
4. River Basin and Rural Development Authorities, which began in 1973; its nonwater projects came under the policy of privatization and commercialization from 1989
5. World Bank Integrated Agricultural Development Projects (ADPs) in the 1970s
6. The Guarantee Minimum Price Scheme, 1975
7. The Operation Feed the Nation, 1976
8. The Land Use Decree of 1977
9. Harmonization of Marketing Board Operations, 1977
10. The Agricultural Credit Guarantee Scheme, 1978
11. The Green Revolution, 1980
12. The National Rinderpest Control Scheme, 1983
13. National Accelerated Fish Production Projects (NAFPP), 1981
14. Agricultural Bank of Nigeria, 1988
15. Strategic Grain Silos, 1986
16. Word Bank Assisted Intergrated Fisheries Program
17. Special Agricultural Program for School Leavers, 1987
18. Rural Banking Program: Peoples' Bank of Nigeria. Community Banks, 1976 to present
19. National Directorate of Employment (NDE) and Agriculture Employee Program, 1986
20. Directorate of Food, Roads and Rural Infrastructure (DFRRI). 1988
21. Better Life for Rural Women Program
22. World Bank–Assisted National Agricultural Research Project (NARP)
23. National Accelerate Industrial Crop Production and the Cotton Revolving Fund Management Committee Program 1994
24. National Agricultural Extension Research Liaison Services (NAERLS)
25. The National Agricultural Land Development Authority (NALDA), 1990
26. World Bank–Financed Second Livestock Development Program (SLDP)
27. The Agricultural Projects Monitoring and Evaluation Unit (APMEU)
28. National Agricultural Technology Support Program (NATSP)
29. National Fadama Development Program (NFDP)

The aftermath of the composition of this category of farmers was the establishment of large farms of different category of input. However, most of the farms consisted of animal husbandry and other secondary forms of activity. For instance, between 1974 (the indigenization exercise) and 1983 (the fall of the Second Republic), there were 500 such private capitalist farms, with a total capital investment of N900 million. By 1990–91, the number had increased to 1,000 farms scattered over the whole federation. Their total capital investment stood at two billion naira.[3] In addition to the capitalist farmers, indications are that more of the conglomerates in Nigeria are either in part or in full engaged in some agricultural or agro-allied ventures. Organizations like UAC, John Holt, Texaco, Agip, Dunlop, Lever Brothers, PZ, SCOA, etc., are constituting a significant part of the agricultural active group in Nigeria. It must be added, however, that their real significance lies outside actual staple foods (roots, grains) and crops activities. They are significant in the services like feeds and fertilizer products. The total contribution of both the capitalist farmers and the conglomerates to agricultural production by 1988 was put at 35 percent. By the end of 1991, it had gone to 37 percent.[4]

The general poor food situation, low agricultural productivity, and the overall depressed economy determined to a large extent the SAP of 1986, which informed the policies in agriculture and agricultural productivity from the mid-1980s to date. That policy package as it affected agriculture is our next attention.

STRUCTURAL ADJUSTMENT PROGRAM AND AGRICULTURAL POLICIES

All policies of the Babangida administration in Nigeria, including those on agriculture, were predicated on the SAP. Broadly, the structural adjustment policies in agriculture were designed:

1. To increase domestic food production with a view to improving nutritional standards and reducing and eventually eliminating external dependence on food supply;
2. To increase domestic supply of agricultural raw materials, such as cotton, cocoa, oil palm, sorghum, rubber, millet, sugar cane, and maize, to the manufacturing sector, thereby increasing local value-added and reducing dependence on imported raw materials;
3. To increase production of exportable cash crops, thereby diversifying the export base of the economy;
4. To raise rural employment and income; and
5. To achieve regional optimal crop production mix, reflecting the comparative advantage of each agroecological zone (SAP) for Nigeria:

The administration believed that with this series of policies, the objectives would be achieved.

In relation to specifics, one of the early policies on agriculture during the period was the dissolution of the agelong marketing board system. Others were the establishment of the export credit scheme, privatization of government holdings on agricultural service schemes including the non-water projects of the river basin and rural development authorities, the soya beans, and wheat accelerated projects (CBN Annual Report, 1984–86).

Also, programs of Directorate of Food, Roads and Rural Infrastructure (DFRRI), National Directorate of Employment (NDE), Peoples' Bank and Community Banks, and Better Life for Rural Women were conceived to have positive contribution to agricultural activities. There was also the establishment of Nigerian Agricultural Insurance Company, which aimed at funding agricultural guarantee scheme. The scheme provided money to compensate farmers in cases of farm disasters or unexpected crop failures. Also, a fertilizer plant at Onne in River State was opened to increase fertilizer input in agricultural activities.

Between 1986 and 1992, a vigorous attempt was made by the federal government in carrying out an enlightenment campaign about agriculture as the lifeline of the SAP. Also according to the figures, most graduates of the NDE were in agricultural or agro-allied activities (CBN Annual Report, 1987–92). Most of the state governments had well-articulated youth programs for agriculture (e.g., the Rivers State "School to Land" program). Indeed, effort was made to mobilize the youths of the country into agricultural productivity, particularly through the Agricultural Employment Program of NDE, which by 1994 granted loans to over 3,091 farmers nationwide worth about N31.0 million (CBN Annual Report, 1994: 109). By 1988, most of the programs of agriculture were already promulgated, and those yet to be implemented were incorporated into the Agricultural Policy for Nigeria, which, because of its supposed centrality to agricultural development now and hereafter, may need some review.

THE AGRICULTURAL POLICY FOR NIGERIA

This is a comprehensive blueprint and the first of its kind (APN, 1988). The policy package consists of programs of intent designed to guide the practice and activities of all aspects of agriculture in the country. Presented in five broad parts, the main thrust of the document is to harmonize agricultural productivity, marketing, distribution, and technology in Nigeria.

The introduction of the document treats as an overview the problems and prospects of agriculture in Nigeria's developing economy dating from the colonial period to the year 2000. The second chapter focuses on macropolicies, which government has formulated in the areas of pricing, trading, exchange rate, agricultural land, and how these impact agricultural productivity and distribution.

What may be considered the most vital contribution of the document to agriculture is in the areas of specific subsectors of agricultural and support services as contained in chapters 4 and 5 of the document. According to those two chapters, the pricing policy is meant to address current changes, particularly in enhancing income of farmers. This is to be achieved partly by attaining realistic exchange rates and also by constantly reviewing the exchange rate. Government will provide subsidy to inputs and also use trade policy to consolidate the growth and diversification of agricultural production. It will further attain these through strategies like trade liberalization, export promotion, tarrif regulation, and backward integration and agricultural investment promotion. It also intends to use appropriate exchange rate through the two-tier system and uniform land policy to promote agricultural activity.

As discussed in chapter 3 of the policy document, every subsector of agriculture has special attention given to it: land crop production, livestock production, fish production, forest products, and wildlife. For these subsectors to be developed, certain objectives, targets, and strategies were identified. Of particular reference was the use of the National Agricultural Land Development Authority (NALDA) agricultural agencies, ADPs, their policies, and the use of large-scale or contract farming.

The major objective of all these was specialization and self-sufficiency in food production. One significant objective of the policy is that of reattracting the youths to the farms. Animal health care and the training of the personnel handling different aspects of animal and fish protein and products would be intensified. Emphasis was also placed on the need for sufficiency in industrial raw materials.

Chapter 4 of the policy stated the policy options in encouraging support services like agricultural extension, technology, development and transfer, agricultural credit, agricultural insurance, agricultural produce marketing, agricultural commodity storage, agricultural commodity processing, agricultural research, agricultural cooperatives, land resources, pest control, agricultural mechanization, water resource development, rural infrastructure, agricultural statistics and databank, agricultural investment and management advisory services, and agricultural human resources development and training. The objectives and strategies for attaining each of these support services were exhaustively articulated.

Chapter 5, which is the last chapter, focused on the complementary but delineated role of the three tiers of government in the country: the local government, the state government, and the central government. It is the hope of the government that such streamlining will avoid overlap, duplication, or waste of resources in the implementation of the programs.

A REVIEW OF THE AGRICULTURAL POLICY OF NIGERIA

The new agricultural policy as presented is a large and comprehensive policy package. The greater part of the document was incorporated into the Vision 2010 report, which was prepared by the federal military government (under General Sani Abacha) in 1997. The Vision 2010 document was meant to serve as a blueprint for all aspects of national development policies between now and the year 2010. However, my review of the policy will focus on the original policy of 1988, which is still being implemented.

Perhaps one of the few thoughts about the policy is to examine its objectives against the concrete realities of the Nigerian economy under SAP and beyond. For instance, the main goal of the policy is the attainment of self-sustaining growth in all the subsectors of agriculture as well as the realization of the structural transformation necessary for the overall socioeconomic development of the rural areas (APN, 1988: 8).

These goals are to be attained through the following objectives: self-sufficiency in basic food commodities within periods ranging from two to five years; increasing production of agricultural raw materials; increasing production and processing of export crops in order to boost nonoil exports; modernizing agricultural production, processing, storage, and distribution; boosting rural employment by improving infrastructural facilities so as to productively absorb an increasing labor force; and improving the quality of life of rural dwellers and improved protection of agricultural land resources from drought, desert encroachment, soil erosion, and flood (APN, 1988: 8–10). These are some of the ways of raising the usual and common objective of sufficiency in food and fibre (industrial raw materials) and of providing guaranteed employment and income for citizens.

The first observation to make is that the goals and objectives are not new. They have been restated over the years. Secondly, the timing of the policy, under SAP, creates doubt about their sustenance. This is because adjustment has only succeeded so far in establishing a "money economy," that is, the growth of financial institutions, while at the same time weakening other sectors of the economy; for example, capacity utilization of manufacture is put below 42.4 percent (CBN Annual Report, 1989: 30) and did not averagely meet a target of 45 percent from that date to present (CBN Annual Report, 1990: 76–77; 1992: 85–88; 1994: 81; 1996: 100; 1997: 102; 1998: 103).

Another observation on timing under the SAP that is dependent on the privatization exercise is to ask, how does the government hope to implement or monitor policies through institutions and organizations, which came into being as a result of the policy of privatization, and which does it not control? That is to say, with privatization in the agricultural sector, how does the government ensure that its policy objectives are enforced and realized? For instance, how does the government insist that root crops and not cash crops are cultivated, or foods/cash crop and not animal husbandry? Or how does government enforce more of agricultural productivity than the marketing of agricultural produce and inputs? Also, how does government enforce an appropriate percentage of financial allocation to specific subsectors of agriculture? In other words, with privatization and the nature of financial investment in agriculture determined by those who control the financial resources, it may be difficult for the government to provide the needed directives or enforcement of the agricultural policy, especially in the area of balance between agricultural productivity and agricultural commerce.

A third issue, and one of the most common objectives raised against government in planning for the people, is often the end result of excluding the very citizens who are considered the center of the policy and program from participation. Over the years, there has been the long-standing criticism against government leaving out the real farmers in decisions affecting them. In the Nigeria situation, the criticism is still valid in the sense that the rural farmers who constitute the mainstream farming activity are left out of the agricultural policy. This has constituted disincentive to successful agricultural policy.

Accordingly, it is pertinent to inquire about the extent of the rigor by policy makers in identifying the problem of agriculture in Nigeria. The posture of the policy appears that the problems have not been adequately identified and sharply articulated. In this regard, the chapter has identified the plethora of illiterate peasant farmers whose illiteracy impedes agricultural mechanization and the lack of mechanized farming, which will incorporate the peasants and their farming methods, as major problems of agriculture. What the policy has done so far is to avoid or sidetrack the peasantry who constitute 90 percent of the farming group.

Also presently, the new policy has internationalized agriculture in Nigeria. This is another problem. The new policy will end up establishing a new form of dependency on international capital through the agribusiness; more remarkably, it will establish the control of food production by multinational organizations. The response to the illiteracy of the peasantry, therefore, is not to make them proletarian farmers employed by large-scale farmers, thereby bypassing the smallholders. This is a situation the new policy seems to be fast creating, particularly since the 1980s and more intensely since 1986 (Beckman, 1985a, 1985b; Nzimiro, 1985). We shall review in the next section how the situation is affecting agricultural productivity between 1986 and now.

In addition to budgetary allocation, agricultural activity received more funding from the various bodies, agencies, or institutions that had been established since the 1970s to speed up agricultural productivity. The first on the list is the Agricultural Credit Guarantee Scheme, which though in operation since 1973, received increased attention and funding during the period. According to the CBN Annual Report, the loans granted by the Scheme increased appreciably over the period. Loans granted stood at N102.2 million in 1987, N118.6 million in 1988, N129.3 million in 1989, but they declined to N98.5 million in 1990. By 1994, it stood at N103,186.0 million, in 1996 N225,502.5 million, and N242,038.2 million in 1997. It dropped to N215,700,000 in 1998 (CBN Annual Report, 1994:

163; 1996: 178; 1997: 189; 1998: 178). Also, commercial banks, for instance, granted various loans to the agricultural sector during the period under review to the tune of over 15 percent of the banks' total loans and advances, except in 1986 and 1987 when loans and advances to agriculture were 11.8 percent and 12.9 percent, respectively. These figures are clearly represented on Table 10.2. From 1994–1996, the loans and advances stood at 17 percent for the commercial banks, also as contained in Table 10.2.

Loans by merchant banks also increased with the years. As Table 10.2 shows, the performance of the merchant banks was impressive. Between 1988 and 1991, and 1994 and 1996, the banks exceeded the prescribed amount of loans they were to make by an average of 3.5 percent; although CBN prescribed 10 percent of their loans to go to agricultural activity from 1988 to 1990 and 13 percent from 1994 to 1996, the banks gave loans and advances to agriculture in the order of 11.5 percent in 1988, 14.3 percent in 1989, and 14.5 percent in 1990. They also exceeded the prescribed targets from 1994 to 1996. Classification by "agricultural loans" was not made in the CBN Annual Report of 1997 and 1998.

Also, Nigerian Agricultural and Cooperative Bank, specifically established for the development of agricultural productivity, expanded its loan facilities to agricultural productivity by 15 percent from 1986 to 1997 (CBN Annual Report, 1986–97). But loans and advance dropped, while investment fell, in 1998 (CBN Annual Report, 1998: 43). There were contributions by other agencies like ADPs to agricultural productivity, as will be examined in full shortly.

Ordinarily, therefore, the financial allocations to agriculture would appear as significant contributions to agricultural input and productivity. However, two observations may be made here. Firstly, when allocations to agriculture and defense are compared, what appeared significant to agriculture will clearly be seen to mean little. (See Table 10.3 for the allocations.) Also, if one were to compare the budgetary allocation to agriculture in countries like China, India, and Brazil, it becomes more convincing that what appear to be large allocations to agriculture are indeed small. Agriculture is a crucial sector for all economies. And in a situation where most countries allocate close to 20 percent of their annual budget to it, and Nigeria allocates barely 5 percent, the indication is that we may not be close to reality where all others are wrong. When compared with defense, the impression one gets is that agriculture, a productive and economically sensitive sector, is cheated out, and defense, a nonproductive sector, has taken an upper hand and claimed preeminence. Table 10.3 abundantly exposes this paradox. The neglect of agriculture became worse during the 1990s, while at the same time more money was being committed to defense.

The second observation regarding financial allocations to agriculture is the common one about what constitutes agricultural activity, which should

Table 10.2
Agricultural Loans by Financial Institutions: Percentage of Their Total Loans and Advances

		1986	1987	1988	1989	1990	1991	1992	1993	1994	1995	1996
Commercial banks	(a)	15.0	15.0	15.0	15.0	15.0	15.0	15.0	15.0	18.0	18.0	18.0
	(b)	11.8	12.9	15.3	15.3	15.9	15.7	14.9	16.4	16.9	17.0	17.0
Merchant banks	(a)	8.0	10.0	10.0	10.0	10.0	10.0	10.0	10.0	13.0	13.0	13.0
	(b)	7.2	7.7	11.5	14.3	14.5	14.7	15.1	14.7	13.7	14.0	12.0

(a) Prescribed by CBN
(b) Monthly average performance by bank

Source: CBN Annual Report: 1987: 71, 76; 1990: 42, 46; 1994: 43, 44; 1996: 50, 51.

Table 10.3
Federal Government Capital and Recurrent Expenditure on Agriculture and Defense, 1985–1997 (* million)

Agriculture	1985	1986	1987	1988	1989	1990	1991	1992	1993	1994	1995	1996	1997
Recurrent expenditure percent share of total expenditure	41.1 (0.6%)	38.1 (0.5%)	72.6 (0.5%)	83.0 (0.4%)	151.8 (0.6%)	258.7 (0.7%)	208.7 (0.5%)	464.9 (0.9%)	1,083.7 (0.8%)	1,183.3 (1.3%)	1,510.4 (1.3%)	1,818.4 (1.2%)	2421.2 (1.7%)
Capital expenditure percent share of total expenditure	305.8 (4.0%)	374.3 (9.5%)	442.9 (7.0%)	659.9 (7.9%)	1,733.2 (11.5%)	1,598.2 (6.6%)	1219.0 (4.3%)	941.3 (2.4%)	1824.4 (4.4%)	2178.8 (4.2%)	2414.2 (2.0%)	3894.8 (2.5%)	6247.4 (3.0%)
Defense													
Recurrent expenditure percent share of total expenditure	1,100.9 (15.2%)	732.8 (9.5%)	1,973.1 (12.6%)	1,340.4 (6.9%)	1,680.5 (6.5%)	1,760.5 (4.9%)	1834.0 (4.8%)	2753.8 (5.2%)	4644.7 (3.4%)	4205.1 (4.6%)	6597.6 (4.7%)	11,902.2 (9.2%)	13,342.5 (9.1%)
Capital expenditure percent share of total expenditure	284.2 (3.7%)	70.4 (0.7%)	181.9 (2.9%)	379.7 (4.6%)	538.8 (3.6%)	524.7 (2.2%)	877.7 (3.1%)	2067.9 (5.2%)	1736.9 (4.2%)	2402.6 (4.6%)	2762.8 (2.3%)	3784.0 (2.4%)	4943.4 (2.4%)

Note: Capital expenditure for agriculture includes water resources.

Source: CBN Annual Report, 1987: 83, 85; 1988: 86, 87; 1989: 88, 89; 1990: 54, 55; 1994: 56, 57; 1997: 67, 68.

attract loans and advances. The criticism of the Nigerian policy is that more of the loans to agriculture do not go into actual agricultural productivity—actual arable or pastoral farming—which includes poultry and other forms of animal husbandry. Most of the loans go to commercial agriculture, which deals with the buying and selling, including export, of agricultural produce. Indeed, as will be discussed shortly, export loans schemes, through an Export Promotion Council, were established by the administration to encourage export drive of some of the agricultural products like cocoa, rubber, ginger, etc. The Export Promotion Council operates under the frame of the Central Bank of Nigeria Financing and Rediscounting Facilities (RRF), introduced in 1987. By 1991, a total of N16.6 million was lent to banks to finance agricultural exports. By 1993, disbursement by RRF had reached a peak of N3,026.7 million. It was hoped that such export drive would attract good domestic prices for the agricultural commodities, thus encouraging the cultivation of such products domestically. But by 1994, disbursement had begun to decline (CBN Annual Report: 1994: 133; 1996: 150; 1997: 153).

Achievements were also reported in the area of crop development and technical development in the processing and preservation of foods, crops, fish, meat, etc. For instance, the National Institute for Fresh Water Fisheries Research at New Bussa, Kwara State, reported achievements in fish transplantation, propagation, and the production of hybrid fish and improved feed for fingerlings. The Lake Chad Research Institute in Maiduguri reported the development of improved variety of wheat, millet, and barley, which are available to farmers for cultivation (CBN Annual Report, 1989: 27). Also, the Federal Institute of Industrial Research, Oshodi (FIIRO) reported the development of a new technique and equipment for processing benniseed oil, and improvements were reportedly made on the techniques for processing protein-enriched garri, using soya beans (CBN Annual Report, 1989: 27). The National Center for Agricultural Mechanization reported the development of rice parboilers, solar cookers, weeding hoes, cassava lifters, and groundnut decorticators, as well as new techniques of integrated weed management and improved cassava and groundnut harvesting (CBN Annual Report, 1989: 27). There was also the establishment of a livestock development project with the assistance of loans from Nigerian Agricultural and Cooperative Bank. The project was involved in animal fattening (CBN Annual Report, 1990: 68). Similarly, a total of 651 doses of viral and bacterial vaccines were produced by the National Veterinary Research Institute between 1988 and 1992 (CBN Annual Report 1994: 84). The federal government in 1989 established the Nigerian Agricultural Insurance Cooperation with the amount of N3 million. It was to be operated by the National Insurance Corporation of Nigeria (NICON) (Federal Ministry of Information, 1986a; The Punch, 1989, 9).

Also, because of the government's belief in the crucial role of agriculture to sustained growth and development, several other agencies and institutions were established to improve agricultural productivity, as well as the life chances of the rural majority who control agricultural activity in the country. Two of these bodies stand out clearly and have been in focus all through the days of the SAP. They are in 1986 the National Directorate of Employment (NDE), and in 1987 the Directorate of Food, Roads, and Rural Infrastructure (DFRRI). Both were already identified in Table 10.1. Closely related to these two was the School to Land program, a special agricultural scheme for school leavers that began in Rivers, Lagos, and then Oyo State in 1985. The idea became adopted in all the states and was incorporated into the federal government's NDE.

The NDE and DFRRI seem to have created some measure of impact in expressing the government's concern about agricultural productivity. This is best shown by the very large financial allocations made to them for agricultural activity. For instance, at the first year, 1987, DFRRI received N700 million, in 1988, it was allocated N550 million, in 1989, it received N400 million, and in 1992, it received N250 million. By 1994, the functions of the agency had become reorganized and rationalized at the state and federal levels (CBN Annual Report, 1994: 110).

The function of DFRRI was to develop agriculture and open up the rural areas by linking up or developing the seasonal roads so that they would become all-season roads, which were greatly needed for the success of agriculture. DFRRI was also to provide water and light to the rural communities predominantly inhabited by the farmers, so that with improved environment and health conditions, there would be increased agricultural productivity. A Presidential Task Force, Final Comprehensive Inspection team was usually detailed to inspect the conditions of DFRRI projects (CBN Annual Report, 1987–91). The contribution of DFRRI to agricultural and rural development is still debatable. Perhaps the debate may have been reduced by the reorganization and rationalization of the functions of DFRRI, as mentioned earlier.

NDE has produced many young farmers and others whose activities center on agricultural and agro-allied projects. Established in 1986 (along with DFRRI), one of the four areas of NDE was to create a crop of self-employed modern farmers in the rural areas. By 1987, the project had recruited 100 participants from each state of the federation. Each participant was allocated five hectares of land and a loan of N11,500 as working capital. By the end of 1987, 45,000 new jobs had been generated by the project (CBN Annual Report, 1987: 23).[5] By 1989, the agricultural scheme of NDE employed 159,355 new hands, including 147,515 seasonal jobs. A total of 122 Agricultural Development Projects were also executed, while 11,840 people were enlisted under the agricultural program to cultivate 19,800 hectares of land during the year (CBN Annual Report,

1989: 45). By 1994, 3,091 NDE farmers, under the Agricultural Employment Program, had benefited from a loan of N31.0 million (CBN Annual Report, 1994: 109). Between 1994 and 1997, emphasis shifted to rural/industrial food processing (CBN Annual Report, 1996: 127; 1997: 129). One of the major contributions of NDE is not only the shift of emphasis to farming, but more importantly the idea of self-employment, which within so short a time is now an accepted social value among young Nigerians, particularly the higher school leavers (including university graduates). But again, the overall contribution of NDE to agricultural productivity, to be discussed shortly, is still being debated.

To the efforts of DFRRI and NDE may be added the efforts of Better Life for Rural Women and the Family Support Program (FSP), which have succeeded, at least, in mobilizing the consciousness of women toward their role in national development through the occupation where the rural women are predominant (that is, agriculture). These are organizations that were formed under questionable political-military circumstances. Their contributions are still arguable, particularly because there is a tendency among Nigerians to argue that the two agencies were more political than assisting farming and rural development. The rest of the work examines in greater details productivity in both arable and pastoral farming.

ARABLE FARMING

According to the CBN Annual Reports, 1986 to 1987, agricultural productivity was on the increase, except in 1987 when there was decline in some subsectors; the decline was attributed to "adverse weather condition and high incidence of pest and disease infestation" (CBN Annual Report, 1987: 14). The increased productivity was a result of increase in land under cultivation and in per hectare output, particularly with the land acquisition efforts of the National Agricultural Land Development Authority, established in 1990 (see Table 10.1). Although bad weather affected cultivation in 1987, there was no prolonged significant hostile weather during the greater part of the period under review (1988 to 1997).[6] Instead, there were favorable weather conditions most of the period, especially a good spread of rainfall (CBN Annual Report, 1988–97).

Also, overall capital input, such as tractors, machines, harvesters, fertilizers, insecticides, herbicites, vaccines, etc., has increased. In addition to large investments in farm inputs, storage facilities were constructed in Oyo, Niger, and Benue states to assist preservation and storage of agricultural products (CBN Annual Report, 1987–97). There were increased fund allocations, extra dedication by research institutes, particularly in the development of appropriate vaccines, more local raw materials for industry, and improved seedlings for further cultivation under the National Seeds Service Program (CBN Annual Report, 1989: 18; 1990: 68). The index of agricultural productivity by type of activity stood at 5.2 percent by 1990 to 1994, and it declined to 3.5 percent between 1994 and 1997 (CBN Annual Report, 1994: 71; 1996: 91; 1997: 92).

According to official statistics, as indicated in CBN Annual Reports 1987–97, the total increase in maize, guinea corn, millet, rice, soya beans, sorghum, cowpea, groundnuts, wheat, yam, and cassava (staples) increased by about 8 percent over the 1987–91 period. By 1987, the nation was said to have attained self-sufficiency in maize, cassava, guinea corn, millet, and yam, and self-sufficiency in rice in the future. (Federal Ministry of Information, 1987). Also, with the activities of the National Agricultural Land Development Authority compiled with the participation of private large-scale farmers—the agribusiness—more land came under cultivation (CBN Annual Report, 1994, 1996, 1997).

The increase in productivity was also recorded for cash crops, in particular cocoa, palm oil (produce), groundnuts, cotton, rubber, etc. There was also remarkable increase in the export of these commodities, particularly cocoa. With the abolition of marketing boards early at the inception of the Austerity Program and with government encouragement of export trade through the establishment of the Export Promotion Council (referred to in Table 10.1), the cultivation and export of the cash crops like cocoa and palm produce increased remarkably. According to CBN Annual Reports, the production and export of cocoa increased sharply from N7,500 to N11,000 per tonne between 1986 and 1988, about 46.7 percent increase (1988: 19), but the increases became unimpressive by 1992. However, they increased again in 1994 (CBN Annual Report, 1992: 123; 1994: 124).

An observation to be made is the exceedingly high prices of these commodities that the individual farmers earned, particularly in the cocoa belt of the country between 1986 and 1992. The large prices attracted new and expansive land for cash crop cultivation, especially cocoa, and more attention was paid to palm oil farms. In the case of palm oil, which also attracted high prices, many more palm oil commercial merchants emerged. The palm oil belts of Ondo, Edo, Delta, Cross River, Akwa Ibom, Rivers, Imo, and Abia developed new palm oil merchants whose trade and exploits are yet to be studied in full, particularly those whose base was the Calabar-Ikot Ekpene-Aba-Port Harcourt-Onitsha basin. The growth started gradually in the 1970s, and both the size of merchants and the revenue attracted increased appreciably between 1986 and 1997 (CBN Annual Report, 1985: 15; 1990: 70; 1994: 73). However, weak international demand for several of these export commodities, particularly cocoa, coupled with the general state of oversupply, ineffective management of the bufferstock, and export-quota arrangements, largely contributed to the weakening of the world prices of most agricultural export commodities (CBN Annual Report, 1990: 70; 1996: 94).

Of particular interest in the federal government's effort in agricultural productivity is the attention given to wheat production—the accelerated wheat production scheme. The existing wheat belt was mobilized with special funds (about N53 million only) given to Bauchi, Borno, Kano, Kaduna, Katsina, and Sokoto and with the injection of varieties of fast-yielding wheat seeds. The aim was to attain self-sufficiency in wheat production in about five years (Federal Ministry of Information, 1998; CBN Annual Report, 1987: 88). Several opinions and criticisms were generated by the "wheat trap," which the nation set for itself because the conditions for wheat production and all known aspects of economies of scale did not appear to support the policy (Andrae and Beckman, 1985).[7] By 1991, however, the emphasis appeared to be dead. What was left behind appeared to be increased wheat smuggling and less mass media campaign for self-sufficiency in wheat production. That notwithstanding, the federal government has not relented in its effort at achieving self-sufficiency in food crops while sustaining the self-sufficiency in areas where it has been attained.

PASTORAL FARMING

Of all aspects of animal husbandry, fish farming continued to attract increasing participation. On the other hand, poultry farming, the previous area of attraction in the 1970s and 1980s, declined steadily because of the cost of maintaining the birds. Cattle, sheep, and goats' cultivation also increased. According to CBN Annual Reports, the average growth rate of livestock and fishery products was 5 percent (CBN Annual Report, 1988–91; 1994: 73; 1996: 94; 1997: 95).

Like in arable farming, the input into animal husbandry has increased. Of particular mention is the special attention paid to the eradication of renderpest, especially cross-border infestations of the disease. Accordingly, an extensive vaccination exercise was carried out during the period. Also, pest and disease control boards have been established to ensure the continued health of the animals (see Table 10.1). As obtained in arable farming, several loan facilities were made available for the purpose of increased and sustained activity in animal husbandry. In addition, animal farmers received extra security from the animal insurance scheme established in 1986 to cover the risks to animals (Federal Ministry of Information, 1986c). The scheme has remained relatively effective since then.

The overall animal population was put at 11 million cattle, 30 million sheep and goats, 20 million commercial poultry layers, 900,000 pigs, 8 million commercial poultry broilers, and 130 million local chicken (Federal Ministry of Information, 1986b). By 1994, the number was put at over 102, 112 heads of cattle, and 676 pastoral families who were settled by the Second Livestock Development Program (SLDP), financed by the World Bank. The cultivation and production in the subsector have increased, with 1991 recording a modest average increase of 0.5 percent, and fishing alone maintaining the highest lead of 2.4 percent. By 1995, there was a 4.2 percent growth in livestock. The growth rate remained fairly steady up to 1997. However, the indications are that these figures are still far between the need of domestic consumption, as food situation continues to show. It is the food situation and other indices of successful agricultural policy that will enable us to adequately evaluate the contribution of agricultural policy under the Austerity Program to agricultural development in Nigeria, as the conclusion endeavours to demonstrate.

CONCLUSION: A CRITIQUE OF AGRICULTURAL PERFORMANCE, 1985–98

Regardless of what policies are made on agriculture, either through the SAP or the comprehensive APN, one of the most effective ways of assessing their result is to ask how adequately such policies have resolved the foods, raw materials, employment, and income needs of the entire economy. In those respects, the public policy and programs of all aspects of agriculture under the period of structural adjustment may be better evaluated in their ability to or the extent to which they were able to meet those four cardinal objectives.

Accordingly, it may be observed that because of the profound nature of structural adjustment, policies and programs in agriculture could not have been excluded from the total package of SAP. Consequently, the inflationary aspect of SAP wiped out whatever high income that might have accrued to farmers through the sale of agricultural products. The price of cocoa beans is a particular case in point. Also, what constituted food scarcity meant that although the foods were physically available, the value of the currency was too low to pay for food sufficiency for citizens, particularly in a situation of wage freeze. Furthermore, high transport cost, arising from the total SAP package, increased the cost of food and the quantity of it purchased, as well as the quantity on the table of workers and peasants.

There was also evidence of shortages of agricultural raw materials for reasons close to the same as the cost of raw materials in relation to cost of production and market price of commodities. Raw materials, most of which competed with food items, suffered the same high cost. Except the manufactured essential commodities, especially foods, demand on manufactured products fell because of low purchasing power, which in turn affected producers' ability to buy more raw materials for industry. Capacity output for manufacture generally was put at 30 percent, which partly indicated low utilization of both agricultural and other industrial raw materials.

Apart from over-production, another disincentive to agriculture was the neocolonial policy of the developed countries that insisted on fixing the prices of agricultural products, despite the adverse effect of that policy on the occupation of farmers. The negative consequences of this neocolonial policy on the farmers' income and general development in the poor nations have remained persistent debate.

Another effort that is of particular interest is the revival of certain products like rubber, which was considered abandoned from about the 1970s—the period of the mineral oil boom. It is now an attractive product both for the domestic and foreign market (CBN Annual Report, 1989—97). Palm oil, which by the 1970s and early 1980s had fallen in production and was often imported, not only became sufficient but it attracted very good market prices and export. But because of high productivity market price, it is now on the downward trend. However, a significant contribution of the adjustment program is that more firms now depend on palm oil produce (including kernel oil) for their products. More of the small-scale industries now produce soap, pomade, magarine, candles, etc., and they rely largely on domestic supply of palm oil and kernel oil for their products. In spite of the increased demand, palm oil is in large supply, and this writer's survey shows that indeed there is a downward trend in prices, particularly on supplies from Calabar-Ikot Ekpene-Aba-Port Harcourt-Onitsha (the eastern part) to the western part of Nigeria where palm oil is most consumed both by industrial and domestic users.

In the big picture, the largest problem to agriculture now is the aggregate consequence of the entire policy of structural adjustment. Although the intentions of the policies of SAP may be forthright, the short- and long-term implications for agriculture, and indeed the whole economy and polity, are adversely far from what may have been anticipated. In the first place, labor in agriculture appears to be growing through the NDE, DFRRI, and other such programs, yet the low rate of the naira eliminates profit, which results in high turnover in the agricultural labor that was recruited through institutions like NDE. Also, loans from Peoples' Bank, Community Bank, and others directed specifically to the poor are not large enough to remove the subsistence level of agriculture in which the poor who form the majority labor in agriculture find itself. This is partly because SAP has created an economy that rarely accommodates marginal participants or inputs, particularly because of the very high cost of factors of production.

However, the Federal Office of Statistics records low rural urban migration in search of wage labor (CBN Annual Report, 1988–97), but this does not show that rural labor on agriculture increased accordingly. What is shown is an increased number of youth unemployment, which is not unrelated to the degree of crime and delinquency. These have been reported as some of the social consequences of the adjustment programs.

Also to be considered is the overall development of appropriate agricultural technology, particularly as employed at the River Basin Development Authorities and other large and mechanized capitalist farms, whether privatized or publicly owned. As presently existing, the agricultural technology in these farms will subject the agricultural program under the interests of the owners of the technology. This is no new argument. It has been extensively discussed by scholars since the early 1970s when government policy on the River Basin and Rural Development Programs began (Wallace, 1980; Okello, 1982; Beckman, 1985a, 1985b; Nzimiro, 1985; Andrae and Beckman, 1985).

Furthermore, the intensity of privatization (a major instrument of SAP) of the agricultural institutions and practices indicates to an extent that policy makers do not seem to be convinced of the dangers to national sovereignty of subjecting a sensitive sector like agriculture to the hands of multinational corporation, international finance institutions, and agribusiness ventures worldwide. For instance, although the indigenization policy of the 1970s placed agriculture in the exclusive list for indigenous participation (later reduced to 80 percent in 1982 and to 40 percent in 1984), the privatization and new business (industrialization) policy of 1988 removed agriculture completely from any restriction to foreign investors (1988). What this means is that with the control of agricultural technology and Nigeria's favorable land policy, the conglomerates will soon take over the agribusiness in Nigeria to the detriment of national food security. High cost of technology, for instance, will not only reduce the ability of indigenous farmers to buy the technology or to compete in the procurement, but it will affect the cost of productivity and price of foods.

Privatization in agriculture need not connote complete disengagement of government at this level of national development. Even the privatization of water/nonwater irrigation projects of the River Basin Authorities is debatable considering the nature of subsidy agriculture given even in developed countries. In other words, the degree of privatization in agriculture should not be such that the government completely hands off activities in agriculture. Presently, agriculture is as crucial, if not more crucial, than mineral oil, Nigerian Telecommunication (NITEL), National Electric Power Authority (NEPA), and others in which government is involved with the aim of safeguarding national sovereignty and security. There is a global drive toward privatization. But in agriculture, policy makers should be careful to integrated indigenous farmers more than the overconcentration of multinational corporations in agribusiness in Nigeria.

What may be suggested as the government's role to the success of agriculture is the state's continuous encouragement and sponsoring of the indigenous control of key aspects of agriculture, especially real arable and pastoral farming. Indigenous agricultural business that will utilize improved local agricultural technology should be encouraged. At the same time, research and technology ventures should be undertaken to improve local agricultural technology, which will reduce dependence on foreign technology. The examples of Brazil, China, and India are worth developing here.

Any technology that excludes the majority of the farming population is defective for a developing country like Nigeria. The tendency now is that the growing large farms reduce the peasant farmers, who are in the majority, into wage workers. This extends the problem of the exploitation and poverty of the majority of the people.

Having observed as follows, it may be necessary to add that the problem of agricultural productivity in Nigeria lies largely on two major areas. The first one is the inability to develop a workable local technology like the Chinese and Indian approaches for the mechanization of all aspects of agricultural practice. What is needed in the Nigerian economy is a technology that will be simple to operate yet be mechanized and that could be fitted for large-scale production.

The second lies in the area of what may be referred to as the national attitude to the role of agriculture to development. This attitude fails to recognize the "historic mission" of agriculture as the point of departure for any sustainable growth and development. An example of this lack of recognition of the historic mission is that of the 10,000 registered large-scale farmers (with the manufacturer's Association of Nigeria [MAN], 98 percent are devoted to animal husbandry, fishery, poultry, feeds, and fertilizers. Only 2 percent are involved in foods/cash crop production, but foods/cash crop production holds the key to successful agricultural activity, which also is the requisite for industrial revolution. This is because foods and cash crop provide the largest input for industrial fibre and domestic food consumption, whereas in Nigeria, foods and cash crop production are still subsistent, using local, unscientific methods. Although there may be policies to change all these, a lot of them are not appropriate. The SAP of the administration under review has not significantly changed this state of agriculture.

Although serious attempts appear to have been made to improve the state of agriculture, some of the contradictions of SAP as analyzed above, as well as the neocolonial dependent economy of Nigeria, will frustrate the major objectives of agricultural policy which include food, employment and income for the population, and raw materials for industry.

NOTES

1. There are brief notes on each of these policies/programs in the Central Bank of Nigeria (CBN) annual Reports for the year of establishment, and there are continuing progress reports of their performances almost yearly.

2. See also the CBN Annual Report for the respective years of establishment and progress reports of subsequent years.

3. Up-to-date information was drawn from Manufacturers Association of Nigeria, Lagos (MAN) and the Nigerian Association of Chambers of Commerce, Industry, Mines and Agriculture, Lagos (NACCIMA).

4. Ibid.

5. The other areas of NDE are Youth Employment and Vocational Skills Development, Small Scale Industries, and special public works.

6. 1998 figures for this discourse were not available at the time of writing.

7. *Guardian* Editorial of 13/5/89, "Much Ado About Wheat," wondered why so much attention was given to wheat when there were too many other food items requiring self-sufficiency.

BIBLIOGRAPHY

Adams, W.N. (1983). *Downstream Impact of River Control, Sokoto Valley Nigeria* (Oxford: Oxford University Press).

Ake, C. (1981). *A Political Economy of Africa* (London: Longman).

Andrae, G., and Beckman, B. (1985). *The Wheat Trap* (London: Zed Books).

Baran, P. (1978). *The Political Economy of Growth* (New York: Penguin).

Beckman, B. (1982). "Whose State: State and Capitalist Development in Nigeria," *Review of African Political Economy*, 23, Jan–April.

Beckman, B. (1985a). "Bakalori: Peasant State and Capita," *Nigerian Journal of Political Science*, 4(1 & 11), 90–101.

Beckman, B. (1985b). "Public Investment and Agrarian, Transformation in Northern Nigeria." In M. Watts, ed., *State, Oil and Agriculture in Nigeria* (Berkeley: University of California Press).

Eicher, C.K., and Liedholm, C., eds. (1970). *Growth and Development of Nigerian Economy.* (Lansing: Michigan State University Press).

Elegalam, P. O. (1980). "An appraisal of Nigerian Agricultural Policy under the Military," in *The Nigerian Economy under the Military,* Proceedings of the 1980 annual conference of the Nigerian Economic Society, Ibadan, Nigerian Economic Society.

Emekekwe, E., and Turner, T. (1984). *Oil, State and the Internationalization of Class Struggle in Nigeria*: memo; Port Harcourt, Nigeria. Port-Harcourt.

Federal Ministry of Information, Lagos. (1986a). Press release no. 624.

Federal Ministry of Information, Lagos. (1986b). Press release no. 625.

Federal Ministry of Information, Lagos. (1986c). Press release no. 629.

Federal Ministry of Information, Lagos. (1987). Press release no. 2399.

Federal Ministry of Information, Lagos. (1988). Press release no. 1373.

Gramsci, A. (1971). *Selections from the Prison Notes* (London: Allen and Unwin).

Helleiner, G.K. (1966). *Peasant Agriculture, Government and Economic Growth in Nigeria* (Homewood, IL: Richard D. Irwin).

Hill, P. (1963). *The Migrant Cocoa Farmers of Southern Ghana: A Study in Rural Capitalism* (Cambridge: Cambridge University Press).

Hill, P. (1970) *Studies in Rural Capitalism in West Africa* (Cambridge, Cambridge University Press).

Miliband, R. (1969). *The State in Capitalist Society* (London: New Left Books).

Myint, H. (1958). "The Classical Theory of International Trade and the Underdeveloped Countries," *The Economic Journal*, 68, 317–37.

Myint, H. (1964). *The Economics of the Developing Countries* (London: Hutchison Press).

Nzimiro, I. (1985). *The Green Revolution in Nigeria or the Modernization of Hunger* (Oguta: Zim Pan-African Publishers).

Okello, O. (1982). "The Political Economy of Planning: The Bakolori Irrigation Project, 1974–80," in Y.B. Usman, ed., *Political Repression in Nigeria* (Kano: Bala Mohammed Memorial Committee).

Onimode, B. (1983). *Imperialism and Underdevelopment in Nigeria.* (Nigeria: Macmillan).

Onuoha, O.B. (1988). "Indigenization in Nigeria; 1972–83: Resources and Income Redistribution," unpublished Ph.D. thesis, University of Lagos, Lagos, Nigeria.

Poulantzas, N. (1973). *Political Power and Social Class* (London: New Left Books).

Poulantzas, N. (1974). *Fasism and Dictatorship* (London: New Left Books).

Poulantzas, N. (1975). *Classes in Contemporary Capitalism* (London: New Left Books).

Poulantzas, N. (1978). *The Crisis of dictatorship* (London: New Left Books).

The Punch, Lagos, 8 August, 1989.

Structural Adjustment Program for Nigeria, July 1986–June 1988 (Lagos: 1986 The Federal Government Printer).

Turner, T. (1978). "Commercial Capitalism and the 1975 Coup," in K. Panter-Brick ed., *Soldiers and Oil: The Political Transformation of Nigeria* (London: Frank Cass).

Turner, T., and Bakear, A. (1984). "Soldiers and Oil: The 1983 Coup in Nigeria," unpublished paper, Port Harcourt, University of Port Harcourt, June.

Wallace, T. (1980). "Agricultural Projects and Land in Northern Nigeria," *Review of African of African Political Economy,* 17, Jan.–Apr, 59–70.

11

Women and Sustainable Development in Africa

April A. Gordon

For many developing countries, the past three decades have not been good years. Economies have stagnated, external debt has ballooned, poverty and illiteracy have grown, while measures of health and well-being have declined. In a growing global marketplace, the gap between rich and poor widens. Even the once flourishing NICs (newly industrializing countries) find themselves facing economic (and in some cases, political) uncertainties that are reversing some of the gains in development they had made. Concentration of wealth and power in the hands of a few, class and ethnic divisions, rapid population growth, and environmental degradation are other negative features of decades of "development."

For some observers, these troubling trends are temporary or else surmountable given the recent triumph of market capitalism and the near demise of socialism in the world. The promise of global economic integration under the mantel of free trade is for a resurgence of economic growth and development that will "lift all boats."

Others have a more sobering assessment of the global situation. They question some of the major tenets of development ideology and practice by raising such unsettling questions as:

What is development?

Is development possible for most of the world's people?

Is development, based on unlimited economic growth, sustainable?

Such questions are especially salient for countries of sub-Saharan Africa—
most of which are among the poorest and least economically developed in
the world. Can Africa hope to emerge from its current economic and political decline and provide a decent life for its long-suffering people? Is sustainable development possible for a region with the highest population growth
rates in the world and mounting environmental problems? Are economic
and political liberalization the answers to the continent's woes?

Although I would not presume to offer a definitive answer to these complex questions, I will examine one variable in the equation: the role of
Africa's women in sustainable development. To do this, I will first present
recent reassessments of what development means, followed by some indicators of where Africa currently stands in its development. Next, I look at
the roles women play in development and the potential of women to
advance development if problems created by gender bias are seriously
addressed. Indeed, there is growing evidence and recognition in official documents that women must be key decision makers and participants if sustainable development in Africa is to have any hope of success.

CRITIQUING DEVELOPMENT

Critics of mainstream development thinking argue that one has only to
look at the results of fifty years of "development" in the world to conclude
that it has been a failure (e.g., Rapley, 1996). Instead of developing, most of
the world's people enjoy few of the fruits of the enormous growth in output
of goods and services produced by the global economy. Looking at the most
commonly quoted measure of economic growth and development—GNP
(gross national product)—one would think that the world's people would be
enjoying much higher living standards than they are. But GNP can be a very
deceptive measure of development. A growing economy or richer economy
may also be one where the wealth is highly concentrated in the hands of an
elite few while the poor, often disproportionately women and children, are
worse off. Economic growth also reveals nothing about what is being produced. How much is the result of expanding education, health care, nutri-
tious food, decent housing, and infrastructure that benefit a majority of the
population and improve their standard of living? How much of GNP is due
to military spending or the production of goods and services that benefit the
rich but not the poor? What share of production causes major, perhaps irreversible, damage to the environment or is a response to damage to health,
property, and social welfare caused by the development process? For example, is a society more or less developed if it is providing low-paying jobs for
people to produce goods for the rich in their own country and for foreign-
ers, which allows jobholders to purchase a few consumer goods (often
foreign-made) while their health and environment suffer due to growing air
and water pollution? (See Brown et al., 1993; Jacobson, 1993.)

By focusing on growth alone, the social costs to people of development also tend to be ignored. It is simply assumed that the expansion of industrial or agricultural output, the appearance of modern cities and shops filled with goods (often imports), and the adoption of Western consumer tastes and behaviors indicate development is taking place. The underside of such development, and there are no comparative indicators for this, may be massive unemployment and impoverishment of small-scale producers due to the invasion of transnational corporations or privatization and concentration of land, urban squalor, and social problems such as homelessness, family breakdown, hunger, crime, and drug and alcohol abuse (Swantz, 1995: 210) The poor are the least likely to experience economic growth as development, because so often it is at their expense. Mexican economist Gustavo Esteva comments that, for the overwhelming majority of the population, development simply means "the progressive modernization of their poverty" and the loss of their way of life and means of subsistence as they are pushed little by little into the cash economy (Hellinger, Hellinger, and O'Regan, 1988: 14).

In recognition of these and other problems of the development economic growth paradigm, many in the development community and many governments are beginning to abandon a narrow fixation on economic growth and to adopt the concept of sustainable development, an idea popularized after the 1987 World Commission on Environment and Development (also called the Brundtland Commission). Although difficult to define and measure, sustainable development includes economic growth but includes much more. Development to be sustainable must be shared and equitable to meet the basic needs of the world's people today while protecting the environment for future generations. Sustainable development also encompasses political and social development, not just improvements in material living standards. It includes a political system that empowers local communities and maximizes citizens' participation in decision making (rather than centralizing power). Empowering women and reducing rapid population are other elements of sustainable development (cf. Rapley, 1996; UNDP, 1995: 11–14; World Bank, 1997: 1–4).

AFRICA'S DEVELOPMENT CRISIS

Sustainable development seems a remote possibility in much of Africa, where de-development is a looming threat. A commonly heard lament is that, in many African countries, people are economically worse off now than they were at independence. Most countries have experienced or currently face war, civil war, coups d'etat, and corrupt, authoritarian rule. Only a small minority of African states are stable, truly democratic governments with a flourishing multiparty system and civil society. Recent World Bank figures give some indication of the devastating failure of development on the African continent compared to other regions of the world. Sub-Saharan Africa's GNP in 1995 was $490, a decline of 1.1 percent between 1985–95. Nine of the ten poorest countries in the world are in sub-Saharan Africa. Africans are now far more dependent on aid than other developing countries; 16 percent of GNP in Africa comes from aid compared to only 1.6 percent in less developed countries as a whole. Meanwhile, Africa's debt burden has grown from $84.1 billion in 1980 to $226.5 billion in 1995 (World Bank, 1997: 214–15, 219, 221, 247).

Human welfare indicators also show the degree to which development gains at independence are being eroded. In developing countries as a whole, 39 percent of adult females and 21 percent of adult males are illiterate, compared to 54 percent and 35 percent of African women and men, respectively. An ominous trend for future development is that a smaller percentage of both boys and girls in 1995 are going to primary school than in 1980 (90 versus 78 percent of males and 68 versus 65 percent of females). Growing illiteracy is inevitable unless declining investment in education is reversed. Also discouraging is the fact that only a tiny percent of Africans in most countries have access to education beyond secondary school (in most countries only 1–2 percent) (World Bank, 1997: 226–27; UNDP, 1995:100–101). As a result of such negative trends in human capital development, the availability of trained Africans has not changed much in thirty years (Green, 1994: 205).

Also a troubling indication of decline, environmental problems such as soil erosion, desertification, deforestation, and water pollution mount as the pressures of meeting the needs of Africa's growing population and debt repayment compel countries to destroy their environment, the natural resource base on which their future depends. Lester Brown of Worldwatch Institute writes, for example, that soil erosion in Africa, precipitated by unsustainable farming practices driven by population growth, may be the fastest of any continent. Crop yields have declined as a result and will worsen if soil erosion is not stopped. Botswana, Lesotho, Madagascar, Nigeria, Rwanda, and Zimbabwe are among the countries suffering the most damage, but the problem is widespread elsewhere. "The next generation of farmers in Africa," Brown warns, "will try to feed not the 719 million of today, but 1.45 billion in the year 2025—and with far less topsoil" (Brown, 1998: 9). In southern Africa, additional problems are caused by mineral resource extraction (e.g., copper, gold, iron, and diamonds), mines scar the landscape and pollute the water, and cattle and sheep ranches have denuded vast areas of vegetation on marginal, semiarid land (Kalipeni, 1994). In Nigeria, the tragic execution of Ken Saro-Wiwa and other Ogoni environmental activists protesting pollution caused by the oil industry provides another dramatic illustration of the high environmental costs of the development process in Africa.

Africa's development crisis has many causes, both external (e.g., unfavorable terms of trade for Africa's commodities) and internal (e.g., mismanagement of the economy and state corruption). But a major factor in the poor performance of most of Africa's economies has been a neglect of the needs and interests of women. Women have always played a central role in African development, albeit a role not accurately reflected in most official statistics or appreciated in mainstream development writings or practice. The importance of women to the economy has increased during the past decade and a half of SAP because many men have seen their incomes fall and female-headed families have increased in number. Recognizing women's contributions and empowering women so that they have more opportunity and access to productive resources will be vital to Africa's economic recovery and hopes for sustainable development in the future.

This recognition is growing. For example, the World Bank writes that providing more opportunity for women is a "sure route" to "faster and more sustainable development." Assisting women has been given more attention in the Bank's lending programs as well as its writings with the justification that "no country can afford to underequip and underutilize more than half of its human resources . . . Alleviating poverty, ensuring food security, reducing population growth, improving the quality of a country's future labor force, and properly using the natural resource base all depend substantially on women" (World Bank, 1990: 32). A series of United Nations conferences in the 1990s similarly stressed the link between empowering women and achieving development objectives. The 1992 UN Conference on Environment and Development (in Rio de Janeiro) addressed the link between women's issues and sustainable development. In 1994, the International Conference on Population and Development (in Cairo) highlighted the importance of the status of women and population growth along with other economic, political, and social development objectives. The World Summit for Social Development held in Copenhagen in 1995 raised these issues yet again. In all these global forums, the negative impact of failed development on women, including environmental degradation, were given international exposure along with the recommendation that women's participation in solving these problems was essential (cf. World Bank, 1996; UNDP, 1995).

Some basic facts about the contributions to development of African women can explain why women are receiving more attention. Women grow about 80 percent of the food for their households and cultivate about 50 percent of all cash crops (Jacobson, 1993: 67). In Kenya, for instance, women provide 75 percent of the labor on smallholder farms, half the labor on cash crops, and 95 percent of the household labor (Munyak'ho, 1994: 8; see also von Bulow and Sorensen, 1993). In Malawi, 71 percent of seasonal agricultural work is done by women (Malindi, 1995: 121), and in Tanzania women are working double or triple work days while producing 80 percent of the food and performing other productive and household duties (Vuorela, 1992: 111–12). Women are often the main providers for their families, especially in female-headed households, which comprise from 43–48 percent of all African households. Lesotho has the highest proportion of female-headed households—2/3 (Picard, 1995: 37; James, 1995: 6–7).

Because agriculture is the main source of livelihood for most Africans, the importance of increasing the productivity of women to ensure both food security and the growth of the cash crop economy can hardly be overemphasized. Africa's dependence on agriculture will continue well into the foreseeable future. In food production alone, the World Bank estimates that a growth in production of at least 4 percent per year between 1990 and 2020 will be necessary to meet the needs of Africa's rapidly growing population (World Bank, 1991: 73). African economies will also continue to depend on processed and unprocessed primary products, which is "tantamount to a dependency on women to find the resources and time to achieve more in the economic sphere" (Palmer, 1991: 3).

Women's economic contributions are by no means limited to the agricultural sector. Their entrepreneurial activity is also substantial. Insufficient attention is given to women's role and their potential in this area partly because women's business activity tends to be largely in small-scale, informal sector enterprises. But such businesses have been crucial to the economic survival of many households in recent years due to the hardships wrought by economic decline and structural adjustment. Women's enterprises have become a vital source of cash and affordable goods and services. Many men in the formal economy have lost their jobs or had their wages slashed. Others have suffered declining incomes due to falling commodity prices in global markets. Women have turned to such income-earning activities as beer brewing, animal husbandry, pottery production, and trading agricultural commodities in order to provide for their families. As basic products like soap, milk, and medicine have become more expensive, women have begun to produce them as well (cf. Swantz, 1995: 199–200; Moghadam, 1995: 124–25). Even in the cities, women's businesses, including urban farming, are making women the primary income earners in their families. In Dar es Salaam, for instance, an estimated two-thirds of women are now self-employed, and they bring in as much as 90 percent of household income (Vuorela, 1992; Tripp, 1992).

Most of these businesses in both rural and urban areas are women's response to the survival needs of their households and the failure of the African state and formal economy to sustain even basic needs for most of the population. The same is true in the area of providing basic community and social services. Governments have cut back on expenditures under SAPs, largely shifting the burden onto the shoulders of women. Women are more likely than men to contribute their labor to such projects as building clinics and schools or for conservation projects despite their already heavy workloads (see Thomas-Slaytor, 1992; Safilios-Rothschild, 1990).

Despite the contribution to development of the income-generating and community activities of women, they are usually not calculated in most measures of economic growth. The multiplier effects of women's activities also remain invisible. However, as numerous researchers have found, women's activities on behalf of their households and communities create new skills and jobs for themselves and others; provide essentials such as food, clothing, education, health care, and housing for children, the sick, and the elderly; and are reinvested. Although many men are making similar contributions, men are more likely to spend money wastefully or on luxury items for themselves, such as alcohol, cigarettes, gambling, women, bikes, watches—even if their wives and children lack adequate food and other necessities (see Elson, 1992: 36; Staudt, 1987: 206–7).

Environmental protection is another area of sustainable development in Africa where women's role is crucial. The World Bank writes that "caring about the environment in Africa is not a luxury but a prime necessity" (World Bank, 1996: ix). Already severely degraded in many areas, the environment will become an even greater problem in the future with population expected to grow to over 1 billion by 2025. Over half will be living in already congested, polluted, and underserviced cities (World Bank, 1996: 3). Protecting the environment is also linked to poverty alleviation— "the overarching goal" of development—because the poor often suffer the most from environmental problems. Women are the key, says the Bank, to protecting the environment and alleviating poverty because they play a greater role in environmental management than in any other region of the world (World Bank, 1996: 4, 53).

The centrality of women in environmental management is a reflection of their roles in the gender division of labor that exists in many rural areas of Africa. Women usually have only use right to natural resources such as land, forests, and water rather than titled ownership. Women's access to resources are primarily to enable them to provide for the subsistence needs of their households over time. Sustainable use and protection of environmental resources are, therefore, likely to be in women's interest. For this reason, women engage in practices such as fallow periods, crop rotation, intercropping, mulching, and using manure to conserve soil fertility. Because women depend on forests for multiple resources, including nuts, fruit, fodder for domestic animals, medicine, and fuel, they conserve the forest by using only deadwood or branches rather than cutting down live trees. From experience, they recognize the role trees and other vegetation play in protecting the soil and water supplies. It is not surprising then that women are most involved in such community work as terracing and reforestation (Thomas-Slaytor, Rocheleau, and Kabutha, 1995: 195–98; Livernash and Rodenburg, 1998: 14; Jacobson, 1993: 68–69). Making better use of women's knowledge and experience in farming and resource management as well as helping them in these areas will not only help to protect the environment but improve both food and cash crop production as well (Jacobson, 1993: 76, 78; Harrison, 1990: 69–70).

ECONOMIC LIBERALIZATION AND GENDER BIAS

SAPs designed to eliminate waste and inefficiency and create freer markets to boost investment and productivity are currently in force in most countries in Africa. In the effort to eliminate "market distortions," policy makers need to be mindful of the fact that gender bias is one of the greatest sources of distortion in African economies; and it will not be eliminated with "gender-neutral" economic reforms. It is a fallacy to say that an economy is a free market when half of the population faces systematic discrimination because of sex. Until women have equal access with men to land; equal rights to make contracts, own a business, and control their own labor and that of others; control over the fruits of their labor; equal access to non-stereotypic education and jobs; equal access to resources such as credit and extension services; and an equitable sharing of domestic responsibilities; there are no free markets in Africa. Gender bias is not just an issue of equity, although equity is one of the criteria for sustainable development. Equally, if not more, important is discrimination against women, which is wasteful and inefficient and hinders the economic transformation to a more productive and sustainable economy (Gordon, 1996b).

The magnitude of the problem is indicated by economist Ingrid Palmer in her research on gender bias and structural adjustment in Africa. "If the gender bias, the weakest link in sub-Saharan economies, is not resolved, these economies may have an absolute advantage in no product and a comparative advantage only in lines of production based on the superexploitation of women and a demand for children's assistance" (Palmer, 1991: ix).

The superexploitation of women Palmer refers to originated with the colonial system. All African labor was exploited, not just that of women. Men were compelled to grow cash crops or to migrate to the towns to work for low wages. Women, on the other hand, were primarily relegated to producing food crops, helping their husbands with cash crops, and maintaining the family with little or no compensation or assistance. In essence, women's unpaid labor allowed the colonial economy to pay below-subsistence wages and prices to men. But these inequitable and exploitative labor practices persist largely unchanged today (cf. Berman, 1992: 134–36) and are increasingly counterproductive. They were not designed to produce development in Africa but cheap commodities for industrial countries—and that is mainly what results they continue to achieve.

GENDER BIAS IN AGRICULTURE

Initially, it was believed that the path to development in postcolonial Africa depended on rapid industrialization, especially import substitution industrialization. Achieving development would require squeezing surplus from the agricultural sector, which would be reinvested in industry. The failure of this strategy has led to a new emphasis on grassroots development, especially smallholder agricultural development in order to ensure food security and poverty reduction (Harrison, 1990: 69; Palmer, 1991: 74–75). To achieve higher productivity in agriculture, more investment needs to be made in this sector, and prices to farmers must be raised. Because women do so much of the cash and food crop farming, boosting women's capacities and incentives to increase production is the key to grassroots development.

Unfortunately, the supposedly gender-neutral market reforms and price incentives of current policies in place in most African countries will not have the desirable results intended because they do not take into account gender bias. Therefore, most women do not benefit from reform, and many are, in fact, worse off. For example, the goal of increasing the output of export crops requires the use of high-yield, often expensive seeds and chemicals and more labor—mostly from women (Vuorela, 1992: 113). Yet men usually own the land and the crops and receive the cash income; therefore, women are often unwilling to expend their labor on these crops when they will not benefit (cf. Rapley, 1996: 91; also von Bulow and Sorensen, 1993: 41). Instead, many women prefer to focus their energies on their own food crops, from which they do control the income (cf. Blumberg, 1994: 14–15). Even if they are willing to do more work on their husbands' cash crops, it may be at the expense of work on their food crops, thus threatening food security, or the need for children's labor may increase. This reinforces high fertility and population growth and results in less schooling for children, especially girls, because their labor is needed at home (Palmer, 1991: 112). So even if current policies result in some short-term increase in agricultural production, the costs of growth may jeopardize long-term welfare and sustainable development.

Men receive most of the benefits of increased agricultural output because few women are able to buy or inherit land or get the access they need to other agricultural resources. Even when they can legally own land, as in Kenya, only 4–5 percent actually do because of the resistance to change of patrilineal customs and gender bias (World Bank, 1989: 6). Yet, men usually own the land and the crop and receive the cash income; therefore, women are often unwilling to expend their labor on these crops when they will not benefit (cf. Rapley, 1996: 91). As long as such discrimination against women continues, however, it will remain a major source of market distortions. For instance, rather than market forces determining the allocation of land and the ratio of cash to food crops to be planted, men have the authority to make such choices because the land is theirs. Because men grow cash crops, their decisions tend to favor them rather than women's food crops. It is not unusual for men to allocate the poorest and remote plots to the women while keeping the best land for themselves and their cash crops. Women are further disadvantaged and may be unable to respond to price incentives to grow more crops because they are unable to get credit to purchase the inputs they need. The reason they are unable to get credit is that they are not able to own land (Picard, 1995: 50; Nwomonoh, 1995: 176–77). Women are also discriminated against in their access to technology, agricultural research, and technical training (cf. Blumberg, 1994). As Picard notes, farmers included to participate in agricultural research are usually men, and even the research literature always refers to farmers and researchers as "he" (1995: 45–47). Until women are given more equitable access to improved and appropriate technology, their work will remain, as Palmer writes, "laborious, time-consuming and wasteful" (1991: 176).

Yet even when women do get access to some improved technologies, it can make things worse. For example, ox-drawn plows allow for more land to be cultivated and for additional crops. But this entails more planting, weeding, and harvesting time. Therefore, for women to benefit, other labor-saving devices are needed; otherwise, women's agricultural work increases on top of all the other work they are expected to do. Women certainly need technological improvements in performing their agricultural work. But under the current gender division of labor, women also spend hours fetching water because wells or other clean water sources are not nearby; gathering fuelwood, which is burned in inefficient and polluting stoves; preparing and processing food; caring for children and animals; and performing other domestic chores. When cash is needed to purchase necessities, women often work for other farmers, market their surplus crops, or undertake small-scale, income-generating business activities (cf. Vuorela, 1992: 113–17).

Numerous studies exist that demonstrate the high price African societies pay for the perpetuation of gender bias. Women simply won't or can't be as productive if males continue to control the land, money, and labor on the farm and if women do not receive substantial relief from the excessive burden of work for which they are responsible. Overwork of women alone results in delays in land preparation, planting, and weeding as well as other inefficiencies that cut yields as much as 30 percent (Harrison, 1990: 69). When women do benefit from their efforts, significant gains in productivity occur. Currently, because of gender bias, the yields of women farmers growing the same crops as men are lower (Picard, 1995: 50). But, according to Palmer, if women enjoyed the same access as men to information, inputs, and technology, the results would be very different (Palmer, 1991: 123).

Supporting Palmer, Gittinger et al. (1990) report that in Kenya when women had access to extension services and had the ability to make decisions on their farms, they adopted innovation more quickly than men. It was also found that, while in general yields increased when women did more weeding, in households headed by women, yields increased 56 percent compared to only 15 percent in households headed by men. Women had more incentive to do a good job when they stood to gain from their time and effort. The difference in productivity gain between female-headed and male-headed households was "about equal to the gain in yield from applying phosphate and nitrogen fertilizer" (Gittinger et al., 1990: 19). In Nigeria, after women farmers were given more access to extension services and resources, agricultural output began growing by 5 percent per year (Gittinger et al., 1990, 28, 30). Similarly, the World Bank reports that female farmers in Kenya produced 7 percent more per acre than men when they had the same access to inputs, extension, credit, and education (World Bank, 1990: 5). Women's ownership of land has also been found to result in greater productivity and higher living standards among Haya women in Tanzania compared to that of women who did not own land (Henn, 1983). Finally, Nwomonoh reports that when women can control the benefits of their labor, they are eager to increase their output and efficiency in all aspects of their work: farming, processing, storage, and marketing (Nwomonoh, 1995: 178).

These studies suggest that market competition and growth in agricultural output would improve from a reduction in gender bias. This is essential for food production but could improve cash crop production as well. Although women already play a significant role in producing cash crops, many women farmers would like to grow more cash crops—if they could be assured that the crop and income would go to them and not their husbands (Palmer, 1991: 25–26).

Increasing agricultural output is only one of the benefits of increasing the women's income. Income controlled by women is more likely to be spent on food, education, clothing, medical care, and other basic needs for the family. This can have a significant positive impact, especially on the welfare of children. In Kenya, for instance, children from female-headed families were less likely to be malnourished than children from male-headed households. By contrast, studies from several African countries found that improvements in income in households headed by men did not translate into a proportionate improvement in food or other necessities for women or children in the household (Gittinger et al., 1990: 3–4, 19–20). Another positive result of women's control over income is that the basic goods and services purchased by women are more likely to be locally produced and, therefore, a stimulus to the domestic economy. Many of the goods purchased by men—radios, watches, bikes, and cigarettes—are imports, which add to Africa's balance of trade deficit and debt burden (Palmer, 1991: 119).

Unfortunately, market-oriented structural adjustment reforms are not effectively addressing the issues related to gender bias. The pressures placed on rural women to produce more can have deleterious consequences for their families. In Zambia, for example, both men and women farmers are increasingly producing cash crops. This has resulted in such an increase in women's work on the farm that they are spending less time on child care, infant feeding, and food preparation for their families. Consequently, children's health and nutrition are suffering (Picard, 1995: 35).

This problem could be solved and productivity increased as well if the domestic burden borne by women were more equitably shared between men and women and if more labor-saving technology was developed for women (Picard, 1995: 43; Malindi, 1995: 121; Gordon, 1996b: 100–106). In Orvis's (1993) study of households in rural Kenya, he found that in general the farm families who had more egalitarian gender relations were more productive and had more stable marriages. Among the Kofyar of Nigeria, men appreciate women's labor contributions and help with such time-consuming jobs as gathering wood, processing crops, washing clothes, building homes, and even fetching water (Stone et al., 1990). Also, in Iringa District in Tanzania, men began to help women gather firewood after viewing a film on "Sharing the Responsibility," which showed how difficult and time-consuming women's work was (Gittinger et al., 1990: 32).

More typically, however, men resist assuming the work of women. They refuse to help with productive or household chores even when they have free time. In their research in rural Kenya, Thomas-Slaytor et al. found that the men quit working on their coffee farms when prices dropped in the 1980s, but they did nothing to help their wives. They left the burden of family well-being on the women. The men also until recently seldom contributed their labor to community self-help groups; that work, too, was done almost entirely by women (Thomas-Slaytor et al., 1995: 205–6).

The gender division of labor in domestic work is perhaps the most resistant to change. It tends to be ignored by politicians and development workers alike. As Mikell observes, politicians are mostly male, and they see women in largely stereotypic terms and in subordinate roles (1997a: 338–39). Although the need to increase women's productivity has won widespread agreement, there is little challenge to the sexual division of labor (Scott, 1995: 82–85). The refusal to address African women's "double day" means that structural adjustment is less market liberalization where women are concerned than a policy that depends upon "the deepening of women's subordination within peasant agriculture under male heads of household" and "the intensification of women's labor as unpaid family workers" (Mbilinyi and Meena, 1991: 847).

GENDER BIAS IN THE NONAGRICULTURAL ECONOMY

Despite gender bias, some African countries have been able to increase their output, but mainly in the area of primary products for export with little value added. Food production, however, has not kept pace with population growth, and manufacturing has stagnated or declined in most countries. This pattern of producing primarily raw materials in an undiversified economy is more reminiscent of the colonial economy than an indication of sustainable development. Africa's long-term development will require domestic industries using local inputs and encouragement for indigenous entrepreneurs (cf. Rapley, 1996: 81–83; Palmer, 1991: 74–75).

The potential is there. Africa already has a multitude of indigenous businesses, but most of them are small-scale and in the informal sector. If properly nurtured and supported, many could blossom into prosperous, formal-sector enterprises. Many of these small businesses are owned and operated by women. Currently however, gender bias along with the obstacles that impede male-owned businesses limit the potential of women-owned enterprises (cf. Vuorela, 1992). Most are low-growth, low-return, and concentrated in a narrow range of activities—usually derived from women's activities in the gender division of labor. These include trading, dressmaking, soap making, baking, food processing, hairdressing, and handicrafts.

Gender bias in education also limits most women's entrepreneurial possibilities. Women get less education on average than men and are far more likely to be illiterate. They are also steered toward stereotypic female fields rather than toward more lucrative fields of manufacturing and technology (cf. Stamp, 1989).

Furthermore, women face discrimination in access to credit and other support services, such as training and information. This discrimination is often related to the fact that women are not allowed to own land or businesses or get credit in their own names. Another problem, one that can affect men as well as women, is the myriad bureaucratic obstacles (e.g., registration, regulations, taxes, and bribes) with which business people must contend. These act as a disincentive for many, especially women, to formalize and expand their enterprises (Osirim. 1994: 65–66).

Although men face some of the same obstacles to starting and expanding a business as women do, men do not have to overcome gender bias. Lacking men's education and formal-sector contacts makes the "normal" process even more daunting for women.

Gender bias rooted in the gender division of labor in the household also holds back many women entrepreneurs. According to Swantz, for example, urban women in the informal sector in Tanzania prefer to keep their enterprises small not only to avoid dealing with government bureaucracy but also because they must combine business with their domestic responsibilities.

They cannot work full-time at their business like men, who are unencumbered with domestic responsibilities (Swantz, 1995: 203–4).

GENDER BIAS, POPULATION GROWTH, AND THE ENVIRONMENT

Rapid population growth exacerbates economic and environmental problems and, therefore, undermines possibilities for sustainable development in much of Africa. Gender bias makes it difficult to effectively address either population or environmental issues. For instance, reducing women's access to land often forces them to cultivate ecologically fragile areas and puts pressure on women to increase crop yields by shortening fallow periods. Both practices are among the ways that soil conservation is threatened, a key element in Africa's long-term ability to feed its growing population (cf. Wacker, 1994: 131–35).

Another problem associated with women's lack of secure access to land is that women may have little incentive for conservation or tree planting, which helps to prevent deforestation and desertification (cf. Braxton, 1995: 77). In customary law in many parts of Africa, tree planting is associated with establishing a claim to land; therefore, husbands may not allow their wives to own or even plant trees. The problem is that the men have little interest in planting trees themselves (cf. Rocheleau et al., 1995). Women, however, would plant trees if they could, because they would gain many benefits. Trees provide fuelwood; having their own trees could save women hours of labor they currently spend gathering wood. Trees that provide nuts, fruit, honey, and other valuable products could provide women with a source of cash income and subsistence for their families (Harrison, 1990: 69–70).

There is also good evidence that lack of access to land and other aspects of gender bias promote high fertility. Lack of access to family planning and modern contraceptives play a relatively minor role in the high fertility found in Africa. Because most women are unable to attain economic security on their own and must bear such a heavy workload, women have a rational reason for having large numbers of children. Because women often can't own or inherit land, women want sons who can. If the woman is divorced or widowed, she can continue to gain access to land; sons help with chores as well. Daughters provide essential labor on the farm and help with child care and housework. Even if women want to have fewer children, their relative lack of decision-making power in the household can extend to their fertility. Husbands can override their wives' preferences in the areas of sexuality and childbearing, and they may compel their wives to have more children than the women would choose themselves. Among the reasons for this is that men gain the advantages of children but often do not have to contribute much to their care or financial support. For the same reason, men may have little incentive to use birth control or to allow their wives to practice family planning (Dasgupta, 1995: 42).

Educational discrimination also contributes to high fertility and population growth in Africa. Generally, fertility is higher in countries where female illiteracy and dependence on the unpaid work of women in the household are greater. As already discussed, both of these factors are structural characteristics of most African societies. By contrast, fertility declines when females have more education and access to employment opportunities outside the household. Education and control over income are also positively associated with women who have more decision-making power in their households; they also have more resources to ensure their own health and that of their children. This in turn translates into lower fertility (Gordon, 1996a: 174–181; Sen, 1994; Dasgupta, 1995: 42; World Bank, 1996: 53; Green, 1994: 182–83).

EMPOWERING WOMEN FOR GRASSROOTS DEVELOPMENT

To date, few donor agencies or governments have done much to utilize African women's potential to participate equally with men in their societies. They tend to stereotype women as primarily wives and mothers—not potential engineers, managers, or skilled workers. This carries over into the development projects aimed at women. Most are in the areas of health, nutrition, family planning, and basic education. Although these are important, more resources need to be directed toward the full range of productive as well as reproductive activities in which women are engaged (cf. Kabira and Nzioki, 1993: 72). Developing women's ability to enter new productive areas from which they have been largely excluded could dramatically improve the rational allocation of human resources currently limited by gender bias.

This would mean a shift from the traditional welfare approach of "integrating women in development (WID)," which encourages women to pursue primarily income-generating microenterprises while doing most of the unpaid household, farm, and community labor as well (Moser, 1991: 96–110). Instead of accepting the limiting gender status quo upon which such views of development are premised, governments need to embrace policies that can transform such limitations in the interests of genuine and sustainable development. Rather than continuing the superexploitation of women, what is needed are measures that would counter the unpaid domestic labor of women and expand women's opportunities so that they can compete on a more level playing field. For this to occur, women would need what Palmer refers to as "counterbalancing taxes and expenditures," such as child care, maternity benefits, safe tap water, and electricity (Palmer, 1991: 165). This would contribute to a major goal of sustainable development (that it be equitably shared and poverty reducing).

Such policies are consistent with current stated views of the World Bank that recognize the positive role the state plays in development. To achieve development, the state and markets must work together. The state must create an "enabling environment" for people at the grassroots level so that they can develop themselves and their societies (cf. Hyden, 1990; World Bank, 1997: 4). "The state is essential because it must develop the institutional foundation for markets to work. Public policies and programs are necessary to ensure that growth is shared through investments in basic education and health, regulatory frameworks, and protection of the environment "(World Bank, 1997: 4).

Such goals are impossible without gender equity because an enabling environment is one that fosters entrepreneurship and encourages contributions "by all agents of development and change." It also "empower[s] people at the local level, invest[s] in them and channel[s] resources to them to gain their participation in increasing productivity and production" (Rashid, 1994: 46).

Transforming WID so that it empowers women is not an idealistic, theoretical proposition. There are elements of it in the Asian model of development, so often touted as an exemplar for other, less successful developing economies. Part of the success of the dynamism and growth of the best performing Asian economies is that they have invested in women. This is not to say that these countries have eliminated gender bias and exploitation of women; that is clearly not the case. Nonetheless, they have implemented several measures that benefit women and that have paid off in terms of development. For one thing, in Asia, the efficient, small family farm has been considered the model for development, and rural dwellers have received much more government investment than has been typical in Africa. In Indonesia, for example, the government invested heavily in infrastructure and rural development (World Bank, 1994: 32, 38). Of special significance, in many Asian countries, women's land rights have been assured by various laws (for example, marriage, child custody, divorce, and widowhood). Agricultural training for women in Asia has also been provided on a much larger scale than in Africa: 47 percent of Asian women farmers have received such training compared to only 17 percent of African women (Palmer, 1991: 163). Also, most Asian countries have surpassed those of Africa in part because since the 1960s they have invested in universal primary education, which is viewed as a key to rapid and equitable economic development in the best performing Asian countries (World Bank, 1994: 32, 38). The Asian growth with equity (including gender equity) model has so impressed the World Bank that it concludes that expanding social services, "especially for girls," is crucial "both as an input for high growth and as a mean of ensuring broad participation in the growth process" (World Bank, 1994: 162–63). By contrast, "neglecting these social fundamentals can be fatal" (World Bank, 1997: 25).

There are examples of efforts to promote growth with equity, including gender equity in Africa. In Nigeria, for example, the International Institute of Tropical Agriculture (IITA) has been working to improve food crop production and food processing technology to lessen women's workload. They have achieved some notable results. For instance, cassava normally took twenty-four hours per ton to process. With new technology, the time was cut to six hours. In one village where the new technology was installed, women's average income increased by 126 percent. In another village, labor was reduced 70 percent, and losses during processing declined 50 percent. Women reported that for the first time they had some leisure time. IITA was also working to include more women in its training programs and to expand the number of women agricultural scientists (Ajayi, 1991).

Agricultural development can also be coupled with grassroots rural industrialization to enhance technological innovation and entrepreneurship. Originally used in China, rural-oriented smallholder industrialization (ROSH) has been shown to lead to the development of efficient, increasingly sophisticated, small-scale manufacturing enterprises in rural areas. Many of these enterprises use agricultural inputs as well as supply affordable inputs for improving agricultural productivity. Rural incomes grow due to the increase in farm output and from the expansion of farm and non-farm employment opportunities. Technological skills also improve, which can provide the basis for further industrialization. ROSH-type rural development could help correct several deficiencies of African development strategies. These include the failure to develop domestic skills and technical know-how, dependence on (often inappropriate) foreign technology, and the lack of linkage between domestic raw materials production and manufacturing. ROSH-style development might better prepare African economies to escape their reliance on raw materials exports and to eventually build a more favorable basis for integration into the global economy than most African countries now have. If gender equity were emphasized, ROSH could be a potentially valuable means to improve women's productivity, skills, and income.

Unfortunately, as Olofin (1991) reports, ROSH has not been popular among African policy elites, who have favored large-scale projects and firms, which depend heavily on imported technology and inputs. For ROSH to succeed in Africa, the state would have to reorient its activities toward creating favorable conditions (that is, an enabling environment). Training and credit would be needed as well as some period of protection for smallholder enterprises from competition from larger firms.

Togo provides an example of a project that exemplifies many characteristics associated with equitable, grassroots development. In this case, local entrepreneurs were in partnership with international business and an NGO (nongovernmental organization). The project began in 1986 when a group of local business investors created a joint venture with a Danish firm and the

Danish Industrialization Fund for Developing Countries (IFU). The locals provided the land, the Danish firm the financing and technical, managerial, and marketing knowledge. The IFU contributed financing and experience with other African investments. The location was a rural area about 20–25 kilometers from Lomé; the product was fine herbs for export to Europe. Over half of the initial 170 local employees were women. By 1994, after an international firm bought out the Danish partners, employment grew to 700—still over half women. The workers were organized into a trade union, all received training, and some got advanced education. The farm had significant, positive multiplier effects in the surrounding area, becoming one of the biggest sources of private-sector jobs in Togo. Local living standards have improved greatly. Worker families can afford to send all of their children to school for the first time. They can afford fertilizer and pesticides for their farm plots and have gained new agricultural knowledge and skills that enable them to expand their own crop production. Consumer goods such as TVs, bikes, and radios are now found in workers' homes, and workers and their families have better access to health care. With women's gains in income have also come more self-respect and self-confidence, and they are receiving help with child care and cooking from grandmothers and girls so that their workload at home is reduced. A quality-of-life benefit of the Togo project is that family and community life are enhanced by the fact that family members—usually men—no longer have to split up their families in order to migrate to the cities to find work. Now work can be found at home. This has the added benefit of lessening the urban congestion and other problems of rapid urban growth (Hasdorf, 1995: 251–52).

In both rural and urban areas of Africa, there are cases of impressive entrepreneurship—many times involving women. Successful women's businesses can be found on any scale, from micro to large, and in many diverse activities. Along with government policies that nurture rather than discourage the informal sector (where most women get their start in business), the success or failure of women's businesses often depends on the availability of both credit and training in such skills as accounting and management. Women's World Banking (WWB), with branches in twenty-four African countries in 1990, works with commercial banks to make small loans available to women. After six years of lending, there had been only one default on a WWB loan. Affiliates provide training in economic skills and in the use of credit. As an example, the Kenyan affiliate, the Kenyan Women Finance Trust, trained women traders in the two largest markets in the country in business management, accounting, and marketing along with guaranteeing their loans from a commercial bank (Gittinger et al., 1990: 27–28).

Several studies suggest that a commonly found characteristic of women's businesses is that women often work and invest with other women (Mikell, 1997b: 32; Freeman, 1993: 95; Gordon, 1996b: 95–96, 155–57). In part, this is a result of women's household responsibilities, which make it difficult for many women to work full-time at their business, but it also reflects a culture of labor sharing and savings clubs upon which women have long depended (Swantz, 1995: 204). Another factor supporting group business activity is that it allows women to protect more of their profits and the business itself from usurpation by their husbands because the "owner" of the business is the group (Gittinger, 1990: 27).

There are numerous examples of these successful women's group businesses. They provide good illustrations of what women can accomplish. In Kenya's Thika township in Kiambu district, women formed a company with 1,025 members, bought land, and began running a prosperous coffee farm. All the directors are women. In Turkana district, four women were given assistance by the Danish International Development Agency to start a bakery. They made their own bricks and ovens and eventually expanded into selling dried fish and handicrafts. They bought land and built a women's center, a bakery-duka, an office, and a butchery. In addition, they started a block-making factory, a catering business, a water-selling kiosk, an education program, and a training center. Women are trained in many useful traditionally male skills, such as carpentry, masonry, plumbing, and accounting (Kabira and Nzioki, 1993: 57–59). In Nairobi, urban farming is providing women working together with sometimes highly lucrative business opportunities. Most women involved in urban farming grow crops on land in or near the city to feed their families, but about 45 percent grow enough to sell or exchange. Many of those who are entrepreneurs (12 percent sold half or more of their crop) are building experience and capital to reinvest in larger, even formal-sector businesses (Freeman, 1993: 9–15). In Tanzania, with factories paying below-subsistence wages, small-scale manufacturing has become the most lucrative form of work in Dar es Salaam for women. They provide cheap goods using local inputs and technology at a time when import-dependent industries suffer machine breakdowns, power cuts, lack of spare parts, and imported inputs due to foreign exchange shortages. These enterprises also provide jobs and a livable income for many. They are also at least five times more efficient in terms of output per unit of investment than large-scale industries (Tripp, 1992: 177).

There are also possibilities for women in export manufacturing. An example is the indigenous textile industry in Nigeria, which is very old and dominated by women. Both rural and urban women are involved at all stages of production: growing the cotton, weaving, management, and marketing. The technology used is local and appropriate, and the raw materials are all locally produced. The textiles are handwoven and of very high quality, with delicate designs and colors. Ikale cloth, made by Yoruba women, is one of the most popular of these textiles, but because they are handwoven, quantities are currently limited. Indigenous textiles have entered the international market, including the U.S. market, with the help of some African-Americans. The Nigerian government has made some effort to promote indigenous textiles abroad along with other products made by rural women; however, more effective distribution and marketing are needed to promote these goods. Unfortunately, women in textiles or other industries producing for domestic or export markets face a major constraint: They have trouble raising capital because legally or practically most can't own land or property. Even if the lack of capital doesn't keep them from starting a business, it often keeps them from getting the technology and business assistance they need to move from small-scale into larger-scale industries (Gabriel and Ikien, 1995).

As was true for women in agriculture, women in business need secure property rights. If women had such rights, along with access to education, training, technology, and credit on a par with men, Africa's dismal record in promoting indigenous entrepreneurs who could transform their countries' economies might look quite different than it does today.

THE GLOBAL ECONOMY VERSUS SUSTAINABLE DEVELOPMENT

Although gender bias is an important factor undermining the prospects for sustainable development in Africa, promoting gender equality within the dominant global capitalist economic system carries no guarantee that development will occur or that it will be sustainable (that is, able to meet current human needs without destroying the natural resource base necessary for future generations to meet theirs). One problem is that in the current global economy, concentration of wealth and power in the richest countries appears to be a structural characteristic that includes few exceptions. Even the Asian NICs, seeming exceptions to the rule that "the rich get richer," are foundering and facing the prospects of a prolonged recession or worse (Heredia, 1997). As Johnson-Odim argues, equal opportunity between men and women is not the only issue when African countries are locked into an unequal position in the global system along with most other developing nations. Under current conditions, gender equality for most means an equal opportunity to be poor. Therefore, gender bias is but one obstacle constraining women's opportunities and hopes for a better life (Johnson-Odim, 1991: 320).

By the same token, more gender equality does not guarantee that environmentally sustainable development will replace current environmentally destructive patterns. The global economy and the neoliberal economic theories that underpin it are premised on unlimited growth, as though there are no environmental limits (cf. Miller, 1995: 146; Kettel, 1995: 242). To most poor countries—including most women as well as men—the Western model of development with its resource-consumptive lifestyle represents the ultimate goal of development, even if few expect to achieve it. It will be hard to convince people who have endured material deprivation and economic insecurity that sustainable development is necessary or even desirable if it requires them to forego the fruits of development so far enjoyed primarily by the West. Such self-restraint by the poor is especially unlikely and unfair given the daunting task of convincing most people in the industrial world that they need to alter their environmentally destructive way of life if development is to be a realizable prospect for everyone in the world, not just the affluent few (Rapley, 1996: 175; Miller 1995: 146).

As long as the structural inequalities of the global system persist, even if women in African and other rapidly growing poor countries lower their birthrates or do more to protect the environment, the global prospects for sustainable development may not improve appreciably without a transformation in the way decisions about resource usage and distribution are made. Amalric argues that, theoretically, curbing population growth should lessen demands on and abuse of the environment. However, "the historical capacity of Northern countries to take over surpluses suggests that if some sort of environmental surplus is released it will be taken over by them. In other words, Southern countries would not collect the global benefits of a reduction in world population growth, whereas they would incur the cost of adjustment" (Amalric, 1994: 236).

Indeed, our current system not only exacerbates the gap between rich and poor, it is also inherently environmentally destructive, as current data on climate change, declining biodiversity, and other environmental problems indicate (cf. Teeple, 1995: 143; Harmon, 1996). Despite some efforts at global cooperation to promote sustainable development, the dominant tendencies of global capitalism remain oriented toward ever greater exploitation of the world's environment and people to increase corporate wealth and accumulation. This approach to development—which focuses on profits, technology, and private interests without regard for the health and well-being of the environment, people, or communities—is not sustainable. At present, women in Africa and in other developing countries tend to be a force for sustainable development in part because they have been exploited by the economic system and played more marginal and subordinate roles within it. With more power, opportunities, and resources at their disposal, women could contribute much more. However, if women simply become incorporated into the global system without working to transform its inequitable and environmentally destructive tendencies, it is questionable how much will be changed for the better.

BIBLIOGRAPHY

Ajayi, Femi. 1991. "Food for Thought." *Africa Report* 36 (September–October): 25–28.

Amalric, Franck. 1994. "Finiteness, Infinity and Responsibility: The Population-Environment Debate." In *Feminist Perspectives on Sustainable Development*, edited by Wendy Harcourt (London: Zed Books).

Berman, Bruce. 1992. "The Concept of 'Articulation' and the Political Economy of Colonialism." In *Unhappy Valley: Conflict in Kenya and Africa*, edited by Bruce Berman and John Lonsdale (London: James Currey).

Blumberg, Rae Lesser. 1994. "Reaching Africa's 'Invisible' Farmers." *African Farmer* (April): 14–15.

Braxton, Gloria J. 1995. "Designing Gender-Specific Interventions in Zaire: A Social Science Perspective." In *Women and Sustainable Development in Africa*, edited by Valentine Udoh James (Westport, Connecticut: Praeger).

Brown, Lester R. 1998. "The Future of Growth." In *State of the World 1998*, edited by Lester R. Brown, Gary Gardner, and Brian Halweil (New York: W.W. Norton)

Brown, Lester R. et al. 1993. "A New Era Unfolds." In *State of the World 1993* (New York: W.W. Norton).

Dasgupta, Partha S. 1995 "Population, Poverty and the Local Environment." *Scientific American* (February): 40–45.

Elson, Diane. 1992. "From Survival Strategies to Transformation Strategies: Women's Needs and Structural Adjustment." In *Unequal Burden: Economic Crisis, Persistent Poverty, and Women's Work*, edited by Lourdes Beneria and Shelley Feldman (Boulder, CO: Westview).

Freeman, Donald. 1993. "Survival Strategy or Business Training Ground: The Significance of Urban Agriculture for the Advancement of Women in African Cities." *African Studies Review* 36 (December): 1–22.

Gabriel, Amakievi O.I., and Augustine A. Ikein. 1995. "Agrarian Women and Indigenous Textile Industry in Nigeria." In *Women and Sustainable Development in Africa*, edited by Valentine Udoh James (Westport, Connecticut: Praeger).

Gittinger, J. Price et al. 1990. *Household Food Security and the Role of Women* (Washington, D.C.: World Bank).

Gordon, April A. 1996a. "Population Growth and Urbanization." In *Understanding Contemporary Africa* (Boulder, CO: Lynne Rienner).

———. 1996b. *Transforming Capitalism and Patriarchy: Women and Development in Africa* (Boulder, CO: Lynne Rienner).

Green, Cynthia P. (ed.). 1994. *Sustainable Development: Population and the Environment* (Washington. D.C.: USAID).

Harmon, Willis W. 1996. "Reassessing the Economic Assumption." *The Futurist* (July/August): 13–15.

Harrison, Paul. 1990. "Sustainable Growth in African Agriculture." In *The Long-Term Perspective Study of Sub-Saharan Africa*, vol. 2 (Washington, D.C.: World Bank).

Hasdorf, Mogens. 1995. "Employment Creation through International Cooperation: Case Studies in Rural Areas in West Africa." In *Global Employment: An International Investigation into the Future of Work*, vol. 1, edited by Mihaly Simai (London: Zed Books).

Hellinger, Stephen, Douglas Hellinger, and Fred M. O'Regan. 1988. *Aid for Just Development* (Boulder, CO: Lynne Rienner).

Henn, Jeanne K. 1983. "Feeding the Cities and Feeding the Peasants: What Role for Africa's Women Farmers?" *World Development* 11: 1043–55.

Heredia, Blanca. 1997. "Prosper or Perish? Development in the Age of Global Capital." *Current History* (November): 383–88.

Hyden, Goran. 1990. "Creating an Enabling Environment." In *The Long-Term Perspective Study of Sub-Saharan Africa,* vol. 2 (Washington, D.C.: World Bank).

Jacobson, Jodi L. 1993. "Closing the Gender Gap in Development." In *State of the World 1993,* edited by Lester R. Brown, Gary Gardner, and Brian Halweil (New York: W.W. Norton).

James, Valentine Udoh. 1995. "Introduction: Sustaining Women's Efforts and Sustainable Development in Africa. Westport, CT: Praeger.

Johnson-Odim, Cheryl. 1991. "Common Themes, Different Contexts: Third World Women and Feminism." In *Third World Women and the Politics of Feminism,* edited by Chandra Talpade' Mohanty, Ann Russo, and Lourdes Torres. (Bloomington: Indiana University).

Kabira, Wanjiku M. and Elizabeth A. Nzioki, 1993. Celebrating Women's Resistance: A Case Study of Women's Groups Movement in Kenya. Nairobi: Africa Women's Perspective.

Kalipeni, Ezekiel. 1994. "Introduction: Southern Africa's Expanding Population." In *Population Growth and Environmental Degradation in Southern Africa,* edited by Ezekiel Kalipeni (Boulder, CO: Lynne Rienner).

Kettel, Bonnie. 1995. "Gender and Environments: Lessons from WEDNET." In *Engendering Wealth and Well-Being: Empowerment for Global Change,* edited by Rae Lesser Blumberg et al. (Boulder, CO: Westview).

Livernash, Robert, and Eric Rodenburg. 1998. *Population Change, Resources, and the Environment.* Population Bulletin 53 (March) (Washington. D.C.: Population Reference Bureau).

Malindi, Grace Margaret. 1995. "Participation of Rural Women in Malawi National Rural Development Program." In *Women and Sustainable Development in Africa,* edited by Valentine Udoh James (Westport, Connecticut: Praeger).

Mbilinyi, Marjorie, and Ruth Meena. 1991. "Reports from Four Women's Groups in Africa: Introduction." *Signs* 16 (Summer): 846–48.

Mikell, Gwendolyn. 1997a. "Conclusions: Theorizing and Strategizing about African Women and the State Crisis." In *African Feminism: The Politics of Survival in Sub-Saharan Africa,* edited by Gwendolyn Mikell (Philadelphia: University of Pennsylvania).

———. 1997b. "Introduction." *African Feminism: The Politics of Survival in Sub-Saharan Africa* (Philadelphia: University of Pennsylvania).

Miller, Marian A.L. 1995. *The Third World in Global Environmental Politics* (Boulder, CO: Lynne Rienner).

Moghadam, Valentine M. 1995. "Gender Aspects of Employment and Unemployment in a Global Perspective." In *Global Employment: An International Investigation into the Future of Work,* vol. 1, edited by Mihaly Simai (London: Zed Books).

Moser. Caroline. 1991. "Gender Planning in the Third World: Meeting Practical and Strategic Needs." In *Gender and International Relation,* edited by Rebecca Grant and Kathleen Newland (Bloomington: Indiana University).

Munyak'ho, Dorothy. 1994. "Kenyan Women Press for Land Rights." *African Farmer* (April): 8–9.

Nwomonoh, Johathan. 1995. "African Women in Production: The Economic Role of Rural Women." In *Women and Sustainable Development in Africa,* edited by Valentine Udoh James (Westport, Connecticut: Praeger).

Olofin, S. 1991. "The Prospects for an Outward Looking Industrialization Strategy Under Adjustment in Sub-Saharan Africa." In *Economic Reform in Sub-Saharan Africa* (Washington, D.C.: World Bank).

Orvis, Stephen. 1993. "The Kenyan Agrarian Debate: A Reappraisal." *African Studies Review* 36 (December): 23–48.

Osirim, Mary J. 1994. "Women, Work, and Public Policy: Structural Adjustment and the Informal Sector in Zimbabwe." In *Population Growth and Environmental Degradation in Southern Africa,* edited by Ezekiel Kalipeni (Boulder, CO: Lynne Rienner).

Palmer, Ingrid. 1991. *Gender and Population in the Adjustment of African Economies: Planning for Change* (Geneva: ILO).

Picard, Mary Theresa. 1995. "Listening to and Learning from African Women Farmers." In *Women and Sustainable Development in Africa.* Edited by Valentine Udoh James (Westport, Connecticut: Praeger).

Rapley, John. 1996. *Understanding Development: Theory and Practice in the Third World* (Boulder, CO: Lynne Rienner).

Rashid, Sadig. 1994. "Africa at the Doorstep of the Twenty-First Century: Can Crisis Turn to Opportunity?" In *Africa within the World: Beyond Dispossession and Dependence,* edited by Adebayo Adediji (London: Zed Books).

Rocheleau, Dianne and Isabella Asamba. 1995. "People, Property, Poverty, and Parks: A Story of Men, Women, Water, and Trees at Pwani." In *Gender, Environment, and Development in Keyva,* edited by Barbara Thomas-Slayter and Dianne Rocheleau (Boulder, CO: Lynne Rienner).

Safilios-Rothschild, Constantina. 1990. "Women's Groups: An Underutilized Grassroots Institution." In *The Long-Term Perspective Study of Sub-Saharan Africa,* vol. 3 (Washington, D.C.: World Bank).

Scott, Catherine V. 1995. *Gender and Development: Rethinking Modernization and Dependency Theory* (Boulder, CO: Lynne Rienner).

Sen, Gita. 1994. "Women, Poverty and Population: Issues for the Concerned Environmentalist." In *Feminist Perspectives on Sustainable Development,* edited by Wendy Harcourt (London: Zed Books).

Stamp, Patricia. 1989. *Technology, Gender, and Power in Africa* (Ottawa: International Development Research Centre).

Staudt, Kathleen. 1987. "Women's Politics, the State, and Capitalist Transformation in Africa." In *Studies in Power and Class in Africa,* edited by Irving L. Markovitz (New York: Oxford University).

Stone, M. Priscilla, Glen Davis Stone, and Robert M. Netting. 1990. "The Sexual Division of Labor in Kofyar Agriculture." Paper presented at the November meeting of the African Studies Association, Chicago.

Swantz, Marja-Liisa. 1995. "Women Entrepreneurs in Tanzania: A Path to Sustainable Livelihoods." In *Global Employment: An International Investigation into the Future of Work,* vol. 2, edited by Mihaly Simai (London: Zed Books).

Teeple, Gary. 1995. *Globalization and the Decline of Social Reform* (Toronto: Garamond).

Thomas-Slaytor, Barbara P. 1992. "Class, Ethnicity, and the Kenyan State: Community Mobilization in the Context of Global Politics." *International Journal of Politics, Culture, and Society* 4: 301–21.

Thomas-Slaytor, Barbara, Dianne Rocheleau, and Charity Kabutha. 1995. "Policy Implications and Opportunities for Action." In *Gender, Environment, and Development in Kenya,* edited by Barbara Thomas-Slaytor and Dianne Rocheleau (Boulder, CO: Lynne Rienner).

Tripp, Aili Mari. 1992. "The Impact of Crisis and Economic Reform on Women in Urban Tanzania." In *Unequal Burden: Economic Crises, Persistent Poverty, and Women's Work,* edited by Lourdes Beneria and Shelley Feldman (Boulder, CO: Westview).

UNDP (United Nations Development Program). 1995. *Human Development Report* (New York: Oxford University).

Valentine, Theodore R. 1994. "Female-Headed Households, Private Transfer Entitlements, and Drought Relief in Rural Botswana." In *Population Growth and Environmental Degradation in Southern Africa,* edited by Ezekiel Kalipeni (Boulder, CO: Lynne Rienner).

von Bulow, Dorthe, and Anne Sorensen. 1993. "Gender and Contract Farming: Tea Outgrower Schemes in Kenya." *Review of African Political Economy* 56: 38–52.

Vuorela, Ulla. 1992. "The Informal Sector, Social Reproduction, and the Impact of the Economic Crisis on Women." In *Tanzania and the IMF: The Dynamics of Liberalization,* edited by Horace Campbell and Howard Stein (Boulder, CO: Westview).

Wacker, Corinne. 1994. "Sustainable Development through Women's Groups: A Cultural Approach to Sustainable Development." In *Feminist Perspectives on Sustainable Development,* edited by Wendy Harcourt (London: Zed Books).

World Bank. 1989. *Kenya: The Role of Women in Economic Development* (Washington, D.C.: World Bank).

———. 1990. *Women in Development: A Progress Report on the World Bank Initiative* (Washington, D.C.: World Bank).

———. 1991. *World Development Report* (New York: Oxford University).

———. 1992. *World Development Report* (New York: Oxford University).

———. 1994. *Adjustment in Africa* (New York: Oxford University).

———. 1996. *Toward Environmentally Sustainable Development in Sub-Saharan Africa: A World Bank Agenda* (Washington, D.C.: World Bank).

———. 1997. *World Development Report* (New York: Oxford University).

PART V

Regional Integration and Sustainable Development

12

Evaluation of the State of Integration in Africa: How to Strengthen the African Economic Community

Aguibou Mouké Y. Yansané

Economic integration has always been considered an important and unavoidable means of development strategy in Africa's new nations. The inclination to unite was an initial response of Africa's founding fathers to the balkanization process of the colonial era. Many cooperative organizations have been created. It is important to draw the lessons of their experiences with a view to effectively defining the nature of the challenges that the African Economic Community (AEC), the continental economic organization established by the Abuja Treaty signed in 1991, will have to meet and determine the strategy of economic development.

The purpose of this chapter is to evaluate the progress achieved in implementing integration policies in Africa by reviewing the current status, problems, opportunities, and challenges of some of Africa's existing regional economic communities (RECs), such as the Economic Community of West African States (ECOWAS), the Union Economique et Monétaire de L'Afrique de L'Ouest (UEMOA), the Common Market for Eastern and Southern Africa (COMESA), the Southern African Development Community (SADC), the Central African Economic Community (CEEAC), and the Communauté Economique et Monétaire de L'Afrique Centrale (CEMAC). What should be the new approach to the institutional aspect of integration to meet the objectives of the AEC?

THE ECONOMIC COMMUNITY
OF WEST AFRICAN STATES (ECOWAS)

Created in 1975 and regrouping in 1977, the sixteen West African states in ECOWAS aimed at successfully achieving a customs union and a common market in West Africa and promoting development. To this end, the Lagos Treaty provides for the harmonization of programs in several sectors. A compensation and development fund was set up to ensure equitable distribution of the benefits of economic cooperation and reduce the disparities in the development levels of the member states and to finance and guarantee foreign investments in the member states. In 1988, it was opened to non-regional governments and financial institutions.

ECOWAS Achievements

ECOWAS has made several positive achievements. The fund has financed several projects in the field of agriculture. There is a relatively free movement of nationals of member states with only an identity card, and of goods and capital. Cooperation has been enhanced in several areas with the adoption of several protocols and policy decisions. Protocols on nonaggression and mutual assistance in defense have been concluded. They have helped to establish a framework of confident relations, security, and settlement of disputes. A new ECOWAS Treaty of 1993 adds the role of regional peacekeeper to the ECOWAS list of objectives. Several institutions, including a regional parliament and a permanent military advisor's office, have been established. A clearinghouse has been operating with the collaboration of the Committee of West African Central Banks to ensure the full monetary cooperation by 2000.

Obstacles to Integration within ECOWAS

Certain obstacles have hampered the integration process in ECOWAS. The ECOWAS authorities have failed to implement the trade liberalization in ECOWAS member states. Indeed, 90 percent of intracommunity exports still come from Nigeria, Ghana, Côte d'Ivoire, and Senegal. The application of trade liberalization before harmonization of external customs will prove to be costly for countries that levy high customs tariffs on imports.

Another difficulty stems from the too-narrow concept of the criteria for determining goods produced within the community. All internal exports (40 percent of the total volume of the transactions, mainly from Côte d'Ivoire and Senegal) cannot satisfy the regulation stipulating that 50 percent of shares should be held by nationals of member states. ECOWAS has placed too much hope in the macroeconomic model of eliminating tariff barriers as a key factor for integration without taking due account of the political, economic, social, national, and international realities, including diminishing funds from external sources and the ever-increasing influence of centrifugal forces such as different monetary zones, bilateral agreements outside the community, political instability, and social unrest.

Other ECOWAS problems include the adverse effects of many inefficient public industries and state enterprises, lack of harmonization of development strategies and investment plans, nonconvertibility of certain local currencies and their negative impact on trade, non- or late payment of member states' contributions, and existence of several similar intergovernmental organizations competing for the meager resources.

The ECOWAS manufacturing sector has suffered from several other policies, such as strategies giving undue priority to import substitution; from preference accorded to expansive and inefficient large-scale projects; from economic policies relying too strongly on government funding, management, and regulation of economic matters; from unjustifiable protection measures in favor of uncompetitive products; from lax customs surveillance of fraudulent products; and from the failure of monetary, fiscal, and social policies.

How to Strengthen ECOWAS

ECOWAS would be strengthened by increasing the competitiveness of the subregion by organizing the disengagement of the state from a protected environment toward a more open-market framework. Hence, two components of a strategy to strengthen the investment climate are in order: the adoption of a pragmatic and realistic approach to investment by assembling government officials, and economic operators in a joint effort to prepare flexible guidelines; and the creation of optimal conditions for a successful agricultural and industrial master plan, whereby governments create an enabling environment for private sector development.

In sum, although ECOWAS has successfully drawn up the legal instruments for the implementation of the Treaty of Lagos in many sectors of cooperation and has authorized the free movement of persons, it is still true that the lack of political will, institutional red tape, the critical economic situation of member states, and the basic concepts of integration that have met with little success have not made it possible to obtain the expected results.

ECOWAS constraints include the deteriorating terms of trade, the debt burden of member states, weak support services, and inadequate levels of entrepreneurship, skills, technological capabilities, and financial institutions. ECOWAS member states need stronger political will consistent to the adjustment of its integration policies and programs. The pragmatic approach to integration is preferable to the implementation of a global macroeconomic model.

THE ECONOMIC AND MONETARY UNION
OF WEST AFRICA (UEMOA)

UEMOA is the successor organization to the Communanté Economique de L'Afrique de L'Ouest (CEAO), the West African Monetary Union (UMOA), and the West African States Customs Union (UDEAO). UEMOA was created in January 1995, and its headquarters is located in Ouagadougou, Burkina Faso. A commission manages the daily activities. One of its major objectives is to create a new framework of solidarity to facilitate a global adjustment process and the realization of common growth. The Treaty of UEMOA is also aimed at enlarging the market in goods and services throughout the West African zone to allow a significant reduction in the costs of production in UEMOA member states. UEMOA was projected to create a customs union by 2001.

UEMOA integration is seen as contributing eventually to the strengthening of the ECOWAS subregion by coordination of member states' budgetary policies; harmonization of business law, investment codes, and fiscal legislation; and establishment of a subregional financial market.

UEMOA Achievements

To date, major UEMOA achievements include: freedom to transfer funds throughout the zone, convertibility of the currency and a fixed exchange rate, and currency stability founded on tight monetary and credit policies formulated by the UEMOA Council of Ministers, which controls the subregional central bank, the Central Bank of West African States (BCEAO).

Lately, UEMOA has established an agenda for integration by the rules, which includes the introduction of a transitional tariff regime set at 30 percent on an approved list of imports; the adoption of all judicial and fiscal changes to allow the free involvement of workers across borders at the end of 1997; the agreement on a common investment code and unified business legislation; the harmonization of national indirect taxes; the creation of a regional institution to train experts in finance and administration; and the current implementation of common sectoral programs in transport and telecommunications, environment, human resources development, and energy.

UEMOA Obstacles

The obstacles of UEMOA are the following: Member states are not allowed to draw more than 20 percent of the previous year's budget receipts; differences between UEMOA jurisdictions are large enough to outweigh moves toward tariff harmonization and other integration measures; value-added, corporation, and personal income tax levels remain highly disparate, with each country sticking to its existing domestic tax legislation; existing industries, similar in all UEMOA member states, are all concentrated around a few growth poles; and trade liberalization has tended to benefit those growth poles, depriving many least developed countries of fiscal resources.

How to Strengthen UEMOA

UEMOA's new industrial policy would promote the manufacture of inputs such as fertilizers, pesticides, veterinary products, agricultural machines, and tools. It would encourage the processing of agricultural products to increase manufactured value-added. It would minimize duplication of industries and stimulate new complementarities of production in the subregion. The success of the new industrial policy would require the following: harmonization of industrial programs, fiscal and customs policies and investment codes, trade liberalization accompanied by transitional tariff policies to improve the competitiveness of industries, the existence of qualified and motivated entrepreneurs with sufficient financial means, and the creation of community enterprises.

In sum, UEMOA integration seems to favor the same policies as ECOWAS through the intensification of interstate economic relations, the multiplication of common investment projects, the coordination of sectoral development for optimal use of resources in the subregion, and programs of restructuration of and compensation for the least developed member states.

THE COMMON MARKET FOR EASTERN AND SOUTHERN AFRICA (COMESA)

COMESA was originally established through the initiative to embrace all the countries of eastern and southern Africa. Now COMESA comprises twenty-three member states.

The aims of COMESA are to liberalize trade; encourage cooperation in industries, agriculture, transport, telecommunications, natural resources, and monetary issues; and establish a regional common market with the goal of strengthening the economy of the entire region. This would raise the standard of living in those countries as well as make them competitive. COMESA was created in 1984 by the adoption of a common list of 209 products (now increased to 319). The mechanisms are the study and reduction of customs duties and tariff barriers among member states and the gradual development of an external common tariff, which would lead to the common market.

A multilateral clearinghouse was created at the Central Bank in Harare, Zimbabwe, on February 4, 1984. A COMESA monetary unit of account (UAPTA), equivalent to the Special Drawing Right of the International Monetary Fund, is used to settle interstate debts every two months, with the balance payable in dollars. A COMESA Trade and Development Bank, initially established in Bujumbura in 1986, has been relocated to Nairobi (Kenya). COMESA has recorded examples of success, and it has also experienced many problems.

COMESA Achievements

The COMESA clearinghouse is reported to ensure the payment of about 70 percent of the interstate trade in 1991. COMESA's traveler's checks were introduced in 1988.

The practical effect of the rule of 51 percent of the capital held by the nationals of member states, at least 45 percent of the value-added ("rules of origin"), which Kenya and Zimbabwe challenge, has been lessened. Furthermore, COMESA agreed on a tariff reduction scale to be applied over a five-year grace period. Companies in which nationals control between 30 and 40 percent of the capital can benefit from 30 percent reduction. This conversion means that many firms that direct their exports to Kenya and Zimbabwe would enjoy preferential treatment.

Generally, the charges of the customs union have been reduced in order to give preference to COMESA member states. Concrete progress has been realized in the formulation of strategies of planning and promotion of cooperation projects. They include the following:

- increased trade volume in manufactured goods;
- rehabilitation of existing industries in priority subsectors;
- identification and promotion of multinational industrial projects;
- promotion of the establishment of institutions of excellence to enhance cooperation in science and technology;
- training of human resources (200 people engaged in cement, iron and steel, fertilizers, food industries, and health sectors);
- exchange of information;
- cooperation on standardization and quality control;
- preparation of an integrated industrial development program and a long-term perspective plan for cooperation in the industrial sector, which formed the basis for the Industrial Development Decade for Africa II (IDDAII);
- creation of an enabling climate conducive to intercountry cross-border investment by preparing a charter for multinational industrial enterprises and adjusting member states investment codes to take into account the integration of leather products from the Leather Products Institute in Ethiopia.

Obstacles to Integration within COMESA

Obstacles to integration within COMESA include the following:

1. Several COMESA member states still have a restrictive system of issuing and controlling import licenses and exchange systems.
2. The Trade and Development Bank has problems in obtaining all its subscriptions and accessions.

3. COMESA member states still maintain tariff barriers in terms of licenses, exchange control, and red tape.

4. The international trade of COMESA is limited by the lack of foreign exchange, which affects the import capacity of member states.

5. The inadequate transportation system keeps trade within COMESA at a lower level than with the outside world.

6. There is little information on local commodities, and the tradition to buy outside COMESA seems to be firmly established.

7. Traveler's checks are not readily accepted in certain member states.

8. The civil strife in Somalia, Sudan, Rwanda, and Burundi has contributed to the weak performance of member states' commitment to economic integration, which was confirmed at Lilongwe, Malawi, in December 1994.

9. There are hardly any links between many of the member states, and a handful of countries (Kenya, Madagascar, Zambia, and Zimbabwe) account for 60 percent of total UAPTA trade.

10. There are structural weaknesses of the manufacturing sector, which are extremely dependent on imports.

11. There is a low industrial capacity utilization in the subregion: 33 percent in Sudan, 25 percent in Tanzania, and 30–50 percent in Zambia.

Domestic constraints include lack of managerial skills, frequent disruptions in power supplies, inadequate technical facilities, lack of information, and marketing weaknesses.

How to Strengthen COMESA

1. COMESA would be strengthened by the increase of prices of member states' primary commodities that dramatically lowered export revenues.

2. The most devastating problems of drought, desertification, and communications have to be solved.

3. Member states' dropping of tariffs and trade barriers will give preference to internally produced goods, thus contributing to keeping the money in the region. When full market integration is achieved, those goods could be competitive on the world market.

COMESA economic integration would be helped by the increased use of railroads, better communications, the alleviation of poverty, and the control of population growth. Integration would also be facilitated by macrolevel demand management, price liberalization, and privatization.

The COMESA governments should maintain peace, security, and law and order to encourage domestic and foreign investment. They should create an enabling environment for the development of entrepreneurship and new markets. Institutional and human resource development and capacity building would be in order. Financial institutions such as commercial, savings, and merchant banks are needed to assist in the improved mobilization of resources.

In conclusion, COMESA is nowhere near the steady reduction of tariff and other nontariff barriers among member states in order to create conditions that would contribute to increasing the volume of interstate transactions. The objective of establishing a common monetary system, as well as that of an effective and profitable promotion of specialization and complementarity of agricultural and industrial production, are as remote as in the case of ECOWAS, even though COMESA has succeeded in adopting many protocols, agreements, acts, and decisions with regard to trade preference and increased trade among member states.

COMESA constraints include increasing debt, deteriorating terms of trade, the effect of external financial shocks, and the problems originating from inappropriate monetary policies. They also include difficulties in mobilizing technical and financial assistance.

But like ECOWAS, most of the development strategies are being reoriented toward the more active participation of private entrepreneurs in the industrialization process, especially with respect to small- and medium-size industries (SMSIs), the strengthening of the African entrepreneurial base, a new emphasis on market culture, and the promotion of regional and subregional cooperation through increased mobility of factors of production, skills, goods, and services among countries. The COMESA governments also realize that national industrial programs, if to be successfully carried out, need the close involvement and commitment of all at every stage of project preparation, evaluation, promotion, and monitoring.

COMESA also chose to emphasize some joint programs of large-scale basic industries to reduce external dependence on certain imports and to achieve greater complementarity of the economies of member states.

SOUTHERN AFRICAN DEVELOPMENT COMMUNITY (SADC), THE SUCCESSOR ORGANIZATION TO THE SOUTHERN DEVELOPMENT COORDINATION CONFERENCE (SADCC)

The 1980 Lusaka Declaration created the SADCC. The nine founding member states are Angola, Botswana, Lesotho, Malawi, Mozambique, Swaziland, Tanzania, Zambia, and Zimbabwe. After their independence in March 1990 and August 1994, Namibia and South Africa respectively joined the SADC. The objectives of SADC today are boosting southern African economic independence, promoting a judicious regional integration, mobilizing support for national and regional projects, and making a concerted action for the mobilization of international assistance for the achievement of these objectives. SADC has set for itself targets for the elimination of trade barriers within two years and the creation of a common currency system by the year 2000. The sectoral responsibilities for each state have not changed. Each member state is responsible for coordinating community projects in specific economic sectors; emphasis should be placed on coordination and increased production aimed at helping the expansion of trade.

To achieve its aims, SADC organizes meetings with representatives of governments and bilateral and multilateral institutions with a view to mobilizing resources within the framework of annual conferences.

SADC has a limited secretariat, and the secretariats of member states maintain relations with the executive secretariat.

Achievements of SADC

The financial resources were estimated at about $8 billion U.S. dollars, relating to 490 projects valued at more than $8 billion by 1994. Four billion dollars have already been secured and disbursed, including 80 percent in the form of foreign aid to member states of SADC.

SADC has rehabilitated the transport and communication networks of member states, particularly those destroyed during the Civil War, such as the Beira corridor and the Harare-Maputo railway line, and has also completed rehabilitation works on other communication projects.

Obstacles to Integration within SADC

Obstacles to integration within SADC include the following:

1. Although, in order to achieve its earlier objectives, SADC has embarked on an autonomous plan of actions toward South Africa, it is obvious that the adopted measures have rather increased the dependence of SADC member countries on the northern ones and the European Common Market. Moreover, the organization has only partly reduced the dependence of member states on apartheid South Africa, partly because of difficulties caused by the effects of Civil Wars on communication lines.

2. To maintain GDP growth of member states at 4.5 percent, it is necessary that aid funds be increased annually by 4 percent. Western creditors should also make concessions to considerably reduce the region's debt service.

3. The trade and industry sectors, the value-added of the subsector of manufactured products, are declining. Agriculture stagnated during the 1980–1990 decade because of limited incentives for procedures. As a result, the volume of interstate trade remains at 5 percent, which is well below its potential.

4. Few concrete results have been achieved to date because lack of industrial planning prevented the implementation of a good number of viable projects, including the rehabilitation of already existing ones.

5. The landlocked member states of Botswana, Lesotho, and Swaziland (BLS) are also members of the South African Customs Union (SACU), created since 1910. SACU's objectives include trade liberalization, establishment of a common external tariff, a standard consumer tax, and fiscal compensation for BLS.

Because the philosophy of SADC was centered on project-led development, there was a strong need for Western aid. For its part, the West was willing to provide aid to SADC countries without having an effect either on SADC primary goal of disengagement from South African transportation and communication system, or facilitate economic growth for the member states. The record of Western aid from the inception of SADC shows that the initial interest in the new organization waned over time. Initial aid was primarily directed at improvement of transport and communications projects over other sectors such as agriculture and industry. Later, Western aid would favor other sectors (food security, energy) again over industrialization programs.

In addition to the need for Western aid, SADC was hopeful to lure Western business away from South Africa and to its member states, giving them expanded trade relations and a new Western position on trade and investment in the region. However, the record of Western trade and investment with the region, prior to the divestment from South Africa, shows the West's unwillingness to look to other SADC markets.

Although these obstacles are formidable, they are not the only ones responsible for some of the failures of SADC. There are internal obstacles to the development of the primary goal of development. These obstacles include among others an overemphasis on project-led development.

Cases of Success in Project-Led Development

SADC sought development through project implementations. Each member state has been allocated an area for research and project development on a cross-border basis. The record shows that there were many successful projects, but the follow-through process was insufficient to act as a catalyst for further development.

For example, SADC argued that there is no point in easing nonphysical barriers to trade if physical barriers still exist. To decrease these physical barriers, Mozambique was charged with the development of railway lines and port facilities in member states, to be used as an alternative to lines crossing to South African ports. To this end, railways were constructed between Zambia and Angola and Zimbabwe and Mozambique. These new routes to SADC member states' ports were shorter and cheaper than transporting goods via South African ports. Despite this fact, one-third of SADC trade still uses longer and more expensive South African routes.

Toward Building SADC Political Strength and Organization

Drawing on the lessons learned by the failures of previous regional groupings, the foundations of SADC are significantly different than previous African organizations of economic cooperation and integration. SADC retains a relatively small bureaucracy consisting only of a Summit of Heads of Government, a Council of Ministers, a small secretariat, and sectoral commissions for each program. The small size of the secretariat limits the cost of SADC. To ensure equitable growth and the independence of member states, SADC is designed to minimize "infringements on national sovereignty and the responsibility for operational programs is devoted to national governments." This would also serve to limit the growth of a bureaucratic SADC with powers to impose rules on member states rather than seek cooperation and coordination. The problem for SADC was compelling member states to implementation, when the foundation of the organization has recognized the need for national sovereignty over the region.

Again, like the individual projects, there is a record of successes and failures. For instance, a major success for the region was the improvement of rail lines, as it was stated earlier. Because this was a cross-border investment, member states involved in the project showed great initiative and cooperation in its construction.

However, the underlying macroeconomic policies necessary to support future development was missing. This type of coordination includes pricing, monetary, and/or subsidy programs. With each member state allowed to maintain its own separate economic policy, the ability for intraregional trade is limited, regardless of the ease of transportation. Although there has been recognition of the need to reconcile economic policy within SADC, there has been little progress toward this goal.

The South Africa's membership to SADC means new markets for its resources (oil, water, and hydroelectricity) and a new local source of imported goods. Additionally with Western aid and markets becoming increasingly hard to access, many African nations see South Africa as an engine of growth. For SADC to fully benefit from a new South Africa, the normalization of trade relations and terms of trade across borders must occur.

Impact of Trade Reform on Trade and Industrial Structures

Studies have been carried by SADC to determine the impact of trade reform on trade and industrial structures on GDP employment exports and imports, but it was assumed that policy shifts would soften the impact of trade reform on trade and industrial structures. These policy shifts would include converting state enterprises into private enterprises through enabling policies to set the private sector free. They would include a competitive industrial and trade policy package, which would contribute to improving the investment environment for private sector. There would be macroeconomic policy reforms to set the exchange rate right and to adopt regulation on capital flows. The region would develop its natural resources (mining, agriculture, forestry, and tourism) downstream. SADC would promote cross-border investment, which could bring the benefits of transferring skills and technology, rectifying regional trade imbalances and enlarging extra regional trade capacity.

How to Strengthen SADC

SADC would be strengthened by the creation of an enabling environment, an attractive investment climate, competitive industrial production, coordination of economic policies and business practices, improvement of the existing banking systems, the simplification and provision of tax incentives, and rationalization of tax regimes in SADC member states.

In conclusion, it should be recalled that although SADC has been associated with a number of projects including food security in the region, its initial raison d'être and first objective were to reduce dependence on South Africa's apartheid regime in transport and communications.

SADC constraints are increasing debt, deteriorating terms of trade, higher taxes, difficulty of financing mechanisms, and elaborate and complex investment codes and land acquisition laws.

After majority rule was achieved in South Africa, SADC member states wanted to increase their access to European markets and secure stable commodity prices under the Lomé Convention. It is therefore obvious that the end of apartheid in South Africa called for a redefinition of the objectives and role of SADC, including relations with COMESA in the context of a wider integration and in the prospects of the establishment of the AEC. In January 1993, SADC decided against merging with COMESA and soon afterwards launched its own trade program, which is designed to create a single common regional market.

THE CENTRAL AFRICAN ECONOMIC COMMUNITY (CEEAC)

The CEEAC was created in Libreville, Gabon, in 1983 on the recommendation of the United Nations Economic Commission for Africa (UNECA). The member states are Burundi, Cameroon, Central African Republic, Chad, Congo, Equatorial Guinea, Gabon, Rwanda, Sao Tome and Principe, and Democratic Republic of Congo. Angola has an observer status. The headquarters of the CEEAC is located in Libreville, Gabon, with the secretariat in Kinshasa, Democratic Republic of Congo. Several member states of the CEEAC belong to one of the two subregional organizations: the Economic Union of Central African States (UDEAC)—now the Economic and Monetary Community of Central Africa (CEMAC), of which the members belong to the franc zone—and the Economic Community of the States of the Great Lakes (CEEGL). The objectives are to gradually set an economic union by creating preferential trade areas. This objective should be achieved in three stages of twelve years each.

The treaty establishing the CEEAC highlights the uneven distribution of the costs and benefits of integration and aims at the rapid development of the landlocked and least developed countries. The objective of the treaty is also to promote cooperation in the fields of agriculture, industry, transport, communications, and energy. The development of the transport sector is emphasized first, and trade integration occupies the fifth place.

CEEAC Achievements

The structures of the CEEAC are identical to those of ECOWAS with a Conference of Heads of State and Government, a Conference of Ministers, a Tribunal, a secretariat, and a Technical and Consultative Committee. CEEAC *also* has a compensation and development fund, which compensates the least developed member states for losses, related to the reduction and removal of tariffs. Like the other aforementioned subregional organizations, the CEEAC has in the first twelve years of its existence adopted several protocols, acts, and decisions with a view to strengthening interstate trade, in particular in the fields of finance, customs, transport and telecommunications, agriculture, industry, etc. Some national highways have even been transformed into interstate roads in order to facilitate the movement of persons, goods, and services. In 1988, the CEEAC set up a clearinghouse to promote the utilization of the five currencies within the subregion. It is not necessary to evaluate CEEAC because it has not had the time to establish units to execute its agreements, acts, and decisions because it is one of the more recent subregional integration organizations.

CEEAC Obstacles

CEEAC has to overcome the following difficulties:

transportation problems in an immense geographical area where a considerable quantity of products perishes;

the lack of enthusiasm of certain member states;

the nonpayment of the equivalent of 54 percent of institutions' budget by certain member states for the operations of the CEEAC secretariat; therefore, CEEAC suffers from a weak mobilization of resources;

the nonimplementation of regional programs partly due to the application of financial reforms and structural adjustment programs (SAPs);

large and inefficient public sector;

underutilization of existing manufacturing capacities;

numerous difficulties experienced by local enterprises to gain access to the markets;

poor functioning of judiciary institutions specialized in business law;

fiscal laws are not encouraging investment in small and medium enterprises;

there is little or no respect for the sacredness of public and private property in some member states;

high costs of the factors of production and lack of several productions inputs;

insufficient support mechanisms provided to small and medium enterprises in the formal or informal sector, especially in terms of information;

inadequate training institutions;

the currency exchange rates are artificially manipulated;

promoters need to overcome too many problems before getting their licenses;

weak competitivity of the subregional environment;

serious human, institutional, physical and economic constraints;

little or no availability of subregional capital for manufacture and commerce.

Different intergovernmental organizations have been able to draw consequent lessons from this identification of constraints. Given the subregion's potentialities, such as immense territories, diverse and important natural resources, and a vigorous working age population, these meetings have made appropriate recommendations concerning the involvement of the private sector.

How to Strengthen CEEAC

CEEAC would be strengthened by accelerating the establishment of economic and institutional programs of reforms, by emphasizing the importance of small- and medium-scale projects, and by associating organizations in charge of the collection and mobilization of the resources to the formulation and implementation of programs. CEEAC would benefit from economic adjustment programs; privatization of many state-owned companies; improvement of the environment of industrialization, manufacturing, and transport and communications; private-sector development through expansion of small- and medium-size enterprises; and expanded opportunities for resources' mobilization and trade.

In conclusion, like the other subregional organizations, CEEAC needs to overcome the following difficulties: the lack of enthusiasm on the part of the member states and the problems of transport in a vast geographical area where huge stocks of produce perish due to their inaccessibility. CEEAC has to resolve the problem of nonpayment of member states' contributions to the upkeep of the secretariat and the nonimplementation of regional industrial programs due partly to financial austerity imposed by SAP.

CEEAC's constraints include the lack of a viable mechanism to coordinate the policies between member states, the lack of technical and financial support, and the absence of good linkages between member states. CEEAC is also suffering from a faulty mechanism to follow-up activities.

CEEAC's potential as a prime mover of the AEC's implementation will be enhanced when at least two members, Zaire and Rwanda, end their current violent political turmoil.

THE ECONOMIC AND MONETARY COMMUNITY
OF CENTRAL AFRICA (CEMAC)

Unlike UEMOA, the CEMAC seems to be moving more slowly, but it is backed by strong studies that were sponsored by the defunct Central African Customs Union (UDEAC). Even though the treaty has been signed, no head of state has ratified it yet.

Many of the achievements or obstacles described about the UEMOA zone franc in West Africa are similar. Many CEMAC conventions are being drafted; they are related to the customs union, the economic union, and the court of justice. Differences among member states concerning the restructuration of the Central Bank of Central Africa have delayed the proceedings of heads of state and government, which was adjourned sine die in August 1996.

CEMAC argues for "an integration by the rules," which will proceed according to the following gradual and pragmatic means:

- the establishment of democratic rights (free election, freedom of thought, press, information, etc.);
- the harmonization of economic, financial, and fiscal policies;
- the liberalization of the markets for goods and the factors of production through the abolition of tariff and nontariff obstacles, creation of a commerce by intensifying exchange within the zone;
- the establishment of a well-adapted formal and institutional framework;
- the definition and implementation of a budgetary policy, consistent with the monetary and credit policy;
- the creation of a common market.

The steps taken to implement the policies of CEMAC are the following:

- enhancing the institutions of CEMAC through the definition of adapted expertise and financing;
- establishing a legal framework appropriate to the take-off of the investment climate and growth.

CEMAC's "integration by the rules" is focused on the following:

- enhancing consistent national macroeconomic policies;
- harmonizing legal, fiscal, and financial policies;

- creating one single market;
- establishing common sectoral policies.

The achievements of CEMAC are:

- the creation of a tax on investment income;
- the creation of an income tax on physical persons;
- the harmonization of fiscal rules on saving, productive activities;
- the adoption of necessary policies to stimulate the participation of the informal sector to the process of economic growth and development;
- CEMAC's study initiative on external common tariff, the single-tax regime, and the harmonization of internal taxes.

CEMAC's fiscal and customs reforms for the Subregional Program of Reforms are aimed at four objectives:

- to eliminate observable subregional economic distortions;
- to promote the competition of enterprises through allowing international competition;
- to simplify the tariff system and differentiate the instruments of protection, which must ensure public receipts;
- to improve the field of fiscal receipts in the CEMAC member states through the reduction of nominal rates of tariffs on imports.

The stage of a perfect customs union would be realized when the rate of preferential tariff is zero (to eliminate tariff barriers) and the rates of the tax on investment income have been harmonized in all member states, and when the establishment of common sectoral policies in transport and communications, agriculture and food, internal trade and industry would have been finalized.

In the industrial sector, CEMAC's objectives include the following:

- the normalization of quality control;
- the promotion of subregional core industries, which would contribute both to the fulfillment of basic needs and to self-sufficiency in priority sectors, especially by creating incentives;
- the organization of economic operators to help to restructure the subsectors and the channels;
- the encouragment of innovation and applied research to the priority sectors through enlisting the support and coordinated actions of institutions of higher learning and research;
- the development of technology transfer mechanisms in the system of production.

These CEMAC objectives seem to be relatively consistent with those of CEEAC's except in the subsector of fiscal and customs policies where CEMAC's written documents abound.

The central problem appears to be that the currencies in different member states need to be enhanced by an adherence to strict monetary and credit policies.

CONCLUSION

The existing RECs succeeded in establishing many legal instruments, protocols, and agreements relating to the free movement of persons, goods, and services and increased trade among member states. But they failed in areas that would be essential to the success of the AEC, such as the increase of the volume of trade (5–6 percent of total trade) and of agricultural and industrial production, the successful step-by-step implementation of the agenda for regional integration, the harmonization of policies between RECs and specific institutions, and the full cooperation by bilateral and multilateral donors in facilitating the integration process by drawing on their own experiences. Yet, in terms of scale, continental integration may offer the only long-term solution to Africa's impoverishment and the only chance for economic stability and growth.

Some difficulties include: poorer states' inability to meet integration commitments, the uneven distribution of benefits and costs of integration for which it remains difficult to compensate, institutional deficiencies including not only the proliferation of intergovernmental institutions but also over-centralization and politicization, political and ideological differences and aggravated militarization that lead to the destabilization of the states, lack of adequate resources and transportation and communication network, and staff based more on geographic representation instead of skills. RECs also suffer from the inability for least developed member countries with a narrow and inelastic tax base to foresee the long-term benefits of economic integration.

The brief review of the various regional experiences of cooperation and integration in Africa makes it possible first of all to assert that these attempts have obviously not been successful in Africa. These unsuccessful attempts are mainly due to the state of undevelopment, natural barriers, inappropriate transport and communication infrastructures, lack of complementarity between economies, national economic disparities, the burden of immediate costs of integration compared with short-term benefits, and especially the lack of political will of member states concerning the effective implementation of community decisions on cooperation and integration.

Larger concerns were the protectionist policies of industrialized countries, the deteriorating terms of trade, the falling commodity prices, the debt burden, the lack of technology transfer from the industrialized countries, and inadequate resource flows. All of these seemed to involve strong political will and persuasion for lobbying and promotion and competitive pricing to reverse the flow of financial resources toward African development.

The recent trends in the RECs have been to define industrial programs, which include the harmonization of industrial policies and plans and the promotion of subregional trade by the establishment of complementary units utilizing the raw materials of the member states. These complementary units will include core industries (chemical, engineering, and construction materials) as well as basic consumer's industries. There is an emphasis on studies and their exchange, joint research, and development for new technologies and products among REC's member states.

The REC's development strategies are also being reoriented toward the following:

- good governance and popular participation in an environment of peace, rule of law and order, and respect for human rights;
- a sound macroeconomic framework dominated by the stabilization, structural adjustment, price liberalization, and better management of national affairs;
- development and a more active participation of the private-sector entrepreneurs in the industrialization process, especially with respect to SMSIs;
- the strengthening of the African entrepreneur base;
- a new emphasis on market orientation;
- the stimulation of an industrial culture and the promotion of regional and subregional cooperation through increased mobility of production factors, goods, services, and skills among REC's member states;
- improved productivity and competition.

To strengthen the RECs, it must be recognized by each African member state that its development program must be rehabilitated by a better policy-making mechanism, good governance, rule of law and order, and a peaceful environment. The development program of nation-states must also be based on an efficient resource allocation policy. There must be a greater mutual participation of the people—the private sector, the public sector, nongovernmental organizations, the civil society, urban and rural workers—in setting the goals of development. There must be a sustained and adequate financial assistance to programs to carry major political and economic reforms. There must be an emphasis on rehabilitation and maintenance of the existing industrial capacities and infrastructure systems. There must be a sound formulation of more efficient programs in health, human, and environment resources and continued internal and external financial support. This requires Africa's nation-states to totally revamp their development policies, and Western donors must continue and even increase donation levels.

At the national level, the RECs are strengthened by emphasizing the private-sector development and the formation of SMSIs, which will make concrete the concepts of self-reliance and self-sustaining development.

At the subregional levels, the trends have been to cooperate on the harmonization of policies on finance, trade, customs, tax, human resource development, infrastructure improvement, and technology innovation.

The efforts of the RECs have also been focused on joint projects in the area of the core industries, which are determined by the criteria of comparative advantage and minimal external dependence.

To develop a strategy for future regional integration, there should be an emphasis on step-by-step rationalization of existing regional organizations to achieve lean and efficient institutions; to harmonize customs, tax, monetary, and financial policies; and to improve their infrastructures. Thus, African governments should work toward achieving an enabling environment, including removal of tariff and other natural and human-made barriers. They should mobilize public opinion, popular support, and financial resources.

13

West African Regionalism Revisited: Cooperative Management of the Senegal and Gambia Water Resources

Nurudeen B. Akinyemi

INTRODUCTION

This chapter examines regional cooperation among African countries by exploring in some detail the experience of West African countries in managing their shared water resources. Some attempts at establishing regional cooperation schemes include the East African Community (EAC), Economic Community of West African States (ECOWAS), Economic Community of Central African States (ECCAS), the Southern African Development Community (SADC), and the African Common Market (ACM).

The EAC is defunct, and the others have not achieved much beyond the initial signing of treaties, although ECOWAS was very busy in the 1990s and the beginning of the twenty-first century with peacekeeping and peace enforcement in the Liberian and Sierra Leonean crises. SADC has found new life with the membership of postapartheid South Africa. Although the economic benefits of regional economic cooperation schemes are well known, symbolic rhetoric of African unity and Pan-Africanism tend to be more important in the statements of African leaders as justification for establishing these organizations.

A common obstacle in all these organizations has been the reluctance of national governments to sacrifice any iota of sovereignty in economic policy making to such supranational organizations. This is despite the fact that member states uniformly recognize and desire the expected benefits of regional cooperation. One may be tempted to conclude that given these experiences, regional economic cooperation among African states is a very remote possibility at best.

This chapter argues that although success in macrolevel regional schemes may have been more elusive, cooperation on microlevel issue-specific areas within the framework of international regimes offers better potential for success. These may create confidence-building measures that become stepping stones toward achieving the much desired macrolevel regional economic cooperation schemes. Shared international water resources are an example of an issue-specific area where such benefits may be derived. The Senegal River basin is shared by Mauritania, Mali, and Senegal, and the Gambia River basin is shared by Senegal, Gambia, Guinea, and Guinea-Bissau.

THEORETICAL FRAMEWORK

Functional theorists present international regimes and organizations as frameworks for interstate cooperation.[1] Realist theorists on the other hand see an international system dominated by the pursuance of uncoordinated self-interest, in an atmosphere perceived as zero sum.[2]

According to regime analysts, if actors are convinced that they can better achieve their long-term self-interests by cooperating with other actors, the tendency will be for them to sacrifice any perceived short-term gains from unilateral actions for long-term, more superior outcomes from multilateral action, preferably within the framework of an international regime. These international regimes are defined as "principles, norms, rules and decision-making procedures around which actors' expectations converge in a given issue-area."[3]

Conventional regime analyses rely on rational choice assumptions, such as egotistical actors deciding whether or not to join cooperative arrangements based on cost-benefit calculations of self-interest. They often overemphasize the benefits of cooperation over the potential for disputes in these arrangements. What they often ignore are the tendencies of dominant actors to cajole and coerce weaker members through the manipulation of incentives and sanctions into conformity in the absence of a negotiated settlement of conflicting interest.[4]

These analyses do not allow for adequate examination of the interests and concerns of less dominant, weaker, and smaller actors; the contests over the fundamental basis of regimes; and more generally, the dynamism that characterize real regimes.[5] We will therefore be paying more careful attention to the interests of the individual riparian states of the Senegal and Gambia River basins. We cannot assume that all the states equally desire a basinwide regime in their respective basins, under any circumstances. This approach attempts to reveal the characteristics of the issue area as "loci of greater or lesser, but not inevitable tension in which actors struggle to define the regime and the space it orders . . . it does not suggest or assume that we should or should not want any specific regime or regimes as such."[6]

SENEGAL RIVER BASIN ORGANIZATION

The Senegal River Basin Organization (OMVS) is the institutional mechanism through which the co-riparians of the Senegal River manage their shared water resources.[7] The Senegal River has its sources in Guinea and the Republic of Mali, from where it flows west forming the border between Senegal to the left and Mauritania to the right, on its way to the Atlantic Ocean. Since its establishment on March 11, 1971, in Nouakchott, Mauritania, the organization has provided a framework for the relatively successful cooperative efforts of these states to develop the water resources of the Senegal River.

The OMVS replaced the former Organization of Senegal River States (OERS), which was formally dismantled in November 1971.[8] The objectives of the OERS, founded in 1968, went beyond the specific goal of water resource development. The OERS was intended by the member states as a vehicle for the integrated and comprehensive development of their respective national economies. The decision-making apparatus of the OERS was therefore very politicized, requiring absolute consensus on every issue. The ultimate decision-making authority was vested in the heads of state themselves, leaving the organization with very little decision-making capability. Stalemate, paralysis, and inaction characterized the period of the OERS. Political dispute between Guinea and Senegal in 1971 completely paralyzed the organization, leading to its demise.

The experience of OERS left the founders of the OMVS determined to depoliticize the new organization and narrow its objective specifically to the development of the Senegal River, with each state an equal partner. In addition to narrowing the focus of OMVS, all decision making and implementation authority was vested in the general secretariat, headed by the Council of Ministers. This body inherited most of the power of the Heads of State Conference under the previous OERS. Under OERS, the heads of state met regularly at an annual summit. Under the OMVS, the heads of state were required to meet only when and if it was felt necessary.

The principal bodies of the OMVS are the Interstate Committee on Agricultural Research and Development, the Permanent Water Commission, and the Consultative Committee. These bodies are responsible for coordinating the agricultural policies of member states, water allocation, and solicitation of foreign funds, respectively. Together, they constitute the cooperative mechanism for the joint management of the Senegal drainage basin.

Two projects were identified as key to achieving optimum benefits in developing the water resources: the Manantali Dam in Mali and the Diama

Dam in Senegal. These projects were intended to provide for hydroelectric power, navigation, and irrigated agriculture.[9]

The Diama Dam was expected to protect land along the river bank from the Atlantic's salt water. Salt water from the Atlantic penetrates 160 miles above the city of St. Louis inside Senegal. Completed in 1985, the dam was expected to make the river navigable all year-round, up to the Malian town of Kayes. About 74,000 acres of land were expected to become irrigable for double cropping.

The Manantali Dam, completed in 1988, is not yet fully operational because of lack of funding. It is expected to generate electricity for the extraction of iron ore in eastern Senegal and the conversion of bauxite into alumina in Mali. It will also irrigate more than 750,000 acres of land for double cropping. Additionally, it is estimated that about 250,000 tons of rice paddy could be grown along the river.[10] This would cut down significantly on the foreign exchange required for rice imports. Senegal currently imports about 280,000 tons of rice a year at very high prices.

With underdeveloped economies, the individual member states of the OMVS each depend to a very large degree on grants, loans, and technical assistance from international financial organizations like the International Monetary Fund (IMF), the World Bank, the African Development Fund, and donor countries like France, Germany, Canada, Saudi Arabia, and the United States. By implication, therefore, the projects proposed by the OMVS were bound to depend almost entirely on external assistance both financially and technically. That fact was not lost on the OMVS member states. On May 23, 1974, the Rural Development Ministers of the riparian states met in Nouakchott, Mauritania, to finalize a 30-year joint development program for the Senegal River basin. This report was intended for submission to a group of international financiers.[11] The report was then submitted to a meeting of about twenty international financial organizations, and interested countries convened in Nouakchott on July 11, 1974, to discuss ways of raising funds for the implementation of the OMVS projects. The Manantali and Diama Dams were estimated at a cost of $250 million. A coordination committee was formed at the meeting with the purpose of putting the financial resources of the donors to work as soon as possible.[12]

The OMVS projects, however, caused some disagreements among the major foreign donors on the one hand and between the donors and the Senegal River Basin states on the other. The West Germans and the French objected to the building of both dams. They each preferred one of the two. The Germans preferred the Manantali Dam in Mali, which was to be built by Germans. West Germany, therefore, increased funding for the dam. The French preferred the Diama Dam in Senegal and increased funding of the project accordingly. The Diama Dam, a mainly irrigation project, would serve French interests better by increasing agricultural production near St. Louis.[13]

A West German study team concluded that the Diama Dam was not needed because (1) the Manantali Dam would provide enough water flow to keep the sea out of the delta; (2) commercial fishing would be hurt by the Diama Dam, because it would render two species—the mullet and the African shad—extinct; (3) the cost of making the river navigable by the Diama Dam project, which included annual dredging, is not justified by the expected river traffic; (4) 10,000 persons would be displaced by the lake, which would flood the area behind the dam; and (5) herders of cattle and sheep would have to choose between becoming farmers or moving to other grazing lands.[14]

On the OMVS side, the organization's planning director, Mr. Sheikh Bati, responded that both dams were needed for political reasons. Costs were only incidental. He emphasized that environmental costs must be weighted against development needs: "Environmental questions don't really have the same place in Africa as they do in Europe or in the United States, because here people don't have enough to eat."[15]

The political considerations of the OMVS projects, which take precedence over economic and environmental concerns, can be stated thus: (1) Mali objected to only the Diama Dam being built because it wanted navigation and access to the sea, which the Manantali project would provide; (2) Mauritania's interest in the Senegal River is irrigation, and only the Diama Dam would fulfill the potential for irrigated agriculture; and (3) Senegal preferred both projects because it would benefit from both in terms of irrigation and hydroelectric power. To keep all the members of the OMVS happy and hence the organization intact, both dams must be built—regardless of financial costs, economic feasibility, environmental impacts, and effects on local population.

Applying the cost benefit analysis proposed by the foreign donors would have removed the original incentives, which in the first place, convinced these countries to join forces for a cooperative development of the Senegal River. They had each hoped to achieve within the framework of the OMVS what they could not achieve individually. Because of close geographical proximity to each other, the benefits from projects on one side of the river are easily transferable across the border, each state is too poor to afford a unilateral implementation of its water project, and international financiers typically demand cooperation among riparian states as a condition for assistance.

Building only one of the projects would have alienated at least one of the riparians and threatened the collapse of the organization. After all, states' decisions to cooperate with other states often depend on the extent to which they perceive their own interests as being served by cooperating. States will join international regimes when they believe the regime framework to be fair and equitable. If they believe the regime framework to be unfair and injurious to their interests, agreements within the regime will be highly unlikely and the continued viability of the organization itself will be in jeopardy. In the case of the OMVS, political consideration was paramount over all others.

This dilemma points out a problem common to regional economic organizations in Africa. Although economic considerations might act as the initial motivator for interstate cooperation, political considerations and perceptions of the equitable distribution of costs and benefits of joint projects often dictate the strength and potential for survival of the schemes themselves. It also highlights the problems with financing these projects. The high costs of initial construction plus the technical skills required are often beyond the reach of African countries, hence the necessity for significant dependence on outside sources for finance, data collection and analyses, feasibility studies, construction and maintenance of projects, and decisions about which projects to build and where to cite them. The international donors for the OMVS projects were Saudi Arabia, Abu Dhabi, Kuwait, West Germany, France, Canada, the African Development Bank, the European Community, and the World Bank.

The foundation stones of the Diama Dam were laid on December 12, 1979.[16] Work on the Diama Dam was not started until June 1981 whereas construction of the Manantali Dam started in June 1982. On November 15, 1985, the Senegalese Minister of Hydraulics, Mr. Samba Yela Diop, announced the completion of the Diama Dam.[17] The Diama was commissioned in 1986. The Manantali Dam was completed on March 31, 1988, with a reservoir capacity of 18 million cubic meters. The cost for the Manantali alone was $575 million, and the total cost for both projects came to $1 billion.[18] This is substantially larger than the initial estimate of $250 million for both projects.

The Manantali Dam is central to the OMVS plan. It has the capacity for large-scale irrigation on both banks, year-round navigation for oceangoing vessels, and electricity for the region. A proposed hydropower plant for Manantali at a cost of $1 million is expected to produce 200 megawatts of electricity.

According to World Bank estimates, the hydropower plant can yield adequate returns only if oil prices remain at $25 to $30 per barrel. The Bank also doubts the economic rationale of the project, which intends to make 900 kilometers of the river navigable at a cost of CFA160,000 million. The ability of the OMVS countries to repay the loans for these projects has been seriously questioned. West Germany converted Mali's debt on Manantali— $42 million—to grants because of Mali's inability to repay its loans and canceled about $500 million of OMVS debt.[19] Other creditors are expected to do the same for the other two Senegal riparian states.

Development of irrigated agriculture in Senegal, Mauritania, and Mali has proven slower and more expensive than anticipated. By 1988, only 54,000 hectares of the targeted 375,000 hectares have been developed. Out of the 54,000 hectares developed, 30 percent was not being used. The unused 30 percent could have produced additional 75,000 tons of food for the three countries, which had a combined food deficit of 660,000 tons in 1987. The cause of the delay is attributed to lack of funds and uncoordinated donor response.[20] This situation has not improved because these countries continue to depend on foreign funding, while sources of such funding increasingly dry up. The domestic constituencies of the donor countries are becoming increasingly hostile to foreign aid as they themselves struggle to deal with budget deficits.

At the local levels, with lands developed at an average cost of $10,000 per hectare, agricultural yields have increased while farm incomes remain quite low—at subsistence level. Farming remains centered on family plots that are generally small in size, with inadequate use of modern farming techniques. Prices typically remain very low. Consequently, family farmers have accumulated large debts. The introduction of double cropping had not been successful because farmers insist on achieving self-sufficiency in food and prefer traditional farming techniques, which require less work and less capital investment.

In an attempt to prevent the disruption of traditional pasturing, which would have occurred by damming the river during the four months of the rainy season, the OMVS states opened the dam for four weeks during August–September 1988, creating an artificial flood. The consequence of such action was very costly because of the reduction in the hydroelectric generating capacity of the dam. The expected benefits from river navigation were also sacrificed due to a substantial reduction in water flood.

Border conflicts between Senegal and Mauritania became bloody in April 1989. Diplomatic relations between the two countries were broken off, and the Mauritanian President, Colonel Maaonyua Ould Sid'Ahmed Taya, demanded the removal of OMVS's headquarters from Dakar, Senegal to Bamako, Mali. The Mauritanian General Secretary of OMVS and three other Mauritanian officials were recalled from Dakar. The Malian President responded by stating that the headquarters could not be transferred without the unanimous consent of all three countries. He advised that the organization must not be politicized in the quarrels between two member states, however serious such quarrels might be.[21]

Although the conflict between Senegal and Mauritania for some time threatened the collapse of OMVS, work resumed on the projects of the organization in mid-1990. The construction of a 71-kilometer-long dike in Mauritania resumed on May 14, 1990, after temporary stoppage in 1989 due to the border conflict with Senegal. The dike, started in 1987, is intended to prevent flooding when the floodgates of Manantali Dam are opened. It is also expected to make all-season river navigation possible.[22]

However, the closure of the Senegalese border added 36 percent to the cost of the project. Because of the border closure, raw materials that were supposed to be procured from the Senegalese banks were replaced with materials from 150 kilometers away. Senegalese workers required for construction were withdrawn by the Senegalese government and replaced with Malians and Mauritanians.

Although the organization had been somewhat paralyzed by the Senegal-Mauritania conflict, the OMVS met in mid June 1991 in Mauritania to discuss ways of making the population living in the Senegal River valley aware of the advantages of the organization. It was the first such meeting since Senegal and Mauritania broke off relations in 1989, and the Senegalese were absent.[23] At the thirty-second Ministerial Council meeting in Nouakchott, on July 16, 1991, the Senegalese Minister of Rural Development represented his country. He was the first Senegalese representative to visit Mauritania since the break in diplomatic relations in 1989. The Senegalese representative rejected suggestions that Senegal was attempting to use OMVS in an effort to impose a Senegalese-drawn boundary plan on Mauritania. He asserted that "the OMVS is a model which has always functioned outside the problems between the states."[24]

During the short history of the OMVS, the organization has proven to be a relatively successful framework for the cooperative management of the Senegal River basin. The efficiency of its projects is subject for debate among international donor agencies, such as the World Bank and the IMF. However, the fact that the organization continues to exist, that it survived the political conflict between Senegal and Mauritania, and that it had actually implemented its major projects, plus some additional smaller ones, is evidence of the political will of these states to continue to tackle their water management problems within the OMVS framework.

The relative success of the OMVS also demonstrates that cost benefit economic analysis alone might not be enough to predict or guarantee the establishment of a cooperative mechanism among sovereign states. For the Senegal River basin states, political expediency dictated that they attach more importance to noneconomic benefits. It was more important that the development needs of each state be taken into account equally, by all the states. This way, the interests of all riparian states became strongly interdependent. No single state could afford to withhold cooperation for long without injuring its own national interests in the Senegal River.

Depoliticizing the organs of the organization was an ingenious way to avoid the paralysis, inefficiency, and eminent collapse that have plagued many regional cooperation attempts on the African continent. The organization has also proven that interstate cooperation in specific issue areas, which by their very nature impose a certain level of interdependency on states, is more feasible and productive than general-purpose cooperative schemes. By creating confidence-building measures, such microlevel regimes can become stepping stones toward larger macrolevel regional economic cooperation schemes.

The establishment of cooperative mechanisms such as the OMVS requires deliberate actions from states. States must believe that benefits from such schemes will outweigh those expected from unilateral actions. The OMVS has not only reduced the cost of operation for individual states, it has made external sources of financial and technical assistance accessible, at a level that would not have been possible for each state acting independently. The basin no doubt continues to share significant dependence on external assistance with other regional development organizations in the developing world. The delay in implementing some of its other programs is attributable to lack of funding. As the OMVS matures in the years to come and continues to learn from its experience, the areas of cooperation among its members are expected to spill over to more sophisticated areas of their economies.

ORGANIZATION FOR THE DEVELOPMENT OF THE GAMBIA RIVER BASIN

The Organization for the Development of the Gambia River Basin (OMVG) is the institutional framework through which the riparian states of the Gambia River—Senegal, Gambia, Guinea, and Guinea-Bissau—seek to develop their shared water resources.[25] The idea for a cooperative management of the Gambia River began to take shape when in 1967 Senegal and Gambia signed a treaty to carry out preliminary studies on the water resources of the river. On December 31, 1976, both states established a coordinating committee for the improvement of the Gambia River.[26] On January 30, 1978, Senegal and Gambia founded the OMVG. In March 1979, Guinea—from where the river has its source—agreed in principle to join the organization, and at the second annual heads of state summit in Dakar, in July 1980, Guinea became the third member of the OMVG.

Guinea's formal decision to become a full member of the OMVG followed the decision of the organization not to build a dam at Sambagalon in eastern Senegal. The dam would have had adverse effects on Guinean agriculture and mining.[27] The water development projects identified as priorities for the riparian states were a dam at a site yet to be determined in Guinea, a bridge/dam at Balingor in the Gambia, and a dam at Kekriti in Senegal. The projects were to be financed by West Germany, Saudi Arabia, The European Development Fund, the African Development Bank, the Islamic Development Bank, and the United States Agency for International Development.

The bridge/dam will link Dakar and the Cassamance region, which is considered vital for Senegal both economically and politically. The dam is expected to stop salination upriver and store freshwater for human consumption and irrigation during the dry season. About 24,000 hectares of land can be irrigated by the freshwater. This project is also expected to allow traffic along the course of the river.

The Kekriti Dam is expected to irrigate 360,000 hectares of land in eastern Senegal, make river navigation possible, supply energy to the iron ore mines in the town of Kedougou, and control the upstream level of the anti-salt barrage reservoir.[28] At the initial stage of planning, the projects took on added urgency because of the unrelenting droughts experienced by the region in the previous ten years. Since then, the widespread Sahelian droughts and the enormous food deficits that resulted from them combined to highlight the significance of these projects for meeting the food needs of the population in the area. At the July 27, 1983, Summit Conference in Dakar, Guinea-Bissau became the fourth member of the OMVG. Two more dams were also added to the organization's projects. They were hydroelectric dams at Saltinho, Guinea Bissau, and Kouya, Guinea.

After several years of inaction, the riparian states met for their seventh meeting in Banjul, Gambia, on February 3–4, 1987, to discuss finance possibilities for the two dam projects in the Gambia and Senegal. The cost of the two projects was put at a total of $276.5 million—$128.5 million for the Balingor Dam and $148 million for the Kekreti Dam. The total operating budget for the OMVG in 1987 was $540,000.[29] The major obstacle to financing the projects—and responsible for the paralysis of the organization itself—had been the insistence of international donors that projects be spread out over several years. On their part, the OMVG states had expressed intentions to build these projects at a relatively shorter time frame—arguing the urgency of the food situation. At the eighteenth session of the Ministerial Council in Dakar in October 1990, this condition was overcome, paving the way finally for the start of the construction.[30]

At the eighth summit of the Heads of state in Conakry, Guinea, on January 30, 1991, the heads of state declared their dissatisfaction at the lack of progress in implementing the projects of the organization. Both the Guinean President Lansana Conte and Gambian President Sir Dawda Jawara lamented that the OMVG had not demonstrated its efficiency and that the potentials of the river basin had not been exploited. However, in the face of the apparent shortcomings, the summit adopted a "minimal restructuring program," the effect of which was to reduce the staff of OMVG from thirty to fifteen and reduce the budget by 50 percent and abolish the High Commission and the general secretariat, to be replaced by an executive committee.[31]

The implication of the restructuring is that the capability of the organization is further curtailed while management of its activities will rely more on executive powers of the heads of state, thus heavily politicizing the OMVG. This is the same practice that has rendered many African regional groupings ineffective and inconsequential beyond the euphoria that accompanied the initial signing of treaties. Additionally, due to lack of funding, its projects remain on the drawing board.

CONCLUSIONS

The problems confronting the OMVG are typical of the growing pains shared by almost all regional organizations on the African continent. Above any other, that problem is access to international financing. The organizational problems are directly related to the state of the domestic economies in the individual member states. The national economies themselves rely on foreign financing to meet national development objectives. That means the organizations they establish among themselves, particularly river basin organizations, of necessity also rely on foreign financing and expertise to implement joint projects. Where international donor countries, agencies, and banks have been forthcoming, such as in the Senegal River basin case, the organizations tend to be successful and their goals tend to be accomplished. Where international finance is lacking, such as in the Gambia River basin, the organizations tend to be ineffective and revert to obscurity, and their objectives remain unfulfilled.

A second source of paralyses has been the tendency of these organizations to revolve around the executives of the member states. The top-heavy personal involvement of the heads of state in the decision making of these organizations, plus the requirement for unanimity in decision making, unnecessarily politicizes the organizations, and nothing gets done. Political jostling overshadows the important social, economic, and environmental considerations. To the extent that the OMVS had successfully avoided these bottlenecks, the organization had been more successful in fulfilling the promise of cooperative water resource management in the Senegal River basin. The Senegal River basin, like the Gambia River basin, remains vulnerable to continued access to international financial resources.

In both river basins, the riparian states clearly recognized their individual interests in the shared water resources. They also demonstrated the political will to manage and develop the water resources within the institutional framework of a cooperative regime. The issue for these countries was not whether or not to cooperate. The problem they continue to confront is how to achieve the objectives of cooperation, given their dependence on economic forces beyond their control. What then can we conclude about the cooperation experiences in these two international river basins? There are clear principles, rules, and decision-making procedures explicit in the institutional frameworks these countries have established for the joint management of their shared water resources. These can be found in the formal treaties establishing the respective river basin development organizations. They are also evident in the policies and practices of these organizations and of the member states. Both organizations have weathered political disputes between member states, which threatened the very survival of the institutions. Where one organization's success in achieving the objectives of cooperation has been directly related to its ability to attract international lenders, the other's failure reflects the inability to attract similar sources of financing. This is a finding that can be generalized to explain a significant portion of why regional economic cooperation schemes among African countries tend to perform less than satisfactorily.

This condition reflects the underdeveloped nature of African economies and the extent of their dependence on external sources of financing and investments. Although this dependency tells us something about the extent to which cooperating states can actually implement joint projects, it tells us very little about the potential for interstate cooperation among countries sharing the same natural resources, such as water resources.

What we have learned from the experiences of the Gambia and Senegal River basins is that there is potential for fruitful interstate cooperation where states perceive the existence of common interests in an issue area. The potential for cooperation (and conflict) is greatest where the nature of the issue area is such that it reenforces an interdependent relationship among the states concerned. However, the decision of states to actually join such formal or informal cooperative mechanisms ultimately depends on the extent to which states perceive these arrangements to be equitable and fair.

The decision of the Senegal River basin states to build both the Manantali and Diama Dams, over objections concerning financial costs, economic feasibility, and environmental impacts, reflects this concern for equitable distribution of costs and benefits. Similar concern is evidenced in the decision of Guinea and Guinea-Bissau to suspend joining the Gambia River basin organization until a dam in each of these states was added to the projects of the OMVG. The guarantee of the equality of legal status in the waters of the Senegal and Gambia Rivers, enshrined in their respective treaties, removed the fears of domination that smaller countries such as the Gambia and Guinea-Bissau might have. The most powerful predictor of cooperative state behavior, in addition to self-interests, appear to be the perception of the fairness of the institutional framework and concerns about equitable distribution of costs and benefits.

On the wider issue of the viability of regional cooperation as a strategy for African economic development, the African experience with shared water resource management demonstrates that the potential for success is greater in substantive issue areas than where such efforts are motivated mainly by ideological and symbolic concerns. The symbolisms of Pan-Africanism, African unity, Francophone, and Anglophone solidarity are useful mobilizing forces. Beyond that, the absence of concrete and specific economic and political interests that states can directly identify with will continue to guarantee that such schemes remain mainly symbolic and ineffective.

The potential for regional cooperation also exists in addressing the environmental impacts of natural resource use, such as pollution, erosion, flood control, population resettlement, and threat to wildlife. Other issues that hold potential for international cooperation beside natural resources include health epidemics, transboundary refugee movements, atmospheric pollution, and desertification. It is assumed that successful regional cooperation experience in such issue areas will have a favorable spillover effect on cooperation in broader regional economic interests.

NOTES

1. See John G. Ruggie, "International Response to Technology: Concepts and Trends," *International Organization* 29 (Summer 1975): 557–84; Robert O. Keohane, *After Hegemony: Cooperation and Discord in the World Political Economy* (Princeton, NJ: Princeton University Press, 1984); Robert O. Keohane and Joseph S. Nye, *Power and Interdependence: World Politics in Transition* (Boston, MA: Little Brown, 1972); Harold K. Jacobson, *Networks of Interdependence: International Organization and the Global Political System* (New York: Alfred A. Knopf, Inc., 1979); Stephen D. Krasner, ed., *International Regimes* (Ithaca, NY: Cornell University Press, 1986); Ernst B. Haas, "Why Collaborate? Issue-Linkage and International Regimes," *World Politics* 32 (April 1980): 357–405; and Marvin Soroos, *Beyond Sovereignty: The Challenge of Global Policy* (Columbia, SC: University of South Carolina Press, 1986).

2. See Nicholas J. Spykman, *America's Strategy in World Politics* (New York: Harcourt Brace Jovanovich, 1942); Frederick L. Schuman, *International Politics*, 4th ed., (New York: McGraw-Hill, 1969); Stanley Hoffman, *The State of War: Essays on the Theory and Practice of International Politics* (New York: Praeger, 1965); Hans Morganthau, *Politics among Nations: The Struggle for Power and Peace* (New York: Alfred A. Knopf Inc., 1978); and Kenneth Waltz, *Theory of International Politics* (Reading, MA: Addison-Wesley Publishing Co., 1979).

3. Krasner, 1986, op cit., p. 2.

4. See James F. Keeley, "Towards a Foucauldian Analysis of International Regimes," *International Organization* 44 (Winter 1990): 83–105.

5. See Nurudeen B. Akinyemi, "Cooperation and Conflict in International Regimes: Water Resource Management in the Nile Drainage Basin." Ph.D. Dissertation, University of South Carolina, 1994; and Nurudeen B. Akinyemi, "Sources of Future Conflicts in the Horn: Water Management and Interstate Relations among Egypt, Sudan and Ethiopia," *The Journal of African Policy Studies*, 1(3) (1995): 23–43.

6. Keeley, 1990, op cit., pp. 98–99.

7. The acronym is from the French, "l'Organisation pour la Misse en Valeur du Fleuve Senegal." The member states are Senegal, Mauritania, and Mali.

8. *Le Monde* (Paris), March 14, 1971.

9. *Fraternité-Martin* (Abidjan), February 2, 1973.

10. *The Times* (London), April 13, 1974.

11. Agence France Presse, May 25, 1974.

12. *West Africa*, July 29, 1974.

13. *African Gazette*, February 16, 1979.

14. *An Nahar Arab Report*, September 3, 1979.

15. Ibid.

16. *Le Soleil*(Dakar), December 12, 1979.

17. See Agence France Presse, November 11, 1985; Fraternité-Martin (Abidjan), November 8, 1985; and *West Africa,* November 25, 1985.

18. *African Economic Digest,* April 1, 1988.

19. *Le Soleil* (Dakar), May 24, 1990.

20. *African Economic Digest,* April 1, 1988.

21. Agence France Presse, September 2, 1989.

22. *Le Soleil* (Dakar), May 15, 1990.

23. *Le Soleil* (Dakar), June 17, 1991.

24. See *Le Martin* (Morocco), July 19, 1991; *Le Soleil* (Dakar), July 18, 1991; and Agence France Presse, July 16 and 18, 1991.

25. The acronym is from the French, "l'Organisation pour la Mise en Valeur du Fleuve Gambie." The members are Gambia, Guinea, Guinea-Bissau, and Senegal.

26. See *West Africa,* May 3, 1976 and *Marchés Tropicaux ET Méditerrancéens,* January 14, 1977.

27. *African Business,* September 1980.

28. Ibid.

29. See Agence France Presse, February 2, 1987; *Le Soleil,* February 3 and 4, 1987; and *African Economic Digest,* February 7, 1987.

30. *Le Soleil,* October 29, 1990.

31. See *Fraternité-Martin* (Abidjan), January 31 and February 1, 1991; *Le Martin* (Morocco), February 3, 1991; and *Le Soleil* (Dakar), January 29 and February 1, 1991.

BIBLIOGRAPHY

Adams, Williams. *Wasting the Rain: Rivers, Peoples and Planning in Africa* (Minneapolis, MN: University of Minnesota Press, 1992).

African Business, September 1980.

African Economic Digest, 1 April 1988; 9 July 1990.

African Gazette, 16 February 1979.

Agence France Presse, 25 May 1974; 11 November 1986; 2 September 1989; 16 and 18 July 1991.

Akinyemi, Nurudeen B., "Cooperation and Conflict in International Regimes: Water Resource Management in the Nile Drainage Basin." Ph.D Dissertation, University of South Carolina, 1994.

———. "Sources of Future Conflicts in the Horn: Water Management and Interstate Relations Among Egypt, Sudan and Ethiopia." *The Journal of African Policy Studies* 1, 3 (1995): 23–43

Collins, Robert O. *The Waters of The Nile: Hydropolitics and the Jonglei Canal, 1900–1980* (Oxford: Clarendon Press, 1990).

Darkoh, M. B. K. (ed.). *African River Basins and Dry Land Crises* (Uppsala: Reprocentralen HSC, 1992).

Eraternite-Martin [Abidjan], 2 February 1973; 8 November 1985.

Godana, Bonaya Adhi. *Africa's Shared Water Resources: Legal and Institutional Aspects of the Nile, Niger and Senegal River Systems* (Boulder, CO: Lynne Rienner Publishers, Inc., 1985).

Haas, Ernst B. *Beyond the Nation-State: Functionalism and International Organization* (Stanford, CA: Stanford University Press, 1964).

———. "Why Collaborate? Issue-linkage and International Regimes." *World Politics* 32 (April 1980): 357–405.

Hoffman, Stanley. *The State of War: Essays on the Theory and Practice of International Politics* (New York: Preager, 1965)

Jacobson, Harold K. *Networks of Interdependence: International Organization and the Global System* (New York: Alfred A. Knopf, Inc., 1979).

Keeley, James F. "Toward a Foucauldian Analysis of International Regimes." *International Organization* 44 (Winter 1990): 83–105.

Keohane, Robert O. *After Hegemony: Cooperation and Discord in the World Political Economy* (Princeton, NJ: Princeton University Press, 1984).

———. "International Institutions: Two Approaches." *International Studies Quarterly* 32, 4 (December 1988): 379–96.

———. "Reciprocity in International Relations." In *International Institutions and State Power,* Robert Keohane, Ed. (Boulder, CO: Westview Press, 1989).

Keohane, Robert O., and Joseph S. Nye, Jr. *Power and Interdependence: World Politics in Transition* (Boston, MA: Little, Brown, 1977).

Krasner, Stephen D. *International Regimes* (Ithaca, NY.: Cornell University Press, 1986).

Le Martin [Morocco], 19 July 1991.

Le Monde [Paris], 14 March 1971.

Le Soleil [Dakar], 12 December 1979; 15 and 24 May 1990; 17 June 1991.

Marches Tropicaux et Mediterraneens, 14 January 1977; 29 July 1988.

Morgenthau, Hans. *Politics among Nations: The Struggle for Power and Peace* (New York: Knopf, 1978).

An Nahar Arab Report, 3 September 1979.

Perrit, Richard. "African River Basin Development: Achievements, The Role of Institutions and Strategies for the Future." *Natural Resources Forum* 13 (August 1989): 204–8.

Ruggie, John G. "International Response to Technology: Concepts and Trends." *International Organization* 29 (Summer 1975): 557–84.

Schuman, Frederick L. *International Politics,* 4th ed. (New York: McGraw-Hill, 1969).

Scudder, Thayer. *The African Experience with River Basin Development* (Boulder, CO: Westview Press, 1993).

Soroos, Marvin S. *Beyond Sovereignty: The Challenges of Global Policy* (Columbia, SC: University of South Carolina Press, 1986).

Spykman, Nicholas J. *America's Strategy in World Politics* (New York: Harcourt Brace Jovanovich, 1942).

The Times [London], 13 April 1974.

Waltz, Kenneth. *Theory of International Politics* (Reading, MA: Addison-Wesley Publishing Co., 1979).

West Africa, 29 July 1974; 3 May 1976; 16 February 1979; 25 November 1985.

14

The Politics of Regional Integration and Development in Africa: Issues, Limitations, and Prospects

Aja Akpuru-Aja

The task of this chapter is to identify, discuss, and analyze the politics of regional integration in Africa. Special attention will focus on the recurrent issues and efforts, limitations and prospects in the present *pull* and *push* factors of globalization. In point of theory, the framework of analysis will be the functionalist-neofunctionalist approaches. Theorists are concerned about integration as a contractual form of interdependent relations of states that share common experience, values, interests, and aspirations and that are agreed to work together for the realization of commonly set goals (Haas, 1976). Integration scheme is supported by two contrasting but highly related approaches. One is the functionalist approach, which is *evolutionary* in process. It holds that states that have common interests, values, and experiences can transfer their sovereign will by a *function* and not formula in the realization of set goals, objects, and objectives in the hope that *in time* the integrating states would shift from working together in certain technical areas of interest to creating a political union (as a higher level of cooperation). The central point of the functionalists is that by cooperating in specific, usually nonpolitical issues, states can learn to trust one another to the point, in the stream of time, where causes of political conflict are eliminated (Mitrany, 1966:31, 38.) Basic about functionalism is the reduction of extreme forms of nationalism to pave the way for greater mutual trust and confidence.

The other approach is labeled neofunctionalism. The neofunctionalists share the same spirit with functionalists about the need for states that have common interests, values, and aspiration to agree and work together, but they are more worried that the timetable of evolutionary process will not move quickly enough to head off too many differences, perhaps, in strategies of action and compliance (Rourke, 1991:440; Axelrod and Keohane, 1985).

The position of neofunctionalists favors the establishment of an institutional mechanism to promote more collaborative tendencies and behaviors rather than stake transition from nonpolitical arms of cooperation to political union. Fearing that an evolutionary process does not hold an absolute guarantee for the elimination of causes of differences and self-interested actions of states, neofunctionalists make a stronger case for an institutional mechanism to respond to early signals of differences with a view to addressing political issues with an eye to greater political cooperation or union (Haas, 1976).

The two images of integration are attractive and fitting to the thrust of this effort. Africa has a checkered history of integration constrained by the vestiges of colonialism, governmental instabilities, high level of distrust and suspicion, poverty of political economy, high and unrepentant official corruption of the neocolonial elite and counterproductive policy choices by foreign powers and other interests. Going by common experiences of the misadventure of colonialism and neocolonialism and by shared values, interests, and aspirations, African states obviously need an integration framework *not by words* but deeds in a highly competitive world system. By extension, given the high degree of self-centered and self-interested states in Africa, the neofunctionalist case for an institutional mechanism is, indeed, very appealing. African states do not just need to agree to live and work together in certain areas of cooperation but they need to work out an institutionalized framework for harmonizing perceptions, intentions, interests, values, and strategies for achieving set goals.

ISSUES AND EFFORTS TOWARD AFRICAN INTEGRATION

For sure, African states are not ignorant of the grave crisis situation in the region. Apart from the climate of insecurity in Africa, the Organization of African Unity (OAU), the Economic Commission for Africa (ECA), the developed nations, the United Nations, International Monetary Fund/World Bank, and scholarly writings or reflections have shed sufficient light on the general deterioration in the quality of life, governance, interstate relations, and increasing marginalization in the global market system (Ihonvbere, 1994:1) Yet, Africa has not fallen totally short of responses and/or efforts. These responses have been incorporated into several major declarations and charters, such as *Charter for Africa* (1976), *African Charter of Human and Peoples' Rights* (1981), The Lagos Plan of Action and the Final Act of Lagos (1981), African's Priority Program for

Economic Recovery and Transformation (1989), and the African Charter for Popular Participation in Development (1990). Since the 1980s and the 1990s, several special summits, conferences, and workshops have debated on the three levels of integration needs in Africa: Subregional, regional, and global efforts have succeeded mostly in identifying the too many limitations against the movement from *words* to *deeds* toward integration of African states. Proposals have remained a paper tiger. As Africa begins the twenty-first century, the region remains the most backward, crisis-ridden, and disintegrative. This trend works against the several efforts towards *group-think* and *group relations*. A brief review of African efforts may be more informative.

AFRICAN EFFORTS TOWARD INTEGRATION

At the conference of Africa leaders in 1958, economic integration and cooperation were recognized as developmentally imperative. In 1963, the establishment of the OAU made this aspiration more significant (Ojo et al., 1985:142–81). Successive OAU summits in 1971, 1973, 1977, and 1979 decided that the ultimate goal is to establish the African Economic Community (AEC) in five successive stages covering various areas: (1) Preferential Trade Area, (2) Free Trade, (3) Common Community by the year 2000, (4) Customs Union, and (5) Common Market. The realization of the broad objective is expected to spring from existing subregional economic groupings in West Africa, East and central Africa, and North and southern Africa.

1. Economic Community of West African States (ECOWAS). It was established in 1975 and comprises sixteen countries.
2. Preferential Trade Area (PTA) for Eastern and Southern African States. It was established in December 1981 and comprises nineteen countries.
3. Economic Community of Central African States (ECCAS). It was established in 1983 and comprises 10 countries.
4. Southern African Development Coordination Conference (SADCC). It was established in 1980. Today, it is called the Southern African Development Community (SADC) and comprises ten countries.
5. West African Economic Community (CEAO). It was established in 1974. It comprises Francophone countries in West Africa.
6. Central African Customs and Economic Union (UDEAC). It was established in 1966 and comprises five counties.

It needs to be observed that a number of African countries had the wrong motives for regional integration. The first was the concern to maintain colonial unity. The second was the security factor arising from fear of larger and more powerful neighbors. A final point was lack of mutual trust among integrating countries (Aning, 1994b: 17–18). The fears of African countries notwithstanding, the OAU Plan of Action in April 1980 resolved generally to:

1. strengthen the existing regional economic communities and establish other economic groupings in subregions, where nonexistent, with a view to covering the whole continent.
2. strengthen sectoral integration at the subregional level, particularly in fields of trade, agriculture, transport, communication, industry, and energy.
3. promote coordination and harmonization among the existing and future economic groupings for a gradual establishment of an African common market.

At the end of the 1980s, no subregional grouping was within the striking distance of attaining the targets set. Since the 1980s, and even up to the early 1990s, the institutional structures have remained largely separated from the objectives. The point being argued is that institutional structures in Africa are far from being instruments of achieving the objectives of the integration process (Martin, 1989:71–79). The regularity of the OAU meetings and resolutions have not redressed this lapse. The picture of the OAU and integration process is that of mere signings of treaties—that in 1991 at the protocols. It was not surprising, therefore, that in 1991 at the OAU summit in Abuja-Nigeria, the date for the attainment of the continental community was postponed from the year 2000 to 2035 (Laporte, 1993:60–61). The community would be achieved over a period of thirty-four years divided into six stages:

1. strengthening the existing subregional communities (five years).
2. stabilization of fiscal regimes applied to intrasubregional trade (eight years).
3. establishment of a free trade area at the level of each subregional economic grouping (ten years).
4. coordination and harmonization of tariff and nontariff regimes between the subregional economic groupings (two years).
5. establishment of an African common market (four years).
6. establishment of the AEC (five years).

Since 1990 there been several "special summits," conferences, workshops, and round tables convened at subregional, regional, and international levels to discuss politics and obstacles of the African integration scheme. The ECA has repeatedly pointed out that integration is the only viable option for African economic recovery in the present globalization process. The treaty establishing the AEC at the twenty-seventh summit of the OAU in Abuja, Nigeria, on June 3, 1991, was indeed a novelty toward integration schemes. The treaty has 106 articles and six stages of implementation expected to overcome barriers to intra-African trade toward strengthened regional economic groupings (African Recovery, 1991:12). It is one thing, however, to have ambitious goals, and it is another thing to realize these objectives. An analysis of the subregional economic groupings in Africa has shown that the trend has been toward stagnation, and in an obvious case, outright disintegration. The other is that African states are rather too optimistic in their desire for integration, and in the process they have underestimated the obstacles strewn across their path.

THE POLITICS AND LIMITATIONS
OF AFRICAN INTEGRATION EFFORTS

Adebayo Adedeji is right after all when he cautions that "no African country, no matter how big it is, can really go about integration alone" (Harsch, 1991:2). Indeed, no African state is big enough in the first place. African states are generally weak and necessarily need an integrative framework to relate with one another from a position of strength and not weakness.

Previous efforts at identifying and analyzing Africa's integration problems and possibilities for their resolutions were understandably likened to the divisive legacies of colonialism, neocolonialism, and underdevelopment. Equally significant has been the call for the integration agenda in Africa. Given the persistence of the integration crisis in Africa, there is need to have an extended analysis of the politics and limitations of integration in the region. The task is a complex one, particularly as an integration scheme stretches beyond what is politically internal to Africa to include virtually all aspects of African interstate and international lifestyle. The specific focus of this effort is not so much of the well-known efforts but the extent to which factors internal and external to Africa combine to constrain the capacity of the region to move in the direction of a successful record of integration more than forty-one years after the initial conception. In this way, it is possible to map out a wide range of issues of nagging concern, such as:

1. lack of mutual confidence and trust
2. low cross-border trade relations
3. poverty of African political economy
4. no sustainable political will and security climate
5. the limitation of institutional mechanism
6. the challenges of the new world order and globalization

In the discussion that follows, an attempt will be made to elaborate on each of the problems or obstacles strewn in the path of regional integration in Africa.

Lack of Mutual Confidence and Trust

In both functionalist and neofunctionalist images, integration is about collaborative behaviors. Integrating units must have to believe first in one another and then in the ideal of integration. As a cooperative effort with a law-creating force, integration derives from confidence-building measures. Where, for whatever reasons, states are unwilling to trust one another against the converging desire to live and work together, the problem of distrust and suspicion becomes a variant of serious constraint to the ideal. Integration is also about sharing, and integrating states ought to accommodate both the strength and weaknesses of sovereignties and their political leadership for the overriding gains of working together under a highly competitive international setting (Adedeji, 1991:12).

Since the 1960s, when most African states achieved political independence, the emerging new nations have *nurtured* and *matured* images of distrust and suspicion, which are mirror images of misunderstanding of one another. From the North to South, East to West, and even central Africa, African states have farsighted images of one another. Relatively powerful states are perceived as subimperial powers, desperate to oppress and repress the weak ones (Aning, 1994b:17–18). Even in a subregion where the possibility of better understanding exists, the inclination presents itself more toward high degrees of distrust and suspicion between states. For instance, Nigeria is one country in the West African region that stretches its influences far into Africa over and above its domestic capabilities and constraints. Yet, Nigeria is perceived either as wasteful, as an interventionist, or as a subimperial power. The Anglophone and Francophone countries do not always move together in practice. Worse still, no real love relations exist, even among Anglophone and Francophone countries themselves. On the whole, unfounded distrust and suspicion remained a negative political trend at the level of perception against the spirit of trust and confidence. As logic would suggest, people who do not trust one another may in words come together and agree to common interests, but they will hardly work together in practice. This is the exact case of the African situation (OAU, 1986:12). It is not always any serious problem for African states to agree on the need for conferences, summits, and workshops. The implementation process will be frustrated by lack of shared commitment. The lack of confidence and trust at interstate levels is, in part, a reflection of internal contradictions within African states themselves. African citizens hardly trust one another or even their national governments.

Addressing the problem of confidence and trust in Africa remains a key element in harmonizing interstate relations necessary for the mobilization of multiple layers of national power for the ideals of regional integration. The Liberian and Sierra Leonean crises revealed a great deal on how distrust and suspicion could work against a well-intended ECOWAS interventionist security climate that hoped to enable member countries to stabilize their governmental systems and economies.

Nigeria, which is the prime mover in the ECOWAS system, not necessarily due to her economic stability but political will, has contributed no less than 80 percent of the funds and troops, to resolve the crisis in Liberia and Sierra Leone. Nigeria's perceived domineering position has a disintegrative motif rather than an integrative one. Kwesi Aning reports a confidential telegram from the U.S. embassy in Cotonou, Benin, to the State Department in Washington: "Nigeria has taken over ECOMOG, and the ECOWAS is too divided to have a common policy for peaceful resolution of the problem" (Aning, 1994b:17).

The decision-making process in the ECOWAS system is not cohesive. The age-old Anglophone and Francophone divide still remains. Decisions are often taken unilaterally without consulting the organization or analyzing the effects on general policy implementation. The many fragmented integration schemes in Africa are not helping the development of mutual trust and confidence among those who face a common threat of real marginalization and irrelevance in the emerging global economic system in the twenty-first century.

The Arab states in Africa certainly display more attitude of Pan-Arabism than Pan-Africanism. The Arabs' memory of participation in African slave trade and Islamization has left a farsighted image of sub-Saharan African states (Akpuru-Aja, 1999:151–52). Nearly forty years after a majority of African states attained political independence, a well-functioning, integrated scheme is still an aspiration. The irony of fate is that while even the developed countries in Europe and fast developing countries in Latin America believe so much in integration schemes, African states who have more need for them are yet to match words with deeds or desires with political empowerment.

Low Level of Cross-Border Trade Relations

Cross-border trade relations indicate the existence of a network of free flow of capital and labor as well as communication relations. It has a built-in integrative value. For about five decades since most African states gained political independence, African states have not learned to trade among themselves (ECA, 1983:13–14). This is sad, considering the obvious that Africa has a large market of 600 million. There exists a persistently low level of cross-border trade relations among African states. The bulk of Africa's transnational trade relations is with the developed countries. Eighty-five percent of Africa's total exports are marketed in the industrialized North, compared to 75 percent for Latin America and 68 percent for South and East Asia (Ihonvbere 1994a:14). Only a very small fraction of officially recorded exports, about 3 to 6 percent, goes to other African countries. In 1988, intracommunity trade in ECOWAS was a mere 4.9 percent. In the CEAO, which was disbanded in February 1994, it was 10.5 percent. For UDEAC, it was 3.6 percent. Noteworthy is that the bulk of cross-border trade relations in Africa is unofficial by ways of smuggling as a lucrative industry. In Africa, smuggling is a highly organized business with local and cross-border networks supported by wealthy syndicates transnationally. This has been the most common form of intracommunity trade relations in Africa because of the highly porous borders of African states, the weakness of political structures, and discriminatory economic and fiscal policies.

According to a World Bank (1989) report, some of Africa's problems include political instability, widespread use of power for individual gain, the neglect of agriculture, increase in food imports, low level of capacity utilization in industry, and increasing difficulty in financing recurrent expenditure. The overall picture reveals that African political economy is structurally dependent, weak, unproductive, and unserviceable.

Poverty of African Political Economy

The poverty of the African political economy certainly works against integration efforts (Ake, 1981). Beyond the lasting legacies of colonialism, the neocolonial elite in African are unrepentantly unproductive and corrupt to pioneer sustainable economic growth and development. In the global economic rating, Africa is increasingly becoming irrelevant due to real marginalization in international division of labor. The general pattern of politics in Africa is the same. High premium is placed on the economic realm as a means of selfish and class enrichment. Policies and projects are *faked* to serve self or class and not the nation. Every sector of the economy is politicized, and little or no interest is shown in technological development. As Omar Ali Juma, the foreign minister of Zanzibar, noted at the conference on Alternative Development Strategies, organized by the institute for African Alternatives (IFAA) in 1989:

Thirty years of independence had not benefitted the people of Africa . . . Leaders had become pawns of extra-continental power, economies remained mere appendages of the metropole and cultural values . . . Thirty years of independence had also brought dictatorship and tyrannical regimes in some countries. Basic human rights recognized by all civilized mankind were denied to millions. (Omar, 1989:6)

The true picture of African integration efforts is that of commitment in words and retreat in deeds. As Professor Julius Ihonvbere notes, over the decades, African leaders have been unable to use integration as a scheme to fight dependence, underdevelopment, foreign domination, and gross inequalities in the region's relations with the outside world (Ihonvbere, 1994a).

It is pertinent also to note that due to the self-centered nature of African leaders, they have failed across the board to sell the ideals of regional integration schemes to their citizens. Integration as a variant of economic growth and development in a global village is hardly given serious scholarship in schools. The press coverage on the values of integration is weak. Given the contradictions of underdevelopment and marginalization in the global economic system, the building of a common market for Africa has remained, not surprisingly, a paper tiger (Ihonvbere, 1994a).

African political economy is plagued by mounting external debt servicing, weak neo-mercantilist policies, and official corruption. As Ibrahim Babangida once lamented, "Africa's indebtedness is the single major obstacle to development in the continent. Africa's external debt is well over $300 billion. In per capita terms, Africa is the most indebted region in the world. In 1990 alone, Africa spent 30 per cent of its export earnings, about $25 billion, on debt servicing alone" (Ihonvbere and Turner, 1993:446). Comparatively, the total value of foreign aid to the region in 1989 was $21 billion, much lower than what was taken out for debt servicing alone. In 1986, ECA observed that 45 sub-Saharan African nations paid out $895 million more to the IMF than they received. Arising from politicized social and political settings, African states do not have a common voice or approach toward external debt management. Thus, weak and nonconvertible currencies, declining terms of trade, declining foreign aid, high debt-servicing ratio, and declining foreign support and interest are working against integration schemes in Africa.

From political and economic indicators, all the subregions in Africa are still heavily dependent and/or reliant on foreign aid and markets (ECA, 1991:VIII) The limited range of production, technology, goods, and services create supply pull from outside. Without achieving an autonomous capacity to control, exploit, and manage natural, economic, and human resources, it would be a far cry to expect increased cross-border trade relations en route to integration as a function.

Lack of Sustainable Political Will and Lack of Security Climate

Integration as a function is dependent on states surrendering part of their sovereign will to the larger framework. As logic expects, political will has to do with political empowerment of every article of association, which includes building a network of trust and confidence between integrating states. In Africa, there is the political vision of integration as a variable of continental growth and development. However, what has been lacking is political will and commitment of states to the functions of integration.

There is no evident political will to search for a solution that progressively leads to cooperation and integration as a development strategy despite intervening national and international obstacles (Laporte, 1993:60–61). In Africa, there is hardly the translation of treaties, conference resolutions, and protocols into actions and commitments.

The high cases of governmental instability create two main problems toward integration in Africa. The first is that the sudden rise and fall of heads of state and governments do not create room for continuity of policy commitments. The second is that there is no favorable security climate to promote transnational integration (Nwokedi, 1992). A situation where no subregion of Africa is spared of woes of ethnic cleansing, interstate border disputes, extreme forms of nationalism, terrorism, and nonmilitary threats such as human rights abuses, food crises, refugee problems, high unemployment rate, gross official corruption and crime waves endangers integration (Aning, 1994a:5–9). Lacking political stability, many African heads of state and governments have not politically empowered African integration and development.

As the experiences of Europe and Latin America show, the future of integration in Africa will depend greatly on the development of the right political perception, thinking, and attitudes among national political leadership. It is a path of honor for integrating states to share common political will and determination to move forward. Invariably, this depends too on an encouraging security climate. Political stability is vital for security factors of integration. Security of the integrating region reinforces political will of states involved. Sadly, Africa lacks both political will and security environment toward integration.

The Limitation of Institutional Mechanism

Neofunctionalists have raised the significance of an institutional mechanism as a collaborative mechanism for harmonizing principles, practices, strategies and, perhaps, differences in perceptions toward the goals of integration (Haas, 1976). In Africa, there is clearly no institutional mechanism for harmonizing interests and strategies among African states, particularly as African states have evident crises of distrust and suspicion (Hazzlewood, 1985:177–78). Charters, treaties, and protocols are no substitute for an established institutional mechanism as typified by the European parliament in the case of the European Union. But then, the place of an institutional mechanism in African integration schemes would logically depend on the development of political stability, political will, mutual trust, and confidence across national, racial, and religious boundaries. Meanwhile, African states lack a mechanism for harmonizing attitudes and commitments toward a viable integration scheme (Laporte, 1993:60).

Challenges of the New World Order and Globalization

The present world system is experiencing *push* and *pull* factors of globalization and regionalization. Globalization for countries and for firms is characterized by openness of economies and a global market in which the strategies of firms focus on efficient resource seeking along with synergies and standardization in market offerings (Mucchielli et al., 1998:xi–xxi). Regionalization for both countries and firms is characterized by preferential trading arrangements among countries and a regional network approach to resources, markets, and organization for firms. Since the 1980s, there has been a steady openness in the flow of international capital, labor, and technology. Multinational corporations of the structurally advantaged capitalist economies have effected, in part, a number of reductions of technological and policy-related barriers in foreign direct investment (FDI), trade, and communications. All these have triggered a world economy that is becoming increasingly globalized with obvious constraints to weak and unstable states, as in Africa, with persistent difficulties toward regional integration (Ihonvbere, 1991:527–32).

According to the *African Charter for Popular Participation in Development,* Africa is becoming further marginalized in world affairs both geopolitically and economically (Ihonvbere & Turner 1993). ECA corrobates that Africa is endangered by the adverse effects of growing protectionism and restrictions on market access. There is also the prospect that resource flow to Africa will dwindle as and when resources are diverted for the depressed areas within the European economic community; by extension the investment opportunities in Eastern Europe will dwindle, as well. Evidently, Africa is entering the twenty-first century as a more vulnerable, crisis-ridden, and marginal participant in the world system (Ihonvbere, 1994a).

Although many regions are responding to the new trend of globalization, Africa is still experiencing deepening internal contradictions, conflicts, and crises that militate against its ability to restructure internal relations of power, production and exchange, sustainable cross-border trade links, and mutual trust and confidence toward sustainable integration schemes. The general atmosphere of insecurity, political and economic contradictions, gross human rights abuse, and the shrinking foreign economic and other interests in Africa contribute to African weakness toward integration schemes. In terms of FDI, Africa will rank lowest in the calculation of European, Japanese, and American investors.

Aid, grants, and trade concessions to Africa relative to Russia and Latin American countries reveal Western bias (Ihonvbere and Turner, 1993: 452–53). In 1991, in support of restructuring efforts in the former Eastern Bloc, Germany gave $34.88 billion, Italy $5.85 billion, the United States $4.08 billion, the EU $3.88 billion, Japan $2.72 billion, Spain $1.36 billion,

France $1.22 billion, the United Kingdom $0.07 billion, and other donors $14.01 billion. Since June 1990, Germany has contributed more than $120 billion to the former GDR and additional $40–50 billion to the Common Wealth of Independent States (CIS). In contrast, German aid to Africa is a mere $2 billion. In November 1991, the OECD estimated pledges from its members to Eastern Europe as $45 billion. This compares with annual official commitments to Africa at the end of the 1980 of some $34 billion (Ihonvbere and Turner, 1993:454).

With the ongoing globalization, our world is witnessing more openness of economies and a global market in which strong push and pull factors have redirected attention and investment interests of firms to Eastern Europe. One result has been a sharp decline in foreign aid to Africa and an increasing loss of interest in FDI in Africa. The successful inauguration of Canada-Mexico-U.S. free trade known as the North American Free Trade Agreement (NAFTA) does not hold a bright prospect for Africa. The rise of tiger economies in Asia (Malaysia, South Korea, and Taiwan) are modern attractions to multinational corporations (MNCs), the IMF/World Bank, and the developed states in resource generation and market offerings.

Given the persistent insecurity in Africa, the Western developed countries do not perceive Africa as a relevant focus for resource seeking and FDI. The twenty-first century is likely to marginalize Africa all the more proportionally to international competitiveness in resource seeking, FDI, and market offerings.

PROSPECTS OF AFRICAN INTEGRATION SCHEMES

The prospects of African integration schemes seek answers to such questions as what possibilities do African states have for improving their capacities to live and work together? What capacities have African states to compete economically in the increasingly challenging and competitive global market? What opportunities are open to Africa for acquiring greater access to markets and for improving balance of payments and scarce resource allocation? What are the imaginable consequences for African integration if these efforts fail?

If Africa must become relevant by moving along with the trends of globalization in a fast changing world system, it must make practical efforts toward strengthening state institutions and other complex political inter-relations in Africa, which make for political boundary questions regarding the spiralling ethnic cleansing and religious revivalism (Aning, 1994a). Developing state-building capacities is of a crucial importance first, for achieving the *security climate* of integration in Africa (Sayigh, 1990:49) and, second, for developing an institutional mechanism for harmonization of interstate interests and relations to promote more collaborative behaviors than discord or discriminatory trade and technical practices. In this direction, Africa must directly confront the increasing personal ambitions and worst of all the dangers of lingering authoritarianism.

Cooperation is a key element in integration as a function. African states need to work together for the purposes of bargaining a new form of partnership with the major powers of the world, particularly the United States, Britain, France, Japan, Malaysia, China, and Russia. This is a demand for the reintegration of Africa in the network of world systems in the twenty-first century.

Two typologies of integration await Africa. The first is regional in focus; the second is global. At the regional level, African states must confront directly the persistent problems of structural economic dependence by looking more inwards, trusting in their own strength to evolve macro- and microeconomic policies as well as strategies capable of substituting for foreign-dictated structural adjustment programs. Africa needs to make it a task to allow the private-sector–led economic growth and development to take the lead in diversification of the economy and standardization of goods and services to meet international competitiveness. Instead of wasteful investment in war mongering and weapons, African states need to encourage, by policy and finance, indigenous investors as part of the designs to create favorable economic climate necessary for attracting FDI. This is a sure way to reintegrate African economies in the global market.

It remains to be noted that corruption is one of the worst "enemies" to African integration schemes. Without public-serving spirit and accountability, it is impossible for African states to develop and implement policies and strategies of self-reliance and development. "Fighting" corruption to a standstill will improve the prospects of both regional integration and, by extension, the attraction of Africa to foreign investors and firms necessary to reintegrate Africa in the international division of labor.

Experience from Latin America and Western Europe further reveals that integration derives from short-term, medium-term, and long-term plans accompanied by a shared concern and determination on the part of integrating states to move in the direction of mutual interest, understanding, and collaboration. It remains an open concern whether pluralism will fare any better than authoritarianism in an unstable, unproductive, and corrupt African political environment. If Africa fails to confront directly its numerous socioeconomic, political, military, and environmental problems, it leaves only itself to blame and must suffer increasing marginalization and irrelevance in the world market of the twenty first century.

Today, the arrays of problems strewn in the path of African integration are, no doubt, beyond the ability of any single nation to solve (Langhammer, 1993:59; Martin, 1989:22). Anglophone, Francophone, and Arab Africa need to explore trade and technical partnership. Political will among African states is indispensible toward a successful regional integration.

There is need for the right political attitude, thinking, and perception for African states to work together. African leaders should learn to send officials who have both the discipline and expertise to conferences, seminars, workshops, and roundtable talks based on their familiarity with the issues involved. This is one way of ensuring that on their return from meetings or conferences, considerable and necessary pressures would be brought to bear on national governments to implement the resolutions adopted and even to set aside funds to advance the goals of regional integration (Laporte, 1993:60–61). Hopefully, this is a path of honor to pursue community or regional interest instead of a sum of sovereign interests.

Another related political problem is overlapping or multiple membership of international organizations. Although the developed countries can afford the high cost of overlapping membership, the African situation cannot accommodate it, particularly due to the weak economic and finance base as well as the persistent attitude of distrust and suspicion. The future of integration in Africa will be brighter if African states play down the syndrome of multiple membership in integration schemes with a view to strengthening such ones with the highest potentials of promoting the ideals of integration process.

Most analysts agree that Africa is seriously burdened by external debt. The burden arises from the size of the debt relative to the area's struggling economics. Africa is simply too poor to service its debt and meet its basic economic requirements at the same time. Without considerable aid and debt relief, African regional integration will remain uncertain. African states should, therefore, brace up diplomatic soldiering to persuade the developed or donor countries in support of bilateral or multilateral debt forgiveness and to reverse the negative trends in trade, fiscal measure, aid, and external debt.

It is now common knowledge that globalization is real. It is an irreversible process that has fundamental implications for integration schemes and/or strategies in Africa. Globalization opens new opportunities and risks for Africa (Ihonvbere and Turner, 1993:449–56). Much of the fate of Africa will depend on how African states perceive and treat the threat of further marginalization of Africa in international division of labor. Besides measures to enhance the productivity of capital through an overall stable macroeconomic environment, there is need for Africa to embrace the information technology revolution if it is to be part of the global integration (Botchwey, 1999:18).

Africa's future lies in its ability, through increased competitiveness, to improve cross-border trade links and break into new dynamic areas of world trade. Manufacturing export-led growth should combine with economic nationalism aimed at protecting African economies from the vicissitudes of the terms of trade in primary commodities. Each African state will, therefore, need to employ its own talents, and its own researchers and experts, to fully appraise its concrete national situation in order to devise appropriate integration strategies in Africa. Regionalism requires the mobilization of all productive sectors and citizens. As Kwesi Botchwey notes, critical to all these efforts is the all-important need for Africa to mobilize existing capacity and build new ones and to develop and maintain both national and foreign policies that would provide incentives for integration schemes in Africa. What becomes of Africa in the twenty-first century will depend wholly on harmonization of policies and actions by African states toward integration as a function and strategy of development and competitiveness. At both regional and international levels, Africa needs peace for increased FDI and improved access to world markets.

BIBLIOGRAPHY

Africa Recovery, June 1991. "Timetable towards Unity."

Ake, Claude, *Political Economy of Africa* (London: Longman, 1981).

Akpuru-Aja, Aja, *Policy and Strategic Studies* (Abakaliki-Ebonyi State, Nigeria: Willy Rose and Appleseed Publishing, 1999).

Aning, Emmanuel Kwezi, "Africa's Security Problematic in the Post–Cold War Era," *Centre for Development Research.* Working paper, Denmark, November 1994a.

Aning, Emmanuel Kwezi, "Managing Regional Security in West Africa: ECOWAS, Ecomog and Liberia," *Centre for Development Research.* Working paper, Denmark, February, 1994b.

Axelrod, Robert, and Robert Keohane, "Achieving Co-operation under Anarchy," *World Politics* 38, 1, October 1985.

Botchwey, Kwesi, "Africa and Global Competitiveness," *Daily Champion,* Nigeria, April 5, 1999.

E.C.A and Africa's Development, "1983–2008: A Preliminary Study, Economic Commission for Africa," April 1983.

E.C.A, African Alternative Framework to Structural Adjustment Programmes for Socio-Economic Recovery and Transformation, A Popular Version, Addis Ababa, April, 1991.

Martin, Guy, "Africa Regional Integration: Lessons from the West and Central African Experiences," Lagos, N.I.I.A, Lecture Series No. 50, 1989.

Haas, E.B, "Turbulent Fields and the Theory of Regional Integration," *International Organization* 30, 2, Spring 1976.

Harsch, Ernest, "Africa Seeks Economic Unity," *Africa Recovery,* June 1991.

Hazzlewood, Arthur, *Economic Integration: The East African Experience* (London, Heinamaan, 1985).

Ihonvbere Julius O. "Nigeria as Africa's Great Power: Constraints and Prospects in the 1990s," *International Journal* XLVI, Summer 1991.

Ihonvbere, Julius O., & Terisa E. Turner, "Africa in the Post-Containment Era: Constraints, Pressures and Prospects for the 21st Century," *The Round Table* 728, 1993, pp. 443–59.

Ihonvbere, J.O., *Regionalism and the Politics of Collective Development in Africa* (New York: The Ford Foundation, 1994b).

Ihonvbere, Julius O., Pan-Africa's in: Agenda for African Unity in the 1990s? Keynote address at the All Africa Student's Conference, University of Guelph, Guelph, Ontario, May 27, 1994a.

Langhammer, I. Rolf, "Integration through the Market: High Costs and Risks of Failure," *Dossier, The Courier,* 1993.

Laporte, Geet, "Integration: From Words to Deeds," *Dossier, The Courier* 142, Nov–Dec. 1993.

Mitrany, David, *A World Peace System* (Chicago, Quardrangle Books, 1996).

Muchielli, Jean-Louis, Peter J. Buckley, Victor V. Cordell, *Globalization and Regionalization* (New York-London: International Business Press, 1998).

Nwokedi, E., "Regional Integration and Regional Security: Ecomog, Liberia and the Liberia Crisis," Bourdeux: Centre d' Étude d' Afrique Noire, 1992.

Ojo, Olatunde J.B., Utete C., M.B., Orwa, *Africa International Relations* (London: Longman, 1985).

Omar, Ali J., "Closing Address." In Institute for African Alternatives (IFAA), *Alternative Development Strategies for Africa* (London: IFAA, 1989).

Organization of African Unity, "Africa's special submission to the Security Council of the U.N. on Africa's Economic and Social Crisis," *Addis Ababa,* March 1986.

Rourke, John T. *International Politics on the World Stage* (Guilford, CT: The Dushkin Group, 1991).

Sayigh, Y. *Confronting the 1990s: Security in the Developing Countries,* Adelphi Pafen 251 (London: Brassey's Publishers, 1990).

World Bank, Sub-Saharan Africa: from Crisis to Sustainable Growth, Washington, DC: World Bank, 1989.

PART VI

Conclusion

15

Redefining the African State: Political Capacity in the Post-Reform Era

Obioma M. Iheduru

Using an institutional analysis framework, this chapter sets out to examine the relationship between the adoption of structural adjustment policies in African countries and the concomitant institutional changes in the state structure. In other words, how do economic changes affect the structure and ultimately the function of governmental institutions that have hitherto heavily influenced the structure of the African economic system? Evidence from this analysis suggests that economic reform measures are a causative factor in the changes in the structure of the state. This inevitability occurs because the changes wrought in the institutions of the state, and of the state itself, affect the ability of the state in the conceptualization, enactment, and implementation of policies. Therefore, in order to understand the dynamics in the development problematique of the African economies, there is a need also to understand the transformations that the state system has undergone, and still continues to undergo, as we enter the new millennium. Finally, I argue that the political capacity to design and implement public policies rather than the extraction of resources is a function the African state has come to learn anew, forced on it by the structural changes that it undergoes during structural adjustment. In other words, the issues that continue to underlie African development are hinged on the nature of, changes wrought in, and the learning curve capabilities of the African state. Thus, in this millennium, the issues that will face development in Africa will probably center around the structure and capability of the state and its ability to handle, channel, and constructively manage these innovations and novelties.

The nature of the African state as inherited at independence was dictated by colonial imperatives. African states are conglomerates of smaller pre-colonial "nations" merged forcibly by the colonizing European powers in order to facilitate the administration and exploitation of these areas' agricultural and mineral resources. At the beginning of the colonial period in the late nineteenth century, the new colonies lacked the basic, infrastructural facilities. There were neither paved roads and railways, waterworks and electricity utilities, nor seaports and airports. After 1885, the colonial administrations were forced by economic necessity to provide the barest of these structures by themselves. Railways and roads were built from the coast to the hinterland, especially through agricultural and mineral-rich areas. Seaports, quays, and wharfs were also developed to facilitate the export of raw materials to metropolitan European industries. In this way, the colonial administration became very much involved in all aspects of the management and control of the colonial economy of African states.

At independence, African countries inherited this centrist function of the state in the economy. This even became desirable and fashionable as these states embarked on huge "development" projects that called for heavier government involvement because local entrepreneurs had neither the expertise nor the resources to undertake them. The result of this inevitable role of the government was that it built roads and markets and owned and managed commercial banks, media houses, mass transit systems, and even small farming enterprises and grocery stores. There was a general lack of expertise on the part of the government to undertake these responsibilities. Consequently, not too long thereafter, economic mismanagement and waste resulted, which in turn led to the economic, political, social, and financial crises of the late 1970s and early 1980s all over sub-Saharan Africa. The pressure arising from these crises necessitated borrowing to stabilize the economy in the interim. Such stabilization measures were a sine qua non for adjustments in the country's balance of payments. The crisis also called for the restructuring of the national economy to make it rational and productive in agricultural and other areas.

From the lenders perspective, it is argued that the irrational nature of the African countries economy is the main factor in its nongrowth. The International Monetary Fund, the World Bank, and other development aid donors insisted on economic restructuring after the short-term balance of payments needs of the nations had been met. By the middle of the 1980s, nearly all of the countries in the region had adopted economic restructuring policies, which emphasized a greater role for the market in the allocation of scarce resources to where they were needed in the economy. The emphasis by structural adjustment on the market allocation of optimal resources and other measures of adjustment have invariably reversed the roles of the state, which had hitherto dominated the management of the national economy and decided where and how resources had been allocated.

In this chapter, I explore how changes arising from economic reforms have in turn led to a redefinition of the role of the state, especially in those African states that have attempted to fully implement structural adjustment policies in their economies. The correlation that is sought here is whether the higher the level of structural adjustment implementation, the greater the variation in changes in the political capacity of the state. In other words, the study seeks to answer the question whether economic changes force governmental institutions, and subsequently the state, to adapt to new role statuses as soon as market forces take over the allocatory functions of the economy. It would appear that as market forces take over the important role of resource allocation, state institutions are inevitably forced to take on the role of regulation, coordination, making and enforcing the rules of the marketplace. Therefore, economic restructuring imposes on the state a new set of defining characteristics that also redefine its functions.

Second, I try to answer the question posed by Crawford Young ("how can [the spiral of state deflation] be reversed?") considering the arguments that some have made that structural adjustment leads to the "softening" of the state. The relevance of the question becomes more stark given that "hegemonic impulses flow[ing] from the logic of the first construction of the colonial state seem impossible to sustain"[1] in the light of the ambivalence that surrounds it.

The argument here then is that economic structural adjustment, in spite of its short-run negative social effects, generates the internal and external impulses that deconstruct the postcolonial state, first toward its reconfiguration as a prelude to eventual economic growth in the country. The forces of structural adjustment weaken the state in the process of reshaping and retooling the economy, and in the meantime, the elements of overload that the postcolonial African state is burdened with since independence are transferred to the private sector of the economy. In this way, the state is equipped adequately for the policy identification, enactment, and implementation that resolves problems, creates opportunities, and subsequently facilitates both political development and economic growth. The process of deconstructing the postcolonial state requires the articulation of the internal and external inconsistencies in which the state system in Africa is mired.

Africa, in this chapter, shall be taken to mean the countries of sub-Saharan Africa. It also needs to be clarified that one is not oblivious of the devastating social impact of structural adjustment policies on the rural poor and those on the margins of the economy who demand "adjustment with a human face." Although these frustrations should be welcome inclusions in a more comprehensive evaluation of the impact of structural adjustment,[2] the concern here is the evaluation of the effects of the reforms of the economy on the state and its institutional structures. The complexities of the postcolonial state and its pervasive elite were the structures that wrecked the African state economy, in the first instance; therefore, an adjustment was called for. Without an understanding of how the economic changes resulting from structural adjustment have affected the state, changes that emerge from it might just be cosmetic in the long run if the same state structures remain intact. It needs no telling that the hitherto postcolonial state structure in Africa had been the superstructure upon which corruption, economic mismanagement, social injustice, and political instability had been built. The increase in additional resources to the state as it is, through capital transfers to help in the economic reform exercise, is most likely to further the interests of state elites and continue to disrupt the economy rather than aid its recovery. This is because the higher the proportion of state resources at the disposal of the state elites, the larger the share of the economy that they control and manage and therefore the greater the perpetuation of corruption, mismanagement, and low economic growth.

It typically goes against conventional wisdom to argue here that the implementation of economic structural adjustment policies affect the political system by freeing up the political institutions from the burdens of the centrist state and in the process reshaping their roles in the political process in the light of a new management agenda. Conventional opinion has it that the greater the amount of resources available to the state, the higher the level of political development in that state. Although this has been the postulatory basis for the capital transfers into Africa, and thereby increasing the resources at the disposal of the African states, such huge capitalization has not translated into an appreciable level of political development along the lines that theorists and policy makers had predicted. Even though this contradicts with the now unsubstantiated argument that it takes a strong political leadership—perhaps in the place of a dictator—to successfully implement the reforms in the economy that would lead to economic growth, economic development has not substantially taken off. Instead political development is beginning to take place at a much faster rate than economic growth in most of Africa. This shows that there is a limit to which the activities of a dominant political individual or party can influence the changes that lead to both economic and political development.

The question then arises as to how the economic restructuring of the economy leads to political changes. The argument is that with economic restructuring in sub-Saharan Africa and the subsequent reordering of the role of the state in a market economy, the capacity of the state is being increased in line with the level of economic restructuring taking place, such that a reformed economy will have a minimalist but a strong regulatory role for the state. It would appear then that the more an African country is subjected to the strictures of economic reform, the more the state recedes to a regulatory role in order to allow the operation of market forces, which allocate resources where they are needed. Essentially, the greater the resources, in the form of capital transfers that a state has, the greater the capacity that it builds through the instrumentality of the market system.

When the market forces are inoperable or blunted, the tendency arises for state elites to manage such resources. In the next section, I examine the nature of the changes that take place in the institutions and instruments of the state and the role of the reforming characteristics of the economy in inducing these changes.

The rest of the work here is organized in four sections. The first section examines the political economy of Africa and tries to relate the structures of the economy in the postindependence period to the realities of state elite dominance. The inevitable centric structure of the colonial governmental establishment is analyzed as the precursor of the postcolonial African state. The role of the postcolonial state under economic reforming conditions is then examined and analyzed. In the second section, a model of the relationship between the implementation of structural adjustment and the development of political capacity is constructed. These results are examined interactively with current evidence from those liberalizing countries where economic structural adjustment proceeded more rapidly than others between 1982 and 1993. In the third section, I define and respecify the political capacity concept, its correlates, and the patterns of its emergence through structural adjustment. In the final section, the analysis and the assumptions of the neoliberal approach are integrated to argue that whereas the literature acknowledges that political development bears a relationship to economic development, economic development in weak political systems could on the converse have a very strong relationship to changes in the political capacity of the state and could invariably be the engine that drives state transformation and the political development of a country.

THE COLONIAL LEGACY OF THE STATE

Any study of the African state must start with addressing the "multiple manifestations of the African state."[3] Although there is certainly no scholarly agreement on a conceptual state entity for it to be adequately studied, there are, however, certain overarching characteristics that the African states share in common. Most of these are predicated on the colonial origin of the state in Africa. The postcolonial African state owes its origin and structure without doubt to the realities of a combination of international capitalism, dependency, and marginalization, but much more so, to the structural imperatives of colonialism. The colonial state managed the economy, determined policies in the public interest, maintained law and order, but paid scant attention to the issues of representation and democracy. The colonial state was also authoritarian, exploitative, repressive, and arbitrary in the drawing of national boundaries.[4] It can be perfectly argued that the level of state development varies from one country to the other and that there are as many states as there are countries in Africa, hence the extent of the states' intrusion also varies.

Regardless of their levels of economic development, regime type, leadership style, and ideological orientations, most of these states have been described as having "a common patrimonial core."[5] The characteristics of the centric colonial state in Africa still manifest themselves in the postcolonial states without the basic elements of the limiting democratic practices that guard state structures in the European tradition such as the rule of law, civil rights and civil liberties, and the constitution. These limiting factors were not fully institutionalized as checks on the excesses of the state prior to the transfer of power to the local political elite.

Despite the belated attempts of the European colonizers at the time of independence in the 1950s and 1960s to shape the African state in the characteristic mold of the European states, the former still defied that expectation both at independence and today. Once political power was transferred to the new African political leadership, in addition to being incorporated into the international capitalist system, they saw the state as a tool for the exploitation of the resources of society just as the colonialists before them had done. The "structures, institutions, and instruments [of the state]" under these conditions were employed by the dominant leadership for the exploitation, repression, and marginalization of the ordinary citizens.[6] The dominant roles of the state in the postcolonial period have resulted in the absence of market forces to adequately operate to direct the economy. The patrimonial nature of the state system has made the state dependent on the support of clients in the society who are reciprocally dependent on the state for the wealth accumulation and class formation. As Marenin has argued, these "contending coalitions" of traditional authority and the new political class now emerging are too weak to present any real challenges to the entrenched state elites and thereby influence the organizational processes of the state.[7]

Authoritarian rulership bears a relationship to state intervention in the economy. As such, actions taken to transform the state are more likely to be sustained when driven by economic change that alters the states' roles in the economy and when such state elites are willing to change *pari passu* or give up power. There are implications here for democracy given the widely accepted theoretical explication that capitalism and democracy have considerable compatibility. There is the contention that increases in the amount of capital resources or financial capital investments in a country lead to increases in economic growth and that economic growth, in turn, drives democratic development.[8] In effect, the more the economic change that a political system experiences, the greater the level of institutional changes that the state undergoes. By shedding off institutional overload, the African state improves its capacity for policy making, innovation and change management, and effective and efficient governance, thereby promoting democratic consolidation both during and after the reforming stages.

As has been argued by social scientists, political and economic development have to be preceded by a phase of institutionalization.[9] The inference from development theory is that there is a relationship between political development and economic development driven by the same kinds of association between the availability of wealth to a country and political development. Also, this bears a relationship to the correlation between democracy and socioeconomic development in Western societies, following a recent observation that political development can be conceptualized in terms of the "qualitative change in values, structures and functions of given political systems, where new values, structures and functions are seen to be replacing existing ones."[10] If economic reforms are set to alter and improve the values and structures of economic management, then political development must incorporate changes in the structure, values, and functions of the state adequate enough to meet the challenges of the new economic structures and thus coalesce with them in building both new economic and political systems.

Consequent upon the actions of the state elite, the governmental control of the African economies was to increase in the course of time as they fell under dictatorial, one-party, and sometimes autocratic regimes. Between 1979 and 1990, economic development in a great many of these countries suffered a reversal in growth. The political and economic crises that have emerged consequent upon this are explainable in terms of the capacity of the state to undertake meaningful development initiatives. Scholars have variously referred to these states as "weak," "soft," or "irrelevant." The interventionist postcolonial African state is apparently incapable of galvanizing the resources and combining them in such a mix to enable it to achieve economic development. This state structure is challenged by the structural changes arising from the implementation of economic structural adjustment policies.

THE AFRICAN STATE AND INSTITUTIONAL CHANGE

The problems of the African state are a combination of historical, internally generated, and systemwide international factors with the results that there are fundamental theoretical and methodological problems that need to be overcome in discussing it. The postcolonial status of the state apparently stamps unavoidably inherent but contradictory weaknesses in the state structure, which paradoxically affects political and, consequently, economic development. The African state inherited a colonial legacy of authoritarianism that continues to affect the present state structure. Some scholars see the problem of the state in Africa from this perspective. Others perceive the problem as arising from the nature of the international capitalist system that imposes a dependency status on the continent.[11] The state is manifested as the central public domain comprising a network of public officials, rules, regulations, and sanctions by which all social actions and conflicts are directed and regulated, and by which the state itself competes with the political, economic, and social institutions for limited resources.[12] Evidently, the state is simultaneously an institution in its own right and also an autonomous actor that oversees the actions of other institutions. By implication then, the changes that affect the resources that the state plays guardianship over or in most cases owns inevitably affect the nature of the relationship between the state and the other institutions. On the other hand, the deterioration of the state demonstrates that the state is neither able to play its associational roles of mediation in the contest between the institutions nor able to allocate and manage the resources at its disposal either because they are inadequate or nonexistent or the state is plainly incapacited.

The centrality of the African state in the political, social, life, and management of the African economies was consolidated not necessarily to enhance its capacity to influence and deliver policy outcomes but with the overt objective of increasing the authority and staying power of the political elite. This consolidation meant the translation of the control it had inherited into centralized power. Unfortunately, however, state consolidation generated the milieu for the strictures on the fledgling democratic institutions inherited at independence. The peoples of these new states were shut off from the public policy processes of their states. The state system and its pattern of perquisites and pay-offs became institutionalized for the private and collective benefit of a few.[13] The lack of open debate and discussion about issues and policies, absence of a menu of human rights to undergird political participation and behavior, and a non-conducive political environment that guarantees liberty and choice led to mammoth misguided policies, barefaced corruption, and inefficiency in the management of essential public services. Meaningful grassroot political participation became virtually nonexistent as the ordinary citizens were excluded from the political system. The rule of law embodied in the democratic institutions inherited at independence was disdainfully treated; laws excluded the wealthy and the powerful and their application was thus subordinated to status and social location. The consolidation of the state was carried out in so far as the leadership exploited the trust of the masses of the people to secure the reins of power and to impose political hegemony.

This deliberalization of the political system in the immediate postindependence period led to the loss of confidence by sections of the population in the political leadership. The state or the conceptions of it became tantamount to an agent of the political leadership. The lack of openness in the policy-making process and probity in implementation and the subsequent exclusion of the large sections of the majority of citizens from government's operations resulted in the withdrawal of the people from the state. This painful disengagement alienated the state from the masses of the people, and they in turn came to identify it as nonrepresentative of the collective interest of the people.[14] State consolidation reached its apogee thereafter and turned into state deterioration. Cases in point were in Kenyatta's Kenya, Mobutu's Zaire, Banda's Malawi, and Nguema's Equatorial Guinea. Further deterioration resulted in the failure of the shoddy and misguided policies that the closed political systems had engendered. Industrial, agricultural, and trade policies failed to reach their targets. Compared with the colonial period, economic growth considerably lagged behind while the needed foreign reserves pivotal for the implementation of public policies were thoughtlessly depleted and squandered on nonessential economic but political endeavors. In Nigeria, Cote d'Ivoire, and Zaire, white-elephant projects were embarked on in order to accomplish this plundering of the state treasury while providing a mock smoke screen of national development. The consolidation and the deterioration processes constituted one dynamic continuum that shaded into one another rather than constitute two distinct historical epochs in study of the postcolonial African state.

It is critical that the historical context within which the state and its role in the economic and political development of African countries are examined must be properly identified and understood. The antithetical point in the development of the state reached a crescendo in the late 1980s, which also corresponded with the emergence of civil society that began to challenge not only the policies of the state, but in addition the legitimacy of the political leadership to make policies. The point actually is that the deterioration of the state, as a result of faulted consolidation efforts in the postindependence period, created the conditions, first for the suspicion in which the state is held, and second for the challenge to its legitimacy. The ensuing cynicism about the legitimacy of the state and the unwillingness of the citizenry to accede power to it to enact and enforce policy arose not only as a result of the absence of meaningful participation by a great majority of the people but inevitably due to the obvious contradictions in the state structure that also made the state an actor. This contradiction was further reflected in the lack of the political capacity to make and implement relevant policies. The state as constituted lacked the ability to make the people obey its commands without resort to coercion or maintain a level of acceptance beyond the juridical political sovereignty that the acceptance of the international political community offers. These shortcomings and limitations drained the powers of the state and constrained whatever ability the state possessed to enact and implement policies resulting in what some scholars have described as "the delegitimization of the state and its institutions."[15]

This outcome was disappointing to the early scholars of development who had argued that the institutionalization of central institutions under the aegis of the state was necessary to stimulate development. Though institutionalization was vigorously pursued through political parties, legislatures, and the judiciary, these too were manipulated by the political elite in their heedless drive to consolidate and centralize power in the executive branch of their governments. The state structure that emerged became an arena for political struggle between the multifarious components of the society and the political class itself masquerading as the state. Victor Azarya has argued that the state came to be regarded as an arena for contesting for resources between the different groups that comprised it; hence, the integrative notes resonant in the earlier studies of political development in Africa were replaced by conflict studies. This situation arose because the the state controlled the more important central resources as well as peripheral resources. Correspondingly, the centrality of the state became more relevant with regards to the distribution and exercise of power, and of course, resources. The initial efforts resulted in "incorporation" (association with the state) whereas the conflict studies have led to "disengagement" (withdrawal from the state) by the people.[16]

The basic assumption of development theorists that development was spatially diffusionary is exemplified by the work of W.W. Rustow, in his "stage theory." That is to say, the process of modernization flowed from one stage, usually the preindustrial stage, into the next stage until the stage of mass production, known as the industrialized stage, has been achieved. In other words, there is a unilinear directional growth from the simple to the complex. This approach, known as the classical method, became the dominant paradigm for marshaling change in preindustrial societies. Acknowledgedly unilinear, the measure of this transition from preindustrial to the industrial was the rate of change in economic growth. The neoclassical approach, which came after the Rostowian models, on the other hand posits that the tools for the recording and tracking of social transformation lay in altering the structures of the economy; hence, it later came to be known as structuralism. For the incipient African leadership, the urge to develop led to the adoption of the structuralist approach to development. It was perceived that the leaders had to take control of the state structure so as to steer development diffusion in the direction they wanted. Claude Ake, in *Development and Democracy in Africa,* argues that the leadership distrusted "the price mechanism" and relied instead on the "interventionist role of the state" because "the general concern was how the national income could be facilitated by the state." Ake however disagrees with the neoliberal paradigm and wonders why the approach was not questioned even in the face of the deterioration of the African state.[17]

Certain questions are left unanswered by Ake's assertion because it ignores the basic assumptions that underlie the neoliberal approach and that could make policies based on them workable in Africa. Even though structuralism and neoliberalism have failed to lead to substantial development in Africa, the efforts to identify the role of the state in this colossal failure have been weak at best. This is so because economic conceptions argue that the free enterprise, market-led allocation of resources have been proven to be still by far the best methods of economic management.

One other characteristic of the African state is that the notions of rationality in both public policy making and human rights as elevating of the human spirit toward conceding legitimacy to the leadership were lacking. The related absence of popular sovereignty due to the imposition by the political leadership of hegemonic political orthodoxies was manifest everywhere in Africa. Perhaps, the emphasis on particularistic rather than universalistic criteria in the selection of persons to design and implement development policies spoke volumes about the muddled perceptions of state authority. These conditions did not discriminate in their location and environment as they were found in single mass-party states (Ghana, Kenya, Zambia, Cote d'Ivoire), pseudosocialist states (Tanzania, Benin, Congo, Guinea), as well as in peripheral capitalist states (Nigeria, Zaire, Uganda, Central African Republic, Sudan, and Togo). The point is that the leadership did not make the conditions propitious for the operation of the neoclassical development paradigm in the African state. The single-minded concern for political power by the leadership suppressed institutional deliberative factors that facilitate the evolution, enactment, and implementation of development strategies. Though the neoclassical paradigm of development was adopted by most of the African states in the late 1980s to early 1990s, most often at the bidding of international financial institutions, the various state deliberative institutions and the constitutional arrangements of a liberal polity—the rule of law, the price mechanism (the market), and the associational factors of an open economy (labor unions, employers and employees)—the fiscal/monetary instruments were ignored due to what has been described as the "predominance of political rationale over economic rationale" in governmental choices.[18] The pervasive centrality of the state and its unrelenting control of the various aspects of the social, economic, and political life of the African state benefitted the political leadership who were determined to protect the status quo ostensibly in their own interest.

Unfortunately, though, the state in Africa is still in its incipient stage and lacks the vitality to address the issues of development three decades after the end of colonialism, in spite of its centrality. The dominance of the state in all areas of human endeavors in the new nations has stifled creativity and development. In the immediate postindependence period, the state's urgency to assert itself and command the national loyalty from the disparate entities comprising it led to the suppression of institution seen as obstructionist, although the state assumed more responsibilities in order to assert its presence. By its dominance, the state overextends itself and becomes unable to function effectively to harness, coordinate, and manage development. Although it is a reality that the present state structure was the inexorable outcome of colonialism, so little transformational change has taken place within it in the past four decades to adequately prepare it for the challenges of development.

Various approaches have been suggested for dealing with the "development problematique" of Africa. The neoliberal approach suggests that changes in the structure of the African economy would be the starting point for challenging these problems. It is argued that previous development programs in Africa failed to promote growth essentially because of the failure of political leadership to restructure "the distorted and disarticulated basis of African political economies."[19] If this were to be done, the state would be better able to undertake the new responsibility of guiding and leading development through effective policies rather than "managing" the economy. To accomplish this, economic structural adjustment policies provide the separation of the state and the economy such that the state does not have a controlling upper hand that could obstruct development.

A cardinal point in the neoliberal argument is that developing nations must allow foreign capital inflow into their economies in order to stimulate economic growth because the lack of capital has been identified as the major problem for these countries. But before this can be done, certain conditions and requirements must be met; the economy must be structurally adjusted. Structural adjustment involves the devaluation of the currency, the liberalization of trade, and removal of government subsidies that had hitherto vastly supported social programs, and above all else the operation of a free enterprise economy such that scarce resources are optimally allocated by the forces of the marketplace rather than by whimsical executive fiats. This is the point of intersection between the state and the economy; the latter condition has proven to be a potent force in the changing of the state in Africa.

As market forces take over the allocative functions that the state has hitherto dominated, the state is diminished in importance. The unproductive state-owned enterprises that carry out economic functions that otherwise could be performed by the private sector and the sometimes sinecure positions that their officials hold disappear once the institutions are either dismantled, commercialized, or privatized. The overbloated state structure is in place invariably through its usurpation of the functions of the markets. Structural adjustment changes the role of the state in the economy. As structural adjustment proceeds, the state begins to shed the structural overload arising from its prior centrist position in the economy, which in turn slowed down the rate of development. Structural adjustment sets in motion the process of economic transformation that simultaneously leads to state transformation.

The transformation of the state proceeds in two phases: the economic phase and the political phase. The economic phase begins with the implementation of the conditions of structural adjustment. The devaluation of the currency, the reduction in social programs, removal of tariffs, the rationalization and reduction of the public service, and privatization and/or commercialization of unproductive state-owned enterprises indicate that the forces of the market are beginning to optimally allocate resources and that "the political logic of decisions" no longer hold sway as used to be the case.[20] For every function that is returned to the market, an equal diminution occurs in the functions that the state used to perform under consolidation and centralism. Some ways in which this occurs are through program shutdowns, privatization, and commercialization. The implementation of structural adjustment policies thus starts off a chain of reactions that operates to the disadvantage of the state.

If it is recalled that the management of the economy by the state provided the spoils of office that sustained the bureaucracy of the postcolonial state in Africa, structural adjustment aimed at curbing the source of the resources was bound to create problems in the society. Dictatorial regimes and one-party states that dotted Africa in the prestructural adjustment period were essentially supported by their unlimited access to state resources and through manipulative macroeconomic control. The continued centrality of the state depended on the availability to the state of resources most often derived through hegemonic property rights over the nation's mineral and agricultural resources. There was little need of the African state in this situation for political capacity, in the narrow and limited sense that this involved the ability to extract resources, because it controlled the resources and dispensed them the way it saw fit, most often to shore up its stranglehold on political power. The state control of the national resources and the patterns of its allocation were the superstructure upon which dictatorial regimes and one-party states in Africa was built in its composition, recruitment, cooptation, and continued existence.

If the postcolonial state was designed as a recipe for authoritarianism, its dismantling by economic structural adjustment policies paved the way for restructuring the state in order to build political capacity. The operation of the state in this situation conceptualized the state as it is and not as it ought to be. The political phase of this transformation of the state then comes when this state reconstruction begins, and economic functions are reassigned to the market and performed through price mechanism in favor of less public intervention through which the state acquires managerial burdens. The unburdening of the state places it in a position to make and implement policies that elevate it as the guardian of the economy rather than as its manager, while leaving it reformed and more ready to perform its role in the economy. We will presently show how this transition takes place through the building of political capacity by the state. But first, as the critical basis for this transformation, we must contextually operationalize political capacity as used here.

REFORM AND STATE POLITICAL CAPACITY

How do we measure the political capacity of a government? Two ways in which political capacity has been operationalized in the literature have relevance here. First, it has been conceptualized as the ability of the government to extract resources in the form of taxes and as the state's ability to penetrate society.[21] Considering that much of the resources that African countries have plowed into their economies in the past four decades have come from non-domestic sources, the operationalization of political capacity as the ability to extract resources leaves the concept unmeasurable in the African context because African states have been unable to extract resources as earlier measures postulate. The citizens of many countries (Chad, Niger, and Central African Republic [C.A.R.]) are too poor to be taxed, and in many countries (Nigeria, Mozambique, Cameroon, and Ghana), the mechanism for tax and other revenue collection are rudimentary and severely inadequate in addition to the corruption of public officials. This raises the need to seek out what might be relevant to the African situation.

In terms of economic restructuring and in regard to its importance in the African economy, political capacity is measured by the ability to design and implement policies relating to the changing economic structures and to achieve the intent of the policies so made. For a state to achieve its policy goals, it must demonstrate a measure of autonomy from competing groups in the society and be able to anticipate, enact, implement, and evaluate policies. These groups may include the military, the business class, the professional group (lawyers and engineers), and the peasants of the countryside. Political capacity should therefore encompass the power of the government, weighed against the strength of these groups, to undertake policy formation and implementation against the possible objections of these groups or some of them. The argument about the failure of the so-called Washington consensus or policies of the Bretton-Woods institutions (the IMF and the World Bank) in African capitals has most often been as a result of the opposition mounted against the full implementation of structural adjustment policies by these groups.

Restructuring has its winners and losers, and most of the time, the vociferous urban professional classes are on the losing end and they seek to alter the outcomes of structural adjustment to their own benefits. But the governmental ability to follow through with changes required of the state, arising from the terms of its international loan facility agreements places it, if it is not beholden to these interest groups, in a strong bargaining position against them. Although the extraction of resources may be vital to the maintenance of the state's responsibility as a political entity, to the extent that it is uncompromising or not succumbing to the pressures of subnational or professional groups or blocks and thus changing the original policy, it then has developed political capacity. The inability of most countries to privatize or commercialize such state-owned enterprises as communications, oil and gas industries, the media of mass communication, and even hotel chains arises from the stubbornness of groups who feel they would lose from such economic rearrangements. Nigeria, Kenya, and Zaire are the typical examples. Nigeria's case is more ethnic than professional. The economically backward northern states oppose these policies on the ground that privatization at this point in time would place them at a disadvantage vis-à-vis their economically advanced southern counterparts. In former Zaire and Kenya, ethnicity also plays a role in reform policy implementation in certain key areas. Here, they are delayed or shelved as a way of shoring up much needed support for the incumbent leadership. Sometimes these instances of class reaction to threats to clientelist interests and certain economic parasitism are confused with the genuine popular and street-level opposition to structural adjustment. This view is consistent with the position of several scholars who argue that political capacity must "consist of disciplined, competent bureaucracy and the establishment of the rule of law rather than arbitrary degree."[22]

In any case, the government must have also developed such democratic processes and institutions like the legislature and the judiciary that legitimize its actions, thus making the need to succumb to subgovernmental pressures unnecessary. The manner in which policies are conceptualized, enacted, and implemented is an outcome of the structure of these institutions. Restrictive political systems produced closed, nondeliberative institutions of the recent past, be they the personal rule of Houphet-Boigny in Cote d'Ivoire in the 1970s or the African socialist experiments in Nyerere's Tanzania up to the late 1980s, or Mariam's Ethiopia in the late 1980s and early 1990s. Open political institutions are associated with open economies and a vibrant civil society. The changes in the state structure also affect the pattern and activities of these institutions.

In order to measure the political capacity in a reforming state, we turn to the ability of the countries that are implementing structural adjustment changes to install the technocratic framework for the enactment, implementation, and regulation of policies. As indicated then, an African state has political capacity to the extent that it has the autonomous ability to make the abiding technocratic decisions to enable it formulate, enact, and implement the policies relating to structural adjustment and hence development, to the exclusion of competing groups and subsequently for the realization of the intended goals of such policies. In so doing, it is the responsibility of government to establish the propitious environment for the successful translation of the factors of production into economic growth. It is also imperative that in adopting the neoliberal paradigm that stipulates free enterprises and economic openness, the state structure be strengthened so that it is better able to guide the economic and general development policy. The emphasis then is on the strengthening of the "declined," or "disengaged," Africa state to make it capable of leading development in an open, market-led economy. It might appear counterfactual and paradoxical that the restructured state will lead economic advancement in the new dispensation. The quality of leadership in terms of policy outcomes and "coherent development strategies" are the factors that underlie the political capacity of the state. State intervention in the market thereafter would be for the provision of guidance to national development rather than to manage the economy. As has been argued, the issue is not that of the state-versus-market dichotomy that characterizes market or capitalist economies but an organizational framework that straddles both the structuralist and the neoliberal paradigms. For instance, the dismantling of agricultural products parastatals in Nigeria, Ghana, Kenya, and other countries and allowing farmers to sell their products directly to international buyers forced the state from economic production and control in that sector, concentrated resources, and paradoxically strengthened the state in regulating that trade.[23] Other cases may be made, such as Nigeria's establishment of the Nigeria Deposit Insurance Corporation as an insurer of bank deposits, thus moving the government away from the ownership and management of commercial banks especially given the history of rapid failure of government-owned banks and finance houses. In Ghana, a similar regulatory institution, the Ghana Non-Performing Assets Trust, was established to stem the tide of mismanagement and corruption in the state-owned enterprises.

Political capacity so conceptualized, it has an important distinction that separates it from previous measures. In this case, it measures the performance of a political system regardless of its ideological leanings or regime type, more so because ideology alone is not enough to explain economic growth rates across countries. Using political capacity as operationalized, it is able to determine, in empirical terms, the rate of change in economic growth on bureaucratic decision making, and hence on the state. In this way, we are able to determine the extent to which a politically capable state is able to make the relevant and critical decisions that generate a market-led economy and that stimulate economic growth.

Some scholars have argued that as an economy becomes wealthier, the effect of political factors on economic growth diminishes.[24] The converse of this is that the poorer a country is, the more political factors become important in explaining economic growth. This ties in with the argument made earlier about the origin of the colonial state and the transformations that resulted in the state dominance of the economy in the postindependence period because political factors matter the most when a country is poor. As every imaginable report on the state of economic development in Africa pursuant to the implementation of structural adjustment indicates, Africa is getting poorer rather than richer, in which case the political capacity of the state should be of utmost concern to aid donors and to the international lenders if economic growth will ever be achieved. This is so because in conformity with the relationship between poverty and the primacy of politics, political considerations, that is political capacity will be uppermost, in the African political economy.

In Africa, it has taken economic structural adjustment to force this separation of the political and economic functions in the African state. Evidence as to the impact of economic changes on political capacity is growing. The independence that the separation of political and economic functions created in the economic arena facilitated the formation of civil society of the groups who under the old state structure would have been unable to come together. Civil society is composed of those individuals who hitherto had been denied property rights, denied access to the political process, or persons desiring further changes in the political system. The transfer of institutional functions to these new groups in the economic arena takes away from the state the burdensome overload that is the genesis of its shortcomings in the prereform period. The civil society has been at the head of the call for political reforms that swept Africa, beginning in the early 1990s. Until March 1991, when the former dictator Mathieu Kerekou of Benin Republic was voted out of office, no incumbent African leader had lost an election. But by that year's end, most of the dictatorships had heeded the voice of democratic change and allowed opposition political parties to form. Where the long-established political regimes had not been voted out of office (Zambia, Benin, and Cape Verde), they had allowed national conferences to determine the future of popular political participation (Cameroons, then Zaire, Kenya, Niger, Togo, and to a limited extent Nigeria with its stillborn 1992 constitution). The upsurge in these democratic institutions will certainly aid African countries to consolidate their political capacity and be better able to manage their economies. They were hardly anticipated at the outset of the implementation of structural adjustment, but these policies have succeeded in strengthening the African state.

CONCLUSION

In studies that essentially focus on the same concept of political capacity in Western political systems, it is argued that there is a relationship between political capacity and the wealth of a country. The more revenues a country raises, the more it is said to have political capacity. If this reasoning is applied to Africa, countries such as Nigeria, Congo (former Zaire), and Gabon that are resource-rich would have a lot of political capacity because they do not need to even extract resources. But this is hardly the case in these countries. Therefore, in addition to the extraction of resources, African countries require the technocratic political capacity for effective management, not only of structural adjustment, but of all policies. What has been done here is to use variables emerging from economic restructuring to design a new measure of political capacity. Such rethinking of the causal flow has helped redefine political capacity in terms of the implementation of policies and the realization of policy goals. The goals of economic reform are to ensure economic liberalization, with the transfer of certain functions hitherto performed by the state to the private sector of the economy in order to empower the state. I have demonstrated that the economic management role of the state through intervention in the economy bleeds it of its proper role in the political arrangement and has been responsible for the lack of democracy in Africa.

Paradoxically enough though, the state must be weakened for it to be strengthened under a new political dispensation of democratic institutions.

The unanticipated consequence of structural adjustment has therefore been the separation of the economic from the political aspects of the national economy of African states. Both the economic and political processes are essential for the achievement of a society's developmental goals. For this to happen, there is need for a better understanding of the processes of both domestic policy and the social implications of economic decisions in the process of integrating economic and political analyses. In this regard, it must be maintained that the political management of structural adjustment must be dependent on sound economic policy as much as it depends on relevant democratic institutions. Thus resource-poverty or the abundance of wealth would not guarantee state political capacity without the autonomy that creates the congenial milieu which state political capacity building on a decadent centrist state must exercise. African states must be deconstructed to be active again.

NOTES

1. See Crawford Young, "The African Colonial State and Its Political Legacy," in Donald Rothchild and Naomi Chazan, eds., *The Precarious Balance: State and Society in Africa* (Boulder, CO, and London: Westview Press 1988, p. 60).

2. There are widespread debates about the social impact of structural adjustment programs. See for instance the works of T. Parfit, B. Onimode, J. Loxley, and M. Lofchie. See also the recent works by Jean-Paul Azam, "The Uncertain Distributional Impact of Structural Adjustment in Sub-Saharan Africa," and Venkatesh Seshamani, "Structural Adjustment and Poverty Alleviation: Some Issues on the Use of Social Safety Nets and Targeted Public Expenditures," in Rolph van der Hoeven and Fred van der Kraaij, eds., *Structural Adjustment and beyond in Sub-Saharan Africa* (The Hague: Ministry of Foreign Affairs/Portsmouth, NH: Heinemann, 1994, pp. 99–148).

3. Zaki Ergas, ed., "Introduction," in *The African State in Transition* (London: Macmillan, 1989, pp. 1–22).

4. C. P. Potholm, *The Theory and Practice of African Politics* (Englewood Cliffs, NJ: Prentice Hall, 1979, p. 35).

5. Zaki Ergas, op cit., p. 7.

6. See Julius O. Ihonvbere, "The Irrelevant State, Ethnicity, and the Quest for Nationhood in Africa," *Ethnic and Racial Studies*, 17(1), January:42–60, 1994. See also Aaron Gana, "The State in Africa: Yesterday, Today, and Tomorrow," *International Political Science Review*, 6(1):120–29, 1985. These studies are interpretations of the state from a dependency/Marxist perspective that basically disagrees with the neoliberal approach as another grand scheme in the periphalization of the African state.

7. Otwin Marenin, "The Managerial State in Africa: A Conflict Coalition Perspective," in Zaki Ergas, ed., *The African State in Transition* (London: Macmillan, 1987).

8. The following works are classic examinations of the relationship between economic resources availability and democratic development: Larry J. Diamond, "Economic Development and Democracy Reconsidered," in Gary Marks and Larry J. Diamonds, eds., *Reexamining Democracy: Essays in Honor of Seymour Martin Lipset* (Newbury Park Calif./London: Sage Publications, 1992); Kenneth A. Bollen and Robert W. Jackman, "Economic Determinants of Political Democracy in the 1960s," *Research in Political Sociology,* 38, 1985; Arthur K. Smith, Jr., "Socioeconomic Development and Political Democracy: A Causal Analysis," *Midwest Journal of Political Science,* 13:95–125, 1969; and Philip Cutwright, "National Political Development: Its Measures and Analysis," *American Sociological Review,* 28:253–64, 1963. See also Obioma M. Iheduru, *The Politics of Economic Restructuring and Democracy in Africa.* Westport, CT and London: Greenweed Press, 1999.

9. See for instance the earlier development studies, especially Samuel P. Huntington, "Political Order and Political Decay," in Samuel P. Huntington, ed., *Political Order in Changing Societies* (New Haven, CT, and London: Yale University, 1968).

10. See Chai-Anan Samudavanija, "The Three Dimensional State," in James Manor, ed., *Rethinking Third World Politics* (London and New York: Longman, 1991: pp. 15–23).

11. See Claude Ake, *Democracy and Development in Africa* (Washington, DC: Brookings Institution, 1995, pp. 1–8); and Claude Ake, *The Political Economy of Africa* (London: Longman, 1981) for a more detailed neo-Marxist examination of the ways in which colonialism and colonialist structures set the stage for the underdevelopment of Africa.

12. This explication of the composition of the state is taken from Eric Nordlinger, *On the Autonomy of the Democratic State* (Cambridge, MA: Harvard University Press, 1981, p. 3).

13. Otwin Marenin, op cit.

14. See Naomi Chazan, "Patterns of State Society Incorporation and Disengagement in Africa," in Donald Rothchild and Naomi Chazan, eds., *The Precarious Balance: State and Society in Africa* (Boulder, CO, and London: Westview Press, 1988).

15. D.K. Bani and Julius O. Ihonvbere, "The State, Non-Governmental Organizations, and Development in Africa," *Foreign Affairs Reports* 46(6), June: 1, 1994.

16. Victor Azarya, "Reordering State-Society Relations: Incorporation and Disengagement," in Donald Rothchild and Naomi Chazan, eds., *The Precarious Balance: State and Society in Africa* (Boulder, CO, and London: Westview Press, 1988).

17. Claude Ake, op cit., p. 11.

18. Christian Morrisson, Jean-Dominique Lafay, and Sebastian Dessus, "The Political Conditions of Adjustment in Africa, 1980–90," in Rolph van der Hoeven and Fred van der Kraaij, eds., *Structural Adjustment and beyond in Sub-Saharan Africa: Research and Policy Issues* (The Hague: Ministry of Foreign Affairs/Portsmouth, NH: Heinemann, 1994). The authors' ideas are based on rational choice theories drawn from the works of R.H. Bates, *Toward a Political Economy of Development* (Berkeley, CA: University of California, 1988); and J. Nelson, *Economic Crisis and Policy Choice* (Princeton, NJ: Princeton University Press, 1990).

19. See D. K. Bani and Julius O. Ihonvbere, "The State, Non-Governmental Organizations, and Development in Africa," *Foreign Affairs Reports,* 43(6), June 1994.

For more detailed discussion of the dependency approach to examining the African development problem, see other works by Julius O. Ihonvbere and Claude Ake op cit.

20. Christian Morrisson, et al., op cit., p. 2.

21. A. F. K. Organski and Jacek Kugler, *The War Ledger* (Chicago: University of Chicago Press, 1980). See also Jacek Kugler and William Domke, "Comparing the Strength of Nations," *Comparative Political Studies,* 1986; and Alwyn R. Rouyer, "Political Capacity and the Decline of Fertility in India," *American Political Science Review* 81(2):453–70, 1987; Marina Arbetman, *The Political Economy of Exchange Rate Fluctuations.* Ph.D. Dissertation, Vanderbilt University, Nashville TN, 1990; and David Leblang, "Political Capacity and Economic Behavior," Conference on Political Capacity and Economic Behavior, The Claremont Graduate School, CA, 1994.

22. See Robert Dibie, "Cross-National Economic Development in Indonesia and Nigeria," *Scandinavian Journal of Development Alternatives and Area Studies,* 15(1):65–85, 1996.

23. John Toye, "Structural Adjustment, Context, Assumptions, Origin and Diversity," in Rolph van der Hoeven and Fred van der Kraaij, eds., *Structural Adjustment and beyond in Sub-Saharan Africa* (The Hague: Ministry of Foreign Affairs/Portsmouth, NH: Heinemann, 1999).

24. David Leblang, op cit.

Index

About the Contributors

NURUDEEN B. AKINYEMI is Associate Professor of Political Science at Kennesaw State University, Kennesaw, Georgia. His most significant publications include "Sources of Conflict in the Horn: Water Management" and "Interstate Relations among Egypt, Sudan and Ethiopia," in the *Journal of African Policy Studies*. Dr. Akinyemi's research interests include international resource management, regional cooperation, and the African refugee crisis.

AJA AKPURU-AJA is a Senior Lecturer in the Government and Public Administration department at Abia State University, Uturu, Nigeria. His recent publications include *Fundamentals of Modern Political Economy and International Economic Relations* (1998) and *Theory and Practice of Marxism in a World in Transition* (1997). Dr. Akpuru-Aja's research interests are international political economy, strategic and peace studies, conflict resolution, regional integration, and globalization.

VINCENT J. FERRARA is a Professor of Philosophy in the department of Philosophy and Religion at Indiana University of Pennsylvania. He is co-author (with Laszlo Kecskes) of *An Introduction to Private Law* (1991). Professor Ferrara's research interests are law, human rights, the arts, African issues, and political thought.

HAROLD A. FISHER is Professor Emeritus of International Communications at Bowling Green State University, Bowling Green, Ohio. His most significant publications are (co-author) *The World's Great Dailies* (1980), with contributions to *The New Third World* (1998) and *Critical Issues in Communication* (forthcoming). Dr. Fisher's research interests are in international communication and sustainable development.

APRIL A. GORDON is Director of Women Studies and Professor of Sociology at Winthrop University, South Carolina. She is co-editor (with Donald L. Gordon) of *Understanding Contemporary Africa* (1996) and author of *Transforming Capitalism and Patriarchy: Gender and Development in Africa* (1999) as well as numerous chapters and articles in various publications. Her research interests include African gender development issues, and African immigration to the United States.

KINGSLEY O. HARBOR is Head and Associate Professor of Mass Communication at Mississippi Valley State University. He has published in *Resources in Education* and has research interests in international communication, national development, global news flows, communication, and African stability.

OBIOMA M. IHEDURU is Associate Professor of Political Science, Co-Director, Center for Social Science Research and Director, University Honors program at Fort Valley State University, Georgia. He is the author of *The Politics of Economic Restructuring and Democracy in Africa* (1999) and several articles and chapters in a number of publications including Charles F. Bahmueller's *World Conflicts and Confrontations* (1999). Dr. Iheduru's research interests include economic and development policy, democratization, comparative political economy, regional integration, and globalization.

JULIUS O. IHONVBERE is Professor of Government at The University of Texas at Austin and program officer at the Ford Foundation, New York. His most significant publications include: *The Emerging Constitutionalism in Africa* (2000), *Africa and the New World Order* (2000), *Illusions of Power: Nigeria in Transition* (with Timothy Shaw) (1998), *Labor, State and Capital in Nigeria's Oil Industry* (1998), *Multiparty Democracy and Political Change: Constraints to Democratization in Africa* (edited with John Mbaku) (1998), and *Economic Crisis, Civil Society and Democratization in Zambia* (1996). Dr. Ihonvbere's research interests are in democratization, constitutionalism, militarization, and globalization.

KELECHI A. KALU is Associate Professor of Political Science at the University of Northern Colorado. He is the author of *Economic Development and Nigerian Foreign Policy* (2000). Dr. Kalu's areas of research are political economy of development and underdevelopment, politics of economic development in less developed countries, political economy of foreign relations, ethnic politics and state reconstitution (Africa), and conflict resolution and prevention (Africa).

SANDRA J. MACLEAN is Assistant Professor of Political Science at Dalhousie University in Halifax, Canada, where she teaches courses in Comparative Politics and International Development. She is co-editor of *Prospects for Governance in Asia and Africa: Globalizing Ethnicities* (forthcoming). Her recent work has appeared in *Third World Quarterly,* and she has co-authored chapters in *Globalization and the Politics of Resistance* (Barry Gills, ed.), *The New Agenda for Peace Research* (Ho-Won Jeong, ed.), and *Great Ideas for Teaching about Africa* (M.L. Bastien and J.L. Parpart, eds.). Her research interests include governance, peace building, health, and human security.

ALI A. MAZRUI is Albert Schweitzer Professor and Director of the Institute of Global Cultural Studies, State University of New York at Binghamton. He is also Senior Scholar in Africana Studies at Cornell University, Ithaca, New York. Dr. Mazrui has published more than twenty books and hundreds of scholarly articles with his best known being the television and video series, *The Africans: A Triple Heritage* (1986) with a book of the same title. Dr. Mazrui has taught at Makerere, Uganda, and University of Jos (Nigeria). Among his most recent books is *The Power of Babel: Language and Governance in the African Experience* (1999), co-authored with Alamin M. Mazrui.

JULIUS E. NYANG'ORO is Professor and Chair of African and Afro-American Studies at the University of North Carolina, Chapel Hill. He is widely published in the fields of development and African politics. Among his publications are *The State and Capitalist Development in Africa* (1989) and *Discourses on Democracy: Africa in Comparative Perspective* (1996). His current research interests are democratization and globalization.

BROWNE ONUOHA is Senior Lecturer in the Department of Political Science at the University of Lagos, Nigeria. He is the co-editor of *Transition Politics in Nigeria, 1970–99* (forthcoming). Dr. Onuoha has contributed various articles on political economy, democratic transitions, and political theory—areas in which he researches and teaches.

TIMOTHY M. SHAW is Professor of Political Science and International Development Studies (IDS) Director of the Centre for Foreign Policy Studies and Coordinator of the MA in International Development Studies at Dalhousie University in Nova Scotia, Canada. He has taught at universities in Nigeria, South Africa, Uganda, Zambia, and Zimbabwe and presently is visiting professor at universities in Mbarara, Stellenbosch, and the Western Cape (South Africa). He has co-edited a special issue of *Third World Quarterly* on "New Regionalism" (with Julius Nyang'oro), contributed to Richard Stubbs and Geoffrey Underhill (eds.), *Political Economy and the Changing Global Order.* He is currently researching issues around new regionalism, ocean/island governance, peace building, and triangles.

AGUIBOU MOUKÉ Y. YANSANÉ is Professor of Black Studies and International Relations at San Francisco State University. He has also taught at Stanford, UC Berkeley, San Jose State, and University of Ibadan, Nigeria. His publications include (as editor) *Development Strategies in Africa: Current Economic, Socio-Political and Institutional Trends and Issues* (1996), *Prospects for Recovery and Sustainable Development in Africa* (1996), and *Decolonization and Dependency: Problems of Development of African Societies* (1980).